AF608244

Befriending the *Commedia dell'Arte* of Flaminio Scala

Befriending the *Commedia dell'Arte* of Flaminio Scala

THE COMIC SCENARIOS

Natalie Crohn Schmitt

UNIVERSITY OF TORONTO PRESS
Toronto Buffalo London

Toronto Buffalo London
www.utppublishing.com

ISBN 978-1-4426-4899-9

Toronto Italian Studies

Library and Archives Canada Cataloguing in Publication

Schmitt, Natalie Crohn, author
Befriending the commedia dell'arte of Flaminio Scala : the comic scenarios / Natalie Crohn Schmitt.

(Toronto Italian studies)
Includes bibliographical references and index.
ISBN 978-1-4426-4899-9 (bound)

1. Scala, Flaminio, active 1620 – Criticism and interpretation.
2. Commedia dell'arte – Stories, plots, etc. I. Title.
II. Series: Toronto Italian studies

PQ4634.S224.Z55 2014 852'.5 C2014-903349-4

University of Toronto Press acknowledges the financial assistance to its publishing program of the Canada Council for the Arts and the Ontario Arts Council, an agency of the Government of Ontario.

University of Toronto Press acknowledges the financial support of the Government of Canada through the Canada Book Fund for its publishing activities.

To Joel

For more than I can say

Contents

Illustrations

Cover: Jacques Callot's *Round Dance,* 1617. By permission of the British Museum.

Preface

This book began as the result of a class I was teaching on acting period plays. First, as is customarily recommended in *commedia dell'arte* acting manuals, I introduced my students to the characters of *commedia dell'arte.* Having collected various masks similar in style to those of characters in the *commedia dell'arte,* I had the students playing the typically masked or made-up characters – the old men, the male servants, and the captain – wear these masks as they worked through a number of the *lazzi* or gags collected in Mel Gordon's book of *lazzi.* I suggested to the students that they might wish to use these *lazzi* in the scenario that I had randomly selected for them to perform from Henry Salerno's readily available translation of the Flaminio Scala collection. It was Day 5, *Flavio Betrayed.* Had I known at the time that the translation was somewhat unreliable, it would not have concerned me much because I had read that *commedia dell'arte* scenarios were "skeletal" and that the scenario merely provided a pretext for the entertainment.

While the students had a good time and laughed a lot at their doings in working on the scenario, I became increasingly uneasy. During the following summer I spent a week meticulously working through that Scala scenario, scene by scene, while sitting on the floor and moving miniature plastic cowboys and Indians around in lieu of the scenario's characters. I discovered not only instructions for action, as Tim Fitzpatrick had described, but also character motivations in a very artfully designed plot. Whether the intricacy of the plot had been worked out by the actors, by Scala, or both I could not say, but it became clear that in performance it could not be, as I had read it was, radically different in the hands of different players. Subsequently I worked through a couple of other Scala scenarios, carefully translated, with the same mindfulness. The process was similarly revelatory. In many cases I could not understand much of what was going on in the scenarios or the significance of it, and so I began to read extensively in cultural history. My work, by means of reading and personal queries, was a treasure hunt with serendipitous finds even up to the very end. When I thought I was all but finished, for instance, I came across Deborah Shuger's essay on Renaissance mirrors, a piece that indirectly sheds light on the otherwise incomprehensible scene of recognition that concludes Scala's scenario Day 16, *The Mirror.* Near that time, I also fortuitously learned that musicologists Lucia Marchi and her husband, Robert Kendrick, knew the meaning of singing in the Roman style that is specified in Scala's scenario Day 6, *The Jealous Old Man.*

The result of my labyrinthine process is the present book, which combines close reading and cultural history to redefine many of the Scala scenarios as carefully crafted works of art that are rich in cultural history. Early in my process, I conducted a class for graduate students, in which, working with reliable translations of the scenarios, they tried to provide reconstructions, as I had done – without knowing any cultural history. I studied with Antonio Fava, a noted *commedia dell'arte* performer and mask maker. I directed one of the Scala scenarios with University of Illinois at Chicago students as performers. The latter activities served to convince me that, although I had written about *commedia dell'arte* performance elsewhere, my focus in this book would not be the performance but the scenarios, which continue to be given too short shrift.

While I intend my work to be of use to performers as well as scholars, I do not intend it to be proscriptive. Actors now frequently use improvisation to free themselves from a text. I show the extent to which Scala's actors were dependent on a text and further that the full impact of the scenarios relied on the audience's familiarity with the culture in which the scenarios are imbedded. That culture not only gave significance to the scenarios but also meant that actors, like all those who were part of the early modern rhetorical tradition, had at their command a large amount of memorized material. Actors today do not. In addition, the performances depended on a variety of very diverse dialects and on a kind of verbal exuberance, including long speeches and flowery language not popular today.

I am grateful to University of Toronto Press's editor Ron Schoeffel who began this book's process through the press and whose unexpected death on 4 July (after he had, just a few days earlier, cheerfully and affably wished me a happy fourth of July) shocked and saddened me. Suzanne Rancourt, executive editor for scholarly publishing, proceeded with efficiency and grace despite the fact that she had to suddenly assume many of Schoeffel's responsibilities in addition to her own. The anonymous readers for the University of Toronto Press provided painstaking and invaluable suggestions. Maria Carrig usefully critiqued parts of the manuscript and cheered me on. Nancy Cirillo quickly answered all kinds of questions that seemed to me urgent at the time. Brepols granted me permission to publish, as chapter 3, my essay in *Viator* 41, 1 (2010), "Life in the Street in the *Commedia dell'Arte* Scenarios of Flaminio Scala." Taylor and Francis granted me permission to publish in revised form, as chapter 6 of this book, the essay that originally appeared in *Text and Performance Quarterly* 29, 4 (2009) as "*Il finto negromante*: The Vitality of a *Commedia Dell'Arte Scenario* by Flaminio Scala." The University of Illinois at Chicago Library supplemented its own collection by tirelessly providing me with innumerable books shipped from near and far.

PART ONE

Context, Culture, and Aesthetics

chapter one

Befriending the Text

ORAZIO	*arrives reading a letter, and, while reading, knocks at the [door of his own] house; at that*
PEDROLINO	*dressed in felt [probably a felt hat] and boots, telling Orazio that Flavio wants to go to the countryside. Orazio: that there are other things to be done; at that*
FLAVIO	*getting dressed in country clothes to go to the villa. Orazio says that one of them must go to Pisa and to Livorno right away, saying that he has received a letter from one of his friends in Venice, by which he is informed that in one month an Armenian merchant, named Hibrahim should arrive in Florence, bringing with him two slave brothers, ransomed in Persia from the hands of the Turks.*

Flaminio Scala, *The Two Old Twins*

So begins act 1 of the first scenario in Flaminio Scala's collection of *commedia dell'arte* scenarios entitled *Il teatro delle favole rappresentative* (*The Theatre of Representative Plots*), 1611,[1] probably the single most important document remaining to us from one of the most significant Western theatre movements. The collection provides a vital link to our understanding of *commedia dell'arte* at its height, 1570–1630, shows the *commedia dell'arte* to be full of the life of its times, and includes spirited works of art. With this book I elaborate upon these claims. I seek to dispel a number of common misconceptions: (1) the Scala scenarios are only minimally about social reality and more about an autonomous world created by previous theatre; (2) because the scenarios are limited to domestic encounter, they do not take up social and political issues; and (3) Scala was merely a rearranger of prior texts, a facilitator of performance, but not a creator. At the end of the sixteenth century in Italy the *commedia dell'arte*, known at the time by various names including *commedia a soggetto* or *commedia all'improvviso*,[2] became far more important and influential than the Italian literary drama. Indeed, it was the most important theatrical movement in sixteenth- and early-seventeenth-century Europe. Its performers spread rapidly throughout Europe, affecting both popular and literary theatre. It was more widely known than Elizabethan theatre and, in its time, more influential. Thereafter, although in decline, the form continued to be popular for another one hundred and fifty years. Throughout the centuries the *commedia dell'arte* has captured the imagination of playwrights, artists, writers, musicians, choreographers, and film-makers.

Scala's is the oldest collection of *commedia dell'arte* scenarios, and the only one to have been published in the seventeenth century. Moreover, Scala, as a successful actor-manager, provided us with a first-hand view of some of the best theatre of his time. The publication of his collection of fifty scenarios was, in the words of theatre historian Louise George Clubb, "an event of the first importance to theatre history." Although the scenarios represent "the repertory of a company that never existed," Clubb continues, "Scala's compilation gives a fuller idea of the dynamics, tropes, and variety of improvised comedy than any other single text has done."[3] That text is central to our understanding of *commedia dell'arte* at the time.

The first modern edition of the Scala scenarios in Italian was carefully provided by Ferruccio Marotti only in 1976. A pioneering translation into English of the scenarios by Henry Salerno appeared in 1967, but, while it attracted the interest of actors and accordingly has gone through four editions, it was neither accurate nor literal enough to facilitate scholarly work.[4] Studies of the scenarios have been few. Observing the paucity of attention directed to the Scala scenarios, Richard Andrews comments that one would "expect that scholars would be buzzing around this text like bees round a honeypot."[5] He himself provides considerable attention by making available his careful translation of thirty of the fifty scenarios in the Scala collection and by appending a commentary to each of them, the primary purpose of which is "to set each individual scenario in the context of existing theatrical expectations, and of resources of material already available to actors."[6] Andrews's primary aim, in addition to making scholarly translations of many Scala scenarios available, is to establish the extent to which materials in the Scala scenarios were borrowed from earlier literary material, including scripted plays.[7] Elsewhere he has commented that "it begins to look as though nothing which appears in *Il teatro delle favole rappresentative* was actually created by … [Scala] at all." The "scenes are opportunities or invitations to the performers." Scala was "a re-arranger, or a facilitator, rather than a creator."[8]

My own effort, quite different from Andrews's, is to see the comic scenarios in the collection in relationship to early modern life in Italy, to consider their value as works of art, and to establish the extent to which their performance can be reconstructed. I shall have a great deal to say about the context, common to all the arts in the period in which Scala worked, in which "borrowing" from earlier material needs to be understood. I argue that Scala's claim to creation – he calls it "invention" – is fitting.[9]

In addition to Andrews's work on the scenarios (2008), two other extended studies of the Scala scenarios exist. In 1995 Tim Fitzpatrick argued, in a pioneering and painstaking work, that the Scala scenarios "are quintessentially practical documents, admirably suited and structured to serve the purposes for which they were originally written, containing nothing superfluous (in the sense of moving to readerly and literary constructions), and manifesting pragmatic features which reflect dramaturgical solutions for performance." To establish this, Fitzpatrick broke down Scala's "notational practices" into linguistic schemas and subschemas.[10] In 2005, apparently without awareness of Fitzpatrick's work, Quirino Galli provided a similar diagrammatic linguistic study, also partitioning the scenarios into performance units, to establish that the value of the Scala scenarios resides in their prescriptive efficacy, whose goal is the theatrical performance.[11] Despite their work and perhaps because it is schematic, the scenarios have continued to be described as they have long been described, "as skeletal."[12]

They are, after all, decidedly not play scripts. Indeed, to overcome the dismissal of the Scala scenarios as secondary sources recollected from their performance for the benefit of readers, and to argue instead that they could be reliably read as performance guides, both Fitzpatrick and Galli evidently felt the need to assert that the Scala scenarios, in Fitzpatrick's words, "are quintessentially practical not literary constructions."[13]

Andrews decries the amount of time that has been spent on the argument about whether Scala was trying to create a genre of recreational literature or rather blueprints for performance, and notes that those who have written on the subject are often less in disagreement with each other than they claim.[14] Robert Henke, who briefly but eloquently champions Scala,[15] takes the perspective of Scala and his famous actor friend Francesco Andreini, both of whom, in their prefaces to Scala's collection, affirm that Scala was writing for both readers and performers. He reconciles the seemingly opposing views quite simply, explaining that, while the book by the actor and *capocomico* (theatre manager), *Il teatro delle favole rappresentative* is "undoubtedly a product of literary memorialization," it "contains both internal and external signs that render it a fairly reliable source for knowledge about performance practice."[16] It is, after all, hard to imagine what Scala might have been doing in any accommodations for publication (and we know that there were some) other than representing *commedia dell'arte*, and his scenarios in particular, in the most favourable light possible.

It may well be that precisely because Scala wrote with an eye to an audience of readers as well as performers that his scenarios serve as such valuable guides to *commedia dell'arte* in its golden age. Uniquely, Scala's scenarios provide an "Argument," a description of the action and/or what preceded it. And, indispensably, his scenarios specify actions and their attendant emotions. Other contemporary scenario collections, Corsini and Correr, for instance, often rely on a mere short-hand for actors, like they "have their scene of reciprocal jealousy," they "play their various antics," and Zanni "replies with his trick of 'Didn't I tell you I didn't believe it?'," making attempted reconstruction of their performance difficult.[17]

To establish the value of examination of the Scala scenarios, rather than offer a schematic and diagrammatic analysis I provide something of a literary study of them. I begin with literary theorist Mark Edmondson's passionate argument that the first job of a critic and teacher is to "befriend" the text (that is, to frame a reading of it that would meet with the author's approval); to analyse it sympathetically; to treat its words with care, caution, and due respect; and, further, "to develop a vision of what the world is and how to live that rises from the author's work."[18] That is precisely my intention in this book.

My process is closest to that of Roberto Tessari, who in a remarkable twenty-seven pages describes Scala's scenarios as a poetry not of words but of gesture, in which dialogue, the sole "gesture" of the characters in the Italian written drama, becomes one gesture among many.[19] While Scala rarely provides dialogue, he does provide, instead, descriptions of actions, intentions, emotions, and prop use. Through examining these, like Tessari but in more detail, I strive to establish that many of the scenarios are artfully constructed, various, and full of invention. Unlike Tessari, I further show that to appreciate the interest the scenarios had for their contemporary audience, it is necessary to read them in light of information about early modern Italian society and the tensions within it.

As the majority of *commedia dell'arte* scenarios and of Scala's scenarios are comic, it has been assumed that they are not serious. Ludovico Zorzi perceived a "lack of ethical and social import" in the *commedia dell'arte.*[20] Similarly, Andrews remarks that the dramatic tradition meant that the scenarios were "limited largely to what we would call domestic encounter."[21] Social historian Guido Ruggiero makes clear, however, the extent to which the distinction between domestic and everything else is misleading.

> Marriage [was] at the heart of social and political institutions, ... [its] layers of signification crucially colored perceptions not only of love and sexuality, but also of social order, stability, and organization. And significantly it appears that as this discourse of civic morality became more and more of a given in ... [the period in which Scala was working], it helped to formulate yet stricter gender stereotypes and increased pressure to restrict and place women firmly in a disciplined domestic space.

The family was the building block of a civic and moral society, and "control of the family was the central issue, both in the moral and the political spheres."[22]

I show in detail that an understanding of the social context in which the scenarios were written informs them at every point, not only with respect to the matter of marriage and familial relationships but also with respect to relationships between friends, between masters and servants, and with outsiders. All were causes for anxiety within the culture. What was at stake, argues cultural historian John Jeffries Martin, was the fundamental question of how the relation between the "social and conforming self" (one's correspondence to one's well-understood place in the social hierarchy) and "the internal dimensions of experience ... should be understood or, where there was conflict between them, resolved."[23] Martin sees the question of the relationship between the social and conforming self and the interior self as a "recurring, if not the dominant theme of Renaissance theatre."[24] This question repeatedly manifests itself in the social relationships in Scala's scenarios. *Commedia dell'arte* audiences would have regarded the issues taken up by the scenarios as serious. As

Scala claimed, the scenarios reflect not just a prior theatrical tradition but "human behavior in all its vagaries and contradictions."[25] In their social and cultural remoteness from us it has been too easy to regard the scenarios as only reflections of theatrical traditions.

STATUS OF THE SCALA SCENARIOS

We know very little about Scala himself that might inform us about the status of the scenarios. In 1614, at the age 62, following the invitation of Don Giovanni de' Medici, Scala became *capocomico* of the prestigious theatre troupe, the Confidenti. He held this position until Don Giovanni died in 1621. Scala's correspondence concerning theatre business from his time as manager of the Confidenti is extant and now in print.[26] In 1619 Scala published a play entitled *Il finto marito* based on one of his scenarios.[27] Another play from 1601 is attributed to him. Several months before his own death at age seventy-three Scala sold his perfume shop in Venice (which had evidently provided him with a supplementary income for some time) and became perfumer to the Duke of Mantua.

Even less is known of Scala's life in the years prior to 1611, when he published his scenario collection. One can infer from several documents that he had served as manager for the well-regarded Desiosi and Uniti troupes and had played the lover Flavio and, probably later, the *senex*, the Frenchman Claudione. Although the troupes with which he worked in the main travelled a circuit of northern Italian cities, from 1600 to 1601 there is record of his having toured in France with the Accesi. It is as *capocomico* that Scala would have composed and collected the scenarios in his collection.

In his preface to the collection Scala's friend, the distinguished actor Francesco Andreini, tells us that Scala's scenarios "in all time and places gave him very great honor," but there is no direct evidence of this.[28] It is reasonable to believe that Scala was invited to assume the position as head of the Confidenti on the basis of that reputation. Near the very end of *Le due commedia in commedia* (act 5, scene 10) by Giovanni Battista Andreini (son of Francesco) a character, the French pastry chef, reveals that he is really the character Flaminio Scala, who will, he says, make a play that will shine like the sun; it will be about the events he has just seen in the play that he is in. Perhaps this framing of his own play is merely Giovanni Andreini's tribute to his family's old friend Scala, who died the following year, in 1624. However, for the joke to have effectively served the ending of his own play, Andreini had to have assumed the audience's familiarity with Scala's work and their high regard for it.

Apart from his own letter to readers prefacing his scenario collection and his two prologues to *Il finto marito*, Scala provides no information about his intention or process in composing the scenarios. In the preface to the scenario collection Scala tells us that he had not thought to publish the scenarios until various enthusiasts urged him to do so. He readily accepted this idea, he says, so that others could not claim the scenarios as theirs. In publishing the scenarios, a genre with no other named authors and in which no one had previously published, Scala was evidently also attempting to raise both the status of *commedia dell'arte* and his own as a creator of scenarios and to claim himself as an author. The first of the two prologues to *Il finto marito* tells us about the regard in which he held the scenarios, not least because, ironically, it serves as a prologue to his fully scripted play. It is a defence of improvised performance and of his earlier publication of scenarios including the scenario on which *Il finto marito* is based. In it Scala emphasizes the centrality of scenarios to drama and performance: "plays properly and in essence consist in actions and only incidentally in narrations," that is, in the words spoken.[29] Further, in an argument akin to that of natural philosophers, newly emphasizing empiricism rather than reliance on authority,[30] Scala affirms the quality of the scenario plots, implying that they are even superior to those of the earlier scripted, that is literary, *commedia erudita*, because they had resulted from "learning by doing" rather than from merely "observing the rules and imitating as much as possible." "Experience produces art," Scala writes. "The only rules and precepts are those of good practice and good dramatists ... it being the case that rules are always taken from usage and not usage from rules."[31]

At the end of his preface to the scenario collection Scala promised a second volume of scenarios "quite soon," but for reasons unknown it never appeared. Perhaps the first volume did not garner the reading public he sought. It had no other successors.

Scala wrote in Tuscan, the vernacular model for Italian literature in the sixteenth and seventeenth centuries, the language of Bembo, Dante, Petrarch, and Boccaccio. Remaining scenarios in other dialects also exist, the monumental Casamarciano collection in Neapolitan, for instance. Assuming that Scala aspired to publish another fifty scenarios, scholars note that that would have brought Scala's total number of scenarios up to the number of fables provided by Boccaccio in his *Decameron*. Fabulists regularly aspired to provide the number of fables that Boccaccio had provided and quite regularly fell short.[32] Indication that Scala was inspired in his effort by Boccaccio is his numbering of the scenarios by days. Unlike those of Boccaccio, however, and more akin to those of Matteo Bandello, Scala's days are set in no narrative framework and are not ordered by topic. In designating his scenarios not just by titles but by days, Scala probably intended for the work of Boccaccio to lend status to his own and to give credence to his plots or fables as acceptably literary.[33] The scenarios were not plays but also were not in any familiar literary genre. Scala, additionally, may have been advertising the large number of wares that he could provide. A troupe with an extended stay in one place might quickly exhaust its repertoire.

SCALA'S FORMAT

For readers and performers, Scala, as I said, added an Argument to each of the scenarios, describing what had happened to some of the central characters before the scenario starts. The Arguments vary in length from a brief paragraph to, in Marotti's modern edition, two single-spaced pages, the length to a large extent dependent upon the amount of back-story that the reader needed to have or the actors needed to supply piecemeal, often at points specifically designated in the scenarios, making some scenarios considerably more narration heavy than others. Occasionally the Argument simply duplicates information to be found in the scenario, as if once Scala had committed to the idea of providing an Argument, he had to provide one whether or not it was necessary. It is not known what, if any, of the Argument Scala intended for inclusion in the evidently customary spoken prologue.[34] In a few instances there are minor inconsistencies between the Argument and the scenario. While the style of the scenarios is as repetitive and inelegant as directions for actors would naturally be, the Arguments, with their long compound sentences and adventures spun out over extended periods of time, reveal greater literary aspiration. However, the effort expended on them appears to have been erratic, and they are not even always self-consistent.

The Arguments are followed by a list of characters, grouped by households, with the relationships of the characters specified: "an old man," "his servant," "his son," et cetera, along with the guise in which they may at first appear: "Fabrizio, his servant, later revealed as his daughter Isabella," for instance. When Pantalone is in the scenario, as he is in all but one of them, his household is listed first. It is often specified that he is a merchant. Graziano or Doctor is the second most commonly listed householder, but he also can be listed otherwise: as a mountebank, a friend, or alone. Characters with no house on stage, for instance some young men or the Capitano, are listed after the households. Occasionally Scala forgets to list characters appearing in the scenario, usually but not always minor ones. Copy-editing, at the time, was often not what we might wish, and the means of printing did not help.

To give continuity to the whole and to borrow the fame of various actors, and perhaps also to make it easier for contemporary readers to imagine the scenarios in performance and in their best performance, Scala changed the names of characters in his scenarios (apart from those of Pantalone and Graziano or Dottore, which were fixed by convention) to the names used by famous actors for their roles. Alongside the cast list appears a prop list that is not always complete. Important props like jewels, weapons, and lanterns are sometimes not listed, perhaps because, although they were not the usual accoutrement of the character, they were always ready to hand.

Andrews notes that, in the 1611 edition of the Scala scenarios he examined, the first few scenarios have the name of the city in which the action is set, squeezed on to the probably already typeset page seemingly as an afterthought. Surprisingly, for all the scenarios, the time of day is similarly squeezed in.[35] That Scala at first omitted the city, which rarely had any bearing on the action and may have been changed in performance to the name of the city in which the scenario was being performed, is understandable, but whether it was day or night, when the characters could not readily have seen one another in the unlit street, would have profoundly affected the way in which the actors were to behave.

Following the city designation are the three acts of scenarios, as opposed to the five acts of fully scripted plays. Each of the unnumbered scenes lists each of the entering characters beside it, although some of the information provided within the scenes appears too late for actors to have taken instruction from it and seems to have been added as an afterthought for readers. If the character is disguised, Scala often refers to that character by the sex in which he or she is disguised, as if he were recalling the action rather than aiding readers. Pronoun referents are sometimes difficult to follow.

How many changes Scala made in the scenarios themselves to accommodate his reading audience or the players in his ideal troupe we cannot know. It is clear that he made such changes, not only because no single troupe existed with the character names that Scala employed but also because his revisions to employ these character names were not thoroughgoing. In Day 15, for instance, entitled *The Troubled Isabella*, Isabella never appears, but a Flavia does. Changes to accommodate the particular audience, the conditions of presentation, and the actors must have been usual all along. Influential audience members, like Hamlet in Shakespeare's eponymous play, had special interests and requests, cities had particular prohibitions, performance conditions varied, and troupe membership was not stable. New troupe members and different troupes had different strengths and skills, and these may have suggested scenario revisions or even new scenarios. Actors themselves would have provided scenario revisions. In that sense, the debate about whether the scenarios were written, *a priori*, for actors to perform, or *a posteriori*, in retrospect is misleading.[36] The scenarios were likely always in process not only before their publication but thereafter. Whether any of them were written especially for the collection, we cannot know; it is easy to believe that the ones requiring large casts may have been. In addition, there is no indication of the order in which they were written. On the whole, those towards the end of the collection show more forceful women and are more various in their stories and in a wider range of moods than those at the beginning, perhaps suggesting that they were written later than many of the ones appearing earlier in the collection.

MY PROCESS

Commedia dell'arte performers became famous for their comedy, but they worked in a variety of genres and performed scripted as well as improvised plays. To unify and limit my work, I restrict my examination of Scala's scenarios to his forty comic ones, rather than also take into consideration the ten scenarios in other genres that are included at the end of his collection: tragedy, pastoral, and what Scala called "mixed," "royal," and "heroic." My focus on the comedies more readily allows me to show their relationship to the social context than do the more fanciful and sometimes experimental works in other genres at the end of the collection, one beginning, for instance, "A bear and a lion come out of the wood fighting." Dorinda having saved the bear from the lion, "The bear caresses Dorinda." Scala also experimented within the comedies themselves with *commedia grave*, for instance.

Scala's comic compositions most often include but are not necessarily restricted to the characters present in a usual troupe: two each of middling-elite[37] old men, young men (when that seems more appropriate I refer to them as youths),[38] young females and lower-class male servants, perhaps one female servant, and a captain, the latter often pretending to nobility.[39] It is very common for a work on *commedia dell'arte* to begin with detailed descriptions of these various characters, the "masks." While it is useful to read the Scala scenarios with the composite descriptions of character masks in mind, it is also necessary to see the extent to which it is essential to infer characters from the scenarios. As Ferdinando Taviani observed some while ago, *commedia dell'arte* actors had "characteristics worked out, but not character which varied from play to play."[40] Scala was describing not fixed characters but characters' behaviours, reasons for them, and feelings about them, and these in relationships. Within a range of possibilities, guided by ideas of verisimilitude and proper decorum but, significantly, also calling that decorum into question, each of the characters serves a variety of functions and has various relationships. Actors would have brought their distinctive costume; their distinctive facial mask (if comic and male);[41] their usual hand prop; speeches and speech mannerisms in the appropriate regional dialect or foreign accent; as well as class, sex, and character-appropriate gestures and movement that made them readily identifiable. Beyond that, to a considerable extent, Scala's plots define the characters. Accordingly, in attending to the scenarios, I have found it more useful to show the characters as functions of the plot and to describe their interactions. Without an understanding of these, it is easy to see the characters merely as pure manifestations of the theatre rather than of life.

My concentration on interactions rather than on masks makes clearer what the interest of these scenarios was for their audiences. The scenarios reflect the strains in personal relationships, and the repeated presence of these in the scenarios is an expression of their importance in real life. The strains were long-standing, but Martin, along with other recent scholars, believes that they were exacerbated at the time because the traditional idea of the self as communal and defined by one's social role was being challenged by newly "conflicting social roles and tensions – between men and women, masters and servants, parents and children, ... and so on."[42] Observing Aristotle's influential assertion that drama was to be about the actions of men (interactions, really), in the second chapter I look at Scala's representations of relationships between (1) citizens and society, (2) fathers and sons, (3) female lovers, wives and widows and men, (4) lovers, (5) friends, (6) citizens and servants, and (7) outsiders, examining the tensions within these relationships, and the links to these relationships and the tensions in them in actual life. As evidence of these tensions, Stefano Guazzo's third book of *La civil conversazione*, 1574, presents a discussion on the nature of the proper interactions "between husband and wife, father and son, brother and brother, and master and the servants."[43] *La civil conversazione* went through fifty editions in Italian, Latin, French, English, and German within fifty years of its first publication in 1574.[44] Scala humorously reflects some of the ways in which, in their individual lives, people acted within and against the rules, customs, and norms set out in this and similar books of the period on household management.

In the third chapter I establish the appropriateness of Scala's fixed street setting and suggest, in so far as possible, how it may have been represented. Traditional as the use of a street setting was, it was also uniquely appropriate to Italian life, to concepts like honour, and to activities like gossip, name calling, and violence. I take up the effect that the street setting had upon representations of women. I show the ways in which the setting is of a piece with the world the scenarios represent and how, accordingly, it contributes to the vitality and excitement the scenarios would have had for their contemporary audiences. Thus, with chapters 2 and 3, I show that the scenarios reflected life and took up matters of central interest to their audience.

In the fourth chapter I examine Scala's aesthetics. Scala adhered to the accepted guidelines for comedy, and, moreover, he borrowed "theatregrams," that is modules of structure, characters, situations, actions or words, and thematic patterns[45] from the earlier written comedy. I argue that such borrowing, far from diminishing Scala as a creator, was regarded as essential to creation. I further show how the historically important concepts of copiousness and variety enable us to appreciate Scala's craftsmanship.

Finally, in the second part of the book, in each of four chapters, I provide a detailed scenario reconstruction, respectively, for Scala's Day 6, *The Jealous Old Man* (*Il vecchio geloso*), Day 21, *The Fake Sorcerer* (*Il finto negromante*), Day 25, *The Jealous Isabella* (*La gelosa Isabella*), and Day 36, *Isabella [the] Astrologer* (*Isabella astrologa*). Through a careful reading of these scenarios scene by scene I am best able to establish how particular aspects of social history inform them throughout and to demonstrate Scala's skilfulness in composition. The painstaking tracking of obscure references, as I suggested in the preface, has often been richly rewarding. Through reading about uroscopy and the state of medicine at the time I came to understand how in Day 21[46] both the prescription of medication by a doctor before he even sees his patient, and the nature of the examination he would conduct when he does see her, would have made sense to a contemporary audience. Conversely, reading about seemingly familiar topics, like honour, marriage, and friendship, in the context of early modern Italy gave me a far better understanding of what was at stake in the actions in the scenarios. Reading about duels, disguises, and ghosts in historical context gave me an appreciation of them as being considerably more than overused theatrical devices.

The reconstructions are attempts to see Scala's scenarios whole, to demonstrate in detail the extent to which they reflect life, to show their integrity, and to elaborate on the rich performance information they provide. I show how much we can retrieve about the staging, character dynamics, and actions, and the interest of this kind of theatre for its contemporary audience. From the scenarios we can begin to see the extent to which the success of *commedia dell'arte* performance under Scala's supervision would have depended on them. Each quite different scenario I have selected provides a very detailed *res* or gist of its performance. Francesco Andreini, in his preface to the Scala collection, claimed that with its publication Scala had, in fact, provided "plays" with all but the dialogue.[47] The present book defends that proposition.

Every effort has been made to read no more into a scenario than a critic ordinarily reads into a play. Each reconstruction, however, is premised on the assumption with which one begins when reading a play: that it is good. My purpose, as I said, is to befriend the scenarios. By no means are all of them good. We would not expect forty good plays from any playwright, and we would recognize that even in good plays there are weaknesses. I refrain from providing a list of my favourite scenarios because to do so would simply re-inscribe our or my values rather than call attention to what we can learn by applying the aesthetic and social values of the period. I confess, however, to having chosen for reconstruction some of the many scenarios that I like. They are deliberately from different parts of Scala's collection and reveal various aspects of his art.

Through my various approaches I hope to establish the great value of Scala's scenarios in telling us about *commedia dell'arte* at its height and about the form's appeal for its contemporary audiences. By detailing the skill with which many of them are crafted, I show that they are not just formulaic iterations of a theatrical tradition but resourceful inventions. Through my reconstructions I demonstrate the considerable extent to which the scenarios' performance can be recovered.

A spate of recent scenario publications makes a sizeable number of the seven hundred and fifty known extant scenarios available for scholarship for the first time in other than their manuscript form.[48] A complete edition of fifty-one anonymous scenarios was published in 1996 as *Gli scenario correr: La commedia dell'arte a Venezia*. *La Commedia dell'Arte*, edited and introduced by Cesare Molinari, 1999, includes a selection of scenarios from the Correr and Magliabecchiana manuscript collections and from Scala's publication. In 2001 Francesco Cotticelli, Anne Goodrich Heck, and Thomas Heck provided a bilingual edition of the 176 legible scenarios in the anonymous Casamariano collection. In 2007 Annamaria Testaverde made available in Italian some scenarios from that collection as well as Scala's, but from a number of other collections as well.[49]

I mean for my work to suggest contexts in which other extant scenarios – many now readily available for the first time, either in Italian or in reliable translations – can be studied and to provide possible methods for going about such study.

chapter two

Character Relationships

Traditional *commedia dell'arte* characters are routinely seen in isolation from one another. The scenarios, however, show relationships between characters in a large variety of situations, and these relationships reflect, in theatrical form, actual interactions within society at the time. Early modern selfhood was experienced relationally. People were largely defined by their part in a nexus of relationships.[1] In this chapter I therefore direct my attention to the nature of interactions between people in the society, the tensions within them and the representations of these in Scala's scenarios. In the last half of the book I read characters primarily through the lens of cultural history and through their interactions.

Scala worked within the well-established theatrical tradition for comedy that restricted it to the imitation of private citizens. He represented the domestic concerns of these citizens, and even then, principally but not exclusively, the marrying off of their children satisfactorily. In this and the resulting interactions between professional men, and merchants (the middle elite),[2] their families, and servants, and a few but various outsiders, including a captain, there was, however, plenty of real life. In the cultural gap between Scala and us, the social significance of the interactions he represents has too often been lost.

Speaking as a character called Player, Scala makes clear in the first of his prologues to his fully scripted play *Il finto marito* that he sees the *commedia dell'arte* as an art of imitation of nature, "verisimilar," including in the imitation of various dialects. Yet another fourteen times in that prologue he repeats that *commedia dell'arte* is imitative, and in contexts that make clear he means imitative of nature.[3] In the second prologue to the same play Scala again takes up that idea, telling us that his scenarios are "a mirror of life." In this, Scala, like virtually every dramatist of the period, followed Donatus, or rather the fragment entitled "On Comedy and Tragedy" in which the author, purported at the time to be Donatus, claims to cite Cicero, defining comedy as "the imitation of life, the mirror of manners, and the image of truth."[4] But what can it possibly mean that *commedia dell'arte* characters and their behaviour mirror nature?

Domenico Bruni, in 1621, and Hamlet help to clarify the matter. In the prologue to his unwritten comedy *Lo specchio* (*The Mirror*) Bruni spells out the relationship between theatre and mirror: the mirror is the most "faithful counselor" and the most "severe censor" because it will honestly uncover every flaw. The mirror of comedy exceeds all others because "amongst all mirrors that are most profitable to man, I would dare to affirm that comedy may be the principal one ... In this mirror everyone should gaze, since in it everyone will find material to regulate himself."[5] Most famously, Hamlet reminds the players that "the purpose of playing, whose end [and not just in comedy], both at the first and now, was and is to hold, as 'twere, the mirror up to nature, to show virtue her own feature, scorn her own image, and the very age and body of the time his form and pressure" (III, 2). This is not what we would think a mirror actually reflects. Hamlet's mirror interprets what it reveals and evaluates it in moral terms.

In Day 16, entitled *The Mirror*, Scala utilizes an actual mirror to provide his scene of recognition, but, like Hamlet's metaphorical mirror, Scala's mirror is not what we would think of as literally reflective. It shows not the image of those in front of it but the truth about the past behaviour of the mischievous servants. Deborah Shuger, in a revelatory essay on Renaissance mirrors, observes the following: "The majority of Renaissance mirrors – or rather, mirror metaphors – do reflect a face, but not the face of the person in front of the mirror. Typically, the person looking in the mirror sees an exemplary image, either positive or negative, the inward self but generic rather than individual."[6] It is thus that Scala can claim that his characters and their actions mirror human life. It is how in the second prologue he can logically argue, if only in the usual defence against antitheatricalism, that the goal of comedy is to help the audience by example, even in "seeing those who live badly."[7] We can learn from Pantalone's failings.

Another way in which the verisimilitude of the early modern period may not fit our conceptions of it is that decorum required the characters to act and speak according to their nature, sex, age, fortune, nation or city, art or profession, and relations and associates. Characters were verisimilar if they were made to behave and speak according to these conditions.[8] Thus, the imitation of nature in the early modern period did not mean then what it means now. With these caveats in mind, I turn now to the interactions between people in early modern Italy and to Scala's representations of them.

In the main, the interactions that Scala shows have gone awry. Harmony and obedience – unlike fear, conflict, rage, tears, and deviousness – do not make interesting theatre. I am reminded of the first line in *Anna Karenina*: "Happy families are all alike; every unhappy family is unhappy in its own way." While Scala shows us those who lived up to the ideal – good citizens, sons and daughters, servants, friends, and captains – he shows us an enormous range of untrustworthy and foolish fathers and husbands, disloyal sons, wayward daughters, faithless friends and lovers, disobedient and surreptitious servants, and military captains who try to disrupt the plans of the others. It is primarily the problems in the relationships between members of these groups that gives Scala the variety of his actions and the range of characters' behaviour.

Scala seems to have accepted Piccolomini's elaboration on Aristotle's idea that comedy ought to show people as worse than they appear in normal life: "that is to say, the old men more avaricious, the young men more dissolute, the servants more untrustworthy, the courtesans more deceitful."[9] But in so doing, and this is the important part, Scala also shows the actual tensions within the society, the dialectic between the conforming self and individual desire. In the seven major sections of this chapter that follow and in their subsections I examine the various relationships in real life that Scala makes use of in his scenarios. An understanding of these relationships and their tensions helps make clear to a modern reader the vitality of the interactions represented in Scala's scenarios.

PATRIARCHY AND PATRIARCHS

In early modern Italy the family was both the foundation of and the model for the structure of civic life. The republic was the family writ large; the ruling elite were regarded as the civic fathers. Just as the fathers of the families were to have control of their wives, offspring, and servants, so too were civic fathers to have unquestioned authority over everyone beneath them in the hierarchy.[10] Patriarchal control was paramount in both the social and the political spheres.[11] Challenges to fathers were potentially challenges to the political authority. To regard the scenarios as wholly apolitical because they attended to domestic situations is misleading. The contemporary audience would have understood problems within the family to be of considerable actual and symbolic societal significance. Increasingly, scholarship has come to attend to these fault lines in the patriarchal ideal, stylized to comic effect in Scala's scenarios.

It was the responsibility of those with enough seriousness of purpose, dignity, and maturity – the citizens, the fathers – to preserve transgenerational continuity: the social order, goods, families, and family names. Citizens – the tax-paying males – constituted a small minority of the population. The vast majority of the population – females, boys, young men, and those of the lower classes – were presumed to lack the gravity, the dispassionate reason, and the controlled sexuality that were the necessary moral qualities of governors.[12] All presented the possibility of discord and even social revolution. Women's sexuality, uncontrolled, because women naturally lacked reason, could destroy the family honour and lineage; youths, regarded as yet lacking in adult reason, could dissipate the family fortune; and the lower classes, who naturally followed their baser instincts, could trick their betters in any number of ways, and such tendency towards social inversion hinted at social revolution.[13] Women, youths, and servants all provided the possibility of disorder within the patriarchy.

The elders, if guided by passion, could themselves disrupt the social order. Social mastery was based on the presumed superiority of masculine rationality. The patriarchal ideal was one of controlled passion and moderation. The troublesome emotions of fear, anger, and sexual desire were to be repressed.[14] Scala regularly shows patriarchs surrendering to these emotions. Frequently they abandon their rationality in pursuit of young well-to-do girls or lower-class women. Ian Moulton observes that "in a patriarchal culture in which social mastery is based on the putative superiority of masculine rationality ... the surrender of the rational faculty to sensual pleasure – constitutes a larger social failure"[15] It was the responsibility of the elders to keep the passions of the young in check, not to indulge in them themselves. In Day 12, fearing that his son is his rival in love for a young woman, the father plans to send the son away to school. In Day 28 two old men come to blows in their rivalry for a married lower-class woman. With such behaviour, old men weaken both their masculine vigour and the commonwealth. Thus, in Day 31 one patriarch reprimands another for keeping mistresses, especially because he is an old man. In Day 32 the potential threat to society is intensified by the possibility of incest: when Pantalone is found chasing after a girl he presumes to be a gypsy but who is actually his own daughter in disguise, he is told that his children run away and go mad because of his own sins.

Scala always mocks such self-degradation, and the old men get their comeuppance for it. Northrop Frye, speaking from the point of view of youth in comedy, rather than, as I have, from the point of view of the patriarchs, stated that "the fury with which these characters [with less youth and more money] are baited and exploded from the stage shows that they are father-surrogates, and even if they were not, they would still be usurpers, and their claim to possess the girl must be shown up as somehow fraudulent. They are, in short, impostors, and the extent to which they have real power implies some criticism of the society that allows them their power."[16] From either point of view, the old men's behaviour in Scala is a source of social anxiety.

Scala makes clear the impropriety not only of the old men's lust but also of their uncontrolled rage at what they see as the misbehaviour of their offspring and servants. This rage is always a source of humour and, as in Day 12, justification for the servant's revenge. Both lust and rage diminish the dignity and authority of the citizens, particularly in the public displays necessitated by the scenarios' fixed street setting.[17]

Marriage

Central to the family was marriage. It was the means to institutionalize sex and to reproduce a paternal biological line in a nurturing and moral environment, while instilling in the offspring an internal discipline based on the all-important qualities of honour and reputation. Among the upper classes the right marriage could enhance individual status: "Tell me whom you marry and I'll tell you who you are" runs an old Italian proverb.[18] More than that, the right marriage affirmed and could elevate the social position of the whole family. Marriages of the well-to-do were a way to build alliances that would facilitate exchanges of material resources and promote social and economic advancement by establishing webs of familial alliances. Thus, the arrangement of the appropriate marriage was of great concern to the families involved, for which the concerted effort to elevate their honour and wealth was regarded as essential.[19]

Further, marriage lay at the heart of social and political institutions. Machiavelli cites an example of how in ancient Rome a woman without a father was advised by her guardian to marry a plebian and by her mother, a noble. A resulting great battle arose in the country. Machiavelli advises princes and governors of republics to learn that disputes arising from such incidents can injure and disgrace their state or republic and to head off such a "corruption of marriages" as was marriage to a plebeian.[20] Marriage was a complex and unwieldy arrangement invested with layers of signification that crucially affected perceptions of love, sexuality, and, more largely, moral and social order, stability, and organization.[21] Arranging a marriage for his young daughter that served the family honour and finances was a time-consuming and important fatherly obligation. "In our social life there is nothing more difficult," wrote the historian and political thinker Francesco Guicciardini (1483–1540), "than marrying our daughters suitably."[22]

While it was hoped that the bride and groom would be companionable,[23] long-standing social norms were to condition the marriage partners to accept that familial rather than personal interest governed marriage decisions. The assent of the prospective partners was required, but it was not assumed that they would provide it.

Scala's scenarios, whatever their most memorable aspects (theft, madness, threatened castration), are almost always structured around a marriage, following not only theatrical convention but also audience concerns. Marriage was the central institution in sixteenth-century Italian culture. In the Argument preceding each scenario Scala, often in the very first sentence, points to the class of persons involved in the main action: "In Genoa lived a well-born and wealthy young man;" "In Perugia lived a gentlewoman;" "In Venice lived an old merchant." He thus makes very clear what is at stake in the dramatic actions represented. Everyone was very status conscious, and marriage was an important way of achieving or, at least, maintaining status. For the upper and middle classes, marriage was critical to their doing so.

In contradistinction to the marriages of the well-to-do arranged by the parents for the social and economic benefit of the families involved, Scala's scenarios feature heterosexual love relationships arranged by young lovers with sole regard for their mutual satisfaction or sometimes the satisfaction of a friend. We see the determination of young people to marry those of their own choosing, often in conflict with the wishes of their fathers. Thus in Day 28 "there was in Pesaro a young man of modest fortune, who loved a girl who was daughter of a certain Pantalone, a rich merchant ... However, ... by pretending to be a magician and playing various and diverse tricks, he acquired the young woman in marriage." After many travails, in the rushed endings of the scenarios, both the fathers and the young people are happy with the marriages effected. Upper-class marriage was intended to preserve and perpetuate the bloodline and to advance the family as a whole financially and socially; it was not designed to provide the couple with happiness. The scenarios represent an improbable reconciliation between love and marriage, between the assertion of individual identity and the reassertion of the communal one.

John Hale trenchantly comments that plays of the period do not end happily ever after with a reinstitution of the old order but rather that they had to end because what followed next would not in fact have been very happy.[24] Laura Giannetti, in her examination of the *commedia erudita,* the written Italian comedy from the early sixteenth century, expanding on the comments made by both John Hale and Jackson L. Cope, points out that the ending of the written plays seems tacked on at the point where continuing the action might destroy the illusion of the couples' living happily ever after. [25] She comments that the marriages made are "not the sensible marriages arranged by the parents or fathers undistorted by youthful passions – in fact, they are often just the opposite."[26] The gap between what the patriarchs want and what results is considerable.

Scala's scenarios, like the earlier written comedy, are consistent with social historians' increasing perception of conflicts, inconsistencies, and ambiguities beyond and beneath the patriarchal ideal.[27] During the course of the sixteenth century the unstable marriage had increasingly become a cause for concern.[28] In the latter half of the sixteenth century, in an attempt to address the problems, there was a deluge of publications on marriage that idealized it and supplied advice about it. Trying to accommodate the desire for marriage based on physical attraction and emotional love, the manuals emphasized love and fidelity, albeit within the arranged marriage.[29]

The Protestant Reformation had tried to accommodate at least some of the difficulties within marriage by allowing divorce for adultery, wilful abandonment, chronic impotence, life-threatening hostility, or wilful deceit. To this the Catholic Council of Trent responded in 1563 that the bond of matrimony could not be dissolved for any reason, including abandonment, adultery, "irksome cohabitation," or absences of one of the parties, and it inserted itself into the marriage process, with the result that clandestine marriages, made to avoid the arranged ones, were no longer recognized. Marriage required the presence of an authorized priest and two witnesses. Tridentine marital law placed the consent of children above the marital plans of parents[30] but, in doing so, set itself against the hierarchical structure of early modern households. In the secular model of parent and child relations each family member had a natural, God-ordained place, with the father in control not only of the household until his death but also of its goods. In Venice, at least, the right of fathers to disinherit children who married without their consent made almost worthless the Tridentine principle of the free choice of a marriage partner.[31]

Neither popular guidebooks nor religious edicts seem to have quashed the conflicts. Joanne Ferraro shows that in court cases women petitioned for annulments, claiming that their parents had forced them into unwanted unions, and they demanded separations from abusive husbands. Her book *Marriage Wars* concludes that "what the marriage wars reveal is that individual desires ... overrode the broader principles of state" but often not without a real fight.[32] Scala, whose scenarios are filled with conflict between arranged marriages and the desire of young people to marry those of their own choosing, was speaking to an audience that was very concerned about the nature and quality of the institution of marriage.

Patriarchs: The Professional

The characters of the patriarchs in the scenarios, principally Graziano and Pantalone, reflect not only theatrical convention but also, more particularly, their relationship to society at the time. Scala uses the Doctor, whom he often calls Doctor Graziano, as his primary representative of "the liberal professions (law, medicine, the humanities) whose practitioners held university degrees." In the social hierarchy, below those in the liberal professions were, in order, the international merchants, the retail shopkeepers and craftsmen, and, at the bottom, the salaried labourers and menials.[33] Of those in the liberal professions, teachers below the university level were held in the lowest regard. Data from Venice shows that about 30 per cent of Latin masters served as private tutors to one, two, three, or a handful of students.[34] In Day 31 Scala shows such a master, the pedant, a scoundrel, who gets no respect at all.[35] Scala only rarely specifies the profession of his doctor. In Day 28 he is a lawyer. In Days 15, 32, 36, and 38, he is a medical doctor. In Days 8, 17, 20, and 37, in which someone else is called in as a physician, we can infer that he is not a medical doctor. In Day 2 he is a sham of a doctor, a mountebank.

In the *commedia dell'arte* the doctor's dialect suggested that he came from or was educated in Bologna, home of the oldest continuing university in Western Europe. He is said to have employed a macaronic Latin, a free, comic Latin incorporating newly coined onomatopoeic words and Italian stems with Latin suffixes. Everywhere, students learned to write like Cicero, and Ciceronian style became the standard of the educated.

It became such a severe and rigid standard, and students became so filled with the excesses of it, that Erasmus found it an easy target for his scorn.[36] The learning, as it was applied, was mocked even by the learned as irrelevant, trivial, and pedantic, and the ideas, texts, and institutions that were the authorities of learning were similarly mocked.[37] Not surprisingly, since Scala was concerned primarily with action, there are no indications of the doctor's speech habits, except perhaps in Day 27, in which his speech is described as all higgledy-piggledy and senseless, and in Day 9, where he is described as stupid.[38]

In Scala the doctor is usually an object of laughter, we must assume, not only because he is a patriarch but also because he is educated. For men not belonging to the upper elites by birth, education, particularly in legal studies, was an important means of raising their social status and political influence. The demand for educated men was rising so rapidly that some descendants of the established elite tended to be squeezed out, although the middle elite seldom reached the highest professional posts. The resulting social mobility disrupted the presumed natural order and resulted in unease and resentment.[39]

Patriarchs: The Merchant

The patriarch as merchant is represented by the character Pantalone. In Scala, he is a figure of fun because he is a patriarch and because of his role in society. In the early modern period, middle-elites could enhance their status through the professions or through their involvement in trade and finance, essential to business in all the major seaports, industrial centers, and market towns. The merchants and financiers engaged in business both at home and abroad. They had to be capable of handling large capital resources and of managing risk. By means of their wealth, the businessmen gained social status and political influence, thus, like the university educated, they also disrupted the supposed natural order. Historian Henry Kamen documents the good sense of a French merchant who died in 1597. He chose for his younger son to become a doctor of law and for the older son to remain in the business. That way, while one branch of the family directly sought position, the other would continue to accumulate wealth.[40]

By the time Scala was writing, the locus of power had shifted from the landed gentry, who for centuries had sought to hinder and discredit the merchant,[41] to the cities and their businessmen and their production and trade, where as one priest observed, "Money is the vital heat."[42] The

Church's objection to usury of any kind, and its suspicion of merchants' avarice and materialism, had been much ameliorated by the merchants' use of the sacrament of confession and by the institution of purgatory, which allowed them to contract for divine favour with donations to welfare and to religious institutions, commemorative masses, and private chapels.[43] Still, the notion persisted that business, particularly banking and money lending, was disreputable.[44] In Scala the merchant is therefore frequently subject to practical jokes and derision. He is doubly vulnerable as both a patriarch and a merchant.

Scala often specifies that Pantalone is from Venice, a centre of commerce. The character of Pantalone is known to have spoken with a Venetian dialect. Nevertheless, excepting in two scenarios, Scala sets his comic scenario in a city other than Venice. In real life the merchant was frequently on the move to find better business opportunities.[45] The prosperity of cities led to great population movements from the countryside to the city and then from one city to another in search of better opportunity. In his ceaseless quest for earnings as a means to enhance, if not his own honour, the honour of his children or his children's children, the merchant travelled more widely and more frequently than any of those on the move in Europe except soldiers and perhaps pilgrims.[46] He travelled and lived where business took him, leaving his extended kinship group for a house of his own with his nuclear family and a self-sufficient way of life.[47] Nor did the merchant restrict his movement to Europe; business interests took Italian merchants to the whole of the Mediterranean basin. In Day 1 Scala makes this clear by telling us that the fathers are two rich merchants who were on their way to Egypt to trade.

The conduct of business required not only the merchant's mobility but a great deal of correspondence.[48] Although he likely had only an education in the vernacular schools, the merchant may well have been more literate than the noblemen and clergy whose status did not depend to the same extent on their ability to read and write.[49] In Day 1 the young businessman, Flavio, receives a letter from Syria that initiates the action. One scenario, Day 23, is even entitled *The Letter Carrier* (*Il portalettere*). The marriage arranged for the daughter by the father in the scenarios, often to a man in another city, as in Day 7, makes clear that he had business correspondents in cities other than where he lived. Letters between men often play an important part in the scenarios. Like the ports of call mentioned, they bring the larger world into the scenarios, incite action or a change of direction in it, and reflect their importance in real life. The correspondence of the leading actor-managers of the late sixteenth and early seventeenth century is itself testament to the importance of letters in the conduct of business.[50]

The merchant understood the importance of not only amassing money through his hard work and professional outreach but also protecting the money that he had earned. He was well aware of the importance of frugality. "Thrift is a holy thing," remarks Giannozzo in Alberti's *I libri della famiglia.*[51] The merchant knew the rapidity with which his savings could be lost to chance, to speculative business ventures, and to what Piero Camporesi describes as "the undergrowth of fraud, trickery, cunning, malice, and malpractice" from which there was no escape. Mistrust, which was only practical, ran high.[52] Giulio Cesare Croce, 1629, summed up a common sentiment: "Don't boast of having too many talents, / But always act the poor man, and the beggar / So that people won't bump you off."[53] In Day 27 Scala tells us that the rich merchant, much envied for his wealth, was attacked and left for dead. Scala's Pantalone seems to be named Pantalone de Bisognosi (of Need) on occasion because of his felt need to accumulate wealth and to protect himself. In the scenarios, suspicion and fear inform the personality of the merchant. He is all too ready to fall into fits of rage, suspecting his children and servants of malfeasance, financial and otherwise. Unfortunately, these underlings do take advantage of him and subject him to practical jokes that reaffirm his greatest fear, his vulnerability.

There are no clear indications in Scala for merchants' set speeches on thrift, like speeches in, say, Moliere's *The Miser.* Only in Day 7, when we are told that Pantalone buries his daughter at night because he is stingy and night burial is cheaper, is it explicit that the merchant is thrifty. In several other scenarios we can deduce that there were comments about his miserliness – in Day 39, act 2, scene 3, for instance – but the merchants' calculating approach to life [54] can be observed in the marriages they arrange for their children to compatriots of their own generation, who are unknown to the offspring involved. In scenarios, like Day 21, in which two old men between them negotiate marital arrangements for themselves and their daughters, the negotiations would inevitably have included financial considerations because, in reality, there were no marriages without them. In the scenarios they would have provided good comic material, and the actors would have known to provide it.

In Days 11, 16, 22, 26, 30, and 35, for their spendthrift escapades, the sons feel impelled to steal from their fathers or, as in Days 22 and 26, have a servant do so. The planning for these thefts includes the ready opportunity for the sons' rationalizations and complaints about the fathers' tight financial rein on them. At the fathers' discovery of the thefts there is opportunity for the fathers' speeches on the sons' fiscal irresponsibility. The great fear of the well-to-do that they would succumb to their own moral weaknesses or to the trickery of their inferiors is amply explored.

FATHERS AND SONS

A number of the well-to-do, unmarried, young men in Scala's scenarios appear unfettered by any familial relationships. In reality, fathers died and some unmarried sons moved away, but, as in the scenarios, the majority of them resided with their fathers. A description of the actual relationship between fathers and sons shows how much the scenarios are representative of daily life.

The son remained under his father's financial control at least until his marriage in his mid-twenties to early thirties.[55] He was dependent upon the father for inheritance and reputation. With the exception of the time he might spend travelling for his father's business (as in Days 8, 9, 19, 32, 34) or away at a university, receiving an expensive education (as in Days 11,13, 26), the son lived at home and, even when he married, he might continue to live in the father's house. In the more and more urbanized Italy, however, those who were well to do, like those in Scala's scenarios, increasingly lived apart from the kinship household and set up their own.[56] The son, though, might well have continuing business dealings with his father and engage with him in public life. The son was to remain subordinate to his father, always addressing him in the polite form.[57] According to the humanist philosopher Marsilio Ficino, 1455, the father was to be a "second God," and the son a "mirror and image" of the father, whose commands he should fearfully and reverently obey.[58] It is natural that in Day 1, Isabella, seeking Flavio as husband, tells him that she can provide him with the dearest thing he has in the world, not herself but his father.

The father's emotional investment in his sons is well expressed by Lorenzo Alberti, the dying patriarch in *I libri della famiglia*: the young should not "imagine that any contentment or joy of the old surpasses that of seeing the young turn out well and worthy of love."[59] Virtuous children brought honour to the family and evidenced the diligence of the father in their upbringing. The fathers' highest expectations were for the sons, through whom the family line was to be maintained.

The son's obligation to his father was considerable. Lorenzo Alberti explains that young people ought to "refer every wish, thought, and plan of their own to their fathers and elders and to take counsel with them about everything ... They should listen eagerly to them as to very wise and experienced men, and gladly submit to the guidance of men of judgment and age. Nor let the young be slow to help any of their elders in their old age and infirmity."[60]

The family constituted a moral entity consisting of people and property to be defended at all costs. Its interests were to supersede personal desires or ambitions. Loyalty to the father and his house in defence of their honour was something for which the son was to risk his life. "Sons," Torquato Tasso writes at the end of the sixteenth century, "are by nature defenses and fortresses for their fathers."[61] Thus in Day 36, when Flavio, the son of the Spanish regent of the high court in Naples, observes the Italian Orazio covertly courting his sister, he fights him seemingly to the death.

Most often in the scenarios, however, we see sons who do not live up to their father's lofty expectations. It is not merely that bad sons are more dramatically interesting than good ones; young men from well-to-do families were, in fact, troublesome. This is not surprising, because they were put in a very difficult position. They were under their father's control, had no economic autonomy, and were denied any role in civic society. They were youths or juveniles until their marriage. In their very long and powerless adolescence (*adolescenza*), which the influential humanist Matteo Palmieri described as continuing until age twenty-eight, their only tolerated expressions of power seem to have been in sexual activity (which was expected of them), violent street fights (which were an inconvenient and frightening constant of city life), and soldiering.[62] The recognized outlets for their sexual activity were poor or immodest women, including other men's wives, and young men.[63] In Scala, young men are shown pursuing ostensibly sheltered and out-of-bounds, well-to-do young women (in virtually every scenario) and fighting (in scenarios too numerous to name). Examples of soldiering in the scenarios are present in Day 40, in which Flavio had gone off to fight in the Hungarian war, and in Day 19, when the Capitano is told that Flavio is dead, so that he will not take Flavio with him to war in Flanders. Scala thus represents youths' activities both feared and actual.

The powerlessness of youths, necessary to keep the patriarchy intact, was conveniently justified by the patriarchy as natural.[64] There was a societal expectation that sons would evade the civic and moral discipline of their elders. Giannozzo in *I libri della famiglia* observed, "They live a life of idleness, ... waste their own resources, neither caring as much for their honor as they ought nor valuing moderation of any kind."[65] Some elders, having themselves been young once, viewed this profligacy with some tolerance and sympathy.[66] Thus in Day 26, when Pantalone tries to blame the bad behaviour of his son on the influence of Graziano's son, Graziano responds that his son is innocent and that anyway youth must follow its own course.[67]

In Scala's scenarios most of the time, however, the fathers are far from accepting the sons' bad behaviour. They lament the bad fortune that they have had with their children and, in utter exasperation, forgoing all semblance of calm reason and authority, lose their tempers at them or even resort to beating them, as in Day 35 when Pantalone's son steals from him. In the main, in fact, elders viewed the self-indulgence and illicit behaviour of the youths with anxiety and feared that their families would be brought low, their fortunes dissipated, and their honour destroyed and that these events would lead to a general breakdown in society.[68] The fathers, as Lorenzo Alberti says, were expected to exercise control so that the sons were not "depraved and corrupted by their own native inclinations." Badly behaving sons reflected badly on the father. They were a result of "the negligence of those who did not restrain them."[69] Thus, the pedant in Day 31 can credibly blame Orazio's failure to study on his father's failure to maintain enough discipline in the household.

The clearest remedy for wayward sons, as Pedrolino tells Pantalone in Day 30, was to marry them off – to someone at least of the same social station. This remedy, however, could not be effected until the youths were of an appropriate age. With their marriage, males were expected to come of age socially and politically. The conclusion of the scenarios implies the abrupt character reversal that was evidently to take place in real life. Madeleine Doran, writing about the Elizabethan theatre, posits that "the belief that one passion drove out another combined with a tendency to view passions as detached from character – that is, a tendency to regard any man as subject, under proper stimulus, to any passion." This tendency may explain the sudden repentance, quite apart from any theatrical reason.[70] Doran's additional idea that the "belief in the enormous persuasiveness of eloquent speech, especially if accompanied by expressive countenance and gesture," serves to explain the swift repentances of the youths.[71] The seemingly pat endings correspond to an actual pivotal moment in male lives. The characters may not develop but they do change. Just as, with marriage, young sheltered girls were expected to become wives, mothers, and household managers, so young men were to fully and responsibly enter into public life.

DAUGHTERS, WIVES, WIDOWS (AND MEN)

To compose a scenario in which a well-to-do female appears is to include her relationship to her guardian because these women had little and rare independence from them. "Women are born to be men's subjects," Torquato Tasso explains.[72] Control of the woman's body was a major patriarchal preoccupation. Women, and particularly their sexual behaviour, had to be strictly regulated to preserve the patriarchy. Discipline and control were particularly difficult to effect, it was thought, because the sexual appetites of women were more voracious than those of men and they were accordingly more prone to sin. Michael Rocke quotes a 1524 commentator: "The laws presume that all women are usually bad because they are so full of mischief and vices that are difficult to describe."[73] Consequently, the upper-class woman was under the supervision first of her father or other protector and then of her husband or, if she did not marry, of a convent to which she was sent.[74] Thus in Day 2, act 1, Flaminia states that her father is the master of her body and soul. While a number of the Scala scenarios have young men who appear as free agents, only one upper-class woman, not identified as a widow, is shown without a supervising family or guardian member. In the scenario in which she appears (Day 15), Pantalone, to whom the woman is unrelated, asks Orazio's father for permission for Orazio to marry her, as if, even though she is alone, she needs a patriarch to provide this.[75] The woman's honour and that of her family depended first upon her chastity and then upon her faithfulness in marriage, and families went to great lengths to protect these. Protection was critical to the purity of the male bloodline, the continuity of the family, and the certainty of legitimate inheritance.[76] Chastity protected the honour of the men, their families, the patriarchal structure of society, and, as Margaret King dramatically puts it, "the world's property."[77] The woman was the conduit through which these passed.[78] "In a woman," remarked Lodovico Dolce in 1553, "one does not look for profound eloquence or subtle intelligence ... or anything else except chastity ... because in a woman this is worth every other excellence."[79] Thus, unlike a son who was married in his late twenties or early thirties, a daughter was married off between the ages of fourteen and eighteen, and sometimes shortly after she had reached puberty, in order to try to ensure her virginity and thus to safeguard the whole of the political, economic, and social order.[80]

To further ensure her chastity and faithfulness, the female was kept sheltered within the home throughout her life. She was to observe *mod-*

estia, avoid pomp and ostentation in her gestures and deportment, hold her head still, and speak seldom.[81] She was to refrain from listening to impudent words and from allowing her eyes to wander; she was to shun immoderate gestures and dress and avoid idleness, excessive refinements, dancing, and male company.[82] She was to display no disordered passion, undue sadness or gaiety, impatience, or anger.[83] She was to keep herself occupied with household management and with devotional literature, spinning, weaving, and needlework.[84] She was to leave home for no destination other than church, and even then she was to be accompanied.[85] Conveniently, the restriction of well-to-do women to the house was thought to suit their nature. Women are "almost all timid by nature, soft and slow," and "therefore more useful when they sit still and watch over our things," remarks Lionardo in Leon Battista Alberti's *Family in Renaissance Florence.*[86] Similarly, Paolo Caggio, in his family advice manual of 1552, describes women as weak "and of little spirit."[87] Since well-to-do women were not expected to have worldly dealings, and since learning could corrupt simple minds, their education was generally limited. While practically all sons of nobles and wealthy merchants and sons of professionals attended school, usually a Latin school, and (as Scala shows) sometimes university,[88] girls' education was generally much more limited and in the vernacular. Girls were rarely taught Latin on the rationale that they had no public role to play. If they were from a wealthy family they were schooled in a convent, otherwise by their mother. Their education was to be sufficient for them to manage social obligations and household affairs.[89] In late sixteenth-century Venice, while 33 per cent of adult males, nobles, merchants, members of professions with high status and income (law, medicine, and some civil servants), master artisans of many kinds, and some petty shopkeepers could read, only 13 per cent of females could do so, these being primarily nuns and the wives and daughters of the wealthiest citizens.[90] If they could read, they were to restrict their reading to saintly teachings.[91] Girls were not to be applauded for writing "saucy rimes" and "love letters" but for writing what was necessary, honest, and appropriate to an "honorable woman."[92]

Daughters

The young age at which daughters were married off and the sheltered life they had lived reinforced the view that, inexperienced as they were, their own judgment in the matter of the choice of a mate would be too easily overwhelmed by passion and improper motivations. Thus, in Day

12, act 3, Flaminia, in a fit of pique at her rejection by the Capitano, whom she loves, decides to love Flavio. Such decisions are not a rational basis for marriage. Indeed, in most of his scenarios Scala shows young girls, as well as youths, overcome by jealousy, irrational suspicion, and sexual passion. Girls were considered to be by nature weak and irrational.[93] "Unless you catch them when they're young, their chastity is all undone," pithily observed an old man in Alessandro Piccolomini's play *L'alessandro*.[94] Unlike youths, girls moved away from their natal family and, at a young age, to that of their spouse.[95] Consequently the ties of a daughter to either parent were not as strong as those of a son. What is more, if the son had a wet nurse, she was likely to be in the home, whereas the daughter with a wet nurse may have been sent off to her until the age of two.[96] She might subsequently be sent off to a convent for her education. As, Stanley Chojnacki observes, the relatively distant relationship between father and daughter helps to explain the coldness and apparent scheming with which fathers negotiated away their daughters.[97] This, in part serves to explain how the daughter, as we see in Scala's scenarios, might be paired with a considerably older man, sometimes in another city, whom she might not meet until her betrothal, and that perhaps very shortly before her marriage.[98] The bride in real life, sometimes even described as merchandise (*mercanzia*), could be bargained away like other goods.[99] She played an even less important role in marriage arrangements than did the groom.[100] Even the most caring of fathers was under considerable pressure to forge financially and socially advantageous family alliances by means of marriage.[101] It was quite natural that marriage and business relationships should go hand in hand.

In the main, Scala shows young girls resisting the arranged marriages, writing letters to secret loves, speaking to them at windows and in the street, enlisting the help of servants in their love affairs, travelling in disguise to pursue their loves, and feigning madness or even death to be with them and to avoid the marriages arranged for them. In Day 21 the daughters are pregnant by their lovers. None of these indulgences had a place in the serious business of arranged marriages. Some of them were greatly feared by fathers and necessitated the daughters' being married off at a young age. Young women travelling in disguise to find their lovers, at least in the numbers they do in Scala's scenarios, is a dramatic fiction, so far as I can tell, as is the feigned death induced by drugs (another kind of disguise).[102]

The girl's requisite assent to the marriage arranged for her was not assured; fathers must have worried about getting it, and the girls must have fantasized about lovers, not about arranged marriages – especially with old men. In Day 4 Flaminia reads stories of love and chivalry. The danger of this was great. Erasmus cautions that "storytellers who corrupt innocent minds with their far from innocent tales must be kept away from young girls, for it is poison that they drip into those tender ears."[103] Despite the admonition that females confine their reading to religious matter, Paul Grendler points to the enormous popularity of chivalrous romances among both sexes.[104] Scala and, in the last twenty-five years, critics have made clear that the relationship between precepts and women's actual lives was in some cases more complicated and varied than such strictures allowed.

Dowry

Although Scala always refers to the class of the lovers, he only rarely makes explicit reference to dowries. In real life dowries would inevitably have been a central part of the marital negotiation. "Second only to the girl's formal assent," remarks E.R. Chamberlin, "was the problem of the dowry." Actually this was the first.[105] The dowry was what Sharon Strocchia calls "the twin sister" of marriage.[106] Fathers of males sought dowries as large as possible. Fathers of females sought to pay out as little as possible.[107] As a powerful determinant of who might marry whom, the dowry penetrated deep into the social system. Almost unavoidably, the subject would have arisen in the dialogue.

Wives

In the tradition of Roman drama and the *commedia erudita,* Scala's scenarios contain few upper-class wives. Scala includes them in only five of the comic scenarios. In real life, the love of the good wife for her husband was expressed in her obedience to him. It was revealed in the moderation she demonstrated in every aspect of her behaviour, including her downward gaze, her gait, speech, and dress.[108] She took care of the house and children[109] and provided no drama. The interactions between such self-effacing wives and their husbands presented no tensions in the society and thus were not a good topic for Scala's comedy. Scala shows only one unequivocally good wife, in a minor role in Day 7: she grieves along with her husband at her daughter's supposed death.

The upper-class wives in the remaining four scenarios play larger roles and their interactions with their husbands are memorable. Scala clearly intended for the wives to garner audience sympathy, despite the fact that they are not altogether good. In Day 17 a wife who has waited for her husband's return for six years, knowing nothing of his whereabouts, does not continue to wait patiently but rather sets her sights on another man – until her husband returns. In Day 31 the wife seriously considers becoming unfaithful to her whoring husband, but then, turns her energies to cleverly devising a means to expose the adulterous intentions towards her of a deceitful pedant. In Day 39 two wives, whose foolish husbands are infatuated with an actress, acquire secret lovers, at least until the husbands promise to reform themselves and take charge of their marriages.

Widows

Scala presents more widows than wives. Because most of them in the scenarios remarry, they, unlike wives, allow for the expansion of Scala's central topic: marrying. Often the widows, like unmarried girls and wives, are under the close supervision of a guardian, most often, a brother or the father. In Day 1, for instance, one of the widows, Flaminia, is unable to spend time at widow Isabella's house without her father's permission and he arranges a marriage for her. The more interesting widows, occasionally living alone, in Days 1, 22 and 35, tend to exhibit greater maturity and independence than inexperienced unmarried girls. Scala's representation of widows, then, not only gives him more range in plotting in the representation of marriageable women but also is in accordance with a growing literature showing that widowhood gave women their best chance for social and economic autonomy.[110]

Given the age disparity between upper-class males and females at the time of marriage, many women, if they did not die in childbirth, became widows while they were still of child-bearing age.[111] Even discounting the high infant mortality rate, life expectancy was considerably lower than it is now. In Venice between 1610 and 1620, for instance, only 30 per cent of the population lived beyond the age of thirty-nine.[112] When a marriage had lasted some years and had produced children, the husband probably hoped that upon his death the wife would remain in his household to look after the children, who legally belonged to him. He generally specified in his will that she be generously supported from his resources – provided that she lived chastely and did not reclaim her dowry.[113] She was excluded by primogeniture from the actual inheritance of her husband's property.

During the lifetime of her husband a woman had no access to her dowry. It was given to the man to "support the burdens of matrimony."[114] At her husband's death a woman did have the right to reclaim her dowry if she left the husband's household, including the children.[115] The mother gained custody of the children only if the husband had so specified in his will. If she did reclaim her dowry, she deprived her sons by that marriage of what would have become part of their eventual inheritance (although even with the period's continuing dowry inflation the dowry never came close to what was left to a male child as part of the father's estate).[116] If she was under forty and therefore had a chance of remarrying, there was strong pressure from her natal family for her to reclaim her dowry and, with the aid of it, forge a new marriage alliance.[117] If she did so, she was portrayed as a dutiful daughter by her kin and as a "cruel mother" by her husband's family.[118] Both widows and widowers who could, often remarried.[119]

The widows in Scala are of a mind to remarry and their efforts to do so show them as remarkably unconstrained and resourceful. After the death of their husbands, dowry inflation did, in fact, allow some upper class women real financial independence and some modicum of authority.[120] In Day 1 the widowed Isabella passes herself off as a magician and proves instrumental in arranging her own marriage and that of the other widow, Flaminia. In Day 12, when old Pantalone desires the widow Isabella, and plans to send his rival in love, his son, Orazio away to university, Isabella poisons Orazio so that he is unable to leave and promises Pantalone to cure him only on condition that Orazio marry whomever she chooses – namely herself. Further, she stipulates that Flaminia, Pantalone's daughter marry her brother Flavio. In Day 4 the widow functions as a trickster and, although she is under the supervision of her brother, she announces that, as a widow, she will marry whom she pleases. She takes Flavio into her house, where their union is consummated, effectively marrying them, assuming honour was to be preserved. In the rather grim Day 40 Orazio had promised to marry the widow Isabella. But then, he behaves treacherously and deceitfully, both towards her and towards another woman. Isabella assumes the authority to make him go off to live in solitude, unfit for life among human beings, and she marries another.

In two of the scenarios Scala shows widows living on their own, evidently with custody of marriage-age children. Caroline Castiglione has recently provided limited evidence from Tuscany to suggest that the courts had, in actuality, begun granting widows the right to live on their own, managing the upbringing of the children in houses of their own.[121]

The stereotype of the cruel mother was gradually being replaced at the end of the sixteenth century by that of the "cruel uncle," the brother of the deceased husband with whom the children were ordinarily left.[122] The widows with children in Scala's Days 16 and 22 are no more successful at trying to arrange marriages for their offspring than are the old men in other scenarios.

Lower-Class Women

In contrast to the conflicts surrounding the arranged marriages of the well-to-do – the centrepiece of most but by no means all of Scala's comic scenarios – Scala usually simply throws in marriages between servants at the end of the scenarios to add to the festivities and to the sense of the scenarios' completeness. On his own volition Pedrolino or, not as often, the generally less resourceful Arlecchino chooses to marry Franceschina or another servant. Occasionally the comparatively liberated Franceschina is even allowed to choose between them. Scala makes no to-do about the matter.

There is indication in the scenarios that Scala's servant marriages may sometimes have been preceded by the partner's considerable sex play on stage.[123] Among the lower classes premarital sexual intercourse was common as long as relations were based on intent to marry or at least to create a stable bond.[124] Members of the lower classes were less likely to be involved in arranged marriages. When they were financially able to establish their own households, usually in their mid to late twenties, they selected their own mates, hoping to have found a dependable worker, rather than the right family with which to form alliances.[125] At marriage, lower-class females tended to be older and have had more life experiences than had those from well-to-do families. There were no marriages at any class level without dowries.[126] Those from the lower classes had to save up their earnings and, in addition, given their small salaries, rely on the help of their employer and others.[127]

Some lower-class women had sexual experiences prior to marriage if for no other reason than that, when servants and other women of modest means had to go about in the street in the course of their daily business, they were subject to sexual assault.[128] Even within the houses servants were exposed to sexual molestation by employers and social superiors.[129] If they were thus assaulted or tricked into sexual acts, the courts provided no satisfaction for their grievances in these matters. Purity of the lower-class line and their non-existent patrimony were not a concern to the courts. "Women were commonly differentiated between those leading 'honest' and those leading 'indecent' lives, with virgins, wives and widows in the former category, and servants, slaves and prostitutes in the latter."[130]

Scala does not take the honour of the lower classes very seriously either. In the scenarios any lower-class woman, or any woman disguised as such, is subject to sexual assault, always to comic effect. The humour in fondling women who are presumed to be lower class follows from the fact that they are not, in fact, lower class. In Day 26, when Pedrolino tries to rape Flaminia disguised as a gypsy, Orazio and Graziano laugh. The intended rape is funny in the context of the times because, if Flaminia, an upper-class virgin, were raped, particularly by a lower-class man, serious consequences would follow. In Day 15, when Franceschina laughs, knowing from first-hand experience that her employer is impotent, we realize that he had attempted to have intercourse with her. We are not to wonder whether she willingly participated in such attempt; our response is only to be amused at the master's sexual inadequacy and her disclosure of it. At least in Day 4 Pantalone, this time evidently potent, having stolen the maidenhead of Franceschina, does what was required by canon law but not enforced in the case of servants: he provides a dowry.[131] He does more than that; he promises money for a first male child. Thus, he publicly acknowledges his responsibility and the woman's "honesty," despite her class. He was, as Pedrolino remarks, charitable in doing so.[132] His marriage to a lower-class woman like Franceschina, as any lower-class woman was expected to know, was out of the question.[133]

Scala regularly substitutes servants, female or male, married or unmarried, for upper-class girls in bed-tricks, again to everyone else's amusement. The important point is that in the bed-trick the well-to-do lecherous old man falls victim to a practical joke. In Day 6, when Pasquella, a lower-class married woman, is used in a bed-trick, it is a laughing matter. The societal anxiety that surrounded upper-class female sex outside marriage did not surround that of lower-class women.[134] The adulterous upper-class wife threatened the political and social order and was accordingly punished by the courts, but, as Pedrolino observes in Day 3, lawyers did not bother with cases against lower-class whores and cuckolds, and Scala treats instances of them as jokes that are no more serious than the intended rapes and deceits that get lower-class women into bed.[135] In the scenarios lower-class female sexual adultery is a source of humour. In Day 3 the matter of the unfaithful lower-class wife is resolved by her husband's being duped into believing that he was not cuckolded.

He is forced to beg forgiveness from his adulterous wife for having even thought that she had been unfaithful.

LOVERS

With the exception of one marriage that proceeds without demurral in a little-developed third act, Scala's scenarios never show obedient and silent upper-class girls and youths who merely assent to the marriages arranged for them. We see two marriages that had been arranged at the onset in Days 14 and 23, which after many complications and tribulations come about by other means. In mere assent there is no conflict, no societal tension, no comic potential. Excepting those I describe in the fifth section of this chapter, the youths and the girls in the scenarios marry for love. In representing the conflict between love and marriage, Scala takes on a very important societal issue.

Love was a topic of considerable contemporary interest. In Italy a great many discussions, *novelle*, and treatises were devoted to it. Records show that the Academy of the Apatisti, founded in 1631, one of many academies of the period that, in addition to being a social organization, was devoted to orations upon solemn occasions, lectures, critical essays, the reading of poetical compositions, et cetera, had among the topics for serious debate "Which is the greater passion, love or hate? Which prevails more in love, pleasure or sorrow? Which is the more vehement anger or love? Is love the result of choice or destiny? Does love end in pleasure or sadness? Whether the flame of love is kindled more by the sight of the beloved's smiles or tears. Whether it is preferable to see the beloved without being able to speak to her, or to speak to her without being able to see her. Whether it is better for a jealous lover to conceal his passion or to disclose it."[136] Questions for discussion of love elsewhere included: "Which love is the greater and more ardent, that of a man for a woman or a woman for a man? Who suffers more, the courtier whose lady has died or the courtier who loves a lady who does not love him?"[137] The terms of these debates and the discussions, which were strongly influenced by the idea of medieval courtly love, may seem strange to us, but they infuse Scala's scenarios and provide the actor with possible topics for speeches on love. And Pietro Bembo's rhetorical question about the torments of love are reflected in Scala's very plots: "Who does not know how many regrets, insults, alterations, griefs, and vengeful thoughts, and bonfires of disdain a thousand times consume and reconsume the lover before he gleans one satisfaction?"[138]

The lovers in the scenarios spoke Tuscan, the language of Petrarch's sonnets, 1327–68. Their florid speech revealed not only their refinement but also their great love, it being widely believed, even into the second half of the eighteenth century, that figurative language occurred spontaneously to the mind in a state of emotion.[139] Historian John Hale remarks that despite the influence of classical literature, writers of love lyrics rarely went back further than Petrarch for their model because of the technical virtuosity and beauty of Petrarch's sound patterns and because the personal psychology of his verse better suited contemporary sensibilities than did the poetry of the classical pagan world.[140] And in spite of the fact that young ladies were not to waste their time reading love poems, any more than stories of love and chivalry, Petrarch's love lyrics were read throughout Italy by upper-class young men and literate women.[141] Rosalind Kerr demonstrates that the celebrated actress Isabella Andreini directly imitated and even incorporated Petrarch's love lyrics into her own.[142] That the actors could speak this beautiful language was cause for admiration.

Petrarch's love for Laura, however passionate, was from afar and chaste. The lovers in Scala are determined to consummate their relationship and get married, sometimes in that order. Following the consummation, if honour were to be preserved, their marriage was all but a *fait accompli*, necessitating the belated agreement of the fathers.

Even when the love relationship was with someone of the right social class, as it is in every Scala scenario, and even when it was also with someone of the appropriate economic status, as it is in all but Scala's Days 9, 24, and 28 (where the financial inequality is overcome by other means), love matches were made without consideration of the family's economic, social, and political strategies that sought to guarantee the status of the lineage over time and that provided the social fabric of daily life. Moreover, they circumvented patriarchal authority and, thus, *ipso facto*, threatened the larger societal discipline, order, and rationality.[143]

At the time, love was regarded as one of the most powerful forces.[144] In Scala the word *love* is capitalized, as it is in Bembo's *Gli Asolani* and in Petrarch. "The power Love has over us," Bembo declared, "[is] a sufficient justification for making him a god."[145] The lovers in Scala's scenarios are frequently given to rail against Love and Fortune as if both were external forces outside their control. Love was considered irrational and even dangerous. In Day 15, even after Pantalone and others had publicly warned two brothers against courting his daughter under her window, thus dishonouring him, the young men persisted in doing so and even openly scorned Pantalone. His honour so threatened, Pantalone consequently attempted to murder them.

In Scala's scenarios the force of Love could be very spiteful. Love could lead people to betray both friends and lovers: in Day 29 the youth cannot help loving his best friend's woman. Love could be fickle: in Day 13, in his love for Isabella, Orazio forgets his love for Flaminia; then his dormant love for Flaminia is aroused, and he forgets his love for Isabella. In Day 38, after Isabella, the Turk, has left her husband, country, and religion and murdered her husband and child in her love for Orazio, he promptly forgets her in favour of a renewed passion for an old love.[146]

Even with lovers suitably matched economically and socially, then, the resulting marriages in Scala seem to forebode problems. They often follow much suspicion, jealousy, and unpredictable transfers of affection. How serious a matter for concern these were in a society marked by persistent fears about trust[147] is difficult to evaluate. It should be noted that at the time it was believed that jealousy increased love. Debates were actually held on the question of whether love could exist without jealousy.[148] It was also thought that the suffering of the slighted lover, as in Days 29 and 38, could be persuasive in winning the beloved.[149]

The keen interest in love expressed by the upper classes was not assumed to be shared by the lower classes. Domenico Pietropaolo comments that "since the diffusion of the courtly love tradition in the late Middle Ages, the lower classes had been accustomed by their culture to the idea that they were not capable of feeling refined sentiments, that courtly love was not for them, and that they should be concerned more with satisfying practical needs and their bestial urges."[150] Whether that is so or not, one can say that the lower strata of the population were represented as incapable of such refined sentiments as courtly love. When, in Day 18, Pedrolino and Arlecchino cast lots to decide which of them will marry Franceschina, the procedure is fully understandable because servants were analogized to "brute animals" that could only "feel the power of love in some ... minimal way."[151] In Scala's scenarios, like Day 21, *The Fake Sorcerer*, while the lovers converse at length, a male servant is sometimes left on stage, evidently to mock them in asides and gestures as they do in some of the learned comedy. Undoubtedly this counterpoint provided the dramatic interest that the lovers' long speeches alone might not. It also provided the supposed perspective of servants on the high-flown language and grand emotions for which the young often risked their lives, and, further, it reflected the practical concerns of the patriarchy about love relationships.

Courtship Exchanges

Girls confined to the house in Scala's scenarios communicate from their windows to their lovers on the ground below. Such communication would have been a dangerous practice that jeopardized the honour of the house. As recklessly, the girls also communicate by means of letters delivered by servants, albeit faithful servants, who act as go-betweens.[152] It was, in fact, partly to restrict such communication that the wives and daughters of most citizens could not read.[153] In Day 4 we learn that Flaminia, who appears at the window with a book in hand, reads a great many stories of love and chivalry and is exchanging love letters with Flavio. Inappropriate reading was thought to lead to inappropriate behaviour.

Exchanges of gifts were a form of social interaction that had even more serious implications than did reading and writing about love and exchanging letters. In the late sixteenth and early seventeenth centuries Venetian women considered handkerchiefs to be appropriate gifts for their future spouses. They were even given as part of the dowry. Handkerchiefs were used to clean away the blood after the first sexual contact and so carried an extremely intimate and specific sexual meaning. Accordingly, they were typically exchanged only after a long period of courtship and intimacy.[154] "When Shakespeare had Othello kill his wife for a dropped handkerchief," comments social historian Thomas Cohen, "the playwright made good Renaissance sense because such a gift was not a symbol but a sign, a pledge, with all the solidity the culture of the time invested in things given."[155] When Isabella, the wife of Pantalone, drops her handkerchief for the Capitano at the onset of Day 31, she reveals that she is so angry at and resentful of her husband that she is ready to pursue an adulterous relationship. This readiness provides suspense for the central plot of exposing the pedant to her husband, when she might, as he offers, conveniently have had sex with him right in her own house, her husband none the wiser. The dropped handkerchief makes clear that Isabella prefers loyalty to her husband to adultery with the loathsome pedant, not altogether because she is so honourable but because the pedant is so vile.[156]

While women were encouraged to engage in embroidery and thus would have had labour-intensive but inexpensive gifts like handkerchiefs on hand, men were in a position to provide gifts of monetary value like jewellery. The Capitano in Day 31 responds to the dropped handkerchief with the gift of a ring, ostensibly proving his emotional commitment. The gift was often given as the man's public investment in an otherwise unequal exchange; the woman would give her chastity for the man's promise of marriage backed up by something of monetary value.

Even more significant is the gift of the portrait in Day 39, after which the scenario is named and around which the drama is centred. Thomas Cohen provides an interesting historical analogue: "One evening from her balcony Maria Dusin witnessed Girolamo giving Regina his portrait. This act was far more than a simple transaction of a material object: it carried a greater meaning. Symbolically he was giving himself away."[157]

FRIENDS

A great many of the Scala scenarios, even when they are ostensibly about marrying, are about male friendship. Several scenarios have titles that make clear they are really about friendship: Day 5, *Flavio Betrayed* (*Flavio tradito*), Day 19, *The Three Loyal Friends* (*Li tre fidi amici*), and Day 29, *The Loyal Friend* (*Il fido amico*). In Days 6 and 18, Flavio's only role is that of faithful friend. In other scenarios also, the friend does everything to help, aiding his friend in his love pursuit and defending his honour, even in sword fights. In Day 38 Flavio is seriously wounded in the process of trying to get his friend Orazio to behave honourably. In Day 34 a friendship between men entails extending every hospitality to the offspring; Graziano lodges the daughter of an out-of-town friend, her two servants, and her tutor in his house and does "her every honour." In Day 33, friendship entails assuming guardianship of a friend's child when the friend leaves the city on business.

Male friendship was exalted to a degree that is hard for us to imagine today. According to Federico in the *Book of the Courtier*, friendship contains the best of life. The true friend is someone "whose love is constant and without deceit, and bound to endure in all intimacy until death."[158] Similarly, Leon Alberti asserts that "true friendships engage a kind of love more durable and more powerful than any other."[159] We cannot know how much the idealized male friendship, often described in the rhetoric of courtly love, actually reflected an erotic relationship. Even chance meetings in the street entailed the same elaborate, revived classical rhetoric.[160]

In any case, friendship bonds were very close, and the expectations for them very high. With one's friends, Lorenzo Alberti declares, "you ought to share every thought, every possession, every gift of fortune."[161]

Adovardo adds that friends are those "who spare no trouble for the sake of a friend, who offer to bear trouble, expense, and injury for his sake, and who never in any danger or difficulty forget the loyalty and duty they owe to him."[162]

In a society where distrust ran high,[163] friendships were based on trust. This trust meant that a friend could be counted on to assist another friend in all his enterprises and, further, to enlist all the members of the friendship circle or patronage network to assist and intercede on behalf of the friend. Friends and friends of friends were obliged to help one another as if they were brothers. Friendships, like business relationships, with which they were frequently intertwined, were based on the model of the family. In each, trust was essential. It served to protect the man's all-important honour.[164]

In the patriarchal society, friendship was regarded as a male prerogative and pleasure. Women, considered imperfect and incapable of virtue, were incapable of ideal friendship.[165] They had no role to play in the civic world that was the essential context of male friendships.[166] Scala does occasionally show women aiding one another and even conspiring together; he does not show either the depths of friendship or the betrayal of it that he illustrates with his male characters. Males are shown making sacrifices for other men; females only for males. No plots are based on female friendship.

The standard for male friendship was so high that, not surprisingly, friends too often failed to meet it. Thus, the Florentine merchant Giovanni Morelli wisely counselled his heirs, "You should never trust anyone so much that he can destroy you."[167] In a number of the Scala scenarios the primary plot concerns serious betrayals of friendship resulting from a youth's pursuit of his friend's love interest.

At the end of almost all of the scenarios in which friendship has been betrayed, the friend comes round and is forgiven.[168] As Madeleine Doran observes, a normally good man could be overcome by passion (as detached from character as the capitalization of the word *love* in the Scala scenarios suggests) and could as quickly repent, particularly when moved by persuasive speech.[169] While such reconciliations between friends may seem to us merely plot convenience, they were, in the idealized view of friendship at the time, not impossible and were deeply moving. Both the extent to which friends might go to help one another and their failure to prove trustworthy would have been of considerable interest in a culture where friendship between males was a very important matter. When, in the end of a Scala scenario, one friend gives up his love interest in a woman so that his friend may have her instead, and the woman in the process is traded like so much goods, we may find it improbable and distasteful, but the sixteenth-century ideal of friendship required that male friendship take unquestionable precedence over heterosexual love and that accordingly in cases of conflict the latter would yield to the former. In Day 16 a widow plans to marry her daughter Flaminia to her stepson Orazio, a sound financial plan. But Orazio, knowing that his friend Flavio loves Flaminia, declines the plan, yields Flaminia to his friend, and agrees instead to marry Flavio's sister, whom he does not know. In Day 29 Orazio abducts his love, Isabella, and hides her in the house of his best friend, Flavio. Flavio stays away from his house because he too loves Isabella and does not wish to betray his friend. In recognition of this loyalty and friendship Orazio gives Isabella to Flavio and takes Flavio's sister, who loves him, for wife. In this case, at least, the seeming harshness of this trade-off of Isabella is mitigated by Orazio's apparent neglect of her, the pity she feels for Flavio, and her gratitude towards him. No matter, she unquestioningly accepts the primacy of the male friendship. In Day 8 a similar regard for the importance of friendship, this time between two brothers, leads to several bewildering switches in intended spouses. In these scenarios, where the friendship is at stake, the male does not marry for love of a woman but out of friendship with a male.

Most moving in the scenarios would have been the instances where the friend is faithful despite the fact that he has every reason to harm his friend. Adovardo Alberti expresses the belief that, while the benefits received from someone who has no reason to harm you are great, the benefit from someone who has reason to harm you but chooses instead to be conciliatory and human is "a double gift and benefit." "Who could possibly deny that one owes real gratitude to a person who could and perhaps should be harshly vindictive but prefers to be kind and generous ...? He is doubly generous, first because he does not harm you, second because he gives you a gift and a reward ... Whose character would be so egregiously treacherous as to fail to commend such a man to perpetual honor?"[170] In Day 5, when Orazio falls in love with Flavio's woman, Isabella, and, as Flavio discovers, does much to deceive and betray both him and Isabella, Flavio nonetheless comes to Orazio's rescue when Orazio is beaten in a fight and almost killed. Orazio, much moved by Flavio's great kindness, kneels before him, repents, and, blaming the forces of Love and Fortune, begs forgiveness for all he has done. This Flavio grants, as Orazio and Flavio admit their great love for one another. The great powers of Love and Fortune being overcome by male friendship provided the contemporary audience with a stirring conclusion to the scenario and the fulfilment of a hope.

CITIZENS AND SERVANTS

The relationships between citizens and servants play a large part in Scala's scenarios. They also played a significant part in early modern life. To judge by the period's many treatises on household management, the relationships were often a tension-fraught aspect of citizens' everyday experiences. The tensions, moreover, were seen to threaten the whole of society. They thus constituted obvious and essential material for Scala's domestic comedies, and not only because they were traditionally an important part of comedy.

In Venice, from where figures are available for 1563, there were approximately two and a half servants for every citizen's household. These households are represented in the scenarios, often with the same relative proportion of servants as borne out by the statistics. Two-thirds of household servants were, in fact, female, although, perhaps under the moralizing influence of the Church, the actual percentage gradually shifted towards the less sexually vulnerable male servants.[171] The most frequently named servants in Scala's scenarios, Pedrolino and Arlecchino, appear in virtually every comic scenario; Franceschina, the most frequently named female servant, appears in fewer.

It was not because of moral scruples that Scala represented more male servants. As I have shown, he does not take the sexual violation of lower-class women as more than a joke. It was presumed that male servants, like males in general, were by nature capable of taking more initiative than were women, and, like their forebears in Roman drama, they realistically could play a more active and visible role in the street.[172] In sixteenth-century Italy the male servant was a mark of prestige for his master,[173] and thus male servants were attached in greater proportion to households of wealth. The male servant was often closely associated with the master, whom he escorted about the city and whom he was expected to protect from danger and defend in quarrels. He was also dispatched to run errands.[174] Scala shows him doing all these things. In several of the scenarios, like Days 21 and 29, Scala shows us a comically athletic Arlecchino. The athleticism befitted a male character; women were limited in movement because of the decorum required of them, which was reinforced by their dress.

Good Servants

The treatises on household management make clear that domestic service was a manifestation of the "natural" hierarchy and order that governed the social order. As Torquato Tasso explains, "some are by nature born to command and others to obey." Servants, Tasso continues, "are not qualified to fulfill the duties of a citizen because their virtue is defective – they possess just enough virtue to make them able to obey, but no more."[175] Servants were to know their proper place in that hierarchy and not challenge their master or disobey him but rather perform their assigned tasks with alacrity and humility.[176] Female servants, in particular, were to dress very plainly in common cloth dyed in drab colours – tan, black, or white – so as to remain in the background, subservient.[177]

Every treatise made clear that the servant's primary good attribute was obedience.[178] Not only was the obedience of the servant of use in itself, but also it affirmed the master's importance and showed that he knew how to command, preferably without having to resort to beatings.[179] "Servants," Giannozzo Alberti explained, "are as obedient as masters are skilled in commanding."[180] Obedient servants, demonstrating their master's skill in commanding, brought him honour.[181]

The best servants, ones who were not only obedient but also able to constantly adapt to whatever were the changing needs and whims of the employer and to meet them unobtrusively even in advance of their being expressed, were a great tribute to the master and an honour to the household. They could become indispensible to the running of the elite household. There might be long-lived affection between the families and the servants.[182] In Day 27 Pedrolino, having heard of his master Pantalone's death, raises Pantalone's daughter as his own, all the while protecting her honour, that is, her chastity. Highly regarded servants might gain financial security and favours, and they might even be included in the will of the master.[183] In Day 10 Pantalone honours Pedrolino, who has been a servant in his house for many years, with a wedding ceremony for him in his house, complete with musicians.

Bad Servants

Scala shows many more servants who misbehave than those who are obedient. Good servants and slaves were traditionally less common in drama, presumably because they are less interesting. And in the sixteenth-century, unlike bad servants, they did not necessitate the manuals of the period on household management, the sheer number of which suggested the very real problems that existed.

The manuals reflect the underlying belief that servants were by nature untrustworthy and disloyal.[184] "We have as many enemies as we have servants" ran a popular proverb.[185] In the natural hierarchy servants were deficient in both intelligence and wit, close to the animal kingdom and subject to vice. They were analogized to asses – known for their stubbornness[186] – or, if not asses, dogs. According to the frequently reprinted writer Stefano Guazzo, 1574, "servants have three faults common to dogs: gluttony, barking, i.e., telling all their master's secrets, and biting, i.e., backbiting their masters. They are also proud and lying, and faithless."[187] The equally widely reprinted Tommaso Garzoni, in 1586, provided a somewhat more generous assessment of haughty and disloyal servants, analogizing them not to dogs but to the lowliest of humans, "'the scum of laziness' capable of 'vile kinds of trickery,' 'unfaithful like the Moors, thieves like Gypsies, assassins like the Arabs, traitors like the Parthians' – people who 'were created from nothing' and deserve nothing but discipline and labour."[188] This distrust and contempt, conveyed to the servants, only served to undermine the trustworthiness that their masters so desperately sought from them.[189] Even though ideally the head of the house was capable of exercising self-control, Pantalone's frequent desperate rages when faced with his servants' behaviour would have been fully understandable to Scala's audience.

Servants were shown as a threat to the honour of the household. The mere presence of servants in a house, it is true, enhanced the master's status: the more servants, the more status and honour. Their honour, however – and honour was, as I said, a serious concern at all levels of society – was often at odds with that of their masters.

Acts of disobedience and disrespect on the part of servants were more than a part of the struggle of everyday life. Because the household was the polity writ small, they could, by implication, threaten the whole of society.[190] To have evil servants, the philosopher Fabio Glissenti remarked in 1596, is to suffer "a damaging imperialism, a wretched subjugation, and an ignominious condition."[191] What was represented on the stage in Pedrolino's rampant disobedience and Arlecchino's laziness was a matter for humour precisely because, in stylized form, the characters' behaviour expressed vital societal concerns. Servants were seen to represent a threat to the larger society, which the authorities sometimes made quite explicit. When the censors convicted one Francesco Zambat of Gambarare of refusing orders from the wife of a Giulio Valier and of wounding Valier's son, they noted that he had acted "in disrespect of the law and of the ordinances concerning servants, as well as in disrespect for the nobility of this city."[192] Similarly, in the prologue to an ordinance of 1595 the censors referred to the "insolence and *tyranny* that male and female servants exercise in the households and against their masters."[193] There was significant societal concern about servants gaining the upper hand in the household.[194] Even when a servant merely offered his advice, as Pedrolino does so impertinently, for instance, in Day 21 he might thereby suggest that the master had no right to command or expect obedience.[195] Masters needed to be vigilant in their control.

The point of view of the servants was, not surprisingly, quite different from that of the masters. Even those regularly employed faced grinding poverty.[196] The position of the servant, always dependent upon the fortunes and whims of the master, was precarious. He or she might be praised as loyal and obedient one day and berated unjustly for bad faith and ingratitude the next day.[197] In Day 24 Pedrolino is falsely accused by his master, Pantalone, of pimping for Pantalone's daughter. Unreasonable demands were placed upon servants: in Day 10 Pantalone tells Pedrolino that if he does not make Pantalone's daughter, Flaminia, take Orazio for husband, Pedrolino will never get his intended, a servant of Pantalone's brother, for wife. In Day 28 Pantalone tells Pedrolino that if he wants to stay in his employ, he must get Franceschina for him to bed and he must beat the Capitano. In Day 30 Pantalone, believing that a servant impregnated his daughter, says that he would like to poison all of his servants. More common than the threat of being murdered was the more realistic threat of being replaced.[198] In Day 33 an enraged Pantalone says he will drive Pedrolino, whom he has falsely accused, from the house. Similarly, in Day 11 the falsely accused Arlecchino is summarily fired. In the growing city populations, half those born in town never reached the age of twenty. The population was maintained and expanded through the constant influx of relocating rural people[199] who were only too anxious to serve as replacement for those who might be let go from their jobs. As many as half the growing population in cities may have been people relocating, many from destitute farming regions.[200]

The acts of disobedience by the servants that so incensed their masters, however, might bring sympathy, even honour and dignity from their peers.[201] Pedrolino's request for Pantalone's pardon at the end of Day 26 for all the tricks he has played, which he then enumerates, serves not only to allow the audience to relive the play but also, in effect, to allow Pedrolino to boast about his many outrageous covert acts.

Glissenti claimed that he would rather be subject to the whims of the sea or fortune than have his fate in the hands of servants because they could destroy one's reputation by recounting "the sorrows, the insidious acts, the shameless deeds, the robberies they have perpetrated on their masters, *winning praise for themselves in these ribald deeds as if they were honorable and beautiful ones*" (his emphasis).[202] In Scala the insidious acts, shameless tricks, and robberies might also bring gratitude from the offspring whom they enabled to steal, or for whom they themselves stole, and in whose love affairs the servants often assisted, often going to great lengths. Most notably, in Day 9 Isabella's nurse feigns death and leaves town, only to return disguised as a gentleman who "marries" Isabella in order to fend off her marriage to the man her father had intended for her and to enable her to marry her true love, Orazio, upon his return. To what extent servants and youths conspired against the masters in real life I do not know. That fear on the part of the fathers, and hope on the part of the youths, if that is all it was, was not altogether unrealistic, although, as in Day 9, the conspiracy is obviously far fetched. Most boys and girls first began their time in service during their early teens and sometimes when they were as young as eight. They may literally have grown up with the sons and daughters of their employers.[203] And to the extent that they were both subordinates, the servants and offspring were kindred spirits.

Masters could take some comfort in the fact that the servants' acts of disobedience, like their acts of obedience, served to affirm the social hierarchy by demonstrating the servants' animal-like inferiority and the masters' own rightful place above the servants. In addition, as in the ending of so many Scala scenarios, the servants' confession of bad behaviour provided opportunity for the masters to demonstrate magnanimity in their forgiveness.[204] Thus, both obedient and disobedient servants served to justify the status quo. At the same time, the topsy-turvy world of the Scala scenarios, in which the servants are in control, was consistent with the anxiety expressed at the time by the elite about the security of their own social position and the ordering of society generally.[205] Conversely, it served as wish-fulfilment for those lower in the social order. Their behaviour would have found an interested audience.

Servants and Hunger

Starving peasants from the impoverished Alpine valleys above Bergamo in Lombardy made their way to Venice in hopes of finding employment. It is no surprise that the first known comic servants, paired with Venetian masters, spoke a Bergamasque dialect. However, Venice, the probable origin of *commedia dell'arte*, was not alone in seeing a large influx of emigrants from the countryside.[206] Those employed as servants were the lucky ones, but the competition among unskilled labourers meant that they were not well paid. Francesco Guicciardini advised that, lest they "leave you or annoy you when they get their fill, it is better to be tightfisted with them. Feed their hopes, but give them only just enough to keep them from despair."[207] Their perpetual hunger is reflected in Scala's scenarios.

In Day 1 the servant Pedrolino bemoans the cancellation of a trip to the villa where he could have had a "good feed," the nature of which he likely details for us. In Day 11 the porters eat the confections intended for a wedding party. In Day 12, to disastrous effect, Pedrolino eats the candy he has stolen. Hungry servants even steal from their fellows: in Day 31 Pedrolino receives a dish of macaroni but gets to eat little of it because Arlecchino and another servant, Burattino, suddenly appear and proceed to eat from it as well.

Cunning

The tricks (*beffa*) that the servants play upon masters in many of the scenarios, their manipulation, lies, and deceits, have some basis in reality. More than that, the tricks represent the fears of the citizens and the happy fantasies of the lower class. They are also of a piece with the Italians' love of a practical joke and of the victim's humiliation.[208] Andrews observes that even in popular Italian comic performance today there is an almost "mystical search for the perfect sucker, to whom everyone can feel derisively superior."[209]

Servants from Bergamo developed a reputation, even beyond Italy, as being resourceful and ingenious. The many literary parodies of them suggest that they were resented for their relative success[210] and admired. The craft, craftiness, and cool nonchalance of Pedrolino are very like that of the admired courtier who manipulated the reality in which he found himself, with linguistic prowess and social dexterity. We admire the derring-do of the trickster servant, particularly knowing that servants were very lucky to have jobs at all.

OUTSIDERS AND SOCIETY

There is much dislocation and uprootedness in Scala's scenarios. Drama is often motivated by the stranger or long-lost relative who has come to town. Scala's characters, as we learn in the Argument preceding each scenario, have often travelled, sometimes extensively, to get to the fixed setting of the scenario. In the course of the scenario the characters would have to have provided the information about their journeys – their relocation in search of family members, fortune, or education or because of capture or self-imposed exile. In several of Scala's scenarios the majority of the characters arrive from elsewhere. But the stranger come to town and the long-lost relative are not merely a matter of dramatic convenience. Once again, albeit in an artificial form, the scenarios reflect real life, and understanding the extent to which they do so with respect to outsiders heightens our appreciation of them.

Many people were on the move in Europe at this time – artisans, merchants, students, and exiles. Students could be virtually anywhere because all European university courses were conducted in Latin.[211] The increasing prosperity of the towns meant that merchants might relocate from town to town ever in search of new business opportunities. The starving peasants came in from the countryside in hopes of employment. While the number of times that Scala sets family members and lovers off in search of loved ones, sometimes from city to city and for long periods of time, does not seem realistic, their travels do suggest the great movement of people that actually occurred in the period.[212]

A surprising number of people moved because they had been exiled. In faction-ridden Italian cities a large number of citizens, having fallen out of political favour, were sent into exile.[213] According to the diarist Romolo Allegrini, in 1581, between 10 and 15 per cent of the men from Perugia were in exile or on the run.[214] Exile was also a common punishment for serious criminal behaviour. To fill the endless need for manpower for war galleys, courts in the city-states that fought at sea might send even petty thieves and troublemakers to serve in the grueling jobs of oarsman. To escape that fate, men went into voluntary exile, sometimes with no foreseeable means of support but banditry.[215] In Scala's Day 15, Pantalone, having, as he supposes, killed two men to protect his honour and that of his daughter, abruptly left Venice for Rome, disguised as a beggar. In Day 27 he is in voluntary exile because of an enemy. Day 18 begins with Orazio having been banished.

In eight comic scenarios, including Day 36, Scala shows us men reappearing after long absences that resulted from their abduction by the "Turks," the name used indiscriminately for all Muslims. Formerly insiders, these returning men function as the outsiders who upset the status quo.

In reality, coastal areas and ships in the Mediterranean were subject to "Turkish" pirate raids and abductions to an extent hard to imagine. Pirates and privateers came from the Ottoman East and from North Africa, where the Barbary States developed under indirect Ottoman authority, and their brutal attacks on Italian coastal areas and on ships in the Mediterranean were a continual threat from the Middle Ages onwards. Captivity was an ever-present fear up and down the Italian peninsula and islands. Indeed, after the battle of Lepanto in 1571, in which the Christian allies defeated the Ottoman fleet, the Barbary States probably became more threatening because the Ottoman ability to control them had diminished.[216] Corsairing activity peaked between 1580 and 1640 but continued with lessening intensity throughout the eighteenth century.[217] On land the frequent raids included looting, burning, capture, and murder. Those captured on land or sea who appeared to be well-to-do were offered for ransom.[218] The rest served as slaves, the preponderance of them on galleys. Great tempests sometimes sank scores of galleys and drowned thousands of men.[219] The harsh conditions for the slaves also contributed to their appalling mortality rates. Escape was rare. Robert Davis estimates that between 1530 and 1780, more than a million European Christians were enslaved by Muslims of the Barbary Coast, most of them sailors, merchants, and inhabitants of the coastal villages of Italy, Greece, and Mediterranean Spain and France.[220] Scala's friend, the celebrated actor Francesco Andreini, had been held by the "Turks" as a slave for several years. Fear of "Li Turchi" justifiably loomed large through the centuries. Historian Tommaso Astarita recounts that even in his childhood in Naples in the 1960s, "'Li Turchi,' the Turks [as a general reference to pirates], were still playfully mentioned as a scarecrow for unruly children."[221] Not surprisingly, Turks and enslavement by them figure in a number of Scala's scenarios, as they did in romances.

In the Argument in Day 1 we learn that the rich twin traders who appear as slaves had been taken by pirates and had not been heard from for many years. In fact, it was often not known for long periods of time whether those captured were yet alive. Robert Davis documents someone enslaved who tried and failed for twenty-six years to get a letter through to his sister, informing her that he was still alive.[222]

Interestingly, the Turks actually shown on stage, as opposed to those described in the Arguments in the Scala scenarios are represented favourably. The Turk, turned Christian, in Day 2 marries Flaminia, daughter of Pantalone. Isabella, a Turk in Day 38, has also converted to Christianity and eventually marries Orazio. Also the Turkish girl in Day

36 had become Christian and eventually marries Flavio, the son of the noble Spanish regent of Naples. The sticking point in acceptance seems to have been religion, not foreign birth. There are records of both slaves and businessmen in Ottoman lands having become Muslim, and similarly of Muslims in Christian lands having converted to Christianity, and for the same reasons: their doing so seems to have conferred some advantage,[223] and, in any case, religious assimilations especially of people living in foreign lands are familiar.

The most memorable outsider in Scala's scenarios is the Capitano. In eight of the comic scenarios he is fully integrated into the community as a brother, son, friend, honourable suitor, or husband and householder, and the comic potential of his role is hardly or not at all evident. In the other twenty-eight of the thirty-six scenarios in which the Capitano appears, he is an outsider and a braggart warrior, a familiar comic figure from Roman drama. He is also drawn from real life.

During the sixteenth century the Spanish soldier was much in evidence in Spanish-occupied Italy, extending north from Naples and south from Milan. Half of Italy was under direct Spanish rule, and Spain's influence was felt in most Italian city-states. Tuscany, Savoy, the Papacy, and Genoa, although formally independent, were in fact beholden to Spain.[224] When and where it was sufficiently safe to do so (including in the drama), Italians made fun of the Spanish captains for their apparent vanity, euphuistic language, and elaborate ceremoniousness. The captain in the *commedia dell'arte* apparently often spoke with a Spanish accent. At times in Scala's scenarios we can deduce that the Capitano is Spanish, and he may have been so in other scenarios as well. In Day 17 his brother comes from Spain. In Day 29 Pantalone, residing in Naples, wants his daughter to marry the Capitano, knowing the power of the Spaniards in Naples. In Day 38 the Capitano had been serving his king in Majorca, Spain's largest island.

Most clearly, Scala's comic captain represents the *condottiere* or captain of mercenary soldiers, many bands of whom were employed by the faction-ridden city-states in Italy in the fourteenth and fifteenth centuries. Although these *condottieri* had originally been from foreign countries, by the fifteenth century in Italy they were Italian. Some had become nobles by dint of their military prowess. Many were Italian nobles who, for various reasons, had not been able to succeed in their own land or who had been exiled from their city-state for having been part of some opposing faction.[225] The principal states, complained Machiavelli, were not "armed with their own proper forces."[226] Even into the sixteenth century, Florence was wholly dependent on mercenaries. Humanists frequently reviled the hired *condottieri* and their bands of mercenaries.[227] Francesco Guicciardini and Lodovico Alamanni, respectively, held them responsible for the "horrible calamity" and "the present state and shame of serfdom of Italy" that had resulted from the occupation of Italy, beginning with the French in 1494.[228] Perhaps most influential in perpetuating a negative view of the *condottieri* was Machiavelli in *The Prince*: "The ruin of Italy has been caused by nothing else than by resting all her hopes for many years on mercenaries, and although they formerly made some display and appeared valiant amongst themselves, yet when the foreigners came they showed what they were. Thus it was that Charles, King of France, was allowed to seize Italy" without any effort whatsoever.[229] Scala, working in the tradition of the humanists, shared in the vilification of the *condottieri* and would have found a responsive audience in doing so. Such widely disseminated contempt for mercenaries had a good deal of influence on articulate civilian attitudes.[230] The condottieri, rightly or wrongly, lived on in infamy.[231]

The accusations levelled against them were many. Politician and orator Coluccio Salutati denounced mercenaries as "outcasts who had entered into perpetual conspiracy against peace and order."[232] Mercenaries and auxiliary armies "are disorganized, ambitious, undisciplined, and disloyal ... among enemies cowardly; unfearing of God, unfaithful to man ... In peacetime they plunder you; in wartime, your enemies do. The reason for all this is that there is no love or reason to hold them on the battlefield other than their meager pay, which is not enough to make them want to die for you ... When war breaks out, they flee, they desert."[233]

The *condottieri* worked on contract with individual city-states and sometimes even with a single individual, as in Scala's Days 15 and 23. Many of the *condottieri* knew and were capable of nothing but war. They felt no allegiance to those who had hired them and had scant respect for the lives and property of civilians. They fought for the highest bidder, passing easily from one lord to another, and, because they held a monopoly on the military power in Italy, they were sometimes capable of dictating terms that made a few of them very wealthy landowners.

The band of men they hired, which could be only a very few or as many as three thousand, might be poorly trained.[234] The contracting captain might exaggerate their number to his employer.[235] The *condottieri* sought to avoid capture and death on the battlefield and only reluctantly endangered themselves or their enlisted men. They avoided hard work and winter campaigns whenever possible. They sought to avoid battle by out-manoeuvring their opponents and, when they did fight, had a reputation for grandiose, pointless, and nearly bloodless battles. They were quick to accept bribes to cease fighting and likewise to offer them to their opponents. They valued a prisoner more than a dead soldier.[236] Sheltered from the rest of Europe by the Alps and the sea, the pseudo-chivalric *condottieri* retained armoured knights and medieval weapons long after the rest of Europe had converted to pikemen and musketeers.[237]

In some scenarios Scala's Capitano can be specifically identified with the condottieri: in Day 11 he recruits soldiers; in Day 15 he offers his services as a killer; and in Day 40 the Capitano says that Flavio, in battle in Hungary, died beside him. In others his behaviour matches that for which the *condottieri* were criticized. He presents himself as a nobleman, part of the hereditary elite, who, unlike the merchants, had the right to bear heraldic arms.[238] Domenico Sella explains that "in every Italian state the aristocracy included ... [a group that] traced its origins to a distant and often mythical feudal past and insisted on the deeds of military valour of its ancestors and on some remote imperial investiture to legitimize its present position; it still cultivated knightly or martial virtues and many of its members pursued careers in the armies."[239] Scala's Capitano is quick to take offence and threaten a fight, as was characteristic of his class, among whom to be bellicose, quarrelsome, prickly, touchy, and otherwise always ready to take offence and fight was regarded as a sign of social ascendance.[240] Castiglione mocks such real life men as making "a show of being so fierce that they are always blustering and bragging, declaring that they are married to their cuirasses, and glowering with ... haughty looks."[241] Typically, in Scala, the Capitano draws his sword to kill someone, only to suddenly depart with some ludicrous rationale for failing to fight.

Scala's braggart Capitano always seems to be newly come to town, homeless, unemployed, and alone, except perhaps for his servant, Arlecchino. He is not a successful *condottiere* but rather down and out. At any given time there must have been a significant number of captains and mercenaries unemployed and present in the cities.[242] Robert Davis comments that after 1559 there were thousands of mercenaries wandering around Italy and contributing to the spreading disorder and violence characteristic of city streets. Spavento, the stateless warrior, is perpetually in search of a woman, as many of the mercenaries must have been. He succeeds with none. Always threatening action, he effects nothing. He is made to appear the more foolish by his frequent sidekick, Arlecchino, who mocks him and at the same time urges him on to ever more elaborate boasts.[243]

Like the language of the Spanish captain, that of the Italian captain was a subject for derision. Michael Mallet remarks that because the later *condottieri* came from the noble and educated class of Italians, it is not surprising that, in accordance with the custom of the period, they frequently cited classical examples and drew classical parallels to their actions.[244] Scala's comic Capitano promotes himself as a great warrior who is always ready to fight, but his quick retreat at the least threat to his life is covered with elaborate excuses, including classical references. In Day 5 he excuses himself from combat, explaining that he never fights unless he has the permission of Mars.

Scala shows a great many other strangers, outsiders, and those not part of his upper-middle-class households: a dentist, a pimp, minstrels, mountebanks, card sharps, old bawds, rogues, pilgrims, gypsies, astrologers, magicians, thieves, fortune-tellers, beggars, and actors. In real life such figures, many impoverished, were a regular part of the street scene. Robert Henke makes clear that while *commedia dell'arte* inherited theatrical tropes of poverty, hunger, and degradation that were intended to be funny, representations of poverty also reflected actual conditions in sixteenth-century Europe.[245] The transition from the relatively secure feudal structures to a market-based economy that was responsible for the rise of cities brought new forms not only of opportunity but also of poverty.[246] By no means were all those leaving the countryside for the cities able to find regular employment. Moreover, in many years the food productivity and distribution were unable to keep pace with the increasing population.[247] There were general food crises in much of Europe in the 1520s, 1549, 1555, 1590, and 1602, and everywhere there were local ones as well.[248] As food became scarce, its price rose, making life increasingly hard for the poor. Of necessity many resorted to begging and street hustling. Thus, while Scala's scenarios focus on middle-elite characters and their servants, these characters are often set in a context of poverty and hunger, even in the disguises they themselves adopt.[249]

Scala's Day 15 opens with ten scenes consisting primarily of begging and eating, without the introduction of any substantive plot. What we would call *lazzi*, comic bits, in these instances concerning food and drink, are employed in Days 4, 12, and 21. In each of Days 31 and 15 there are two of them. Scala himself never used the term *lazzi* in his scenarios,[250] and, with the exception of a couple of these hunger and poverty *lazzi*, all other *lazzi* are integrated into his scenarios just as are the innumerable other materials that he or his actors either made up or took from theatrical tradition. Even the few seemingly discrete hunger and poverty *lazzi* may not have seemed as discrete as they seem to us, because food scarcity was omnipresent in daily life. Hunger was the ever-present silent foe. Camporesi observes that "as far back as at least the second half the sixteenth century one gets the very bitter impression that, for two centuries and a half, hunger weighed upon the whole of Italy like a terrible nightmare."[251] Food deprivation and scarcity form the context in the scenarios in which must be seen representations of feasting and generous amounts of food, as in Days 6 and 26.

Hunger may also account for something in the traditional representations of Arlecchino, including his costume of hallucinatory colourful, stylized shreds and patches and perhaps even his clown-like behaviour. Camporesi believes that much of the population of Europe lived in some sort of drugged condition at the time, sometimes as a result of starvation or sometimes as a result of eating deteriorated or tainted food: bread made with mouldy, verminous flour that was accidentally or deliberately adulterated with hemp, darnel, or poppy seeds. The drugged condition might have alleviated the hunger and pain but may also have stimulated wild fantasies and sensual dreams.[252] Camporesi cites Robert Garapon:

> Many people, in the fifteenth and sixteenth centuries, were reduced to living mainly on *beau language* and feasting on names instead of tasting things. For them, these "succulent" enumerations were like a little compensation for everyday poverty. But let us note well; this compensation obtained by force of words is only possible if a certain intoxication first attenuated the feeling of distance which separated the dream from the reality ... Each term in these enumerations, taken in isolation, is nothing but a desire or a lie; it is the magnificent abundance, the uninterrupted flow of words charged with captivating flavours that create the illusion.[253]

In Day 4 even the poor innkeeper, intending to eat a few mouthfuls of a trunk full of food meant for a customer, is distracted by two rogues, who eat everything in the trunk while engrossing him in a story about the life that people lead in the Land of Cockaigne, the place of plenty.

Poverty and hunger were concerns for everyone. The poor streamed into the towns "at times exhaustedly begging for bread, at other times violently and concertedly demanding it."[254] Their hunger often drove uprisings and lootings that were a source of worry for groups in power. In the unstable economy of early capitalism up to 50 or 60 per cent of the population could, in a crisis, be forced into poverty.[255] The representation of poverty and hunger would have tapped into a deep anxiety even among the well-to-do.

Throughout this chapter I have argued that to appreciate the Scala scenarios in particular and *commedia dell'arte* scenarios in general, it is important to see them in their social context, particularly in the context of the patriarchy. The *commedia dell'arte* performances enjoyed enormous popularity, in part because they expressed the fears and fantasies of their audience. While Scala focused on the upper-middle-class urban family, thus abiding by the theatrical norm for comedy, he was also representing relationships of critical importance to the family and to the state. In chapters 5 to 8, in which I provide reconstructions of Scala's scenarios, I show these character relationships in action. In the next chapter, extending my demonstration of the degree to which the scenarios represent life, I show the close relationship between characters' actions and the setting.

chapter three

The Setting and Life in the Street

In accordance with the convention established earlier for Italian scripted comedy, the comic scenarios of *commedia dell'arte* were devised for fixed street settings, however simple their representation may have been in practice, given the expense of set construction and the difficulties of travel for the itinerant performing troupes. In this chapter I first take up the theatrical appropriateness of the fixed street setting and describe the set. I then show how it is of a piece with the life represented in the Scala scenarios, and, in recovering that life, I continue to put on view an important part of the interest that the scenarios would have had for their contemporary audience. I consider the relevance of the urban setting in general and then focus on various of its aspects: houses, inns, night-time, and the street or *piazza* itself. I move from there to considering the suitability of the street set for the display of certain kinds of behaviour, in particular the presentation of the self, the attacks or perceived attacks on that self-presentation, and the attempts to restore one's public image. Finally I take up the unrealistic representation of upper-class women in the street. Again I choose these particular matters for consideration because they are omnipresent in Scala's scenarios.

The action in all but one of Scala's comic scenarios takes place in what may be either an urban street or a *piazza*. Day 6 is set in the country but appears to utilize the same kind of road-and-house configuration as does the urban set. Andrews calls the convention of the fixed exterior setting that never allows a scene to take place inside a domestic dwelling "a crippling restriction on the development of [all] Italian comedy."[1] By comparison, English drama of the period, including that of Shakespeare, had no such restriction to an exterior setting, much less to one that was fixed. As Andrews points out, "as long as the setting was restricted to the public street, the appearance of a respectable female either automatically broke social taboos, or else had to be justified by extreme developments in the plot."[2] Foreign travellers to Italy remarked upon the dearth of [upper-class] women in the streets. One Englishman visiting Venice, for instance, commented that "Woemen ... if they be chast, [are] rather locked up at home, as it were in prison."[3] Middle-elite women, featured in this drama, could not be realistically represented in the street.

Donald Beecher believes, nevertheless, that the view "that the common setting was deemed an impediment is debatable ... for what could whet the creative genius more than the necessity of creating intrigues so specifically timed that all their component parts must flow seriatim through the local square. Much of the dramatic effect of these works is generated precisely by the near collisions, the fortuitous timings, the unexpected encounters and impromptu explanations, the eavesdropping, and the claustrophobic compactness." The fixed street setting, he argues, provided the scenarist with defined limitations in which to create and generate its characteristic dramatic devices. The very limitation called forth a "consummate skill in the designing of the play."[4]

THEATRICAL USES OF THE SETTING

Andrews' observation that the exterior setting was a limitation to the development of comedy, at least of a particular kind, seems undeniable. I would, however, like to add to Beecher's comments about the dramatic advantages of the fixed setting.

In addition to the plot mechanisms Beecher has observed, there are other theatrical devices that take full advantage of, and indeed depend upon, the street setting. In Scala the double, often parallel, plots rely upon the simultaneous representation of two familial houses. The public gossip and slander, the night scenes including ghosts, and the mistaken identities (of twins and of those in disguise) are of a piece with or are inspired by the street setting. Similarly, this setting fits, or is required for, the out-of-bounds love, the athleticism (including duels, chase scenes, out-of-breath entrances, characters carrying one another), and the stage business with the props and the set (including travelling bags, a ladder, a door bar, and windows, at which people not only presented themselves but from which they threw bread, a letter, a handkerchief, a glove, or the contents of a chamber pot). The street setting suited the arrival of unexpected strangers in town; it facilitated the representation of a postman, innkeepers, a hangman, sailors, merchants, professionals, henchmen, ruffians, rogues, a fortune-teller, a galley captain, an astrologer, a pimp, policemen, gypsies, an actress, animals, a card sharp, slaves, a mountebank, Turks, Armenians, porters, pilgrims, and beggars. In other words, the street setting allowed the great panoply of characters presented in Scala's scenarios and the linguistic bazaar they provided, which in itself seems to have served as a source of comedy. The street, as Domenico Pietropaolo has observed, is where "the representatives of all these classes and professions could cross each others' paths and converse without great prejudice to their social status" – at least, I should add, when they were male or disguised as male.[5] The unexpected street encounters required improvisation on the part of the characters and, to the pleasure of the audience, what was, or at least appeared to be, improvisation on the part of the actors.

The street setting allowed for a particular kind of highly regarded "copiousness." Leon Battista Alberti explained that aesthetic pleasure comes primarily "from copiousness and the variety of things ... I say that history is most copious in which in their places are mixed old, young, maidens, women, youths, boys, fowls, small dogs, birds, horses, sheep, buildings, and landscapes and all similar things."[6]

The many, sometimes breathless, entrances and exits from many places, together with the abbreviated ending and the condensation of events into a twenty-four-hour period, impart the sense of speed and urgency critical to much comedy.[7] So does the double vision provided for the audience by characters both above at windows and below in the street, by disguises and night scenes (in which the audience can see but the characters cannot), by eavesdropping, and by asides – all made possible or greatly facilitated by the street scene. If represented by a perspectival set, the street setting provided the illusion of distance between groups of characters that, as Maggie Günsberg observes, helped make credible the aside as a secret form of speech addressed to oneself or to the audience.[8]

Finally, the fixed setting not only focused scenic composition for the scenarist but also aided the improvising actors, who would have learned well how to move in the specified place with its windows and doors and who would have been familiar with the kinds of encounters they allowed.

THE SETTING AND EVERYDAY LIFE

The various activities facilitated by the street setting – the duels, disguises, eavesdropping, and night scenes – too often seem to be but endlessly recycled theatregrams. For their audience, however, the use of a city street as setting, despite the fact that it may have been borrowed from Roman drama by way of the *commedia erudita*, facilitated the representation in stylized form of early modern life.

The Setting Itself

The set represented two or three dwellings with openings for windows and doors, facing onto a street or *piazza*. In Days 1 and 37 there are four houses. For the most part, the dwellings are those of the middle-elite old men, usually Graziano and Pantalone. Occasionally the houses are those of others, and often there is an inn.

The means of representation of the houses in *commedia dell'arte* was probably dependent on the performance context. We cannot rule out performance on a raised stage in a *piazza*, with perhaps no more than openings in curtains indicating house doors and windows. But it seems safe to infer that for some years prior to 1611 Scala had enough prestige that he would have been writing in the main for troupes that performed for periods of time in the preferred enclosed and largely interior performance spaces that were favourable to construction of a perspectival set. This would likely have consisted of a painted backdrop, foreshortened paintings on wing drops, and downstage buildings represented by angled wings with useable window openings and doors. In Day 36 Scala refers specifically to a set painted in perspective. Owing to budgetary constraints, a built *commedia dell'arte* set was probably reused, perhaps with minor alterations, regardless of the various cities designated as the location for the action.[9] It was not unusual for the written comedy that so influenced the *commedia dell'arte* to have been played before a set that represented no particular city. Donato Giannetti remarked in a letter that his *Il vecchio amoroso*, 1536, set in Pisa, could just as easily be imagined in Genoa. And Machiavelli, in the prologue to his *La mandragola*, 1524, said quite clearly: "Watch now the stage, as it is set up for you; / this is your Florence; / another time perhaps, Pisa or Rome / don't laugh too hard, or you'll break your jaw."[10] In his note to readers in Scala's edition of scenarios, Scala's friend, the famous actor Francesco Andreini, explained with reference to the sets for the scenarios that "since in each good city there is no shortage of excellent men, who take delight in mathematics, out of such respect he [Scala] did not want to attempt that which is not necessary, allowing that each could create as they wish every sort of comic, tragic and sylvan set."[11] Andreini gives the impression that the set, requiring skill in mathematics, would have been perspectival but that the specifics of it were no more important than were the particular words spoken by the actors.

The title pages of scenarios in the Corsini manuscript provide a hundred rather primitive watercolours representing *commedia dell'arte* from perhaps the 1590s and showing perspectival scenery with some actors within the set, at least to the depth of the front houses and the space immediately behind them.[12] Recently it has been concluded that the images sometimes denote a specific event in the text and that otherwise they serve to represent a combination of events based on more than one passage of text or are emblematic of plot elements that cannot be directly related to a specific text passage or to the title of the scenario.[13] In the images, doors are at a height that the pictured actors could not have entered comfortably. In one, *La commedia in commedia,* the play within the play is shown being performed all the way at the back wall. In another, *La battaglia,* figures are represented in a fort at the rear. *Il torneo* similarly shows a figure at some depth. Either these figures were painted onto the backdrop, which seems unlikely, or the artist of the title pages simply imagined them deep within the perspectival view. Actual placement of actors near the painted backdrop would have utterly destroyed the illusion of depth.

The Corsini watercolours are nonetheless probably our most reliable guide to *commedia dell'arte* performance with a perspectival set. They show figures in or having climbed to second-storey windows, and functional entryways, facing front or onto a centre street rendered in perspective. Together, actors at the height of the second-storey windows and at entrances and exits from front- and side-facing doors and window openings allow for considerable variety in the stage pictures, thus contributing to the visual interest of the performance. The space indicated immediately behind the functional two-storey buildings may also have been used for entrances and for hiding. I take these representations of characters at limited depth within a perspectival set and, in one case, *L'amore costante,* either hiding or entering behind the front set of buildings (figures 1 and 2), to be reliable because we can also see similar representations by other artists.[14] It seems less likely that the artists simply copied from one another or independently imagined such entrances for their pictorial interest than that they were representing something they had seen. It is possible that a single reference in one Scala scenario suggests more than the one functional street: "confusamente partono per diverse strade, e via" (in confusion they [the three characters] leave by different streets).[15] We can, however, only be abso-

3.1. Title page of *L'amorosi incanti*, Corsinia Album, Biblioteca Corsiniana, Rome. By permission of the Biblioteca Corsiniana.

3.2. Title page of *L'amor costante,* Corsinia Album, Biblioteca Corsiniana, Rome. By permission of the Biblioteca Corsiniana.

lutely sure that there were entrances from the houses, from stage left and right in front of the houses, and at windows. Day 21 also specifies a loggia or roof where an actor can make an appearance.

Literary critic Lodovico Castelvetro (1505–71) declared that the set represented should be limited "to that vista alone which would appear to the eye of a single person."[16] The earlier *commedia erudita* suggests that, in fact, considerable liberty was taken with Castelvetro's prescription. The set represented the city but not literally; rather, it served as a metaphor for the larger city.[17] In the prologue to Pietro Aretino's *La cortigiana*, 1525, Histrion 1 explains: "Look there's the Palace, St. Peter's, the *piazza*, the fortress, a couple of taverns – the Hare and the Luna – the fountain, St. Catherine's – the whole thing." The city, in turn, served as a metaphor for the world. This is made most clear in the prologue to *L'amfiparnaso*, 1597: "And the city in which is presented this opera, [is] the great Theatre of the World."[18]

The comings and goings of characters in the street or the *piazza* in Scala's scenarios invited the audience to envision it as part of a larger reality. This perception was enhanced by offstage voices, specificity about where the characters were going when they exited, and characters' sightings of characters offstage. In Day 9, act 1, for instance, Pantalone calls for Pedrolino from indoors, and then Graziano calls for Arlecchino from indoors. In Day 6, act 1, Pedrolino leaves because he sees Pantalone and his family and friends offstage, arriving. The setting also predisposed the audience to entertain the illusion that dramatic characters were real individuals who belonged to a community where they lived as ordinary people.[19]

Altogether, Scala specified a large number of cities as the locales for his action: sixteen scenarios are set in Rome; three each in Perugia, Florence, Bologna, and Naples; two each in Venice, and Genoa; and one each in Pesaro, Milan, Mantua, Parma, and a villa near Padua. In his scenario collection there is no discernible pattern to the cities chosen, and it seems unlikely that the cities mentioned refer to actual performance locales, which were in fact probably largely limited to a northern circuit. Written drama like Ludovico Ariosto's *I suppositi*, 1509, was set where it was performed in order to make harmless references to local life or, in the work of Pietro Aretino, 1492–1556, to satirize local phenomena. Whether in performance of Scala's scenarios the city names were changed to accommodate the places of performance we do not know. When entering a new town, Scala's Capitano often praises it and sometimes its women. Flaminia in Day 26 praises the city. The actress, a character in Day 39, praises the city, the Duke, the court, and the city's gentlemen. Although Scala specifies the city in which each scenario is set, with few exceptions (Days 29 and 36, set in Naples), there is nothing in the scenarios that requires the particular locale specified. Opportunities for spoken references to the city in which the performance was taking place may have been afforded by simply changing the name of the city specified by Scala for the action, along with the rare reference to some particulars of that city (like Porta Tosa in Milan in Day 11 or the Florentine eight lords of justice in Day 18), to the name and particulars of the city in which the performance was taking place.

Many cities, place names, and cultural references are mentioned in the Arguments or in the scenarios. In the first scenario in the Scala collection, for instance, Venice, Syria and "other parts of the Levant," "Alexandria in Egypt," Persia, Florence, the Prato Gate, Pisa, Livorno, an Armenian, and a Turk are mentioned; in the second, Constantinople, Rome, the Strait of Dardanelles, Sicily, Pantelloria, Bari, Milan, Palermo, Malta, the Pantallarian Sea, and Naples, as well as Pantalone, a Venetian, a Turkish performer, and Greek wine. The picaresque nature of the scenarios is conveyed not by movement of scenes from one locale to another but by reference to the characters' origins and to what had happened to them before the start of the action. This multiplicity of place references was perhaps calculated to provide a sense of adventure and to appeal to the geographically diverse audiences encountered by a travelling company.[20]

Cities in Italy

The Italian city provided audiences for theatre, and thus logically the city was the setting for the scenarios' comedy. Italy in the sixteenth century was the most urbanized area in Europe and one of the most urbanized areas anywhere, with the possible exception of Flanders. It was made so by the increasing importance of its merchants (like Pantalone), professional men (like Graziano), and craftsmen and tradesmen, who naturally gravitated to business centres.[21] A third of the Italian peninsula was urban. In 1550, forty towns had populations of ten thousand or more and, of those, half had populations over twenty-five thousand. Naples, Venice, Milan, Palermo, Florence, Genoa, and Bologna each had populations of sixty thousand or more. And these urban populations were lower, in some cases much lower, than before the plague had struck. Thereafter the urban populations continued to rise.[22] They rose despite the fact that even in non-plague years the mortality rate was extremely high; the recorded excess of deaths relative to births was probably largely among the poor and numerous peasants relocating to the cities.[23]

Excluding towns that served principally as administrative centres, the large Italian cities were primarily commercial centres, seaports, banking networks, or centres of textile production.[24] The merchant Pantalone, the professional man Graziano, the wily servant Pedrolino (determined to make his way), and the perennially hungry Arlecchino (the latter two both relocated peasants) would all have been familiar urban figures. Reflecting the general age of the population, these are plays of youth. In Venice where we have information from between 1610 and 1620, over half the population was under the age of thirty.[25] The successful exploits are those of the young – servants and lovers alike. The old, or rather those that seemed old at the time and to the young, do not generally fare well.

Houses

In 1455 Marsilio Ficino made clear the relationship between house and family, *casa* and *famiglia*; "the house," he said, "is nothing other than the union of the father with his sons in one residence," the father's house.[26] The houses that we see on stage in the scenarios are at one with the family dramas represented. They stand for the structured world of authority, kinship obligations, and obedience. By the time Scala was writing, however, "the house" may have referred not to the extended family that Ficino had envisioned but to the kind of nuclear families we see in Scala.[27]

The houses usually had two floors, although in the larger cities, where space was at a premium, they might have had three. The main door was massive, iron bound, barred, and locked with a large lock and bolts supplemented with chains. In appearance and in fact, it needed to be capable of withstanding assault, which was a real possibility.[28] Most of the extant renderings of houses in the *commedia dell'arte* show them as two storeyed. In Scala the door and the attempt to gain entry could be a focal point of the action. In one scenario, Day 35, acts 1 and 3, a door bar plays a comic role. Edward Muir's comment that the threshold of the house often served a ceremonial purpose – reinforcing the transitional or liminal phase of the rites of marriage – suggests the possible location of the taking of right hands to signify agreement to marry.[29]

Günsberg points out that the fixed exterior setting of the scripted *commedia erudita* required that, when characters wished to talk without being overheard, they came out onto the street, thereby providing a pretext for being out of doors and onstage, rather than indoors and offstage.[30] In the first scene of Ariosto's *I suppositi*, 1509, Polinesta is instructed by her nurse to come outside Damone's house in order to avoid household spies: "There's no one around; come out, Polinesta, into the street, where we'll be able to see around us, and we'll at least be certain of nothing being overheard by anyone. I think in our house even the bedsteads, the chests and the doorways have ears." Similarly, in Bernardo Dovizi da Bibbiena's *La calandra*, 1521, the adulterous Fulvia decides that it is best to speak to the sorcerer "out here because inside, the benches, the chairs, the chests, the windows all seem to have ears" (act 4, scene 1).[31]

This contrivance, also employed in Scala's scenarios (see, for instance, Day 21, act 2) may not have seemed as improbable at the time as it seems to us now. Upper-class women, to be sure, stayed within and would not have come out into the street to speak. But the house, in fact, provided little privacy. The front door opened directly into the main room, and the interior was essentially a shell subdivided by wooden partitions. Rooms connected immediately with each other, and the space-wasting corridor was used only in large buildings. One of the few places for privacy in the house was the canopied bed, about which curtains could be drawn to make a little private room, but even such privacy might be limited by a servant's truckle bed beneath it.[32] Also, to a greater extent than we might suppose, the street was an extension of the house and often afforded more privacy. Andrea de Jorio observed in 1832 that in the crowded city of Naples the street was, in effect, an extension of the house or apartment and that, therefore, it was more accurate to say not that Neapolitans do everything in the street but that they "*do everything in their house*" (his emphasis).[33] Naples is warmer than the northern cities, and de Jorio wrote two hundred years after Scala, but his observation seems worth bearing in mind.

Travel and Inns

An ordinary day's journey would have averaged about forty kilometres,[34] or even less on foot. Given the great number of people on the move, inns were a central feature of the city, intermixed in the heterogeneous street setting, as they are in Scala's scenarios. Scala makes frequent use of them for the stranger come to town who initiates an important plot element. The few actual women travellers would have been in gypsy bands or *commedia dell'arte* troupes, or they would have been army-camp followers (wives, mistresses, prostitutes, laundresses, food gatherers, and nurses). The women travellers in the Scala scenarios are generally in disguise, often as male. I will have occasion to discuss them in the third major section of this chapter.

Night

The night scenes extended the single day in which comedies were to have been set. Night, like cross-dressing, also served as one of the many kinds of disguises for the characters and facilitated hiding and covert activity, including romance, escapes, and break-ins. Undoubtedly it also lent itself to a lot of comic peering into the darkness, terror, mistaken identity, and bumping into and falling over things and one another. It was one of the many comic devices that allowed the audience to feel superior in knowing what the characters did not know, in this case, because they literally could not see. It was also an iteration of the contemporary drama's preoccupation with the irony of sight and blindness, appearance and reality. The exterior setting facilitated the many night scenes in Scala's scenarios.

Lacking artificial light, night in the early modern street was, in point of fact, dark. It had particular significance in Italy where the hours were counted not from the sun's meridian but from its setting. *Ora di note* and *due ore di notte* are respectively one and two hours after dusk. In accordance with God, day belonged to work, and night to sleep.[35] The distinction made between "Apollonian, virtuous, luminous and active time, and demonic time" was very clear. Where a compulsory curfew was not in force, men knew to be off the streets and safely behind barred doors. As Sabba Castiglione apprehensively warned in 1554, "you will be on your guard when walking at night, if not out of extreme necessity, firstly against scandals, inconveniences and dangers which lurk there continuously; then against the various and diverse infirmities which are often generated in human bodies by the night air ... It is certain that going out at night without need is nothing other than disturbing nature's order."[36] Night was a time of disease and crime.[37] More than that, night in and of itself was a reminder of death: "God created the distinction between day and night for a particular purpose, and that purpose is to serve as a reminder, even a paradigm, of the cycle of death."[38] To know that night was approaching was to be reminded that death was round the corner and to be reminded of all that that implies for the conduct of one's life. As late as 1782 the Jesuit Giulio Cesare Cordara argued against the adaptation of French time, which was counted from the sun's meridian, because it downgraded nightfall to an incidental occurrence that had no definite hour to call its own.[39] The representation of night was a representation of danger. To evaluate Andrews's comment that Scala overused ghost scenes,[40] one has to appreciate the real anguish invoked by the night: it belonged to terrifying apparitions, ghosts, goblins, spells, and collective hallucinations spread by uncontrollable rumours. The perceived porous or permeable nature of the body in the period[41] meant that ghosts were regarded as real. "All it took was a ghost – a supposed masked apparition – to throw a city into confusion and fear." In Modena, as late as the eighteenth century, fear of a spirit provoked a collective hysteria.[42]

Streetscape

David Wiles makes the important observation that *piazza* is a Latinate term with, significantly, no German or English equivalent, "signifying the 'place' that matters, the centre of the community, the space for collective performances." The *genius loci* of the sixteenth-century *piazza* is strong; it is the centre, the seat of collective memories, "where natural topography requires journeys to begin and end." Citing the cultural geographer Don Mitchell and the sociologist Henri Lefebvre, Wiles points to the urban ideal of the "public space" characterized by the *piazza* as one associated with interaction, inclusiveness, and conflict, and subject to constant metamorphosis; its rhythms were constituted by promenading, trading, and scheming.[43] The *piazza* was a space to which people gravitated, and the scenarios reflect this. It is, to use a slang expression, "where the action is."[44]

The climate and the lack of interior space encouraged the preference for a life lived in public. Documenting the family life of three distinguished families in Florence, historian Francis Kent notes that their formal meetings, except perhaps for their more private business, were conducted in the street and *piazzas* near their houses and palaces. One of the families had a wedding feast in the small open area ringed by their family houses.[45] "Men's lives were dramas played out in the streets and other civic spaces."[46] Unlike the impersonal, socially segregated society that one associates with modern urbanization and economic development, Italian sixteenth-century society and capitalism were intimate and personal.

In this face-to-face society, people continually crossed paths in the performance of daily activities, both public and private.[47] The basic units of

Italian social organization in the closely packed towns throughout the early modern period remained family and neighbourhood. The early modern city, even a large one, was in many ways a confederation of villages. The neighbourhood or *vicinanza* provided a tightly knit informal grouping that linked the members of the same parish or the neighbours bordering the same *piazza*.[48] Dale Kent and Francis Kent describe the neighbourhood as "a stage on which many of the events of a man's life were acted out with the co-operation and participation of his *parenti, vicini,* and *amici*."[49] One was always under the watchful eyes of friends and neighbours. Newcomers to the neighbourhood could not stay strangers for long. Everyone knew everyone else. As in the scenarios, the street and the *piazza* were arenas for personal, sometimes emotional, social interactions. These were at home in the street setting.

In his introduction to his English translation of Andrea de Jorio's *Gesture in Naples and Gesture in Classical Antiquity,* 1832, Adam Kendon tries to account for the elaboration of gesture in Naples: it allowed private communication and communication over noise, at a distance, and in both the verbal and visual medium, not necessarily consistent. Although the climate of Naples was, as I have noted, particularly conducive to a life lived out of doors year round, Kendon's observations pertain to the whole of Italy and to the sixteenth century as well:

> for much of the time, people were always co-present in spaces only partly well-bounded and screened, not only with members of their own family but also with others, most of whom would have been at least acquaintances. Life, all facets of it, tended to be carried out ... always in the presence of a widening range of possible witnesses. Even the most private relations either were public or could become public at any time.[50]

Personal privacy was virtually unknown.[51] The theatrical convention of the comment aside was consistent with the street setting, where one might realistically overhear private conversation.

The mixing of high and low classes in the neighbourhoods, which may seem to modern readers to be mere theatrical convenience, preserved the economic and social practices surviving from the formation of cities in the Middle Ages.[52] The neighbourhoods contained both the poor and the rich (whose palaces, essentially fortresses, provided them with a measure of seclusion), and the members of many different professions. Their daily proximity and the presence of foreigners made the early modern city a place of social uncertainty and potential danger.[53] The panoply of figures entering the street scene in Scala's scenarios – pilgrims, gypsies, merchants, beggars, and soldiers – would not have seemed out of place or their unexpected interactions altogether improbable. Historian Peter Burke observes that while the literary multilingualism may have been comic, the humour may also have been, at least in part, a humorous-hostile reaction to country people and foreigners in the towns.[54]

Male life was lived in public on the square. Indeed, there was something shameful about a man remaining at home indoors. While "it would hardly win us respect if our wife busied herself among the men in the marketplace, out in the public eye," remarks a cousin in Alberti's *Della famiglia*, expressing a common view, "it also seems somewhat demeaning to me to remain shut up in the house among women when I have manly things to do among men, fellow citizens and worthy and distinguished foreigners."[55] Merchants conducted their business out of doors in places like the Rialto in Venice where they could be seen bargaining before the eyes of spectators.[56] (Artisans would also have been seen in the street making and selling their wares, but they play no part in Scala.)

Male servants, central to the scenarios, could be seen going about the streets alone, dispatched to collect bills, receive goods, deliver messages, and run various other errands,[57] or with their masters whom they served to escort about the city, clearing a path for them through the crowds during the day or providing them with lantern light at night. They were expected to protect their masters from danger, if need be, by engaging with them in their quarrels. In a humorous reversal of this expectation, in Day 35, act 2, Arlecchino ducks out of a quarrel to which his master, the cowardly Capitano, has been challenged, with the same preposterous excuse just provided by the Capitano.

Serving women could be seen at the windows, lowering baskets for the postman or baker. Their disposal of waste fluids from windows inevitably became a source of comedy (see for instance Day 35, acts 1 and 2). Serving women too were dispatched to run errands, which in real life they frequently did with scarved faces in an attempt to protect themselves from the danger of the streets.[58]

Another street activity represented in Scala (Day 12), although surprising, was also realistic. Dentistry, the profession of barbers and itinerant quacks, was often conducted on seated patients in public places. Other public acts that may surprise us include the procession of a condemned man through the streets, and other public punishments, as shown in Day 18, act 2.[59] Pantalone, frequently driven to despair, had many opportunities to express his rage tearfully in the street. Rage, piety, and grief found expression in tears. Men openly weeping in public was not regarded as unusual or unseemly, at least on certain occasions.[60] In Day 5, act 1, Flavio weeps because he believes that Isabella has betrayed him. In Day 24, act 1, Pedrolino, unjustly charged by his master, weeps in humiliation.

The vitality and variety of the street scene was represented not as it would be at one moment but cumulatively over time and at both levels of the houses in the many scenes of Scala's action-packed, fast-moving scenarios.

Bella Figura, Disguise, and Eavesdropping

People worked hard at creating and maintaining impressions, at manipulating reality to serve their own ends. In public spaces people performed themselves as they wished to be seen. The male sense of identity was affirmed by the successful performance of self with style, *fare bella figura.* Italy was what Peter Burke calls a "theatre society." The facade was far more important than the reality.[61] Showing off, self-presentation, was synonymous with life.[62]

The public square was ideally suited both to such performance and to its observation. Indeed, the architect Leon Battista Alberti regarded the public square as specifically suited to the framing of public action as performance: "Glory springs up in public squares; reputation is nourished by the voice and judgment of many persons of honor, and in the midst of people."[63] Urban historian Alexander Cowan argues for the very close relationship between the stage set that was based on the rules of perspective and the late sixteenth-century reshaping of public squares that were intended for the "dramatic presentation of the elite, both to each other and to observers."[64]

Disguise, so prevalent in the scenarios, was a regular part of life, albeit without a mask or a costume, and not just at Carnival (a time of special liberty from normal rules and social hierarchies that extended from late December or early January to Shrove Tuesday, the eve of Lent). Historian Eric Dursteler points to the extent to which "dualistic self-presentation was widespread throughout the early modern world."[65] The *sprezzatura* that Castiglione recommended for courtiers – the cool nonchalance that concealed all art and made whatever they said or did appear to be effortless and almost without any thought about it – was a kind of disguise. The culture of craft and craftiness was pervasive. In 1609 the Venetian lawyer and historian Paolo Sarpi observed that he was, in effect, "obliged to wear a mask, because no one in Italy may go without one."[66] The mask was a common metaphor for dissimulation in early modern culture. No one knew with certainty whether the face was "already a mask and its owner no different than an actor in a comedy: in the culture of secrecy, the natural was always already artificial."[67] Imposters were potentially everywhere. It was an age of dissimulation in Europe.[68] The French nobleman Louis d'Orléans lamented in 1594 that it was impossible to know the true identity of the dissimulator; all were left as if "in the darkness of night."[69] Adovardo, in Alberti's treatise on the family, declared that everything in the world was profoundly unsure and that the world was filled with deceitful, false, perfidious, bold, audacious, and rapacious men. In the face of the many traps such a world provided, one had to be continually "far-seeing, alert, and careful."[70] In a society in which many people were impoverished and in which appearance was cultivated and deceptive, suspicions ran high. People might not be what they seemed. Surveillance was critical. Not surprisingly, the eavesdropping evidenced in the scenarios was a major literary motif.[71] The period's characteristic consideration of the limits of human perception and of the capacity to make distinctions was of a piece with the prevalence of dissimulation.

Honour

A century and a half before Scala published his scenarios, Leon Battista Alberti forcefully explained the centrality of honour: "[Honor is] the most important thing in anyone's life. It is one thing without which no enterprise deserves praise or has real value. It is the ultimate source of all the splendor our work may have, the most beautiful and shining part of our life now and our life hereafter, the most lasting and eternal part ... Satisfying the standards of honor, we shall grow rich and well praised, admired, and esteemed among men."[72] It was the supreme social value. Virtually everyone, rich and poor alike, male and female, saw honour as more dear than life itself.[73] Dale Kent came across the following telling anecdote from about the same time: Manetto Amannatini was invited to a dinner party with twenty-two friends, almost all of higher rank and status than he. When he did not appear, the friends were miffed by his unexplained absence. They decided to revenge the insult with a practical joke; they treated him as if he were no longer Manetto but someone called Matteo. Having been thus humiliated and dishonoured, Manetto moved to Hungary.[74] In various ways, reflecting the continuing central concern about it, each of Scala's scenarios takes up the issue of honour: its loss, or the struggle to maintain it, or gain it. Honour had altogether to do with public perception. It existed entirely in the eyes of other people and disappeared when their favour was lost. The street was the natural setting for maintaining honour, the "good opinion others have of us."[75] A man's honour derived primarily from his success in business and public life, and it was understood differently according to class. Children, servants, and wives whose character was excellent proved the diligence of the husband and father and brought honour to him, the house, and the country.[76] An orderly society depended upon the good sense of and control by its adult men. Social historian Elizabeth Cohen explains that an attack on honour is anything which shows to the audience of society that a man cannot protect what is his – his face, his body, his family, his house, his property.[77] One family member's fall into dishonour cast doubt on the authority and power of the family, proving its weakness and inability to defend its reputation. Scala's comic scenarios variously pose the threat of dishonour that could be brought upon a family by its members. Patriarchs could bring dishonour upon themselves with their gullibility and foolish lusting after young girls and obviously unobtainable women. Children, servants, and the occasional wife represented in the scenarios could, and regularly do, present a threat to the honour of the patriarch and the family as a whole. One might understand the scenarios' inevitable love matches as merely occasions for raising issues of honour.

A woman's honour (or rather her absence of shame) was defined, as we know, by her chastity.[78] Women who did not abide by their husband's or father's control of their sexuality were regarded as "immodest" or "shameless."[79] Even the appearance of immodest behaviour was a concern. A proper upper-class woman or girl was not even to sit at her window, idly watching the activity in the street. Sizing up a possible marriage partner for her son, the widow Alessandra Strozzi made note of the fact that she "had not seen her looking out of the window every day, which was a sign that she was not frivolous."[80] A low profile, silence, and a consistently modest demeanour indicated that women knew their place in the social hierarchy and served to avoid any hint of sexual provocation. To engage in conversation from the window gave the wrong impression. Conversation across social classes and between genders was associated with liberty and promiscuity.[81] "A man might court a girl at her window only by serenading her and even then in the fellowship of other men."[82] The scenarios regularly show upper-class women both at windows and in the street talking to men, and thus honour becomes an issue in ways we may too readily overlook.

In the streets the chastity and fidelity of women were at risk. Like the representation of night, the representation of women in the street was a representation of danger. In the street, women might act upon the temptation to interact with men or otherwise put themselves in harm's way. The streets and alleys were narrow and unlit, unknown persons lurked about every corner, the police were hardly efficient, and females were in fact always vulnerable to robbery or sexual assault, particularly because unlike men, who regularly carried either a dagger or a staff for purposes of self-defence, they did not go about the city armed.[83]

While upper-class girls were sheltered and married off at a young age, upper-class males presented a challenge to civic society, which depended upon a disciplined citizenry.[84] In their prolonged adolescence under their fathers' rule – at least until marriage, when they were admitted to full manhood[85] – they constituted some of the primary denizens of the illicit world.[86] Scala's repeated representation of upper-class youths in street fights and in inappropriate pursuit of young girls and women, widowed or married, disrupting their fathers' plans and the general neighbourhood, as I have indicated, seems scarcely to have been an exaggeration. The unruly behaviour of young unmarried men provoked fathers' tirades in Scala and, no doubt, in real life.

While the upper classes regarded threats to the *padre di famiglia*, whether from offspring or servants, as threats to the city fathers and to the whole of the social hierarchy, public acts of disobedience, the kind we see repeatedly in Scala's street setting, were considered especially grave because honour was a matter of public perception.

Gossip and Insults: The Public Nature of Dishonour

No one was immune to insults and gossip.[87] Insults could readily damage one's honour and were taken very seriously. For women, who were less able to resort to physical violence than men, such insults were powerful tools and were freely used.[88] However, they were not only the tools of women. Insults by inferiors to superiors, and especially in public, were particularly grievous.[89] Insults could lead to gossip. Gossip, even women's gossip, was a potent form of power that could both create and destroy honour.[90] In the small-scale communities that made up the city, gossip spread quickly. The prevalence of gossip meant that dishonour was widely disseminated and hard to live down.

Ordinary speech was rich in insults against both men and women. Slurs against a woman included the terms *liar, fool, coward, witch, procuress,* but most of all *adulteress, whore, dirty whore,* or *poxy whore.* These latter and most serious insults make clear that defamation of a woman's character consisted primarily in calling into question her chastity and fidelity in marriage. In *The Book of the Courtier* the speaker identified as the playwright, Bibbiena (Bernardo Dovizi da Bibbiena), observes that for men "a dissolute life is not thought evil or blameworthy or disgraceful, whereas in women it leads to such complete opprobrium and shame that once a woman has been spoken ill of, whether the accusation be true or false, she is utterly disgraced forever."[91] As the qualities of men's honour were more various, so were the insults: *liar, thief, rogue, traitor, coward, spy, bugger, pimp,* and *cuckold.*[92] Accusations of dishonesty directly attacked the honour upon which a man's business and social relationships depended, and so called into question his success and stature as a merchant, tradesman, artisan, or labourer. Still nothing was worse than calling a man a cuckold, accusing him of his inability to control or satisfy his wife, and thus threatening the very foundation of the patriarchy. The term makes clear that a woman's honour was never solely her own.

There was not only a rich verbal vocabulary to impugn someone's honour but also a rich gestural one. Such gestures included sticking out one's tongue at an enemy, pulling a man's beard or a woman's hair, singing lewd songs in front of the house of an enemy, spitting in his face, knocking off his hat, and making hand gestures that implied that she was a whore or he was a bugger or a cuckold.[93] There was also the public charivari-like shaming, which served the function of group social control by humiliating those individuals who stepped out of line and discouraging other breaches of custom.[94] Thus in Day 6, without even promising her marriage, old Graziano wants in the worst way to go to bed with Flaminia, an upper-class (and probably young) widow. Pedrolino serves Graziano right by arranging a bed trick in which Graziano lies with a lower-class woman instead and is disgraced at the exposure of this before a large crowd. The larger the crowd, the greater the humiliation.

Lesser insults might be counter-attacked with quick, often witty or biting verbal skills. Effective responses and threats could sometimes stave off violence by allowing participants to verbally repair their honour before the court of public opinion.[95] But defamation of character could also easily lead to blows.

Violence in the Streets

The many verbal fights, chase scenes, and duels in Scala's scenarios may seem to us now to be merely dramatic, even overused, melodramatic devices. All, however, need to be understood in the context of the ready verbal abuse and violence of the sixteenth-century Italian society. At Carnival, sometimes the setting of the Scala scenario, drunkenness and a high degree of sexual licence frequently led to street violence and civil commotion. The masking and the disguises often enabled the perpetrator to remain unidentified.[96] A regular, brutal Carnival amusement consisted of watching or volunteering to participate in a melee of blindfolded men who were trying to break an earthenware pot on the ground with long cudgels. The first to break the pot got the prize contained within the pot.[97]

Verbal and physical violence were not limited to Carnival, nor was drunkenness regularly a significant problem; there was much less of that in Italy than elsewhere in Europe.[98] Violence was endemic. One cause was the number of starving poor flowing into the towns, their overcrowded living conditions, and severe competition for jobs and food.[99] However, the poor were by no means the only cause of violence. Social relations in general, marked by suspicion, jealousy, envy, and rivalry,[100] led to the explosive, murderous quickness of the sixteenth-century Italian temper. It was not mere theatrical convention but a fact of life. However, in life, as opposed to comedy, the consequences of the fights were often grave. A single thrust of the rapier could be fatal. Gentlemen wore swords, not merely for decoration but for violent and sudden use.[101]

The pretext for violence was often trifling: a simple contradiction, the *mentita*, could be enough to spark bloodshed.[102] Over and over again in Scala's scenarios the immediate precipitant of a fight is calling someone a liar. In Day 33, act 1, Flavio says that Orazio is a traitor. Overhearing this, Orazio's servant Pedrolino calls Flavio a liar. As a result, Flavio draws his sword. While the young men of every class were particularly willing to risk death, maiming, or exile on the spur of the moment and constituted a rowdy menace in the streets,[103] no one was immune. To resort to force was a sign of social superiority; to be sensitive to slights and to be bellicose, belligerent, and otherwise always spoiling for a fight was to imitate the behaviour of the great and the good. Turning the other cheek to a challenge was a sign of contemptible weakness and stupidity. Mantegna hired thugs to beat up a rival, Michelangelo had his nose broken in a fist fight, and Caravaggio killed a man over a tennis match.[104]

The evidence of violence is more than anecdotal. There are a multitude of court records of criminal legal cases brought by peasants and artisans in which angry words had quickly escalated to serious and lethal woundings.[105] These cases do not begin to tell the full story of the extent of the violence, because to resort to a court of law in the matter of a private dispute was to risk being thought cowardly and stupid. It was far more honourable to take matters into one's own hands.[106] In Scala's scenarios, youths regularly invoke violence; recourse to the legal system is rare. Even Scala's old men fight one another. In Day 29 old Pantalone accuses old Graziano of conspiring with Graziano's son Flavio to help Pantalone's daughter run off with Flavio. Graziano responds that he is lying through his teeth, and the public fight between them is on. Acts quite regularly end with characters exiting, their swords drawn, and chasing one another. Historian John Hale notes that the popularity of fencing lessons among the upper classes in the sixteenth century reflected not just some new fashion in a costume sword, the rapier, but the need to be prepared for the high incidence of violence that could follow even a jostling on the street.[107] City life afforded frequent occasion for taking offence and provided a wide audience for one's bravado, certainly a wider audience in which to win or lose one's reputation than did the countryside.[108]

One of the primary causes of violence – perhaps the primary cause – was defence of honour. To fail to avenge an injury, no matter the cause, was to lose honour; it was to suffer a loss worse than death.[109] Social historian Gregory Hanlon notes that "young men challenged in public were ready to swing out at acquaintances for reasons historians often find to be pointless, but they were acting with the same concern for their reputation as heads of families."[110] While, "according to the traditional values of the culture, the honorable man must retaliate when attacked or lose his honor ... according to the laws of the state, if he retaliates, he is likely to suffer arrest, confiscation of his property, and exile or execution. If he does nothing or relies on the law courts to exact justice for him, he appears the coward, loses his honor, and makes himself vulnerable to future assaults and the unpredictability of the judge."[111] In Scala's scenarios, as in life, honour takes precedence over the law. A true gentleman tolerates no stain to his name and upholds the chivalric ethos to the death. In most of the scenarios in which he appears, Capitano Spavento is a figure of mockery because, despite his vainglory, the audience knows (as he explicitly says in Day 37, act 3) that, if it comes to that, he will suffer any indignity to avoid death.

It was a further point of honour to fight as quickly as possible after an insult had been given and satisfaction demanded. Taking time to think was tantamount to a declaration of cowardice.[112] The sudden escalation from verbal exchanges to drawn swords in the Scala scenarios is realistic. At the end of act 2, Day 33, Arlecchino tells Flavio that he, Flavio, will never have the woman he loves. At that, Flavio becomes enraged and draws his sword on Arlecchino.

The defence of family honour was as important as or even more important than the defence of individual honour, and a man was expected to defend it even with his life.[113] Any slur on the family's integrity or ambition called for retribution. Defence of the family honour could entail long-term hostilities that passed from one generation to the next.[114] "Just as honor was something one inherited (and which like material wealth, could then be squandered or increased by one's own actions), animosities and alliances were also inheritable."[115] Guicciardini, 1530, explains the account-book model of revenge: "it is perfectly all right to avenge yourself even though you feel no deep rancor against the person who is the object of your revenge."[116] Scala's Day 18 begins with Orazio returning to Florence in protective disguise because he believes that some months ago there he had killed the son of the Doctor who was a long-standing enemy of his family. Honour killing was illegal.

In Scala the upper-class youths threaten one another with duels. This method of fighting was the exclusive prerogative of those who bore arms by profession or by hereditary right: officers, nobles, and gentlemen. Duelling sustained the prestige of a class and also of the male sex, assigning men the role of natural guardian and protector of women.[117] Thus it is that in Day 25 the Capitano grandiosely comes to the defence of Isabella, whom he does not even know. Members of the lower class were left to clubs and sticks, exemplified by Arlecchino's ever-present *bastone.* Women, as Scala shows, resorted to bare hands (or hair pulling). In Day 17, after some name calling (specifically, Flaminia calls Franceschina a "bawd"), the two women engage in fisticuffs. Angry words quickly led to blows. Duelling and brawling mixed; two-on-two and crowd-on-crowd encounters were common; the duelists' "seconds" participated – they did not just watch.[118] In Day 1 Arlecchino comes to take revenge for the slap he received from Pedrolino. When he beats Pedrolino with his stick, all those present on stage – Flavio, Orazio, and the Capitano – join in the fight, and all exit fighting along the street.

While in the Scala scenarios there are few fights that result in injuries, many, including murders, are recounted in the Argument preceding the scenario, which would have served as exposition in the course of performance. The absence of actual physical violence had a basis in reality. Many of the quarrels in real life had a distinctly theatrical quality. They proceeded by a ritualized sequence of words and gestures that could be all the more violent because the opponents could count on being separated by their friends before any serious harm could be inflicted.[119] Scala shows near-death fights in which a friend intercedes. In Day 2, act 3, when Orazio and the Capitano enter fighting, Cinzio and Flavio intervene and stop the fight. The threatened duels and chase scenes that end acts almost never result in any evident untoward effect. In the rare cases that physical harm is actually inflicted in the course of the action, in Days 29 and 38, the victim recovers fully and uneventfully. Most important was to give the appearance of being ready to defend one's honour at all costs, because once it was lost it could not be regained.[120] Perhaps the absurd excuses that the Capitano provides for sidestepping a duel recall the elaborate formal rules for duels. The duel provided a ritual frame to regulate private combat.[121]

The elaborate formal rules and protocols for duels that were propagated in popular manuals followed the anti-duelling decrees issued at the final session of the Council of Trent, 1564, and both the decrees and the manuals seem to have resulted in some decline in duelling in Italy.[122] In the frequent representation of duels or threats of duels, Scala seems to harken back to an earlier period, as he does in the dramatically expedient marriages, which take place without benefit of clergy, and in the intended hunts:[123] by the end of the sixteenth century, the game had been all but hunted out.

Thus far, in this chapter, I have shown how well the fixed street setting served the drama. I have also argued in specific detail the extent to which it accorded with and served to imitate life in what we might think of as a kind of heightened realism. The sixteenth-century Italian city, houses, travel, inns, night, the *piazza* itself, the male presentation of himself, disguise, eavesdropping, the aside, honour, gossip, insults, and violence are all central to Scala's scenarios.

At the risk of appearing to defend the limitation to the requisite street setting no matter what, I want to argue in the last section of this chapter that it was a limitation that was salutary for both theatrical and, from our point of view, socio-political reasons precisely because it was not realistic.

WOMEN IN THE STREETS

Scala acknowledges the restriction of women to their homes, often by having them appear first at their window, and even there alone and silent, as observers to the action below. Jane Tylus has counted 120 appearances at a window in the Scala scenarios. Of these, 109 are made by women, including women of various marital and social statuses.[124] In the relatively safe liminal space of the window the women sometimes go unnoticed by those in the street below. And from the window they can readily absent themselves. When upper-class women come into the *piazza* in the Scala scenarios, Tylus observes, they may be framed by a doorway and thus are only tentatively present in the public space.[125] Even when extraordinary developments in the plot bring the upper-class women out into the street, they often appear in protective disguise or – without regard for such protection – mad. The disguises are of considerable range, including those of a pilgrim, a gypsy, an astrologer, a servant, a porter, a page, a ghost, and a madwoman. Even the disguises do not leave the women safe; as gypsies and servants they are shown to be fair sexual game.

In eighteen of Scala's forty comic scenarios the primary *inamorata* disguises herself as male.[126] In real life women did disguise themselves as male and not just during Carnival, when their disguises may have been deliberately easy to see through. Rudolf Dekker and Lotte van de Pol provide ample documentation from the Netherlands of travel by women in disguise.[127] From the sumptuary laws against cross-dressing in Italy, Laura Giannetti concludes that the practice was widespread there. Transgression of the codes governing dress disrupted the official view of the social order in which identity was largely determined by station or degree and which was, in theory, providential and immutable.[128] Women in men's clothes symbolically became masterless women, and as such they threatened the hierarchy.[129] They also risked the loss of their virginity and of the family's honour. Women travelling are known to have so disguised themselves, particularly on long trips, to make themselves less vulnerable to the frequent highway robberies. Masculine attire was also more practical than travel in a skirt. In Italy young women could successfully pass as young men because the early teenage years of both males and females were seen as sexually androgynous.[130] There was, however, always the risk of discovery resulting in an even greater risk of sexual assault: courtesans and actresses sometimes dressed in male attire because men found it erotic. Thus, while male disguise allowed females the freedom to move outside of the house, to express a spirit of initiative, and even to speak in public, the acute risks involved always contained tragic potential.

However frequent the women disguised as youths may have been in real life, it is most likely that their frequency in Scala's scenarios serves dramatic purposes and expresses societal fears more than fact. Disguise is, of course, intimately related to drama; onstage, actors appear to be other than who they are. In the scenarios, women's disguises, like the women's appearances at the windows, acknowledge the impropriety of women in the street. And, just as in reality upper-class women would not ordinarily have appeared in the streets, they would not have appeared in disguise. However, like women in the street, the effect of the disguises on the drama and on the culture was, from our perspective, beneficial.

In *commedia dell'arte*, unlike in the *commedia erudita*, actresses, not actors, played the roles of females. The disguises, as M.A. Katritzky makes clear, allowed these actresses to escape from the domestic space of women to a variety of roles that permitted them to more fully explore and realize their potential as performers. Actresses "created and starred in a wide range of disguises, drawn from the spheres of gender, race, age, mental competence and social class ... as creative passports to new dramatic territory – in terms of performance modes as well as theatrical space – traditionally monopolized by men."[131] The skill of the actresses in these roles may have suggested, by extension, the capabilities of women. And by bringing actresses into roles that they would otherwise not have had, at least in the instance of some performers (like the celebrated Isabella Andreini and Vittoria Piissimi), the street setting, ironically enough, aided in elevating the status of female performers above the perception of the actress as whore. Both Isabella and Vittoria were invited to perform for the wedding of Grand Duke Ferdinando de' Medici in 1589, and Isabella was invited to became a member of the learned Accademia degli Intenti. Within the troupes the popularity of the female performers, Ferdinado Taviani argues, disrupted the usual sexual hierarchy in "the evident need to recognize a greater weight for those who – regardless of their sex – contributed the most to the success of the company."[132] Some women even became troupe leaders.

The roles themselves may also have served women. I turn to the observations made by Jean Howard about cross-dressed female characters in English drama and to those made by Laura Giannetti about them in the written Italian drama. Their observations can readily be extended to the Scala scenarios.

Jean Howard remarks that one social function of the cross-dressed role was simply "the recuperation of threats to the sex-gender system" at the end of the play where the woman assumes her rightful place in marriage subject to male domination. At the same time, though, Howard points out that the recuperation is never perfect. During the course of the play a space had been opened up for women's speech and action.[133] Simply having female characters playing male roles, however temporarily, calls attention to the constructedness of the roles and thus raises the question of the inevitability of the sexual hierarchy.

With respect to the written Italian drama of the early sixteenth century, Giannetti observes that it often shows a society in which women are not merely objects of exchange in the patriarchy but rather one in which they succeed in satisfying their own sexual desires without regard for the economic and social concerns of their families. In the process they often live on their own for a time disguised as male, risking their chastity and honour, and demonstrating skills usually considered to belong only to men. Giannetti argues that "education, freedom of movement, and culture subtly triumphed over 'nature' in the imaginative vision of these comedies."[134]

It is an easy matter to extend the comments of Howard and Giannetti beyond cross-dressing to all the roles played by women in Scala. One might argue, however, that what Giannetti sees is merely the unintended consequence of presenting women on stage, combined with the limitation to the outdoor setting, rather than the result of any "imaginative vision." The extent to which Scala consciously participated in the lively debate in Italy at the time about the position of women in society cannot be known.[135] The roles that the characters play and the complications in which they find themselves are largely necessitated by the fixed exterior setting. The realm of the possible for women was pushed by it. It allowed characters to engage in and succeed in situations that they would not otherwise have encountered. Even the love matches around which the actions pivot depend upon the exterior setting. It allowed upper-class young people an access to one another that they would not have had. The disguises in the scenarios, at one with the street setting, similarly provide characters with opportunities and actions in which they would otherwise not have engaged and require them to resourcefully confront situations that they would otherwise not have encountered. The women garner our sympathies in so doing, suffer no long-term ill effects of their actions, and, indeed, succeed in their objectives. In these ways the street setting was a fortuitous choice.

Moreover, if the ordering of the scenarios in the Scala collection is in any way chronological, the actresses and their roles to some extent seem to have grown into the use of the setting over time. Particularly in the earlier scenarios in the collection, a number of the young women merely serve as interchangeable marriage partners. In the later ones, many of their roles are more individuated. In Days 36 and 39 the female characters are the plot manipulators, albeit the goal of the female characters remains a marriage in which they will presumably remain faithful.

In the first part of this chapter I argued that the fixed street setting served *commedia dell'arte* as drama. In the second part I argued the extent to which the street setting was linked to the culture represented by the scenarios, that culture having been largely overlooked from a distance of four hundred years and in the focus on the analysis of the scenarios in terms of other theatre. By showing the relationship between the street setting and life, I have called into question, as in chapter 2, the assumption that little information about contemporary history and society can be gained from the pages of the Scala scenarios. In the third section I argued that there are theatrical and, from our perspective, socio-political advantages inherent in the limitation to the fixed street setting precisely because upper-class women would not realistically have appeared there. The setting obliged the female performer and her character to show themselves and to succeed in activities in which women were ordinarily not even allowed to engage, thus suggesting at least indirectly the potential of and possibility for all women. I have called for greater appreciation of the scenarios by attempting to shift the reader's perspective on the scenarios to a perspective more aligned with that of their contemporary audience than with that previously provided by critics.

Having focused for two chapters on the relationships between the scenarios and life, I turn now to the self-conscious artfulness of scenario construction. As, in my discussions of character relationships, behaviour, and setting, I try to adapt my perspective to one that early modern audiences might well have had. I begin with a discussion of Scala's imitation of models rather than of life.

chapter four

Invention

Despite their appeal as social representations and imitations of life, the scenarios would also have appealed as self-defining artefacts with references to prior works of art, distinguishable parts, and qualities of style. In this chapter I explore some of the ways in which the scenarios are highly imitative of models and are artificial constructs. Scala called them *favole* (plots or fables).

I limit my examination of Scala's artifice here to three concepts: imitation of the work of others, copiousness, and variety. In the first part of this chapter I make clear the meaning and significance, in the period in which Scala wrote, of the imitation of models, that is, of the works of others. In the second part I examine Scala's copiousness, artfully knotted and unknotted, and in the third, the variety of which he was justly proud.[1] *Copiousness* and *variety* are terms I take from the influential polymath Leon Battista Alberti, who, in 1436, claimed that pleasure in painting, as in music and food, comes primarily "from copiousness and variety of things."[2] I add theatre to Alberti's list. Imitation of the work of others and copiousness, while they would have been greatly appreciated by Scala's contemporary audience, have caused twenty-first-century critics to founder. Variety is lauded, but imitation of the work of others is derogated, and Scala's copiousness has seemed too convoluted to attend to. The three concepts, which represent attributes much admired in the sixteenth century, do not allow me to say all that I might say, but they do provide me with a means of organizing many of my observations. I explore Scala's art and artifice along with his representations of life in detailed reconstructions of four scenarios in the second half of this book.

IMITATION AND INVENTION

The first concept, imitation of the work of others, is critical because, as Andrews has definitively demonstrated in his recent edition of thirty of Scala's scenarios, the scenarios are closely related to and greatly indebted to the earlier written comedy (the *commedia erudita*) and the novella[3] – and doubtless to earlier *commedia dell'arte* and other street performances lost to us.

The recognition of this indebtedness of scenarios to earlier material, beginning as early as 1935, while it is very important, has not served Scala or other *commedia dell'arte* scenarists very well.[4] In the first part of this chapter I feel impelled, therefore, to make apparent the meaning and significance of the imitation of models in the early modern period and its importance to invention, focusing on Scala.

In the first prologue Scala wrote for his fully scripted play, *I finto marito,* he made clear that in addition to providing imitation that is "good and true to nature," as I have argued that he did, he wanted to follow the "rules and precepts" of comedy that had been established by "good practice and good dramatists."[5] The use of these rules and precepts deliberately calls attention to the ways in which the works are highly artificial constructs. Scala evidently saw no inconsistency between the imitation of life and the imitation of models. Nor did some early modern theorists like Lodovico Dolce who maintained "that to imitate the greatest masters was only another way of imitating nature at its highest and most characteristic."[6] The unity of time and place, understood as an imitation of nature, is a well-known case in point. An argument might also be made that realism can be seen in the division of the multiple plots into protasis, epitasis, and catastrophe – replete with deceptions and misunderstandings, the frequently late point of attack, and the presence on stage of everyone for the final recognitions and reversals, usually resulting in the celebration of at least one wedding.[7] The style known as Realism is itself a simulacrum of reality based on more or less fixed rules, which are themselves artefacts. At any rate, what disturbs critics is that Scala's imitation of models extends further than rules and precepts to include not only characters but also bits of business and plot lines.

During the sixteenth century the imitation of models was central and pervasive. It was taught in the schools and widely practised in literature, the visual arts, music, politics, and philosophy. It was at the core of the period's civilization, even defining conceptions of the self. Medievalist Mary

Carruthers observes that the commonest way for a medieval author to depict himself was as a reader of an old book or a listener to an old story, which he was recalling by retelling.[8] Similarly, Boccaccio depicts himself as recounting stories that were told by ladies and gentlemen, and Castiglione supposedly records four evenings of discussions among friends. Imitation did not at all have the negative connotation it has today. In every endeavour, observed Quintilian, in the first century CE, "it is a universal rule of life that we should wish to copy what we approve in others."[9]

There was no inconsistency between imitation of models and invention. The word *invention* has the same root as the word *inventory*. An inventoried memory was essential to invention. Creative thought came from "remembered structures 'located' in one's mind as patterns, edifices, grids, and – most basically – association-fabricated networks of 'bits' in one's memory."[10] But, like the term *imitatio*, the term *memoria* needs to be understood in its historical context. *Memoria verborum*, the term for word-for-word commitment to memory that today we have come to think of as "memorization," was required of early modern schoolboys. However, the memory of the advanced pupil was to produce a reactivation that was also a reformulation.[11] "*Memoria* refers not to how something is communicated, but to what happens once one has received it, to the interactive process of familiarizing – or textualizing – which occurs between oneself and others' words in memory."[12] *Textus*, meaning "texture," or "weaving," applied to the layers of text, commentary, and gloss that constitute a text.

The significant memory was of the gist of the material, its *res*. *Memoria rerum* was far more highly respected than *memoria verborum* because it compelled the person recollecting to actively shape the material for the occasion, consistent with the moral emphasis given to rhetoric by Cicero, Quintilian, Augustine, and the traditions of monastic prayer. Reshaping was regarded as ethically more valuable. Memory remained central into the early modern period, despite the availability of books, because of the "identity of memory with creative thinking, learning (invention and recollection), and the ability to make judgments (prudence or wisdom)."[13] If there could be such a thing as a person without a memory, that person would be without moral character and, in a basic sense, without humanity.

It is true that the ability to recite material perfectly and both forwards and backwards, and in all sorts of combinations, was a revered skill. The revered skill, however, lay not in the simple retention of even large amounts of material but rather in the ability to move the material about instantly, directly, and securely.[14] The skill was admired because, as in the expression "I know the material backwards and forwards," such memorization indicated that one had thoroughly absorbed the material, made it one's own for use in one's own oratory or writing.

The standard images of this process, of what Mary Carruthers usefully calls "memorative composition," were of mellification and digestion.[15] Epistle 84 of Seneca the Younger (the playwright), ca 4 BCE–65 CE, was frequently cited as a source for both images (themselves frequently reappearing in various formulations) and was itself ostensibly an imitation. Seneca, in an analogy to nature and without any indication of inconsistency, says that he is repeating what other men say and, at the same time, recommending composition by means of the imitation of nature:

> We should follow, men say, the example of the bees, who flit about and cull the flowers that are suitable for producing honey, and then arrange and assort in their cells all that they have brought in ... [Like bees] we should so blend those several flavors into one delicious compound that, even though it betrays its origin, yet it nevertheless is clearly a different thing from that whence it came. This is what we see nature doing in our own bodies without any labor on our part; the food we have eaten, as long as it retains its original quality and floats in our stomachs as an undiluted mass, is a burden; but it passes into tissue and blood only when it has been changed from its original form. So it is with the food which nourishes our higher nature, – we should see to it that whatever we have absorbed should not be allowed to remain unchanged, or it will be no part of us. We must digest it; otherwise it will merely enter the memory and not the reasoning power.[16]

This analogy was itself repeated in various ways countless times and was even to be found in innumerable visual representations of bees.

The concept of the Renaissance entailed the rediscovery and reuse of the ancients. In that concept, however, was an idea of history, an understanding that things had not always been the same. Borrowing from the ancients was necessarily not the same as simply reusing what had been discovered of them. Latin had been the native language of the Romans; it was not of the Italians. Scala wrote not in Latin but, like a number of recognized authors, in the vernacular language of Tuscany. Italians were not the same as Greeks and Romans. They were Christians. Their culture was different. There could be no intention of exact imitation. Nor was it desired. The process was to be one of mellification, turning nectar into honey.

If the material had not been processed, as bees process nectar into honey, that imitation was dishonourable. Simply copying what one had heard or read was not "authentic imitation."[17] Imitation was to be creative. Quintilian scorned orators who simply repeated the words of others as false imitation. Plagiarism was to be avoided because it made one appear ridiculous and shameful in public. It was a failure of invention because it was a failure of memory.[18] Petrarch advised even against repeating oneself.[19] In *commedia dell'arte* the Doctor is an object of fun, representing the pretensions of professional men. He has not digested his learning. He has failed to make what he learned his own.

In the long debate about whether one should imitate a single model or many models, Scala clearly favoured many: "good practice and good dramatists." Again, Scala was not alone in his recommendation for eclectic imitation. Petrarch, for instance, reminded us of this in his iteration of the bee analogy: "We should write as the bees make sweetness, not storing up the flowers but turning them into honey, thus making one thing of many various ones, but different and better."[20]

Thus, too, in Scala's view, one took what worked from experience and from good dramatists and adapted it to the needs of a new scenario. Petrarch observed that "the bees would have no credit unless they transformed ... [the nectar] into something different and better."[21] Scala claimed that he deserved such credit. In his first prologue to *Il finto marito,* speaking as "The Player," he said, "Scala's invention has always been inspired, and that counts for everything in comedy."[22] Accordingly, Scala thought to publish his work. It was invention but, like all invention at the time, it was (and was supposed to be) based on imitation. It was memorative composition. The writer and the audience shared a dialogue of textual allusions and transformations. In recognizing them, the audience could admire the work. Not to engage in that dialogue was the mark, in Mary Carruthers's word, of a "dolt."[23] Not only did imitation have no negative connotations, but it was essential to this dialogue and to invention. No one was a self-contained entity.

Louise George Clubb's term *theatregram* for the pervasive reuse of types of characters, of relationships between and among them, actions and speeches, and thematic design[24]– which term she first used in 1986 to make clear the means by which the drama of Italy influenced that of Shakespeare – was groundbreaking and invaluable. Earlier searches for direct sources of influence had provided no way to establish this self-evident relationship. The concept of theatregram has further served to set out a connection between improvised *commedia dell'arte* scenarios themselves and between scenarios and the earlier written *commedia erudite.* The term *theatregram,* far from Clubb's intention,[25] has sometimes been misleading in so far as it suggests not memorative composition but simply the recycling and reuse of old materials.[26]

Clubb's insight into the manner of the transmission of characters, actions, and speeches from one medium to another and from one culture to another might be usefully contextualized by the term *meme,* which was coined by evolutionary biologist Richard Dawkins in 1976 to extend, by analogy, evolutionary principles to account for the spread of ideas and cultural phenomena.[27] The term *theatregram* refers to a practice unique to theatre, whereas the term *meme* applies to all arts, reminding us that the adaptation of pre-existing material perhaps, above all in the early modern period, was not unique to theatre. Like *theatregram,* the term *meme* enables us to ascribe a source or sources where a direct source may not be evident. It further entails the idea of creative adaptation (and disappearance), whereas the concept of the reshuffleable suggests something fixed. Biologist François Jacob describes evolution as a tinkerer, and biochemist Steven Johnson conceives of the human body as bricolage, old parts (two eyes, one nose, one heart, four limbs, say) strung together to form something new (alligator, elephant, human).[28] Biologist Stuart Kauffman calls these reuses "the adjacent possible."[29]

Whatever the term, it must be clear that reuse can be creative and that the process of creative imitation can apply broadly to both life and art. In her 2010 book, *Unoriginal Genius,* Marjorie Perloff shows the extent to which some of the experimental poetry she champions relies on citation and appropriation and can be described as intertext, reproduction, copying, collage, pastiche, assemblage, or mosaic.[30] She argues that while appropriation, citation, copying, and reproduction have been central to the visual arts for decades, "the Internet has made copyists, recyclers, transcribers, collators, and reframers of us all ... In this new arcade world, writing a poem is no easier than it ever was. Just different." A quotation she provides from the poet Charles Bernstein humourously recalls the frequent restatements on composition made by Seneca above: "I love originality so much I keep copying it."[31] The scholar's use of citations makes evident the extent to which academic writing itself is not free creation but imitation. This is not a paradox. We stand on the shoulders of giants.

What mattered for Scala in his invention was not the particular words the actors used but the *res,* the clearly marked, detailed route map for the actor comparable to what an orator might set for himself. Believing that "plays properly and in essence consist in actions, and only incidentally in narrations," Scala left the actual words spoken by the actors, in Andreini's phrase, to those "who were born just with skill in speaking."[32] Scala divided his scenarios into short scenes. In rhetoric, *divisio* refers to the division of a text into short segments, required for both memorization and composition and putting the segments together in an order, arranging them properly from one to two to three, and so on. Scala's scenes are the divisions of a text into these short segments. Quintilian advised the orator to arm himself with "the order of cues for both the *modus* or 'way' and the *finis* or 'goal'"[33] This order of cues, taught to every orator, and provided by Scala in every scene, allows for digression and all sorts of extempore speaking, while keeping the orator or actor from losing his way by forgetting either how much he has left to cover or his chief points.

In his first prologue to *Il finto marito*, Scala emphasized that good precepts are those that follow from stage practice and not the other way around. When usage resulted only from rules rather than experience, as he suggested they did in many plays written by great men of letters, he said the plays often proved to be lifeless in performance.[34] That the *commedia dell'arte* lasted for two hundred years and became popular all over Europe, while the written drama remained relatively unknown, must have borne some relationship to this truth.

While I would like to show with what effectiveness Scala used his various sources, I cannot do so, for even when we find a fully scripted play similar in important respects to one of his scenarios, as we do with Day 25, we do not know whether Scala was working directly from that source, *Gl'ingannati*, 1532, although it was frequently republished, or from intervening unwritten imitations of it. In my reconstructions I can only illustrate the skill with which much of Scala's work is crafted, observing at the same time that none of it adheres to any known model. I am able to note a number of small very theatrical conventions or topoi that Scala evidently found effective in practice and used repeatedly, in effect borrowing from himself: the servant's breathless or faked breathless entrance (hearkening back to the running slave in Roman drama); his entrance to announce that a character critical to the action cannot be found, immediately after which that character enters, thus delayed and heralded by the announcement; contagious weeping; one actor suddenly carrying another offstage; and the complication that arises unexpectedly just as the scenario is apparently about to reach its happy end.

The only one of these topoi that shows any need to suit a particular actor is the one that requires an actor who is capable of carrying another actor. I instance it here to show how Scala used one of his own theatrical conventions in his scenarios because it is the one that requires the least explanation of its context. Each of Scala's several uses of it is the same in that it provides a surprising resolution to a scene and allows for a display of an actor's strength and agility. With each use, however, the convention is also made new.

In Day 3, act 2, Pedrolino, Orazio, and Flavio deservedly throw the Capitano's cape over his head and carry him off. But then, when Pedrolino tries to carry off the innocent Arlecchino, the Capitano's servant, Arlecchino turns the tables and carries off Pedrolino. In Day 7, act 1, the carrying off results from the Capitano's usual foolhardiness: he decides that the best course of action is to abduct a woman with her father present. In Day 18, act 2, the carrying off is the result of a joyful reunion of lovers, and because the youth carries his love into his house, the audience can infer that their relationship will then be sexually consummated. In Day 21 Arlecchino carries indoors each of the four revellers who have come out of the house and fallen down drunk, thus concluding act 2. In Day 25, act 3, Arlecchino saves Franceschina from a beating by carrying her out of the scene. In Day 32, act 1, the carrying off shows that Orazio has gone mad. In Day 34, act 1, Pedrolino defends himself from an attack by two violent women by carrying off his master who has just defended him and who perhaps serves as a shield. In addition to performing a different function in each scenario, each carrying off is integral to the larger action of the scenario.

With my account of the role of imitation, I have shown Scala's use of the earlier written comedy in a different light than that in which earlier critics have presented it. Andrews describes the process of devising a *commedia dell'arte* scenario as a making do to fit circumstances. "Theatregrams large and small, taken from existing plays or scenarios, were cut, refashioned and adapted for the roles and talents of the company which was going to perform it. It is likely that some scenarios were originally versions of single written plays. These were then ruthlessly adapted to fit circumstances, and their sources became progressively less recognizable." The process was one of continual "distortion" of the original source play or plays.[35] Thus Scala's claims to inspired invention in his scenarios, both in the first prologue to his written play *Il finto marito* and similarly in his letter to readers in his edition of scenarios, are ignored. Likewise ignored are the praise of the famous actor Francesco Andreini in his letter in Scala's volume of scenarios to the same effect and the words, to the same effect, of Andreini's son, a playwright and director.[36] Testaverde reads Scala's claim to invention simply in terms of his means, that is, publication of scenarios rather than of plays written out word for word.[37] Of course, Scala borrowed, as did every writer of the period, including Shakespeare.[38] Such borrowing was essential. Establishing the existence of it in Scala's work is important. This having been done, notably by Andrews, we need to understand imitation as a constitutive element. We need to look closely at the works in themselves as Scala would have us look at them, as inventions.

I have written elsewhere about probable reasons for, the means of, and the interest in actor improvisation upon *commedia dell'arte* scenarios, using Flaminio Scala as a reference point.[39] I only briefly say here, in a coda to this section, that the interest in the use of scenarios rather than fully scripted plays (ironically defended in the first prologue to Scala's only written play) can be explained by other than the practical concerns, like poverty, or additional considerations that have been put forth – including censorship, the instability of the working groups, and the different dialects spoken in the different cities where acting troupes performed – important as these concerns may have been. Jeremy Lopez points out that the success of the drama is fuelled by its potential for failure: "The joy of the drama lies in the space for negotiation between success and failure."[40] When the drama is improvised, that sense of the potential for failure is enhanced. The outcome of improvisation is uncertain. The form seems open, the machinery of the plot fragile. The performance takes on the interest akin to that of a sporting event, especially because improvisation suggests that the performance is provided only for the audience at hand and is a one-time occurrence. The uncertainty specifically calls our attention to the improvising actor, not just to the material improvised. In that respect, the form is non-illusory. Other non-illusory conventions in the *commedia dell'arte* – disguises, night scenes, practical jokes – are of a piece with the intrigue and improvisation in contributing to our sense that the action might fail. Despite our awareness that the trickster and the lovers will prevail, the possibility that the performers and, consequently, the characters will not succeed adds to the excitement. Performers seem to have exaggerated the extent to which they were freely improvising to increase the excitement of the performance and to boast of their skills. In fact, their improvisation was, like Scala's invention, honey made from the nectar of prior texts written or oral, their own or that of others.

COPIOUSNESS

Book 2 of Desederius Erasmus's *De copia* or *De duplici copia verborum ac rerum* (*On the Twofold Abundance of Words and Ideas*), 1512, was reprinted about 160 times before the end of the century.[41] Regularly taught in schools to boys from about the age of ten,[42] it emphasized richness and amplification of style – plenitudinousness. The use of a copious style, including examples, comparisons, and contrasts, was a major strategy of composition. It was certainly Scala's.

"There is no doubt," confidently asserted Lodovico Castelvetro, "that it is more pleasurable to listen to a plot containing many and diverse actions than one which contains but a single one."[43] Scala apparently found this to be so. He intermixed several plots and their diverse actions. His multiple characters, usually a minimum of two old men, two youths, two young women, and two servants, made two plots, and a captain, frequently trying to intervene in one of them, often made another half plot.[44] Sometimes there is even a full third plot.

The audience, when it watches a good scenario, is taken in by the wrenching twists and turns in the plots and, as are the characters, by the urgency of their actions. At their best, the effect of Scala's comic scenarios is to set their readers into a panic lest the scenario collapse altogether. They force the audience to share in the character's, scenarist's, and, at least ostensibly, the actors' peril before, at long last and beyond all expectation, bringing about the long-due conclusion, the very audacity and hazardousness of which adds to the astounding effect.[45] We wonder how the scenarist and his characters will extricate themselves from all the complications and admire him and them for doing so.

At the same time, we, as audience, know, as the characters do not, that the scenario will follow the laws of comedy and end happily and that the characters will be true to form and, for the most part, self-consistent as Horace and Aristotle wished them to be.[46] This double-consciousness makes the events that seem sad, exasperating, or frightening to the characters enjoyable for the spectators and, more important, for my argument here, adds to the copiousness of the audience's perception of the work already provided by the complexity of the interwoven plots. The audience's familiarity with the characters and with comic form allows them an additional frame of reference.

Audience familiarity with the form allowed Scala and the performers to play with audience expectations. We expect that the braggart Capitano, seemingly all set to fight, will come up with a reason to suddenly excuse himself from doing so, and, outside the frame, we look forward to learning how he will weasel out this time. Scala also turns audience expectations on their head. He does so in Day 10, for instance, which begins with the wedding ceremony of servants Pedrolino and Franceschina. Scenarios customarily culminate in weddings of upper-class youths and girls, with perhaps a marriage of the servants thrown in rather cursorily at the very last moment just for good measure. In this case, Pedrolino's pending and interrupted wedding constitutes a major plot line, in the course of which Pedrolino, far from being the usual trickster who controls events, behaves very like a hapless upper-class lover; he is left only to despair at having lost his love, Franceschina, and, increasingly desperate to find her, decides that he wants to kill himself. At the last minute the plot line of Pedrolino's wedding is resolved by a *deus ex machina*, generally frowned upon by theorists influential at the time unless it could be handled plausibly, as it is here with the arrival for the wedding of Franceschina's father, Burattino.[47] As it turns out, Burattino, like Pedrolino, is a peasant from Bergamo.[48] More than that, in a scene no doubt full of rustic dialect and silliness, Pedrolino and Burattino discover that they are brothers. Only after Pedrolino again says that he wants to die because of his love for Franceschina does Burattino point out what the audience has already deduced, that Franceschina is Pedrolino's niece and thus he cannot marry her. Pedrolino, not the shrewd man we have come to expect, is amazed to learn this. The consolation offered to Pedrolino by Burattino is that Franceschina is his niece. Once again, the older man does not get the girl. If the audience is familiar with the more conventional scenarios, in which, in the end, the upper-class *senex* is tricked by the servant and does not get the girl, the familiarity with these particulars about the structure of *commedia dell'arte* and its characters allows this scenario to resonate with those scenarios, adding to the effect of copiousness.

Even the audience member who is not familiar with the form of *commedia dell'arte* is placed both inside and outside the scenario. This double perspective adds to the experience of copiousness. Many scenes are set at night, during which time the characters cannot see, but the audience can. Scala sometimes states that a character speaks in metaphor or ambiguously, and the character whom he addresses does not understand. Two characters are to speak at cross purposes, each misunderstanding the other. In both cases the audience understands. Asides and eavesdropping, sometimes from a window, that is, not on the same level as the characters overheard, provide perspectives on the actions that are different from that of the speakers. In Day 3, Scala plays literally with point of view: Flaminia pretends to speak to Orazio but really speaks to Flavio standing behind him, whom Orazio cannot see but whom the audience can. Tricks (including bed tricks) and disguises (including fake madness, fake death, and cross-dressing that can lead a male character to fondle another male character, presuming him to be female or, perhaps even worse, disguises that lead a lower-class male character to fondle an upper-class woman, presuming her to be also lower class) all provide the audience with knowledge that the beguiled character does not have.[49] Twins, whom Scala uses in only three scenarios, also provide the audience with double vision, inside the action and out. Two incompatible frames are also often provided when the audience is made aware of life taking place, indoors or elsewhere, that the characters onstage cannot know about. In Day 6, for instance, we see the old husband outside zealously guarding the door of the house, dancers dancing and musicians playing, but we know, as most of them do not, that, indoors, the young wife is having sex with her young lover. As Jeremy Lopez says of a Thomas Middleton play, "causing the audience to make adjustments to what it perceives and in what it perceives the characters to perceive, is what the scene, and in fact the play, is all about."[50]

At the same time that the scenarios tell a story, their distinctly overt theatricalism – including the texts that reflect other texts, the use of masks, fixed characters, disguises, tricks and *lazzi*, which are sometimes, like Arlecchino's ladder acrobatics, not necessarily tricks – calls attention to the artifice involved in telling us that story. Interludes performed between the acts, of course, and the act divisions make the audience very aware of the scenarios as scenarios while they are also aware of the stories they present. If the performance is preceded by a prologue and an epilogue, as are the plays of *commedia ridiculosa*, the fully scripted imitations of *commedia dell'arte* that are thought to have been written for amateur performance, these serve to heighten the audience's sense of the performance as performance, regardless of their content. They encourage the audience to become aware of actor improvisation as distinct from character improvisation. An actor's *bravura* performances, the representations of extreme emotions and sudden emotional changes, all call attention to the actor as performer and the scenario as scenario. Applause for such representations, and laughter, also make the audience aware of the presentational aspect of the performance. Moreover, this double awareness at performance increases the copiousness of the audience experience. If the roles were at times doubled, insofar as the actors were both effective and recognized in their added roles, as the characters were in their disguises, the audience's appreciation of the actors' skills would have added to the audience's sense of copiousness and superiority.

The resonance of the experience is increased for the audience in so far as it is aware that the processes in which it engages are very like those in which the characters engage. The audience overhears, it watches, it recognizes, it sees disappearances and reappearances, and it sees both reality and appearance, disguise, transformation, actors becoming what they are not and engaging in acts not theirs by means of disguise, transformation, tricks, magic, or madness. The scenarios are replete with just these processes. Jeremy Lopez even suggests that because the dramatic effects are so "intricately bound up with bringing an audience around to an impossible point of view, comedies ... tend to be built on narratives of conversion."[51]

If a scenario is performed in a *piazza*, its set reduplicates that place and the activity in it, with its representations of comings and goings of various classes of people. The two irreconcilable frames or matrices are quite markedly distinguished and are present simultaneously: the theatre as theatre and the story represented. I have been at pains in earlier chapters to call attention to the ways in which the stories and characters also reflect real life. The audience is aware at the same time of that dimension, further adding to the scenarios' copiousness.

As I argued in chapter 3, the city in which the scenario was actually being performed could easily have been substituted for that named. As Scala suggests, its particulars, including its women, could have been elaborated upon by the Capitano in his grandiose fashion, thus not only suggesting that the scenario had been written for the benefit of its present audience, including women, but also making the scenario self-reflexive. The viewer, necessarily aware both of the actual city sites and women and of the scenario, are kept very busy with any topicality and its use in the story. This audience activity would make the scenario seem more copious than it is on the page.

In certain scenarios Scala plays with the idea of self-reflexivity. Day 39 is about an actress, Vittoria who has come to town and of whom the men are enamoured, suggesting for the audience the actual Vittoria Piissimi, a famous *commedia dell'arte* actress. Day 2 has a stage with a charlatan, a singer, and an audience. These are scenarios, in part, about theatre. Day 6 has professional musicians and so many stories within the main plot that parallel it that Roberto Tessari refers to the effect as like that of "Chinese boxes."[52] In these ways as well, Scala multiplies the number of frames or matrices.

These incompatible matrices can be and frequently are a source of humour and greatly complicate our sense of the action. So do the malapropisms in which Doctor Graziano supposedly spoke, as well as the metaphorical language of the lovers, the sexual puns, and the variety of dialects with which the audience is obliged to deal. Mad Isabella's probable reference to Queen Elizabeth in Day 38, sexual *double entendres* in Day 6, including the tale from Boccaccio, the singing in the style of Norcia (home of pig castrators), the father's instruction to his daughter in how to manage the handle of a hoe, all increase the sense of copiousness. Various remaining *contrasti* (verbal conflicts) make clear that metaphors and similes were much favoured. They also increased the sense of doubleness.

Copiousness is further increased by compression. The great number of incidents in a scenario take place within at most twenty-four hours and in a single setting with the action continuous within each of the acts. The point of attack is characteristically late, usually a turning point in the story. It was understood that if the dramatist could contain his diverse actions within a narrow compass, he had, admirably, done something difficult.[53] The late point of attack not only compressed the action but also required that the considerable backstory, which often took place over many years, and might be very complicated, needed to be supplied within the scenario, thus packing it even more. There is usually a necessity to resolve the conflict in a hurry: the girls are about to give birth; the groom for the arranged marriage that the girl does not want has just arrived in town; the girl who has feigned death must be rescued from the tomb by her lover. The characters' out-of-breath or feigned out-of-breath entrances, occurring at times in acts 2 or 3, enhance the sense of the increasing importance of speed as the scenario proceeds. Strangely enough, so do the delays, which all increase intensity: the long love speeches made by the lovers when instead they ought to be taking action, the long speeches of the Capitano that interrupt the action, and the scenes preceding the entrance of a character who is essential to the action, in which it is announced that that character cannot be found. The many brief scenes with their entrances and exits enhance the sense of speed. So does the street setting. It rarely allows characters to sit. Characters entering together frequently arrive mid-conversation, not only providing a sense of offstage life but also allowing the characters to cut quickly to the information and action relevant to the plot.

What Scala would have asked us to admire in the scenarios is not simply the compressed complexity but also the way in which this complexity coheres through repetitions and contrasts. In the early modern period the finding of similitudes, like copiousness, was regarded as a sign of great wit.[54] In the scenarios they effect what art historian Heinrich Wölfflin called "multiple unity," a coordination of parts, that was at least as significant as, if not more significant than, subordination as a principle of organization in which each part is self-sufficient and equal to other parts.[55] The repetitions and contrasts, in themselves, further add to the copiousness by providing resonance between the parts.

This coordination appears in the plotting, the characters, the use of props and costumes, the emotions, themes, and staging. Repetitions (parallels and contrasts) in the plotting, small and large, are everywhere. The most obvious of these are effected by the parallelism in characters, often from the two different houses represented onstage. With these characters a great many parallels and contrasts can be effected: two youths love one girl; one youth is faithful to his friend, the other is not; an old man and a young one love the same woman; a servant and an old man love the same woman; two women are rejected by the men they pursue; one servant is clever, the other is not; and one old man is of a generous youthful spirit, the other is not. The doubling, in addition to providing copiousness, also provides a sense of coherence that is represented literally by the multiple marriages at the end that often bring two familial houses together. The addition of characters, including a female servant and a captain, can provide relief from the parallelism or add to it: the Capitano loves a woman who does not love him but is loved by another whom he does not love; the two male servants love the same female servant, et cetera.

I can only begin to suggest the nature of some of the other numerous parallels and contrasts found in the actions of every scenario. Day 10 begins with plans for first one wedding and then, in the next scene, another. These scenes are immediately followed by three scenes, each with a person from out of town who has come with the intention of disrupting one of the weddings. In Day 30 Flaminia is pregnant; the father is revealed to be Cintio; Hortensia, Flavio's sister, is pregnant; the father is revealed to be the Capitano. Day 14 begins with Orazio telling his servant how much he loves Flaminia. His servant responds with a speech about how many have come to grief because of Love.[56] Next, the Capitano enters and tells his servant how much he too loves Flaminia. His servant urges him to pursue her, telling him of all the famous men of arms [like the Capitano himself] who have loved and served love. Not only are these contrasting scenes funny in themselves, but they establish the plot.

It has often been observed that jokes and storytelling depend upon the rule of three. Scala uses this pattern, as I have shown above in Day 10. He also uses it in considerably more complex ways. In three separate scenes in *The Tutor*, Day 31, act 1, Pedrolino's mistress badly beats him and/or demoralizes him. Pedrolino, after several attempts at revenge, which have only made things worse for him, stands weeping in pain, his honour virtually destroyed. Arlecchino, servant of the Capitano, then enters with a plate of macaroni for Pedrolino, sent by the Capitano, evidently in lieu of the large sum of money he had promised him. Pedrolino, trying to salvage his honour, if only in front of Arlecchino, provides a noble rationale for his weeping that the audience will understand as mere face saving.[57] In empathy for his supposed plight Arlecchino also begins to weep and to eat the macaroni. Then a third servant from the other house enters and proceeds to do likewise, until the macaroni has all gone. The three servants exit one by one, still weeping. Pedrolino, who failed to get even the whole plate of macaroni, much less his money, again with an ironic comment, exits first. Arlecchino exits last, licking the now empty plate.

This seemingly discrete food *lazzo*, one of Scala's many scenes of contagious weeping, while not integral to the action, is emotionally and morally essential and establishes the pattern of three. In the end of the scenario these three downtrodden servants, previously bound by their hunger and tears (and by another *lazzo* in which Pedrolino and Arlecchino discover that they are from the same village),[58] get their, albeit redirected, revenge and day of glory – dressed and armed as butchers sanctioned to castrate the evil-intentioned tutor. It would not do for the well-to-do family members whom the tutor has actually betrayed to engage in this unseemly behavior, but the servants can. And in the emotional and moral economy of the scenario the weeping *lazzo* justifies their doing so. (This moral economy also serves the tutor, who had evil intentions but was prevented from carrying them out. Consequently, the three servants end up only insulting him, beating him badly with sticks, and driving him away – satisfaction enough but resulting in no lasting harm.)

In Day 19 three loyal middle-elite friends struggle over the same middle-elite young woman; the struggle is resolved amicably. The last scene of the scenario visually parallels the plot of the whole scenario by showing and resolving a physical struggle between three servants for a serving woman. In Day 28 Pantalone, Graziano, and Pedrolino all love the married Franceschina. Cintio, Orazio, and the Capitano compete for the seemingly also unattainable Isabella.

Scala frequently, and in surprisingly various ways, greatly extends the pattern of repetitions with serial entrances or exits. Day 26 has both. Act 1 opens with Pantalone upbraiding his son Orazio for three things: chasing women, gambling, and leading a life of vice. Shortly afterwards, for various plausible reasons, a rather random assortment of people go in succession into the house of the now absent Pantalone; there his son, true to the father's accusations, proceeds to have a party for them, including lavish quantities of food at Pantalone's expense. When Pedrolino, servant in the house of Pantalone, hears Pantalone unexpectedly arriving home, the audience deduces that the partygoers need to vacate the house in a hurry. But how? The solution is a series of very brazen exits, recalling the sequential entrances into the house, but in which the dramatic interest is successively increased by the order of the exits. Flavio, son of Graziano and friend of Orazio, exits first, silently bows respectfully to Pantalone, and goes into the house of the absent Graziano. Pantalone senses nothing unusual in the friend's departure. Next, the youth Fabrizio, unknown to Pantalone, does the same. Then Pedrolino does the same, only, for variety, Scala slightly breaks the pattern established by the previous two characters by having Pedrolino exit up the street. Pantalone may be wondering who sent Pedrolino on what errand. But not for long, because immediately thereafter Franceschina, who is unknown to Pantalone, comes out and for some reason that Pantalone cannot fathom has a large food chest on her head. She too silently bows and goes into Graziano's house. Then a gypsy, of all things, comes out, silently bows, and goes into Graziano's house. Pantalone's own son does the same. By this time, the audience must think that this is the last of the exits, their having built to a climax with the previously upbraided son. They will have forgotten Fabrizio's servant, Arlecchino, who exits last. Often, just before the resolution of Scala's comedy, an unanticipated complication arises from some source, like the Capitano, that the audience may well have forgotten. This minor bump in the road towards the, then inevitable, happy resolution allows the audience to savour the comedy just a bit longer. So, too, the exit of the forgotten servant extends the *lazzo* beyond its seeming end and in a surprising way. He, too, silently bows and enters Graziano's house where, we can imagine, the partying continues. The thoroughly confused and bamboozled Pantalone without a word, like the others, goes off up the street, bowing to unseen passersby or to the audience,[59] and the act ends.

Very often the acts' endings reflect back on their openings, giving the acts a sense of closure and completeness. In Day 27 the scenario opens with Pantalone who is delighted to have just received a letter confirming the match he had arranged between his son and Isabella. At the end of the act, on hearing that the girl is dead, Pantalone exits weeping. Parallels and contrasts provide coherence.

In Day 39 a *lazzo*, used primarily to indicate the passage of time while the husbands are at the theatre, is neatly made to cohere metaphorically with the central action. In the *lazzo* the servants who are gambling at cards literally lose even their pants. Meanwhile the wives within with their lovers are presumably losing their bloomers as well. When the husbands unexpectedly return home early from the theatre, the wives explain that they were merely whiling away the time playing cards with the men within serving as their protectors. This example and the weeping *lazzo* described above make clear how subtle and easy to overlook the relationship between *lazzo* and scenario can sometimes be and why the *lazzi* in Scala's scenarios have been seen as discrete entities. The *lazzi* may well have been ones that Scala borrowed from elsewhere, but he carefully integrated them into his own work.

Act structures can parallel one another. In Day 10, act 2 begins with noise inside Pantalone's house, and then Flaminia fleeing from within, followed by Isabella intent on killing her with a naked sword. Then from Graziano's house Orazio comes out with a naked sword. In the next scene Pantalone appears with a pistol. Act 3 begins with noise in Pantalone's house, and then Franceschina fleeing from within, pursued by Arlecchino with a naked weapon in hand. Pedrolino comes out of the house, holding a club, to rescue Franceschina. In the next scene Pantalone comes out armed.

Emotions may change quickly, providing emotional contrasts between scenes and within a single scene and character. Opposites, like repetitions, pattern the copiousness. In Day 14, act 3, Flavio grieves for the supposed death of Isabella. Then her father, the Doctor, believing his daughter Isabella to be dead, faints from grief, thereby appearing as if he himself were dead. Seeing this, Flavio grieves more. In the very next scene, after a series of recognitions and revelations, Isabella, the Doctor, and Flavio all rejoice. In Day 27 Pantalone's son, hearing confirmation of his impending marriage to Isabella, whom he has never met, is very pleased. In the very same scene, hearing that Isabella is dead, he faints with grief. Such rapid and extreme emotional transformations and contrasts are frequent in the scenarios. Early moderns endorsed the view of both Cicero and Quintilian that in real life one could suddenly be overcome by a violent passion and that it could quickly change.[60] In these instances, however, Scala may be portraying the characters as rather fatuous.

Acts are often tied together by these contrasting emotions that at the same time serve to remind the audience of what has gone before. Day 32, act 2, ends with Pedrolino exiting alone, laughing at the trick he has played on Flavio; act 3 begins with Flavio still frightened by the trick. Day 31, act 2, ends with Pantalone and Isabella very happy; act 3 begins with Orazio enraged. Not only are the emotions contrasting, but they also represent opposing perspectives on the same events or characters, the opening of one act reminding us of the action with which the previous one closed.

There are also repetitions and contrasts in what is said, insofar as the scenarios indicate that. In Day 9 from inside their respective houses first Pantalone calls for his servant Pedrolino, after which Graziano calls for his servant Arlecchino. Then the old men come out. Pantalone complains that Pedrolino is too interfering, Graziano that Arlecchino is too lazy. Pantalone congratulates the Doctor for having married off his daughter and says that he would like to find a husband for the girl who is his ward.

Props and costumes may be repeated, serving as a motif: Day 5, letters; Day 10, brandished weapons; Day 16, rings; Day 26, carpets; and Day 35, door bars and the contents of a dishpan and a chamber pot. In fact, some scenarios are named not after persons or activities but after the prop, or props, that serves to make everything in them cohere and constitute their most memorable feature: Day 16, *The Mirror* (*Lo specchio*); Day 26, *The Alexandrian Carpets* (*Li tappeti Alessandrini*); and Day 39, *The Portrait* (*Il ritratto*). Day 7 presents a sequence of disguises in which each successive entering character puts on the clothing of the preceding character. Such disguising calls attention to the performance itself as artifice. In Day 15 Pantalone, Pedrolino, Capitano Spavento, Arlecchino, Flavio, and Flaminia, for various reasons, all enter dressed as beggars. In Day 25 Isabella is recognized in her disguise as a male; so when her identical twin brother comes to town, he is presumed to be Isabella in disguise. Twins are a kind of repetition.

As Joel Altman has pointed out for scripted plays, the intrigue in the scenarios sometimes serves as an examination of what might otherwise be a debate topic:[61] which is more important, male friendship or love; which is more important, filial duty or love; should an old man take a young wife; is theatrical performance of value?[62] In actions representing the various aspects of the questions in the scenarios, parallels and contrasts are provided.

Scala is also very attentive to visual patterning and rhythms to provide parallels and contrasts. In Day 28, act 1, Flaminia appears at her window and speaks to the Capitano below. Then Isabella appears at her window and speaks to the Capitano below. Later in the act the women appear at their windows in reverse order as silent observers. This is a simple visual pattern.

The use of the windows for rhythmical and even musical effect is most marked in Day 37, *La caccia* (*The Hunt*). The opening, musically structured like a canon, almost entirely comprises sequential entrances. At dawn each of four old men, Pantalone, Graziano, Claudione, and Burattino, in their separate houses come to their windows in sequence, sounding their hunting horns to signal their readiness for the hunt. After each of the four old men has appeared, each goes back in, apparently in the reverse order from that in which they appeared, Pantalone last. Then Isabella comes to her window in Pantalone's house, speaking of dawn and of her lover. The probably florid language, "reproaching Aurora [the dawn] because she does not leave the arms of her old lover Titon," also seems to be a farcical version of something like *La caccia*, a comic madrigal composed by Alessandro Striggio (1536–92), replete with the noises of horses, riders and the cries of animals, which begins, "Sprung from the icy arms of Titon, / dawn appears in the heavens in a shining chariot; /... Brave young men, valiant and strong/ ... bound from out your downy beds, / for a powerful horn / rings out ... / It summons you to the hunt," and ends with the conclusion of the hunt.[63] As is made clear by the title to Lucia Marchi's essay on the musical form *La caccia* (*The Hunt*), "Chasing Voices, Hunting Love: The Meaning of the Italian *Caccia*," the none-too-hidden real object of the hunt in song and visual representations was usually sexual (see figure 4.1).[64] Flaminia comes to her window on the other side of the stage in Burattino's house and speaks of dawn. Then Pedrolino at his window opposite in Pantalone's house comes to his window and speaks of dawn and his lover. After a love scene in the street with Pedrolino who has come from Pantalone's house and Franceschina who has come from Burattino's house opposite, and their exit into Pantalone's house, Arlecchino comes out of Graziano's house into the street and sounds his horn. Arlechinno thus ties together the hunters' entrances at the windows with the ones that now follow from the doors, again following canon form. Graziano enters the street from the same house. Claudione enters the street from his house. Then Burattino enters the street from his house. Pantalone, like Franceschina and Pedrolino before them, breaks the sequence of one person entrances; he enters while beating Pedrolino and Franceschina. The whole sequence is carefully choreographed to provide both repetition and surprise. The second sequence of old men is like the first except that Pantalone, who begins the first, ends the second. Each sequence of

4.1. Giovanni Battista Castello, called "Il Bergamasco" (1509–69), *Huntsman on Horseback Chasing a Stag in a Wood, Watched by a Maiden*. By permission of the Museo Nacional del Prado, Madrid.

one-person entrances, first from the windows and then from the doors, is broken by a multiple-person scene. Each sequence ends with entrances from opposite sides of the stage. Repetitions and contrasts in entrances are so marked that they are a, if not *the,* central aspect of the act. The old men, ludicrously taking up the aristocratic pastime of the hunt but with a cat and a rooster instead of a dog and a falcon, thematically frame and set the tone for the real object of the hunt – the romantic love intrigues that comprise the rest of the scenario. The opening is not "irrelevant padding" but a low comedy parallel to these intrigues.[65]

The hunt itself used traditional instruments and formulaic signals like one for having spotted the prey and another to indicate the gathering around it.[66] Those in the audience who were familiar with the musical references and the aristocratic hunt itself would have appreciated the parodic doubling with these as well.

Jeremy Lopez argues that in early modern English drama "each part of the play resonates with every other part creating a surfeit of coherence, or potential coherence. Playwrights construct plays that contain and interconnect a dizzying number of levels, to the point that the fundamental components of those levels – plot and characters – are in danger of collapsing under the sheer weight of potential significance." These connections, he notes, call attention to the artificial relationships between performer and role, stage and audience.[67] This observation, I have argued, can readily be extended to Scala's scenarios. The internal connections and also the external references like those to earlier works visual, musical, and literary add to the sense of their copiousness. Copiousness does not provide and indeed may disrupt the unity provided by a developing linear action, but, as J.L. Styan has suggested, to insist on this in early modern drama may be to look for the wrong kind of unity.[68]

It is nevertheless the case that in the main the copiousness in Scala's scenarios does cohere in unified actions. Having assembled or generated the various parts out of which the scenario was to be constructed, Scala arranged the material in a clear and coherent sequence that allowed each element to show to its best advantage; he marshalled the "discoveries," as Cicero would have it for orations, "not merely in orderly fashion but with a discriminating eye for the exact weight" to be given to each part, and for the joining of parts.[69] Quintilian observed that even a slight dislocation of the parts was deleterious.[70] Merely assembling and rearranging parts of various plays did not suffice to make a scenario, certainly not a good one. The material used had to be skillfully manipulated. *Dispositio* (arrangement) was, after invention, the second most important of the five parts of oratory. In the detailed analysis of four of the scenarios that follows this chapter, I hope to show the extent to which Scala's abundant actions are "artfully knotted and wonderfully unknotted."[71]

VARIETY

In his preface to his collection of scenarios Scala said that it "contains such a variety of invention that it will be able to satisfy the appetites and tastes of many different intellects." I believe that he referred not only to the invention within scenarios that I show through my reconstructions but also to the variety of scenarios. It is to the latter that I now turn my attention.

Erasmus claimed that "variety is so powerful in every sphere that there is absolutely nothing, however brilliant, which is not dimmed if not commended by variety ... The mind is always looking round for some fresh object of interest. If it is offered a monotonous succession of similarities, it very soon wearies and turns its attention elsewhere ... This disaster can easily be avoided by someone who has it at his fingertips to turn one idea into more shapes than Proteus himself is supposed to have turned into."[72]

Writing about the various Italian Renaissance collections of *novelle*, Janet Smarr argues that they were intended, in the variety of both their forms and their characters, to create a world in small. That sense of completeness, she says, was symbolized by their authors' frequent choice of large round numbers of tales: one hundred for Giovanni Boccaccio; fifty for the less ambitious Ser Giovanni Fiorentino, Masuccio Salernitano, and Giambattista Basile; and three hundred for the tireless Franco Sacchetti.[73] The range of situations in which the characters are employed in Scala's comic scenarios suggests that he similarly set out to provide the variety of the world in small. While working within the given constraints, he was protean. I have already shown the range of societal, principally domestic, issues that Scala takes up through a considerable range of interactions between citizens and their offspring, with servants, between lovers and friends, with women, and with outsiders. From scenario to scenario Scala also varied plots, mood, character roles, even props and their use, and, to a limited extent, setting.

Plot

Often Scala's scenarios begin with Pantalone, attesting to his importance in almost all of the scenarios. Less commonly, but often, the lead youth, Orazio, is given primary focus at the opening. Isabella, the lead female, can also begin scenarios. With these important characters Scala got the attention of the audience. However, he clearly abided by no formula in this matter. On occasion, Flavio, the Capitano, Franceschina, a group of musicians, or even a processions of slaves is given primary focus at the opening. Day 32 begins with scenes of extended exposition; Day 16 begins with a chase scene; Day 35 begins with Pantalone beating his son.

Scala frequently introduces all the major characters at least by name in the first act, except when a surprise, late introduction is central to the plotting. In Day 28, Flavio, whose magic is central to the plot resolution, is introduced only in the second act, and he does not present himself as a magician until very near the end of that act. Occasionally, at the end there appears a character functioning as a *deus ex machina*.

The major characters are initially motivated, sometimes before the scenario begins, by love or lust, honour and friendship, or loyalty. The obstacles to the resolution of an action may be the old men but can also be the protagonists themselves, friends, other lovers, or the failure to recognize the sought-after loved one or correctly understand his or her intentions. Sometimes people are just confused about what they want.

Most of the scenarios begin with a plot complication or with what soon turns into one, usually in the primary plot. But Scala sometimes delays the introduction of any plot complication for many scenes, at the extreme in Day 15 for twelve scenes and in Day 37 for almost the whole of the first act.

As we know, the plots are at least nominally structured around love relationships that usually result in ostensibly happy marriages. Scala played within this given convention. In Day 2 there are two intermarriages between Turks and Italians. For much of Day 9 Isabella has a fake husband who is actually her nursemaid. In Day 13 there is premarital sex that we can infer leads to three marriages, but there are no marriage celebrations within the scenario. In Day 30 two children are born out of wedlock prior to any marriages. In Days 17 and 40 the husbands who are presumed to be long dead return. Day 40 ends with a marriage, but that ending is insignificant compared to Orazio's being sent off at the same time to live in solitude, unfit to live among humans.

Scala endlessly varied the complications in the love relationships. The lover has gone off – to seek his brother or his father or to fight in a war, or he has been abducted by Turks or called home from university. A widow pursues a youth who does not want her; two friends or brothers love the same woman; a man loves two women; the lover is presumed dead; the youth loves the daughter of the family's enemy; the girl does not wish to marry at all or she suspects her lover of faithlessness. The husband is not attentive, has gone off and not returned, or is old and impotent.

Quite a number of marriage plots turn the tables on our expectations for them. Day 27 seems to entail the usual failure of the arranged marriage plan, but in the end it succeeds. In Day 29 a daughter predictably disappears in pursuit of her love, but then the scenario turns out to be about male bonding, and the daughter marries the faithful friend instead of the youth she had intended. Rather than with a plot in which a father arranges a marriage for a child in another city, Scala begins with a widow arranging a marriage between her daughter and a stepson living in the same house.

The most memorable part of the plotting may have little to do with the requisite loves and marriages, as is sometimes reflected in the scenarios' titles: *The Two Old Twins, Flavio Betrayed, The Tooth Puller, The Two Captains Who Look Alike, Flavio the Fake Sorcerer, The Pedant, The Fake Blind Man, The Hunt, The Madness of Isabella, The Proper Punishment.*

Actions are most often both complicated and resolved by any number of misunderstandings including those resulting from misread intentions, mixed-up letters, speaking at cross-purposes, and mistaken identity, including twins being mistaken for one another, and people returning in unrecognizable form after long absences. Frequently the misunderstandings result from deliberate deceptions. Virtually every character engages in these in one scenario or another: old hags, young men, and those on the run or in pursuit of lovers. When he is not a sympathetic lover, the Capitano perpetually tries to misrepresent himself as something grander than he is. He is misrepresentation personified. Graziano can pretend to knowledge he does not have, and Pantalone can pretend to penury. People decide to disguise themselves, or are persuaded to disguise themselves, to both good and bad effect. Women travelling to see their loved ones can disguise themselves as pilgrims and be mistaken for whores. They can take a potion that allows them to seem dead; returning, they can be mistaken for ghosts.

Deliberate misunderstandings can result from tricks. These can be perpetrated by fake magic, fake ghosts, fake doctors, a fake husband. In the scenarios, tricks are primarily carried out by women, youths, and servants – those who are otherwise powerless. Pedrolino is Scala's primary trickster. Through his facility in creating a fictitious reality to engage the credulity of the prospective victim, he sometimes gains enormous power and affects the lives of many people. His tricks are regularly designed to benefit the young, implausibly, never for his own financial gain.

Perhaps the most memorable of the tricks are the practical jokes. The *lazzi* or comic bits can be tricks that, while integral to the plots, generally do not affect them in any profound way. Practical jokes can also play a relatively insignificant role in the plot, in which case the distinction between the *lazzo* and the practical joke is not absolute – for instance when Pedrolino in Day 21 gets back at Arlecchino for a sleepless night by persuading him that an emetic is a sweet wine, which he then drinks. In this case, it serves Pedrolino as revenge, which is seen as part of human nature and necessary to uphold one's honour.[74]

More important, the whole plot can hinge on a practical joke. In Day 12 Pedrolino gets back at his master, Pantalone, for having bitten him, by persuading five people, serially, to remark on his horribly bad breath; as a result, Pantalone has four perfectly good teeth pulled by a fake dentist. Robert Henke observes the curious mixture of pain and festivity that often characterizes the practical joke.[75] The most satisfying tricks, in life and on stage, like this one, fit the offence.

In *The Book of the Courtier* Castiglione distinguished two kinds of practical jokes: (1) someone is clearly tricked in an adroit and amusing fashion, and (2) a net is spread and a little bait is offered so that the victim causes his own downfall – as in the examples of the emetic and the tooth-pulling.[76] The tricks are frequently no less than the characters deserve, particularly the masters or the Capitano. In the moral economy of Day 12, Pantalone gets his comeuppance, not only for biting Pedrolino but also for competing with his son for a woman.[77] We shall see in my reconstructions that Scala employs both kinds of tricks, even in the same scenario.

Tricks, like misunderstandings in general, can both complicate the action and lead to its resolution, as in Day 6 when, with Pedrolino's help, Orazio arranges to sleep with Pantalone's wife, Isabella, thus discovering that she is a virgin. On the basis of that revelation, her marriage can be annulled and she is free to marry Orazio.

In many cases, when the old men lust after young girls, the servants take it upon themselves to deliberately humiliate the old men publicly with bed tricks. In Day 9, after Pantalone arranges a marriage between his ward and another old man and further decides to first sleep with this ward himself, in a trick of ultimate and fitting humiliation Pedrolino gets Pantalone into bed with Arlecchino, an adult male. Such a trick, as Donald Beecher observes, instances the role of the trickster "as self-appointed social critic and illegitimate legislator, ... a kind of culture hero."[78] The trick exposes self-deceptive, overbearing, and misguided behaviour for what it is and deliberately serves as corrective to it. No matter that Arlecchino is tricked, dishonoured, and perhaps raped in the process; he is a servant, collateral damage. Similarly, collateral damage is done in Day 38 when Pedrolino tells Pantalone that his son Flavio is dead, although he is not. The deception helps to quickly bring the confused and badly behaving Orazio to his senses, and as a result he properly marries the long-suffering Isabella. Pantalone is a wholly innocent victim of the deception, but he is quickly disabused, and the deception serves the morality of the scenario as a whole.

The tricks do not always lead to a resolution as they do in the examples above. In Day 26 Pedrolino uses tricks to sell his master's household goods to support the spendthrift son. When the son wants yet more money to spend, Pedrolino points out that nothing remains to sell but the father. He then even thinks of a trick to manage that sale. The tricks are memorable, but the resolution requires Pedrolino's sudden unconvincing change of heart and a *deus ex machina*.

Occasionally the tricks seem merely gratuitous. In such cases they give the impression of having been introduced merely to keep the plot from sagging or even in lieu of a strong plot. In Day 32, for instance, the plot consists of hardly more than tricks played by Pedrolino with the weak justification that he "wants to confuse everybody."[79] Perhaps in Day 3, again in the morality of the scenario as a whole, the fact that Pedrolino is cuckolded and deceived about that is punishment for the seemingly gratuitous and mean-spirited tricks he plays; the trickster is tricked. However, that might not be satisfaction enough for a modern audience who takes no pleasure in mean-spiritedness.

In all the scenarios the main characters are brought together onstage for the final recognitions and resolutions. The relationships, and with them the identities that are largely defined in terms of these relationships, are restored – those of fathers with sons and daughters, of lovers, of friends, and of masters and servants. The trickster, who has worked covertly, confesses / takes pride in the central role that he has played in effecting the resolution. Most often, the recognitions are such that everything is made known to everybody, an important reason for massing everyone on stage. But there are exceptions to the general rule that everything is disclosed. In Day 6, Pedrolino's trick on Graziano is apparently never exposed. At the end of Day 39 the husbands are none the wiser about their wives' adulteries. In Day 21 the fathers remain unaware that their daughters are about to give birth. In Day 25 Fabrizio cannot be brought on stage because his role is doubled, and only the audience can possibly be privy to this metatheatrical information.

The recognitions that resolve the conflicts and confusion are usually followed logically enough by resolutions in the sought-after weddings, for which, conveniently, everyone is already on stage to celebrate. The end of Day 31 brings everyone on stage, not for a wedding but for the festive humiliation of the pedant. When the resolution is effected by Pedrolino's tricks, he is inevitably forgiven. Perhaps we are to believe that no real harm was done; everything ends happily. However, Pedrolino's remorse for what he has done and the subsequent pardon are as unrealistic and unpersuasive as the happily-ever-after marriages that are effected through the trickery. It may not have been only Quintilian's insistence that the conclusion be as brief as possible, an idea "hammered into the heads of many schoolboys" that accounts for the rushed ending of so many early modern plays;[80] it was also best not to dwell on the improbability of the resolution. At the end of Days 12 and 37 Pedrolino even has the temerity to forgive everyone else for the pranks he has played.

Tone

When concepts such as honour, the conflicting demands of love and friendship, and self-sacrifice complicate the love intrigue, the essentially spiritual basis of these issues calls on something less facile than tricksters to untangle them and achieve a happy resolution. Plots involving such concepts also tend to be more serious than those that are resolved by wit alone.

While we know nothing about the ordering of the scenarios in Scala's collection, we do know that in the latter part of the sixteenth century there was increased interest in mixed dramatic genres. The comic scenarios, particularly in the latter part of Scala's collection – with their powerful female roles, their exalted self-sacrifice and fidelity, their tragic potential, and some psychological complexity – are testament to Scala's interest in diversification even within the comic genre.[81] Day 29, like Day 27, is rather sombre, and the resolution is more troubled. Most noticeably in later scenarios (*Isabella the Astrologer, The Madness of Isabella, The Proper Punishment*), Scala experiments with *commedia grave* (serious comedy). As if to call attention to the variety, the commedia grave alternates with some of Scala's most light-hearted scenarios. The variations in tone bear some correlation to the amount of exposition required by the scenarios. Exposition tends to slow down the action and may suggest motivations that are more complex than those present in the purely farcical scenarios.

Most scenarios are set during the day or primarily during the day. Almost all the comic scenarios end during the day, presumably a happier time than the night and a more natural time for clearing up misperceptions. Night could add variety to mood within and between scenarios. All of act 1 and most of act 2 of Day 29 are set at night. The scenario begins with Pantalone's alarm that his daughter has run away. Orazio has secreted her in his friend Flavio's house. In the dark she is stolen from the house, not by Orazio but by the undesirable Capitano who is mistaken for Orazio. Scala sets all of Day 7, *The Woman Believed to Be Dead*, except the resolution, at night. The very dark ending of Day 40, in which Isabella sends the treacherous Orazio off to live in solitude, is suitably set at night. But night was not always correlated with fear, death, and exile; it could also be a time of mischief and merriment. In Day 9, under cover of night and disguise, Pedrolino gets everyone, including himself, into bed with someone. Like character, which I discuss next, the time of day was part of Scala's palette.

Character

Scala generally employed the standard characters in each troupe to serve in the variety of interactions he devised. He would have envisioned and been able to utilize each character in a readily identifiable costume, with distinctive facial mask or make-up, speeches in the character's distinctive dialect or foreign accent, and speech mannerisms, as well as class-, sex-, and character-appropriate gestures and movement, and perhaps with a signature hand prop: a stick, a sword, or a money bag. He would have been further guided by the particular strengths and weaknesses of the actors with whom he worked and by their inventions. He would have been expected to utilize most or all of a troupe's actors in each scenario in some significant way. The actors would have wanted to display, and the audience would have wanted them to display, their particular skills in physical actions including in duelling, impersonations of other characters, acrobatics, *lazzi*, and speaking. They would also have wished for opportunities for the Capitano to display his bombast; the lovers, their arguments and love duets, jealousies, despairs, madness, grief, and shock; and the old men, their suspicion, rage, and lust. These skills and routines would have both limited the variety and inspired it. They allowed considerable range, which Scala explored. Ferdinando Taviani commented that "it is erroneous to say that the same character appeared over and over," and, in that respect, the references to *masks*, the common term for all the characters including the unmasked *innamorate* and female servants, are misleading.[82]

Because the characters in *commedia dell'arte* have received far more attention than has any other aspect of the form, and because I think that for the most part they are most reliably deduced from the scenarios, I point to only two roles, those of Isabella and Burattino, to suggest the considerable range that each of the characters had. Isabella, an upper-class *innamorata*, could be vengefully jealous, a very undutiful daughter, an adulterous wife, a devoted lover, an astrologer, a witless girl, or a very smart plot manipulator. She could travel great distances; she could remain at home; she could feign madness or actually be mad. She could sing, dance, and convincingly disguise herself as a gypsy, a manservant, a gentleman, or a French-speaking widow. I have noted that Scala claimed he published scenarios that had already been performed, in part to keep them from being plagiarized. It seems unlikely, given the various troupes with which Scala worked and the changes of actors in troupes, that any single actress played all the roles to which he later gave the name Isabella. Moreover, unless we assume (contrary to what Scala tells us) that quite a number of the scenarios were written or largely rewritten for the collection, we cannot see the dramatic range of the character Isabella as evidence of Scala's attempt to praise or make use of the skills of one particular actor, namely Isabella Andreini, whose character name he used.

The ordinarily lower-class character Burattino appears in only about half of the comic scenarios. He is never cunning, but he can be perceptive, as he is in Day 25, or foolish, as in Day 28. When an inn is required, Burattino is frequently its host. He can also be a servant, a beggar, a peasant, a postman, a patient father, and a clueless husband, and in Day 37 he ascends to the role of merchant. Each of the standard characters has as much range as have Isabella and Burattino.

In addition to the standard characters in the scenarios, from time to time Scala introduces old hags, musicians, hunters, a gardener, a pig castrator, policemen, postmen, rogues, porters, "Turks," slaves (including white slaves of Christian masters), an Armenian, a hangman, a tutor, an actress, and a regent. While a few scenarios (Days 5, 6, 22, 23, and 38) are notable for entailing no disguises at all, characters could appear and actors could act in a great panoply of disguises including as other characters in the scenario, as females, as males, as dead, as mad, as French, as ghosts, pilgrims, gypsies, Turks, slaves, beggars, rogues, servants, notaries, physicians, dentists, magicians, and butchers.

That Scala's characters, with few exceptions, remain self-consistent from the beginning of the scenario to its end[83] has been taken to mean that within the twenty-four hours during which the action is to have taken place, there is no character development or growth. But this is not altogether true. Friends overtaken by passion do come to their senses. Jealousies are overcome. Fathers forgive their children. Old men recognize their foolishness. Often the changes are abrupt but they are profound. And the implication is that they will be lasting.

Setting and Props

In chapter 3, I had much to say about the appropriateness of the fixed street setting to the representation of sixteenth-century Italian life. For purely artistic purposes, Scala provides some variations in both the setting and its use as well as in the props. Day 36 requires both a palace and a bordello. The set for Day 11, specifying a garden off to one side, suggests something of an experiment and harkens back to a medieval set with two locations in the single space (*décor simultane*). The distance between the houses seems, in imagination, variable, like the distance between actors, depending upon whether they are engaged in a single action or two actions set side by side at the same level, or providing asides. While the houses provide a definite locale and delineate the distinct households, in imagination the locale could represent different cities, and the designated locales offstage to which characters supposedly exit or from which they arrive facilitate the supposition of different settings.

The house doors provide opportunity for vigorous knocking, for surprise entrances, for hiding behind, and, as we have seen, for extended *lazzi* that sometimes involve many characters entering or exiting through them. They served as *loci* for female characters whose required decorum confined them to the house. There could be one functional window or as many as six. Windows were used for the appearance of a single person or, rarely, two people, mostly women. The person in the window was usually either secretly overhearing the action below or openly participating in it. Windows could evidently be at different heights, low enough for a woman in it to have her hand kissed by someone at street level, or to climb out of it, or to close its shutters in someone's face. A window could be at such a height that it was visually interesting when something was thrown from it or it necessitated a ladder to climb up to it.

While in general the street setting and the speed of the action meant that there was no furniture on stage, items of furniture were added for special occasions and places: a chair for the supposedly wounded Capitano, a beautiful chair for the supposedly dead Isabella, a nice one for the patient of the fake dentist, a stool for a supposedly blind beggar, a regal chair for the Regent, a bench and two chairs for revelations in a mirror, benches and tables for a country party, and chairs and a table to establish a park.

I provide only a list of hand props. Relatively few in number in each scenario, collectively they indicate the range of actions in the scenarios and their visual appeal: various musical instruments, weapons of every sort (including a frying pan), flasks of wine, food, silver dishes, a packet of letters, a handkerchief, a uroscopy flask, luggage, shoes, lanterns, cords, jewels, playing cards, fake blood, bandage material, ladders, a hangman's noose, a mirror, a money pouch, a bucket of water, hunting horns, hunting hounds, a live cock, a live monkey, a live cat, hunter's poles with dead animals, eight barrels for water, iron chains for slaves, shoes, a charlatan's wares, blacksmith's tools, a hoe, and a small portrait of a woman.

In short, within the constraints of dramatic convention, including the domestic confine, Scala's scenarios vary greatly in plot, tone, character, settings and their uses, and props. In my detailed analysis of four comic scenarios I establish that each, differing one from another, also provides carefully patterned variety within it. Scala was both imitative of models and inventive.

In each of the four chapters that follow, through detailed examination of a single scenario in each chapter I establish that this is the case. I also show the extent to which each of the scenarios imitates life.

PART TWO

Scenario Reconstructions

With Scenario Translations by David Harwell

Method

The new English translations of the four Scala scenarios that follow, each in a separate chapter, are provided by David Harwell. Margherita Pieracci Harwell was helpful in providing clarification for certain obscurities in Scala's text. I edited the translations. They are based on Ferruccio Marotti's 1976 edition of them and follow Marotti's editorial practices. Marotti's angle brackets for the characters that Scala neglected to specify in his list of characters have been retained, as has Marotti's addition of square brackets for the characters that Scala lists for each scene that are not syntactically integrated into his opening for the scene. The translations of the four scenarios are deliberately literal, providing as much as possible a sense of the style of the writing and leaving intact any textual problems and verbal infelicities. This choice was made to reflect the style of the Arguments and to indicate the problems that there are in reconstruction, and the extent to which Scala was writing for performers rather than readers. In the translation, clarifying material has been added in brackets. So that scenes can be easily referenced and distinguished from the commentary following them, the text of the scenes appears in italics and scene numbers have been added. The name of the character Capitano Spavento (Captain Fear), whom Scala refers to in the margins of his scenes simply as Capitano, is left untranslated for parity with the other characters and in my commentary is referred to as the Capitano. The phrase *in quello* (Scala's shorthand for "at that moment") is translated as "at that" to make it obvious that a new set of entering characters establishes a new scene without delay. Scala's term *via* for exits has been literally translated as "away," again to retain the sense of speed that Scala seems to have sought for the transitions between scenes.

In places in my commentary I use Robert Henke's term *set pieces* for speeches and dialogues that actors would have memorized because the character they regularly played had frequent occasion to use them.[1] Pantalone, for instance, regularly despairs about or rages against his children or servants. The actor would have had a repertoire of speeches for, among other things, despair and rage. Lovers, similarly would have had set speeches. Speeches could be taken from any source. An actor playing a male lover alone on stage, for instance, might have found it useful to have on hand a speech from Pietro Bembo's widely published *Gli Asolani*:

> O Love, may I forever bless the hand with which you have drawn and written in my soul so many features of my lady. On one long canvas I always bear with me an endless line of her fair portraits rather than a single face, and ever read and reread one tall book filled with her words and accents, and in brief compass recognize, whenever I return to them a thousand lovely traits of her and of her worth, so many of them sweet and dear to me that in my thought I feel no small part of that strong pleasure which, thanks to her, I felt when I was first aware of them.[2]

Such a speech could have been adapted to the scenario and situation at hand and, as I argue in chapter 4, would probably have been memorized not verbatim (*memoria ad verbum*) but as a cluster of meanings that could have been adapted to different words (*memoria ad res*). The best improvisers, at least, would have seen it as a point of pride not to repeat their or anyone else's speeches verbatim. In so far as an audience member recognized the source, he would have appreciated the actor's adaptation of it. There are also places for set dialogues, for instance, between lovers. I indicate possible places for both set speeches and dialogues with a single asterisk within the scenes.

In my reconstructions I have assumed that a major task for the actors was to provide exposition that allowed the audience to follow the action and the character relationships, and that entrances from where the characters resided or from where they last exited further served to clarify the action and were the easiest for the actors. In so far as it has seemed appropriate, I have incorporated the characters' traits that are evident in other Scala scenarios, but with care because character traits vary from scenario to scenario.

chapter five

Day 6: The Jealous Old Man

The Jealous Old Man, the best known of Scala's scenarios, is frequently summarized and praised, no doubt because the double plotting proceeds apace, there are no scenes of disguise, which are often difficult for a reader to follow, and the ending even summarizes the central action in a sort of novella.[1] The form seems more familiarly literary than that of most of Scala's scenarios. Scala brilliantly solves the problem arising from the need to have the dramatic crisis (an illicit sexual intercourse between two young lovers) occur offstage, by providing an onstage festivity, consisting of storytelling, musical interludes, eating, dancing, singing, and walks in the country, that variously prefigures the intercourse, colours it as celebratory, provides cover for it, and leads us to imagine its salaciousness. The festivities also provide opportunity for the actors to show off their various storytelling, musical, and dancing skills. The day-long country assembly of family, friends, and acquaintances in turn necessitates Scala's considerable ingenuity in motivating characters' exits to allow for variety in the kinds of scenes, most especially to allow for the intimate scenes that are required to set up the central illicit offstage sexual encounter and the parallel subplot, which is also an offstage sexual encounter.

Day 6
The Jealous Old Man

COMEDY

Argument

In Venice there lived an old merchant named Pantalone de' Bisognosi who had a very beautiful young wife named Isabella. Most passionately in love with her was a very handsome, young man [who was] rich and honourable in his ways, named Orazio Cortesi from Venice.

The old merchant was, most unfortunately for him, jealous of his wife; and to keep her away from the eyes of her admirers, and to reassure himself, he resolved to take her to a villa of his near Venice. The lady was followed by her lover, and, with her consent, they had amorous dealings – and the pleasure was all the more gratifying because it happened while her husband was guarding her. It happened then, that [while someone was] conversing one day with this same merchant, as if in jest, he was told of all that had come to pass with his wife. Having heard this tale, the old man recognized his own impotence and his folly (in living a life of jealousy because of it) and, in a very gracious manner, gave his wife in marriage to the young man.

A useful perspective on the whole of the scenario is provided by Isabella Andreini, wife of Scala's friend Francesco Andreini. Isabella's complaint, in the name of all women, denouncing marriages between old men and young girls, closely parallels the point of view provided by the scenario and supplies the rationale for the primary plot. It also suggests the way in which the role of Pantalone might have been performed. On this account, I quote it at length at the onset:

> The deplorable state of gallantry today requires that some woman should sustain the cause of her sex; we have too long waited for an avenger ... The profanation of our charms in continually uniting us to imbecile old men has been a great enemy of gallantry; for they are a class despised by the whole wide empire of lovers. This strange alliance between youth and old age which avarice has suggested to our fathers permits many abuses. It causes separations and is the opportunity of elegant and dissolute *abbés* who are always on the watch for such incompatible marriages.
>
> Girls do not willingly accept the rewards of such marriages or when accepted, they hate the austerity demanded by spectacled husbands ... Imagine an old graybeard marching under the banner of love! Picture a young girl living with a husband who questions her every hour, counts her every step, is always contradicting her and boasting of his early prowess! A crabbed surly old man who hates to see a new ribbon in her hair; who bribes servants to spy on his wife's most innocent actions. And what shall I say of the legion of maladies characteristic of old age, those insupportable coughs, the common music of an old man. It is true that I find something heroic in the courageous fidelity of those who support such husbands; but for myself I hate an old man who dares to restrain my liberty.[2]

Scala astutely observes that the pleasure of the illicit sex is heightened by the deceit involved.

Characters in the Comedy

PANTALONE old merchant
ISABELLA his wife
PEDROLINO their servant
GRAZIANO a friend of the family

CAPITANO SPAVENTO as a hunter
COMPANIONS hunters

ORAZIO and
FLAVIO friends

BURATTINO a gardener
PASQUELLA his wife
OLIVETTA his daughter

CAVICCHIO a peasant from Norcia

FLAMINIA a widow and sister of Isabella

< *THREE VAGRANTS* >
< *YOUNG GIRLS* >
< *SERVANTS* >

Countryside near Padua

Properties for the Comedy

Hunters' costumes, poles, horns, dogs, and similar things

A basket

Silver saucers

Flasks of wine
Drinking glasses

Confections in silver plates

[Costumes] to disguise the musical players as vagrants

Lute or theorbo[3]

A plate with figs or other fruits

In the list of properties Scala neglects to mention the long bench required in act 1, scene 3. The scenario would also seem to have required non-speaking extras, but Scala does not mention them, and their use would have been exceptional.[4] A number of the roles could have been doubled by the usual ten or so cast members, and the actor who ordinarily played Arlecchino (who is not a character in this scenario) might have played one or more of the smaller parts. However, there are simply too many characters specified as being on stage at one time and not enough females to play the young village girls without there having been extras. The production requirements are great; there are costumes for the additional characters, many set pieces and props, dogs, and perhaps scenery to establish the countryside. The scenery would have been specially constructed if a perspectival set was employed, because this is the only one of Scala's comic scenarios that is not set in the city. The large cast, sometimes seated on enough chairs for all or dancing in the remaining space, necessitates a large acting space. The dances, with scenes aside, would have required careful rehearsal.

Typically, plays and scenarios of the period provide almost no description of the set. We know nothing about where *The Jealous Old Man* was performed, or under what conditions. The scenario, set in the country, like others set in the city, apparently requires two houses, each with practicable entrances.

First Act

1. ORAZIO [FLAVIO] *tells his friend Flavio of having come to this villa because of his love for Isabella, Pantalone's wife, [of] being loved by her in return, and that Pedrolino, her servant, is aware of their love, and that he has never enjoyed her; but that Isabella has promised to satisfy him, with the opportunity [arising from] being at the villa. Flavio says that he [Orazio] has a good go-between and should not worry; at that*

In the midst of conversation Flavio and Orazio enter from offstage, efficiently establishing the nature of the scenario's central relationships and action. Isabella and Orazio will attempt to consummate their relationship. Flavio will serve as a supportive friend. Pedrolino, the go-between, will play his usual role as facilitator in the affairs of the young. As we know, men in this period did not marry until they were twenty-five or thirty, and there was a lack of licit outlets for their sexual drives. The animosity towards old men, presumably on second marriages and married to young women who were thus removed from the marriage market, was considerable. Edward Muir tells us that in fifteenth-century Tuscany, religious paintings of the marriage of old Joseph to the Virgin Mary reflected popular ideas of charivari. He instances Fra Angelico's *Marriage of the Virgin*, in which young men with angry expressions stand behind Joseph, their fists raised against him. Some hold sticks, as if they were about to hit him.[5] Comedy is an outlet for that anger.

2. PEDROLINO *with straw hat and stick, telling Orazio that Pantalone is about to arrive with his wife. Flavio goes to meet him right away. Pedrolino asks whether Tofano, whose villa is only two miles away from Pantalone's, is his friend, and whether Pantalone knows that he is. Orazio says yes. Pedrolino tells him he wants to make use of his [Tofano's] house, when the time comes; at that [he says] that he sees Pantalone coming. Orazio remains; at that*

Pedrolino's straw hat and stick help to establish the countryside. Pedrolino, in his master's employ, has evidently taken to rural life, at least this rural life that is far removed from the impoverished countryside from which his character came. Apparently Pedrolino had seen Pantalone and his companions *en route*; he likely enters from where Pantalone will subsequently enter. Pedrolino enables us to envision the expanse of countryside that becomes part of the offstage action. Flavio and Orazio have entered elsewhere. Pedrolino must establish his relationship with Pantalone and identify his house. He immediately begins to plan and proceeds apace throughout. The action moves quickly, seemingly in a period of little more than a long afternoon. In his usual way Pedrolino, like the playwright that he is in effect, withholds the details of his plan. He exits other than where Pantalone enters, avoiding him. There can be no suspicion of his conspiring with Orazio.

3. PANTALONE [ISABELLA] [FLAMINIA] [FLAVIO] [GRAZIANO]	*leading Isabella, his wife, by the hand; Flavio [leading] Flaminia, a widow. Orazio greets Pantalone and all his company, telling him that he is happy that he [Pantalone] has come to grace this villa with his presence; and, there being a long bench which has been set up, they all sit down to rest, asking Graziano to tell and recount some tale. Graziano first makes them plead with him; in the end, he recounts that tale by Boccaccio, entitled ***. All praise it, except for Pantalone, who says it was not too appropriate where women are present; at that*

Orazio's welcome to Pantalone, his friendship with Tofano, Pasquella's acquaintance with him, shown later, and his readily available lute may indicate that Orazio is a nearby property owner. He greets Pantalone as a social equal.

The relationship of the characters must be made clear: the widow Flaminia is Isabella's sister; Graziano is a family friend. That all six characters on stage sit on a single, long bench suggests comic jostling for seating, a *lazzo* that establishes the various relationships and foretells the action. Graziano, who later tries to bed Flaminia, may go to considerable lengths to position himself next to her; Pantalone may see to it that no one other than he can sit beside Isabella. To avert any suspicion on Pantalone's part, Isabella likely observes proper *modestia,* but sly glances between her and Orazio may signal what is to come.

The atmosphere of the countryside is relaxed and idealized. The setting is both a place and an idea. It is part of the motivation for the action, and it serves to organize it, unify its tone, and invite its sensuality. The perspective is that of the city dwellers, who are the scenario's main characters. It was not uncommon for well-to-do Venetian merchants to have country retreats that were made for carefree parties. They were largely shut off from the problems of field labour. "Anything that implied the use of hoe or ploughshare was considered 'rustic and base.'"[6] In Alberti's *I libri della famiglia,* Giannozzo and Lionardo describe the long-held appeal of the villa and perhaps provide some indication of the set design: In the country, among all the subjects discussed,

> there is none which can fail to delight you. All are pleasant to talk of and are heard by willing ears ... You have a lovely view when you look at those leafy hills and verdant plains. Clear springs and streams go leaping through and losing themselves in the waving grass ... Yes, by God, a true paradise. And, what is more, you can in the enjoyment of your estate escape the violence, the riots, the storm of the city, the marketplace, and the townhall ... You can ... avoid seeing all the stealing and crime, the vast numbers of depraved men who are always flitting past your eyes in the city. There they never cease to chirp in your ears, to scream and bellow in the trees hour after hour, like a dangerous and disgusting kind of beast."[7]

This is a remarkably sunny scenario. There are no night scenes, no duels, and no despairing lovers. Ironically, however, the very danger and evil that Pantalone came to the villa to escape find him there.

The scenario reflects the upper-class passion for leisurely conversation (with love as its principle subject) and everyone's love of storytelling, music, and dancing, all facilitated by the relaxed country atmosphere.[8]

Scala does not specify the story from Boccaccio, which he seems to think has a name. It is merely indicated by three asterisks in Marotti's edition, but the fifth story of the seventh day in *The Decameron* is most apropos. In it a jealous husband posts himself at the door, but the wife admits her lover by way of the roof.[9] The story is only the first of many parallels that foreshadow Pantalone's own. Each, different in manner of presentation and in content, adds resonance and much eroticism and anticipation to the scenario's straightforward story of unimpeded adultery. The pleasure that Graziano takes in telling it contrasts his character with that of the dour Pantalone, who is likely studying his wife for any threat of pleasure that she finds in it. Graziano may use the racy story as a means to seduce Flaminia, probably a very young widow whom he later seeks to bed. The brevity of the human lifespan and the age difference between Isabella and Pantalone mean that Flaminia is what Isabella would likely become in her marriage to an old man.

4. PEDROLINO *all out of breath, tells Orazio and Flavio that some gentlemen from Bergamo have arrived who are asking about them. They leave right away to find them, and all the others remain; at that they hear singing from within.*

Here is an instance of Scala's use of the out-of-breath entrance. It is most often Pedrolino's. His entrance adds a sense of urgency to the action, and his attempt to recover his breath in order to speak is surely comic. The audience is also in on the joke of the actor's having come only a few feet from offstage and can admire the skill of his performance. However, Pedrolino's rushed entrance, in this case to announce the gentlemen from Bergamo, and the subsequent exit of Orazio and Flavio are puzzling. The gentlemen do not otherwise figure in the scenario. With Orazio and Flavio offstage and out of earshot of the group and us, Pedrolino has an opportunity to tell them of his plan. But, at scene 9, Graziano mentions the gentlemen again and so would seem to confirm their existence. The departure of the young men keeps them from hearing Cavicchio's song and story, and it gives focus to the relationships between Graziano and Flaminia and between Pantalone and Isabella.

Cavicchio seems to be heard from offstage, not inside a house.

5. CAVICCHIO *a peasant, singing in the style of Norcia; then he sings about the martyrdom felt by an old husband jealous of his wife; all laugh then ask Cavicchio to recount some tale. Cavicchio recounts the tale of the painter who used to paint the devil as so beautiful [that], etc. They all laugh about the good fable. Cavicchio invites them to a place he rents, so that they can have fun and pleasure. They accept the invitation. Graziano takes Flaminia by the hand, behaving lasciviously with her, and goes ahead; Pantalone remains with Isabella. He repeatedly [tells her] that he is entrusting her with his honour.* She [is] angry about such words.* *

Pantalone appeases her, embraces her, and with her follows the others who have left.

In his cast of characters Scala specifically tells us that Cavicchio is from Norcia. This town in Umbria was known for pigs fattened by castration (and still, today, for its fine sausage). From the practice of pig castration, apparently, arose itinerant Norcini surgeons who were licensed to perform specific kinds of human surgeries, including removal of stones and cataracts, treatment of fistulas and hernias (in a procedure that sometimes included removal of a testicle), and castration.[10] There may be a pun involved in the singing "*alla Norcina,*" perhaps imitating a castrato and suggesting a male who has been rendered impotent, and the song that Cavicchio sings apparently mocks Pantalone's psychological state. His next song, one of many extant songs about the badly or unhappily married, and the story he tells pattern the situation at hand, which Cavicchio has evidently appraised. The beautiful devil in the fable is an analogue for Orazio.

The Norcini regularly rented places in which to stay while they worked in a particular area. They could perform surgeries there or in homes. That the party relocates to Cavicchio's place suggests that the class boundaries are relaxed in the country. There is probably also a rather ghoulish joke involved in the group's taking fun and pleasure in his place. Cavicchio's only function in the scenario is to provide obviously very comic prefiguration and to get the remaining characters off stage while continuing to party.

Pantalone's concern about the threat to his honour that might result from his wife's behaviour would have been familiar. Dennis Romano quotes a merchant of Venice, Andre Bargarigo, who copied the following aphorism into his account book: "*Chi a moger a pensier*" (He who has a wife has worries).[11] Pantalone's exaggerated instance of male fear[12] is further exacerbated here by the fact that he is old and his wife is young. In an analogous situation in Molière's *The School for Wives,* act 3, scene 2, an old man, who is like Pantalone and whose character was probably influenced by that of Pantalone, in one of his set speeches advises his young intended:

> Take care not to imitate those miserable flirts whose pranks are talked of all over the city; and do not let the evil one tempt you, that is, do not listen to any young coxcomb. Remember ... that, in making you part of myself, I give my honour into your hands, which honour is fragile, and easily damaged;

> that it will not do to trifle in such a matter, and that there are boiling cauldrons in hell, into which wives who live wickedly are thrown for evermore ... If you take care not to flirt, your soul will ever be white and spotless as a lily; but if you stain your honour, it will become as black as coal. You will seem hideous to all, and one day you will become the devil's own property, and boil in hell to all eternity.[13]

Pantalone's comments lead us to anticipate his response to her impending unfaithfulness. That he is already suspicious makes clear the difficulty in her carrying it off.

Isabella may respond with a set speech of her own about all the restraints that are put upon her, similar to Isabella Andreini's complaint that is provided following Scala's Argument: "a young girl living with a husband who questions her every hour, counts her every step ..." This would be Isabella's only opportunity to demonstrate the discontent and self-assertiveness that leads to her adulterous relationship with Orazio. Otherwise, consistent with proper decorum, she speaks very little.

6. BURATTINO [OLIVETTA] *market gardener, with Olivetta, his daughter, reproaching her for neither knowing how to hoe nor how to plant, being now old enough for a husband, he gives her a few lessons on manoeuvring the hoe's handle; at that*

The Church was the authoritative source on sexual behaviour. The influential Bernardino of Siena (later Saint Bernardino of Siena) preached in 1427 that "girls about to marry 'had to know how to do it' and sinned if they neglected to learn."[14] The demonstration on how to hoe is clearly full of *double entendres.* Olivetta is introduced into the scenario primarily for this scene, which provides comic prefiguration, now for the fourth time in only six scenes; Isabella, as it turns out, is also a virgin who is about to learn hoeing and planting from practical experience. The sexuality of the young, unlike that of the old, is allied with nature and is a force for good.

7. PEDROLINO *greets Burattino and his daughter, telling them he wants to let them earn ten scudi. Pedrolino orders him to get a dish of the most beautiful figs or peaches and to take them to Orazio, telling him that Tofano Braghettini is sending them to him from his place [and] begging him to go there since he needs to talk to him about a matter of great importance. And he gives him two scudi in advance, and [tells him] to send out his wife Pasquella. Burattino goes inside with Olivetta; Pedrolino remains.*

The two preceding scenes have been devoted to comically foreshadowing the action to come. Now the action moves forward, but the figs, symbolizing a woman's genitals (as in the obscene hand gesture *mano fico*), again foreshadow that action.

In the end, Pedrolino marries Olivetta. There is an opportunity here to establish a relationship between them. Onstage alone, Pedrolino may have time to speak about Olivetta or about how he has plans for Orazio and Isabella.

8. PASQUELLA *comes out; Pedrolino, in Orazio's name, makes her a great offer. Pasquella says Orazio is a most kind gentleman, and that for him she would do anything. Pedrolino tells her that Orazio is in love with Pantalone's wife and that, to enjoy her, he must hide in her house, in one of her rooms; and that, when the time comes that Isabella will wish to urinate at her house, she is to take her to that room, and to let it be known that no one else be allowed to go inside the house except she alone. Pasquella agrees. Pedrolino gives her two scudi. Pasquella [goes] into the house. Pedrolino: that the matter is off to a good start; at that*

The language here suggests a residence in addition to Pantalone's. A typical villa often had secondary buildings for the family of the farmer and for the farm equipment, often directly on the road,[15] which in this scenario serves for exits and entrances as do the city streets in other scenarios. Pasquella comes onstage from her house. She is introduced into the scenario because she is critical to the subplot that begins in the next scene. Pedrolino makes the arrangement for Orazio with her, not with Burattino with whom the young Olivetta is present. Pasquella establishes that Orazio is a worthy fellow. This determination of his worthiness is important in making the audience's view of his planned assignation with a married woman a sympathetic one. His last name, *Cortesi*, which is provided in the Argument, means "courteous" and "courtly" and confirms Pasquella's evaluation of him. There is no indication that Pasquella finds the proposed adultery objectionable. The audience is apprised of Pedrolino's plan now, early in the first act.

Evidently, out in the country, a lady would still have urinated in a chamber pot.[16]

9. GRAZIANO *[says] that those gentlemen have left. He implores Pedrolino [to help him] in his love for Flaminia.* Pedrolino promises to help him; at that*

The announced departure of the gentlemen, as puzzling as their arrival, does provide an excuse for Graziano's entrance and makes clear how it is that the youths can enter with the girls in the next scene.

No sooner has Pedrolino arranged for the first assignation than he is asked to help with another. The audience may already suspect that Pedrolino will play a trick on Graziano, typically an old man, because passionate old men, who in fact may have been no more than fifty, violate the decorum suited to their age. Graziano has already shown his pursuit of Flaminia to be tasteless. A speech here that badly imitates a pure Petrarchan love sonnet, like the one a young lover would characteristically have provided, would clinch that impression. Graziano cannot be a sympathetic figure. The audience must anticipate that a trick on each of the old men, one who married a young woman and one who presently pursues another, is about to be played in which each will get his comeuppance.

10. ORAZIO [FLAMINIA] [FLAVIO] [ISABELLA] [PANTALONE] *with Flaminia by the hand, and Flavio who is leading Isabella, and Pantalone following them. They find Graziano and Pedrolino. [They] ask if lunch is ready. They: [say] yes and that they will be very pleased; at that*

Scala delays the anticipated sexual encounters.

The partnering is not what we might expect. Flavio escorted Flaminia upon her first entrance but now he escorts Isabella. We conclude that Flavio has no love interest in this scenario. He acts only as a faithful friend. The partnering may serve to allay Pantalone's suspicions, but probably not sufficiently. On the need to be on the watch with women, Leon Battista Alberti wrote, "I therefore wisely bore in mind what every husband should hold fixed and emblazoned in his thoughts, namely, that by nature woman is a fickle and inconstant creature, and prone to all sorts of lust."[17] Pantalone's fears, we anticipate, will be borne out. Scala's comedies endorse a more generous view of humankind than does Pantalone and are critical of those who do not.

11. BURATTINO	*market gardener, with a very beautiful dish of figs or peaches; he presents it to Orazio on behalf of Tofano Braghettino, asking him to do him the favour of going to his house after lunch. Orazio accepts the present; he gives him a drink, telling him he will certainly go. Burattino away. Pantalone orders that water be brought for [washing] hands; at that*

The presentation of the fruit and the invitation are staged for Pantalone's benefit, and he must be given focus.

12. PEDROLINO	*with the silver washbasin.*

No mention of Graziano's and Pedrolino's exit into the house at scene 10 is provided but can be deduced here.

13. GRAZIANO	*with the silver jug and a towel; and so they all wash themselves and then they cheerfully go inside to lunch,*
	and the first act ends.

Graziano's useful labour gives his character some focus; the plot involving him does not proceed until late in the scenario. He characteristically loves food and festivities, and his service in providing food here is probably very pleasurable for him.

Scala needs a way to get the ongoing festivities offstage for an intermission, now that both plot lines have been introduced and the first plot has been set in motion. It was customary at the time to offer guests water in a basin for the ceremonial washing of hands.[18] The silver jug and wash basin appear in several other Scala scenarios. If they were on hand, they may have provided the idea for the act's closing. Andrea Perrucci comments that a magnificent theatrical display of silver and luxury items delighted the common people.[19] Water, symbolic of female sexuality and fertility, enhances the construction of the scenario, whether or not Scala was conscious of the symbolism. The young people might provocatively flick it at one another, heightening our pleasure and the promise of the scenario at the end of act 1.

Second Act

1. THREE VAGRANTS	*badly dressed, with their [musical] instruments for playing, who are going through the countryside playing and singing to make a living; they make their instruments heard; at that*

The countryside could not support its population, and vagrant beggars and itinerant performers, who may have been hardly more than beggars, would not have been an unusual sight in any place in which there was hope of obtaining day labour, money, or food. Professional actors were often good musicians, and the actors playing Cavicchio and Spavento could have served as two of the musicians; however, the wording of the prop list suggests that musicians were dressed as beggars rather than that the roles were doubled by actors who played instruments.

2. PASQUELLA OLIVETTA — *come out. The vagrants ask for something to eat, offering to play and sing. Pasquella sends for bread and wine; at that*

It is evidently Olivetta whom Pasquella sends for the bread and wine, there being no one else on stage. Olivetta is then not present for the forthcoming discussion of plot arrangements.

3. PEDROLINO — *from the house, tells Pasquella that the time for that business with Orazio is approaching, with the players providing the opportunity; and they send Olivetta to invite some country girls to come to the dance. Olivetta away. Pedrolino orders the players to play, and that he will see to it that they are very well paid. Vagrants play; at that*

Pedrolino is a master at taking advantage of the situation at hand. He sees the chance arrival of the beggar-musicians as fortuitous; music and dancing will shield the after-lunch adultery. He reminds the audience of the plot set up in act 1 and builds anticipation, promising its imminent enactment. The meal is evidently still in progress; the other characters do not appear, and at act 1, scene 11, Pedrolino had said he was going to arrange the assignation for after lunch, which now he may be in the midst of serving. When Olivetta promptly returns with the bread and wine, he sends her off on another errand. There appears to be a musical interlude with Pasquella onstage to allow for the suggestion of the passage of time.

4. OLIVETTA [YOUNG GIRLS] — *arrives, with the country girls and her friends. Pasquella goes inside for benches and chairs, then returns with her husband.*

Again, little time elapses between when Olivetta is sent off on an errand and when she returns.

5. BURATTINO PASQUELLA — *with benches and chairs, arrange a place for everyone to sit, as the players play; at that*

Ordinarily the scenarios are set in a city street, and therefore chairs and seated characters are uncommon. In this case, they suggest the leisure of the idealized countryside.

6. PANTALONE [ISABELLA] [FLAVIO] [ORAZIO] [GRAZIANO] — *comes out of the house with the entire group; he sits down with all of the others, and here they all begin to dance, now the one and now the other, as is the custom with those women. Orazio, in the middle of the dance, excuses himself from the company, saying he is compelled to go to Tofano, and away. Burattino goes inside for his instrument to play; then they dismiss the players. Flavio pays them; they, away. Burattino [says] that he wishes to go for a stroll with them, leading them as he plays, and so in agreement, they all go away with him, except Pasquella, who remains to look after the house; at that*

Flaminia is not mentioned in the list of those returning from Pantalone's house to the garden. She should be. To give appropriate focus to Orazio's departure, the scene must be carefully staged.

The dismissal of the musicians would allow them to double as hunters at scene 9, and it allows Burattino, as their replacement, to take the group on a walk. His functions in the scenario are multiple. Once again, in the midst of the ongoing festivities, Scala needs to get everyone offstage for the next scene. Conveniently, Burattino will not be in his house when the lusty assignation between Isabella and Orazio takes place. All go off, in a direction other than where Orazio last exited and from where he returns, perhaps singing or still dancing, or both.

7. ORAZIO — *arrives, greets Pasquella, who tells him all that Pedrolino has told her on his behalf; and she leads him into the house to put him in the room already prepared for him to enjoy Isabella, and they go inside.*

For the audience's full appreciation of what is about to happen out of sight, Pasquella explains Pedrolino's scheme again and her preparation of the room. Orazio, like the audience, is all anticipation.

8. GRAZIANO — *[saying] that they have drunk very well at the peasants'*

[PEDROLINO] *houses. Graziano entrusts Pedrolino with his love for Flaminia. Pedrolino: that he will have her for that entire day; at that they hear the sound of horns and the shouts of hunters.*

Again, the two plots of assignation follow one after another. The first secret encounter has only begun, when Pedrolino agrees to set up yet another. To allow for this scene that, like the previous one, requires a discreet negotiation, Scala now justifies the return of only some of the celebrants, who, in fact, have been offstage for only one scene. In the romanticized countryside Graziano has been drinking in Cavicchio's place and perhaps others. The lust of an old man for a young woman, widowed or not, is not sanctioned, and Graziano's inebriation would add to the characterization of him as an unsympathetic gull. He does not even express any intent to marry Flaminia.

There is opportunity for Pedrolino to expatiate on the pleasures of the promised day-long tryst.

9. CAPIT. SPAVENTO [HUNTERS] *[dressed] as a hunter with dogs [and] horns, is coming to the countryside because of his love for Flaminia, Isabella's sister. He asks Graziano about Pantalone, Flavio and Orazio. He [Graziano says] that they are out in the countryside, and goes to inform them; away. Pedrolino tells the Capitano that Graziano is his competitor for Flaminia's love. The Capitano laughs at this; at that*

No sooner does Pedrolino agree to arrange an assignation between Graziano and Flaminia than a wholly unexpected complication to that second plot is first suggested and then laughed off. Spavento's very theatrical entrance into the scenario in the middle of act 2, complete with a kind of musical fanfare, comes as a surprise, except in so far as the audience may have learned to expect the late arrival in a drama of an important character. The hunters' entrance is in marked contrast to the two scenes of arrangements that preceded it and, from the audience's point of view, delays their outcome.

Hunting for deer was a favourite villa pastime and well suited to courtiers as a peacetime substitute for war. The dogs used in such hunts were greyhounds, trackers (*segusi*), and pointers.[20]

Like Orazio, Spavento has come to the country because of a love interest. The style of the hunt suggests that he is well to do. He is on good terms with Pantalone's family and with Orazio and Flavio; he ends up marrying Flaminia. In other words, this captain is not a vagrant braggart warrior; he is apparently part of the hereditary elite, above the merchant class. Whatever he may say about his love for Flaminia, unlike what Graziano may say, is not comic. Countering any expectation that we might have about the character, Spavento must win our respect. Any earlier thought we might have had about the way in which the widow Flaminia might have to settle for Graziano is to be set aside.

10. FLAVIO
[PANTALONE]
[GRAZIANO]
[ISABELLA]
[FLAMINIA]
[BURATTINO]

arrives with the entire group; they greet the Capitano, saying how happy they are about his arrival. Flavio proposes right away that they sit and that [later] they again return to dancing, but first they [should] take some refreshments; they all sit down;at that

The group returns from its walk. Scala needs the group onstage for the crisis to follow. Presumably, the scene-stealing, too freely improvising dogs have been quickly removed from the stage. No further mention is made of them or the huntsmen, but Burattino's narration at act 3, scene 11, suggests the possibility of the huntsmen having been added to the party of dancers. Friend Flavio calls for the distraction of dance. Graziano, who helps with the refreshments at scene 12, probably does not sit but rather enters Pantalone's house.

11. PASQUELLA
OLIVETTA

seat themselves with the others; at that

Pasquella's entrance is a separate scene; she is pointedly on hand for the moment when she must volunteer her house for Isabella's needs. Again, the social classes are equalized. That mother and daughter do not help with the serving reinforces the idea that there are two houses onstage.

12. PEDROLINO
GRAZIANO
SERVANTS

with plates filled with confections, flasks of wine, fruits, [and] with glasses and saucers. They offer the repast, in which each one partakes. Afterwards, they begin to dance, doing the dance of the sentinel, and while they dance, Isabella signals to her husband that she wishes to urinate. Right away, Pasquella, with Pantalone's permission, leads her into the house. Right away, Pantalone, because of [his] jealousy, moves to guard the door, as again they dance.

It is later in the afternoon and time for refreshment. The repast and its service, now with servants, are as visually stunning and extravagant as was Spavento's entrance. Spavento and Graziano each have time for business with Flaminia. Pedrolino can dance with Olivetta. *Il piantone,* the dance of the sentinel, was one of the most popular dances of the period, and Scala seems to have assumed that it was well known to his audience. The dance provides another of the many instances in which the central action is echoed – first in story, then in song and symbols, and now in dance, although nothing in the dance, beyond its name, seems to suggest anything about a watchman.[21] Scala does not abide by Perrucci's caution that banquets on stage, prohibited by the Ancients, were likely to be more sumptuous in the telling than when seen; rather he calls for a visible celebration of the Italian love of food.[22] Pantalone's excessive vigilance and control do not endear him to the party or to us; Isabella is ostensibly out of Pantalone's sight only to urinate. We are however also aware that Pantalone's watchfulness is misdirected; the beautiful devil is already within.[23]

13. FLAMINIA *Flaminia would like to go inside Pasquella's house; right away Pedrolino invites her to dance so that she will not disturb Orazio; and so each one would like to go inside Pasquella's house to take care of some business, and Pantalone keeps telling them: "For goodness' sake, do not go and disturb my wife, who is taking care of certain business." In the end, she comes out.*

If two houses are onstage, it is not clear what prevents Flaminia and the others from going into Pantalone's house. Again, in Pedrolino's dance with Flaminia, we note the idyllic equalization of classes. The audience is led to imagine, not only the sex act taking place offstage, but also everyone having to urinate while dancing, or perhaps by this point merely hopping from foot to foot with the urgency caused by their full bladders.

This is one of the few places in his scenarios in which Scala provides the exact words for the actor to speak. This turns out to be important; later Burattino essentially repeats what Pantalone says here.

14. ISABELLA *all sweaty. Right away Pantalone dries her off with his handkerchief, telling her that when those desires come over her, that she [should] free herself from them and not suffer.*

> *They all stop dancing to go to [find other] amusement, and so they set off, and Pantalone follows them, drying his wife's face, while she plays the shy one, caressing her husband; away.*
>
> *and the second act ends.*

Sweaty Isabella was obviously not a passive participant in the sex. Her shame and probably excessive demonstration of affection for the old man also make clear her complicity. The audience is expected to be fully amused by the adultery and the deception by which it took place.

In real life, adultery was regarded throughout Italy as a serious crime. Practically speaking, it was a crime of wives, and the courts regularly punished an adulteress more severely than they did her partner, the woman being the means by which the purity of the patriarchal line was maintained.[24] However, the punishment was erratically and unevenly enforced. Much depended on the circumstance, social status, and class of the offender. Women were often publicly whipped and had their heads shaved or their clothes torn as a sign of shame.

In Scala's comedy, adultery is a source of humour.[25] The humour here follows from the irrationality of the marriage situation that had been allowed to develop. In Alessandro Piccolomini's play *La raffaella,* 1539, a servant suggests that the very easy remedy for a woman forced to marry a man "of opposite nature and custom" is for her to give herself up "totally to the love of one who with skill makes up for the unhappiness that one suffers with a husband." In the prologue to the same play, Piccolomini tells the women in the audience that if they are careful and prudent, they can enjoy their youth and their loves.[26] A number of critics have argued that *commedia dell'arte* provided no opportunity for satire. We cannot know what actors said or how they adapted the scenarios to times and places. Nothing in the Scala scenarios, from our perspective, satirizes politics or religion. But we must keep in mind that marriage was "at the heart of social and political institutions."[27] The satirical treatment of the lust of old men and of their marriage to much younger women is unmistakable, whether or not Scala intended such satire. Comedy was a version of the "avenger" that Isabella Andreini sought.[28]

With yet another walk, Scala gets his party offstage. The characters' need to urinate is abandoned with Scala's desire to close the act on a high point. The audience is left to anticipate Pantalone's discovery of the adultery and the repercussions of that.

Third Act

1. FLAVIO [PEDROLINO]	*[says] that an hour feels like a thousand [waiting] to see Orazio again to hear how the business went; at that*

The group of family and friends is still offstage. Flavio and Pedrolino, entering from where they exited, remind us of the way that things were left at the end of the last act. They make clear that they endorse and are complicit in the liaison.

2. ORAZIO	*[comes] from Pasquella's house, tells them about the brief pleasure [he]had with Isabella. Pedrolino: that he wants to play a joke on Graziano, who is in love with Flaminia and how the Capitano loves Flaminia with his very life, and how, though pretending to go hunting, he has really come out for her; at that*

The audience does not have long to wait for Orazio's report on the escapade, yet another reiteration of the sexual event. Pedrolino tells the young men that he has arranged another trick – on the other foolish old man who is in love with a young woman. Again the two plots are taken up in sequence, clearly pairing them and lending the frisson of one to the other. With Pedrolino's forthcoming second practical joke, Scala delays our pleasure in Pantalone's discovery of his having been cuckolded. Pedrolino's secrecy about the nature of the trick keeps him in control and us in suspense.

3. CAPITANO PANTALONE ISABELLA FLAMINIA	*arrive, see Orazio [and] tell him that they are happy about his speedy return; they all embrace one another. Isabella begs Orazio to get his chitarrone or theorbo and sing some musical things in the Roman style to entertain the company. Orazio, in a good mood, sends Pedrolino for the instrument. Turning to the Capitano, [he] asks him if he would like to take a wife. Looking at Flaminia, the Capitano says yes. Orazio [suggests] that he charge him with negotiating his marriage. Capitano agrees. And as Orazio is about to speak with Pantalone to negotiate the matter, [Burattino] arrives.*

The villagers, hunters, and vagabonds have apparently gone.

Orazio has evidently played and sung for Pantalone's family before.

The Roman style of singing emerged in Italy at the end of the sixteenth century. Both Orazio and the actor who played him were evidently very *au courant*. They were also very skilled musicians because, according to musicologist John Walter Hill, the characteristics of the style were beyond the ability of the average vocalist; they included a kind of recitative, the improvisation of additional ornamental *passaggi*, and expressive modulation of the voice.[29] The singer in this style customarily accompanied himself by playing chords on a theorbo, guitar, harpsichord or organ, depending on the circumstance. Performers of this new style were in demand but extremely difficult to find even well into the seventeenth century. The songs, largely in the pastoral tradition, are confined to various expressions of sorrow and pain caused by the loss of or failure to gain the intensely desired union between shepherd and shepherdess or nymph. Many of the songs contain references to interlocutors (usually unheard), almost always the beloved. Francesco Rasi, a tenor and a theorbo player – and student of one of the defining figures of the Roman style, Giulio Caccini, also known as Giulio Romano[30] – left us with a song the likes of which Orazio might have sung. It goes, in part, as follows: "When I am far from you I see nothing ... / The gentle breezes may blow, / and the brook may murmur among the trees – / When I am far from you I hear nothing. / Alas, I think so little of myself for when I am far from you I am nothing."[31]

Only that the words are sung and the likely pastoral references would have veiled Orazio's expression of his love for Isabella. In the tradition the songs, as here, could become metonyms for narrative.[32] Despite this, Pantalone, probably pleased at the idea of entertainment, is still none the wiser about the relationship between Isabella and Orazio.

The scene between the Capitano and Orazio is a private one off to one side. The Capitano's intentions, unlike those of Graziano, are honourable. Orazio, perhaps emboldened by his success and in a marrying mood himself, now promises to arrange with Pantalone (whom he has just betrayed) Flaminia's marriage to the Capitano.

4. BURATTINO *who pulls Orazio aside to tell him to be so kind as to pay for his bedstead that he broke when he was in the room with Isabella. Orazio: that he will pay for it; and he sends him away; then he asks Pantalone [to give] Flaminia as wife to the Capitano. Pantalone: that he agrees, if she wants him. Flaminia agrees and touches his [the Capitano's] hand; at that*

Burattino's request, at an awkward time for Orazio, allows the audience to again envision the vigorous adultery and suggests for a moment that the illicit act might be accidentally disclosed. It makes comic and suspenseful a scene that otherwise consists of arrangements. The near disclosure of what Orazio has so recently done also makes his interaction now with Pantalone seem quite bold.

As a widow, Flaminia would have retained her dowry and thus be able to remarry. She is related to Pantalone only by marriage. However, as part of an extended family and absent a more immediate patriarch, he has authority with respect to her marriage. By touching the Capitano's hand in front of Pantalone, Flaminia officially consents to the marriage.

5. PEDROLINO *[enters] with the chitarrone, presents it to Orazio, then everyone sits down; at that*

Orazio's lute is quickly retrieved. Time is foreshortened. At least some of the chairs from act 2 are still on the stage.

6. GRAZIANO *arrives. Pedrolino immediately tells him to go into the house and, into Flaminia's room, shut the windows, and throw himself onto her bed, and she will come to find him. Graziano goes inside. Orazio begins to sing and, singing, sings so sweetly that Pantalone falls deeply asleep; at that, [still] singing, Orazio leads Isabella away. Capitano, Flaminia, and Flavio follow them. Pedrolino remains; at that*

The scene between Graziano and Pedrolino is aside. Pedrolino's direction to close the windows, which would have been shuttered, assures that Flaminia's room in Pantalone's house will be so dark that Graziano cannot see.[33] No elaborate rationale for Graziano's departure into the house needs to be provided; Graziano has frequently gone into Pantalone's house. The second house, like the first, is to be used for a nefarious purpose. The audience knows that Flaminia, off with the group, will not be subject to it. Graziano is tricked to wait in bed; Orazio tricked to wait in bed.

Scala has devised yet another means to get everyone offstage to further Pedrolino's plotting, for which purposes the sleeping Pantalone, left on stage, might as well not be there. But onstage, he is as unaware of Isabella and Orazio together offstage as he was before. We see him tricked again.

7. PASQUELLA *comes out; Pedrolino tells her that Isabella waits for her in the house in her sister Flaminia's room to give her the tip, and that she [should] go quietly, because she has thrown [herself] onto the bed. Pasquella, cheerful, away. Pedrolino remains; at that*

Pasquella's entrance, unless Pedrolino calls or knocks quietly, is motivated only by plot convenience. Finally we learn the whole of Pedrolino's plan.[34] Pedrolino has an opportunity to exult in his success at the way things are going. In contrast to the first adultery trick, this one does not require the distraction of musicians and dancers, and there is nothing onstage to imply anything celebratory about it. Now it is Pedrolino who stands guard, but to see that no one interrupts the trick.

8. PANTALONE *wakes up, sees Pedrolino, asks where Isabella is. Pedrolino: that he too had slept and that he does not know. Pantalone is surprised; at that*

In *The Decameron,* the fourth story of the eighth Day, the old Provost of Fiesole, who is pompous and tedious like Graziano, falls in love with a young and beautiful widow who does not reciprocate his love. His attentions, like Graziano's, are persistent and obnoxious. The Provost is tricked into having sex with the widow's maid instead. He is discovered and dishonoured, including by small boys who taunt him.[35]

Scala's scenario, like *The Decameron,* uses the framing device of city people listening to and telling stories while on a stay in the country.[36] In *The Jealous Old Man* two of the stories, very much like those in *The Decameron,* are enacted. A story actually from *The Decameron* is narrated. In Scala the two enacted stories are very closely related to one another; the story of Graziano is another of the many parallels to that of Pantalone.

9. BURATTINO *[enters and] asks Pantalone if he has seen his wife, Pasquella, and Pantalone asks Burattino if he knows where his wife [Isabella] may be; at that*

The scenario rushes towards three successive recognitions that lead to its conclusion: those of Graziano, Burattino, and Pantalone. Both kinds of practical jokes delineated by Castiglione are employed. Pantalone is clearly tricked in an adroit and amusing fashion. For Graziano a net is spread and a little bait is offered, and he causes his own downfall. The couplings, a right one between Isabella and Orazio and a wrong one between Graziano and Pasquella, are neatly contrasted.

10. ORAZIO [CAPITANO] [FLAVIO] [ISABELLA]	*[enters] singing, followed by the entire party; they see Pantalone and make fun of him because he had fallen asleep, saying to him: "Oh what a fine wife guardian, a guardian who while awake doesn't have the heart to watch [over] her, oh [just] think then what he might do while sleeping!" Pantalone goes into a rage; at that*

Scala gets the group on stage for the recognitions. It is critical to Pantalone's humiliation that it have an audience. Honour was wholly a matter of public perception. The greater the public, the greater the dishonour.

11. PASQUELLA [GRAZIANO]	*[enters] fleeing from Graziano, who is trying to embrace her. Burattino comes between [them]. Pasquella tells them that Graziano has taken her honour by force. Graziano apologizes by saying that he has been betrayed and that he cannot speak, for now, but he will get his revenge. Burattino asks Pantalone if, since Graziano has had to do [sexually] with his wife, he can be called a cuckold. Pantalone says yes. Then hearing this, Burattino says, "Mister Pantalone, Your Lordship should know, that I am not alone. There are other cuckolds and not very far away." And he [says he] would like to tell him about what happened to someone he knows. And he narrates how [while] a jealous old man found himself back in the countryside with his wife over whom he guarded vigilantly, it came about that a young man was in love with her but did not know how he might come to enjoy her found a way, with the aid of a servant of his [Pantalone's] he arranged to be summoned by a friend some two miles away. And thus, having taken his leave, he went to hide in the house of a woman who was his friend, waiting there for the opportunity and the order [to carry out the arrangement] made with the woman. At the same time, the young country girls wanted to dance and after a wonderful group of women and men was assembled to dance, the dancing began to the sound of a fine instrument. And, having danced for some time, the wife of the aforementioned jealous old man pretended to her husband that she wanted to take*

care of her needs; at those words, the woman, being nearby, who had lent her house to the lover, led her [the young lady] into the house, with the husband's leave, and placed her in the arm of the lover. Meanwhile, the good old man, because of his jealousy of his wife, placed himself at the door and said to all those who wanted to enter, not to go and disturb his wife who was taking care of a need of hers. Her amorous work over, the cunning wife, came out of the house all sweaty from the hard work she had done and her pathetic husband said that whenever next such desires might come over her, that she should free herself of them and should not stay and suffer, and drying the sweat from her face, he caressed her. Pantalone, feeling that the conclusion [of the tale] had turned against him, immediately [begins] shouting saying that he has been betrayed and cut to the quick by his wife. Then Orazio tells him that not he but his wife was cut to the quick, for in enjoying her he discovered that she was a virgin and therefore he [Pantalone] was cutting her to the quick with his impotence. Pantalone realizing that he has been discovered, confesses the truth, and agrees that Isabella is to be his [Orazio's] wife. Thus we have the nuptials of Orazio with Isabella, of the Capitano with Flaminia, and of Pedrolino with Olivetta, and, passing over Burattino's dishonor in silence, they prepare to have the nuptials in Pantalone's house.

And the comedy of the jealous old man ends.

Graziano cannot speak publicly of the way in which he has been deceived, for that would make known to Flaminia – and to all – his devious designs upon her. We do not take seriously Graziano's threat to avenge himself; there is no indication that Pedrolino's identity as the trickster is even revealed, and in any case Graziano would be no match for him.

Burattino, who has kept his confidence until now, as if in jest, displaces his anger for his own cuckolding by revealing to Pantalone his. The psychology is finely observed. Scala dramatically puts the recognition of the less important of the tricks first, but the two recognitions are linked, and the one follows from the other.

Not only what happens to Burattino, which the audience already knows, but his telling of the story of Pantalone, which the audience also already knows, serves in yet another way for the audience to experience the story again. The length and detail of the narration suggest that Pantalone listens to it as just another story, until near its conclusion. Pantalone's angry recognition comes only after Burattino has repeated verbatim Pantalone's advice to Isabella to satisfy her desires rather than suffer. Some version of the jealous old man's story has been presented in song, two fictions, twice in fact, in symbol, in dance, and in its recounting. The use of the term *assassinato* (murder) perhaps recalls the violence of Cavicchio's profession. The structure of the scenario is both syntactic (sequential) and paradigmatic (consisting of parallels). Ferruccio Marotti points to a comparison with Sergei Eisenstein's use of rhythmic and tonal montage.[37] The long narration here and, in other scenarios, the long travel narrations make clear the audience's great enjoyment in storytelling as well as drama and in the intermixing of the two.

Pantalone is doubly dishonoured, first by the adultery and then by his impotence. His marriage to a young woman, and one for whom he cannot sexually provide, his overweening suspicion and control, and his gullibility make him the perfect victim of a trick.

Despite the great gender inequality, both partners had conjugal rights.[38] Pantalone's impotence, which was grounds for annulment, partly salvages the morality of the scenario, which otherwise celebrates adultery, at least in cases where foolish old men are married to young girls.[39] In the telescoped ending, no mention is made of a dowry, which would have been crucial. For the sake of dramatic economy in the scenarios, the nuptials harken back to an earlier time, before the 1563 Council of Trent, when mutual consent, without the involvement of the Church, sufficed to constitute a valid marriage.[40]

Unlike Isabella who was an eager participant in the first trick, Pasquella is raped. Rape was not a matter of the woman's autonomy, security, self-respect, or sanity; it was primarily a social, not a psychic fact.[41] Pasquella is a woman at the lower end of the social scale; her rape is of little social concern.[42] If at act 1, scene 8, Pasquella intimates that the anything she would do for Orazio includes having sex with him, Pedrolino's misuse of her here may be more acceptable to our own tastes. But Scala remarks only that it is her husband who has been violated, dishonoured, by her having been raped. Even that observation is hushed up in the rush to the happy ending in three marriages. The dishonour of the lower-class Burattino does not matter much. What matters in the second *beffa*, or practical joke, is that the well-to-do Graziano has been made to look a fool. Neither of the old men has exhibited the decorum appropriate to true patriarchs, and for that they are appropriately humiliated; the audience is intended to take pleasure not only in that humiliation but also in the artistry with which the trickery is arranged and disclosed. Pedrolino's tricks are not gratuitous but are punishments for perceived social sins, and, like the charivari itself, they and their representation serve to effect a kind of social control.

It is time for those of the next generation, fully come of age with their marriages, to take over from the old fools. Perhaps the final humiliation is the planned nuptials inside Pantalone's house. However, the Argument suggests that even old Pantalone accepts the resolution as fitting; he had made himself needlessly unhappy living a life of jealousy; marriages of old men and girls are not suited to either the old men or the girls. Thomas Van Laan observes the extent to which, in Shakespeare's drama, the climax is the conversion of the victim in which he is compelled to accept a new role, and much of the intrigue leading up to this climax is acted out often by the unwitting victim himself.[43] The same can be said in this case. Charivari, which was typically carnivalesque, ended with "a payoff from the victims, a round of drinks and evening of revelry."[44] The group's exit, into Pantalone's house, is probably accompanied by much dancing and merriment.

chapter six

Day 21: The Fake Sorcerer

The Fake Sorcerer does not provide the clearly unified plotting of *The Jealous Old Man.* Instead it provides what Kenneth Burke has explained as a qualitative unity, not of structure but of feeling or tone, that one often finds in early modern drama, here in the relationship of contrasting tones:[1] melodramatic and farcical. The scenario brings together a large number of images of "the grotesque body" (pregnancy, urine, vomit, feces, drinking to excess, and eating) that Bakhtin identified with Carnival. Its further imagery, which Bakhtin would also have identified as carnivalesque, includes "festive" madness, suspension of the social distance between people, clowning (in four memorable *lazzi*), and death, not only in the usual form of the passing generation of old men but also in the form of ghosts.[2] The scenario as a whole is an exuberant celebration of Carnival, suitably for this scenario described by Roger Callois as "an interregnum of vertigo, effervescence, and fluidity in which everything that symbolizes order in the universe is temporarily abolished."[3]

Day 21
The Fake Sorcerer
COMEDY

Argument

In Rome lived two very prominent merchants, the one named Pantalone, with an only daughter called Flaminia, and the other named Graziano, with two children of his [own], the one named Orazio and the other called Isabella. These two friends bought some delightful places near Rome, where, with all their family, they went to stay in the summer to enjoy themselves.

It happened that a young man endowed with nobility, with virtue and with property had a place of his near there. As often happens, this [young man] fell in love with Isabella, Graziano's daughter. And, having become close friends with Orazio, her brother, he disclosed his love to him. He had no other aim than to make her his wife. Orazio liked this, and promised to give him all [possible] help so that he could honestly enjoy his sister. Orazio revealed himself to be in love with Flaminia, the daughter of Pantalone, a close friend of his father's. Flavio (this was the young man's name), to satisfy himself and to give help to the friend, began to banquet the two old fathers with the young daughters, since his place was contiguous with theirs; and in this way, with time, and with the help of the servants and with the opportunity [provided them], both the young men were [able] to enjoy the ones they loved, and to their greatest happiness, they got their women pregnant. But since they were too greedy and eager in their loves, they aroused some suspicion in the old men, and in particular in Pantalone, who immediately went back to the city with his friend Graziano and with the whole family. Immediately when they arrived there, the women (whose bodies were growing larger) pretended – as devised by the servants – the one, to have dropsy, the other, to be possessed. And the young Flavio, to make it seem that staying in the country had caused these illnesses, pretended also to be an idiot a few times. In the end, having agreed [on a plan] with the servants, one of them [the servants] pretends to be a sorcerer [and], with his cunning, makes it so that the fathers agree to give their daughters to the aforementioned young men as wives. When the truth came out, every fault of theirs is pardoned, and from then on they passed their entire lives with the greatest joy.

Characters in the Comedy

PANTALONE
FLAMINIA daughter
PEDROLINO servant

GRAZIANO Doctor
ISABELLA daughter
ORAZIO son
ARLECCHINO servant
FRANCESCHINA servant

FLAVIO alone and noble

PHYSICIAN

< CAPITANO SPAVENTO >

< COPS >

Rome City

Properties for the Comedy

Two ghost costumes

Many glasses with wine

One ring-shaped cake

Sorcerer costume

Mercury costume for Franceschina

Scala neglects to mention either the Capitano or the police in the cast of characters. The omission of the police, evidently non-speaking roles and probably doubled, is understandable. The omission of the Capitano, like the omission of the urine flask, lanterns, and ladder, which are all critical to the scenario, suggests that emendation of the scenario for publication was not thorough.[4]

Guido Ruggiero explains that young women regularly sought a promise of marriage before agreeing to sexual intercourse, and males just as regularly provided it, even in cases bordering on rape. Intercourse followed by marriage was acceptable and occasionally provided a means for a love match that was otherwise not thought to be a good idea.[5] In this case, as the Argument explains to readers, the men's intentions are honest.[6] The evidence of the scenario, as I show, provides reason to believe that the information in its Argument was probably not included in the prologue spoken before its performance. The viewing audience would have learned about the men's honourable intentions only later.

The scenario requires two houses on opposite sides of the stage, each with a practicable window at an upper storey and one with a loggia in which an actor can appear – or, more simply, some means of suggesting these.

First Act

1. PANTALONE [PEDROLINO] *complains to his servant Pedrolino about the infirmity of Flaminia, his daughter, and that she has gotten such a large belly. Pedrolino blames many things out in the country where they had stayed for their enjoyment and [says] that it would be good to give her a husband, proposing Orazio to him. Pantalone, in a rage [says], that he would sooner drown her; at that*

We learn that Flaminia is Pantalone's daughter and that they vacationed in the country last summer. In this case the relaxation of the countryside led to a relaxation of morals.

Immediately, one of the scenario's two plots, that of Flaminia's pregnancy, is introduced. We may hear Flaminia moaning within. In this scenario we are frequently reminded of the ongoing life offstage. The entrance suggests that the characters, perhaps coming from the house, speak as if they were in the midst of conversation, thus supplying efficient exposition. That they speak of such concerns in the street is of course a requirement of the *piazza* setting, but also, as I have noted, the street was an extension of the house, to a greater extent than we might suppose.

The gesture Pantalone would naturally make to demonstrate the size of Flaminia's belly would make the true nature of her infirmity clear to the audience. Pantalone likely also specifies how long it has been since they were at the villa, so that the audience can surely deduce what he does not know and does not wish to believe. Pantalone, although very suspicious of Orazio's behaviour towards Flaminia at the villa, does not realize how far things had actually gone. The audience, however, can readily infer that Pantalone has lost what he tries to keep – the virginity of his daughter and his authority to provide a match for her. He is also in imminent danger of having his honour forever destroyed by his daughter's giving birth to an illegitimate child. Pedrolino must distract Pantalone from the obvious cause of her very protuberant belly and, at the same time, in his unerring faithfulness to the young, move to save Flaminia's otherwise irredeemable honour and, coincidentally, Pantalone's.[7]

Time is of the essence, even more so than in most of the scenarios, because so much is at stake and Flaminia is so very near term. The scenario begins with its primary complication. Owing to Flaminia's "dropsy," it would be best to marry her off immediately, before she becomes the unmarriageable financial liability that a sick daughter would be. This would be the tack to take with Pantalone, who is finely attuned to expenses.

With Pantalone's rapid change from lament to agreement with the suggestion that he marry Flaminia off, and then to anger at the suggestion of Orazio as the choice of husband, the actor playing Pantalone is given a fine opportunity to display his skills and to focus the audience's attention and heighten their anticipation.

Carnival, beginning forty days before Easter, allows an appropriate length of time after the summer holiday for the young women to be near term. The very premise of the scenario, two single upper-middle-class girls just about to give birth under the watch of their oblivious fathers, is carnivalesque. Perhaps the scenario was written not only to celebrate Carnival but also to accommodate at least one very pregnant actress.[8]

2. FLAVIO	*the one possessed goes [around] conversing with himself and circling around Pantalone, saying: "Your daughter will die" and performing the acts of one possessed, to frighten them; he leaves. Pantalone sends Pedrolino for the physician; he leaves. Pantalone, away.*

In the Argument, Scala describes Flavio as a fool or an idiot. Here he describes him as possessed. At the time, no clear distinctions between the two were recognized.[9] Flavio's suggestion that Flaminia, his only child, will die must be deeply disturbing to Pantalone, and apparently his generous-spirited neighbour from the villa has gone mad. Flavio's attempt to distract Pantalone from the actual cause of Flaminia's illness, by pretending to be also afflicted by something in the countryside, backfires. Flavio's ravings make Pantalone more determined than ever to seek the cause of Flaminia's distended belly. The action is intensified.

The time between Flavio's appearance now and his appearance at the villa seems compressed. He has evidently not appeared in the intervening months. He has no onstage abode and perhaps no in-town residence. The madman wanders off.

Madness actual or feigned, to judge by its frequency in early modern plays and scenarios, was very popular with audiences. Three of the lovers, at one point or another in this scenario, take on the guise of madness to mislead the fathers and, temporizing, to stave off their wrath. Like rage and despair, madness provided opportunities for *bravura* performances, instances in which the all-out behaviour blurred the line between actor and role.

Madness in drama was indicated primarily through speech,[10] although Anne MacNeil also observes the extent to which the madwoman's overabundance of passion led to song, as it does later in Isabella's case.[11] Flavio probably makes many illogical, colourful, and perhaps obscene statements, likely playing off and frustrating Pantalone's efforts to reach him. In Day 33 the mad Orazio raves in several different languages. In Day 38, *The Madness of Isabella* (*La pazzia d'Isabella*), Scala provides brief samples of mad speech. The sentences follow normal word order, but the images, for instance, of "the lasagne, the macaroni, and the polenta dressed in brown, unable to tolerate that the clever cat should befriend the beautiful girls of Algiers" provide a conjunction of words that makes them senseless, albeit quite musical in Italian. They exist as what Carol Neely aptly describes as "cultural remnants."[12]

As madness was thought to have brought people closer to a state of nature, its language often included folkloric riddles, jokes, games, proverbs, superstitions, and songs.[13] In Pietro Aretino's *La cortigiana,* 1525, the supposed madwoman is possessed "by maybe ten spirits" and is reported to be speaking "every language under the sun."[14] Similarly, Isabella Andreini spoke many languages in her madness in the work, also called *The Madness of Isabella* (*La pazzia d'Isabella*), in which she performed for the marriage of Duke Ferdinando de' Medici and Christine of Lorraine in 1589.

In his *Anatomy of Melancholy*, 1621, Robert Burton suggests that those afflicted experience rapid mood changes and sometimes think they hear and see phantasms.[15] Rapid emotional changes are evident throughout Scala's scenarios in instances other than madness and, again, to judge by their frequency, were much enjoyed by audiences. So they, as well as the theatrical response to phantasms, were employed in theatrical displays of madness.[16]

Since there was no distinction between the mind and the body (the theory of humours acknowledged none), the madness had bodily manifestations. Mad speech was likely accompanied by odd physical indications like Ophelia's "winks, nods, and gestures," some perhaps obscene (*Hamlet*, act 4, scene 5, line 11). Ludovico Ariosto's *Orlando Furioso*, 1516, described madness in terms of undress. In canto 23, verses 133–4, Orlando, raving mad and in a perfect frenzy, discards his shoes, shirt, and pants and flings them hither and thither. In canto 29, verse 52, he is naked and crazy.[17] Actually, nudity had been part of the folklore of madness for a long time; those who reduced their apparel to rags or cast away body coverings repudiated their place in the social hierarchy.[18] It was assumed that no sane middle elite would do that. Flavio's clothes and hair may have been in disarray, his body partially exposed. A costume actually distressed would have been an added expense and is not mentioned in the prop list. On the title page of the Corsini scenario *La pazzia di Doralice* the madwoman is shown in disarray.[19] For actresses, thus in disarray, the elision of reality and appearance, as in their obscene gestures or even breast exposure, was excused by the madness of the character. But mad men too could be represented in such disarray. Robert Henke observes also that mountebanks portraying madness used soap in their mouths to produce foam to accompany their extravagant acting and copious verbal performance.[20]

Pantalone sends Pedrolino in search of a cure for Flaminia. Very upset, he probably enters his house.

3. ORAZIO [ARLECCHINO]	*complains to Arlecchino about Pantalone's suspicion, because of which he left the countryside so soon, and [says] that the opportunity to talk [to him] was taken away. Arlecchino tells him how, while they were at the villa, Flavio made him tell Pantalone that he [Flavio] was possessed, but that he does not know to what end; at that*

The primary reason for the entrance of Orazio and Arlecchino at this point is to provide more exposition, from which Flavio's mad performance provided a break. The relationship between Orazio and Arlecchino and their relationship to Graziano must be established, perhaps by their entrance from the house.

There was evidently no perceptible distinction between real and pretended madness. Information concerning Flavio's pretended madness and Orazio's honourable intentions seem not to have been presented in a prologue. We learn it here. The audience has already deduced that Orazio is the father of Flaminia's child. We have yet to learn why Flavio pretended madness.

Again, time between the summer at the villa, when Flavio told Arlecchino he was faking madness, and the present seems compressed.

4. PEDROLINO *that the physician wants to see Flaminia's urine; he says this to Orazio, who worries that the physician will discover her pregnancy. Orazio: that he would like to speak to her. Pedrolino goes inside to have her urinate. They remain; at that*

Now, another potential complication arises. Uroscopy, the medical determination of illness by examination of urine for peculiarities of colour, smell, texture, and taste, was the primary means of diagnosis of illness in the sixteenth century.[21] In many kinds of cases, uroscopy was judged to be more reliable than seeing the patient.[22] So it is not peculiar that the doctor seeks first to examine the urine and by act 2, scene 4, has prescribed medicine although he has yet to see the patient.[23]

The urine flask or matula, which Pedrolino carries, was clear and, like a bladder, round bottomed; it had to be carried in a specially made basket, which was readily identifiable because of the common use of uroscopy.[24]

5. FLAMINIA *implores Orazio [to help her], the pregnancy being near its term; they perform a love scene*; at that*

The audience has been well primed to see Flaminia. Scala does not specify where Flaminia appears, but in his scenarios the upper-middle-class females usually appear first at the window to establish that they are carefully sheltered to protect their virginity. In the next scene, in which Scala introduces Isabella, he specifies that she is seen at the window. He also specifies at scenes 12 and 13 that the girls appear at their windows. Flaminia is desperate. The time pressure further intensifies the action. No mention is made of Flaminia's exit, but it seems likely that she withdraws after the scene. Arlecchino has been left on stage, probably to parody the florid love scene in gesture and perhaps in asides.

6. ISABELLA *at the window, implores her brother Orazio [to help her] telling him how her pregnancy is advancing; at that*

Now we are introduced to a second plot line, quite like the first. If Orazio, at scene 1, entered from the house in which Isabella appears at the window, her relationship with him is easily established. One would suppose that Orazio would know that his sister is pregnant and by his friend Flavio, but this has to be specified for the audience, again suggesting that the background information has not been provided in a prologue. Repeatedly, as we shall see, Scala emphasizes the parallels in the situations of the couples by making their actions successive and the stage pictures symmetrical.

7. GRAZIANO *from inside, calls his daughter, asking with whom she is conversing. Orazio leaves with Pedrolino. Isabella remains with Arlecchino, and, seeing her father coming, she immediately begins to sing, and Arlecchino to dance; at that*

Graziano's call suggests his continuing life offstage, the possibility of his overhearing, and the danger for the lovers of his returning to the *piazza* at any time.

Pedrolino comes from the house with the urine flask; it was thought to have been important for the urine to be examined fresh.[25] Pedrolino and Orazio leave hurriedly to avoid any confrontation with Graziano.

To prevent her father from discovering the true cause of her condition, Isabella begins madly to sing. Her madness explains her boldness in appearing in the street. She tries, by this violation of propriety, to distract her father from her true condition. Arlecchino does his best to help because servants, like our sympathies, are loyal to the young rather than to the old fathers.

8. GRAZIANO *seeing Isabella dance and sing, believes that she has gone crazy; with gentle words he sends her into the house; then he sends for Franceschina.*

It must be a sight for Isabella to dance with her very near-term belly, which the audience sees now for the first time. Graziano's manner suggests that he thinks that Isabella is mad from natural causes, not possession. Both causal explanations served at the time.[26] Like Pantalone, Graziano is oblivious to the obvious cause of his daughter's distress.

Isabella may feign tarantism, which was believed to have been caused by the bite of a tarantula, in this case perhaps at the villa. Symptoms of this supposed disease, which received widespread medical attention between the fifteenth and seventeenth centuries, could include acute melancholy, hydropsy, raving, and an irresistible urge to dance with frenetic agitation. Victims of the affliction manifested a distinct tendency towards exhibitionism; they behaved with frenzied abandon, making obscene gestures and improvised movements. They were stung during the summer and often relapsed with the return of warm weather in the spring. Afflicted young women (the disease afflicted mostly young women) might dash out into the street, shouting and leaping during the siesta time or the early hours of the night. Only music, most often the rhythm of the tarantella, was curative.[27] We know from the conclusion of the act that this scene takes place just before nightfall.

Here Graziano is likely to be a doctor of law rather than of medicine; he is able to minister to Isabella only with kind words. True to form, he seems more sanguine about his daughter's condition than is Pantalone about his. And he has something else, more pleasurable, on his mind.

9. FRANCESCHINA *comes out, Graziano leads her [to go] with him to Ripa to buy some wine, ordering Arlecchino to wash the cask, and [says] that he will send it [the wine] by way of the Porta della Caneva. Arlecchino remains; at that*

We know from what Graziano says in act 3, scene 5, that he is making preparations for Carnival. He likely establishes that here. This scene is a relief from further plot complications of the two damsels in distress and introduces the important Carnival motif. To get the wine, as Scala specifies at act 2, scene 2, Graziano will spend the night at his brother's house, presumably near the harbour on the Tiber River where apparently the wine came in. The reference to the harbour is a nice local detail.[28] The explanation is best provided here because it calls attention to the impending nightfall, justifies Graziano's evening departure and very early return the next morning – ready to drink, even before breakfast – and allows Arlecchino to be in the house alone in the night scene that follows. He is in no hurry to work. He has time until his master returns.

10. CAPITANO *speaks to Arlecchino of his love for Flaminia,* * *and that he wants to send her a letter, offering him fifty scudi if he will dare to throw it through the window, and in agreement, they go to write it, away.*

With his entrance, the Capitano, in a characteristic vain and long-winded set speech, establishes that he is a great warrior and lover who could have any woman but has deigned to love Flaminia. He poses and flashes his sword about. As he speaks, Arlecchino leads him on to even more preposterous claims.

Arlecchino, however lazy, is always anxious to earn money and agrees to throw a letter through Flaminia's window. The Capitano promises a sum that the audience must regard as out of all proportion. In the latter half of the sixteenth century a salaried female servant made about five *scudi* a year.[29] Fifty *scudi* is the amount that Pedrolino negotiates for two oriental rugs in Scala's Day 26, *Li tappeti Alessandrini* (*The Alexandrian Carpets*); it is one-sixth the amount that Claudio is to pay in ransom for his brother in that same scenario. But the size of the promised reward evidently does not make the always-needy Arlecchino suspicious of the Capitano's intention to pay.

The difficulty of writing for most people meant that it was often a cooperative venture. Even if the Capitano came from the nobility he may claim, writing would have been difficult for him.[30] Arlecchino would not have been able to write at all. However, the Capitano may think that he can add useful particulars about Flaminia, whom obviously he has only admired in the window: he does not know that she is pregnant.

The Capitano's arrival defers the plots of the impending illegitimate births, which thus far have built to considerable intensity, and suggests a new and ludicrous complication – his pursuit of the very pregnant Flaminia.

11. ORAZIO [FLAVIO] *hears from Flavio how he has pretended to be possessed [in front of] Pantalone and what he has told him. Orazio tells him how Pedrolino has invented a way by which both of them will get inside the houses of their women; then he tells Flavio how his sister is pregnant by him, and that they [the young women] must be informed now that night is approaching; at that*

We learn that Orazio and Flavio, probably entering from offstage where they exited, are friends and finally that Flavio feigned madness to protect Orazio and Flaminia from Pantalone's deducing the true cause of Flaminia's problem. The time between the summer at the villa and the present is again compressed. Contrary to the Argument, Flavio apparently does not know about Isabella's pregnancy. We see that he is quite sane and his intentions honourable. No impediment to his marrying Isabella and thereby saving her honour has been suggested, but so allied are the two plots that this is not likely to occur to the audience. In any case, the two youths seem only to have the ability to fornicate, inseminate, distract their elders from the inevitable consequences, and rely on the plan of a servant, evidently to be effected this rapidly approaching night. We are reminded once again that time is of the essence.

NIGHT

12. ISABELLA *at the window, performs a love scene with Flavio*; at that*

Isabella's appearance can be explained to the audience by the lovers regularly speaking to one another under cover of darkness. They make clear in their extravagant talk that they cannot see one another, surely a torment. One of the debate topics of the time, "whether it is preferable to see the beloved without being able to speak to her, or to speak to her without being able to see her," suggests the predicament of the covert night-time conversation.[31] The love scene importantly affirms the commitment of Flavio and Isabella to one another; it also defers the action.

13. FLAMINIA *at the window, converses with Orazio, to whom she says that her labour pains are tormenting her; Isabella says the same. Orazio advises the women of Pedrolino's invention and that, no matter what they may see, they should not be afraid, because it will all be for [the purpose of] bringing them together. Women, cheerful, withdraw; they [Orazio and Flavio] leave.*

The fraught women provide a symmetrical visual picture. Their lines of dialogue may be interlaced, almost musical. The women share their pains and their anxiety that their children will be born out of wedlock. The action is intensified seemingly to the maximum; the women are experiencing labour pains, and the illegitimate births are imminent. Once again, a resolution is promised. The youths and girls put all their trust in Pedrolino to save them in this most difficult and urgent matter. The particulars of the plan are not disclosed, but we can anticipate from the reassurances to the girls that what we will see might be frightening. The men exit because it is night.

14. CAPITANO [ARLECCHINO]	*with the letter*; Arlecchino goes to get the ladder, saying that he wants to pretend to remove swifts, and that he will throw the letter through the window. Capitano: [says that he] will give him the fifty scudi as promised. Arlecchino [goes] into the house for the ladder and a lamp. Capitano withdraws; at that*

A marked change of mood is effected with the entrance of the comic characters. The promised action to solve the women's problem is sidetracked by this ridiculous enterprise. The Capitano probably reads aloud and admires his letter in which he again boasts of his brave exploits and great desirability as a lover. Arlecchino seeks reassurance of payment.

Should anyone come while Arlecchino is throwing the letter through the window, he will explain that he is removing the nests of disturbingly shrill European swifts, which characteristically nest in eaves at night. The action has been finely imagined, either by Scala or by an actor who played the role.

After Arlecchino leaves, the Capitano is doubtless afraid of the dark. He is a coward, but in point of fact the night realm was, as we know, fearfully full of every manner of frightening thing (see chapter 3, "Night").

15. PANTALONE	*with lamp, hears that the physician has ordered the medicine for the morning; goes into the house.*

We are reminded of Pantalone's intention. Has he, even at night, been out searching for the physician? If so, we know how desperate he is for help. Perhaps he now hears a noise. The lantern calls for comic business involving the near discovery of the terrified Capitano. Just when the situation seems as dire as it can be, a possible new complication is introduced: the giving of pregnant Flaminia a drug for her dropsy. Pantalone and the Capitano are brought very close, but interaction between them is narrowly averted.

16. ARLECCHINO	*with the ladder, says the wine has come; then he leans the ladder at Flaminia's window, falling many times. Capitano encourages him; Arlecchino climbs to the top of the ladder; at that*

Arlecchino's entrance has been delayed by his indulgence in his master's wine; he has started the holiday festivities a little early. Conforming to the common stereotype for servants, not only is he lazy, but he steals.[32] There is much silly business in his drunken attempts to set up the ladder in the dark and mount it. He tries to be quiet but, in his condition, he drops the ladder and stumbles. The Capitano, much fearing their discovery, hurries Arlecchino on and probably offers incompetent help, perhaps in a stage whisper. Finally Arlecchino is perched to deliver the letter.

17. COPS *with large lantern, make a racket. Arlecchino, for fear, falls from top to bottom and runs away. Capitano [does] the same, cops [go] after [them], and here the first act ends.*

The fall must be spectacular.[33] Social historian E.R. Chamberlin notes that "the man who was discovered abroad during the night hours by the officers of the city had to be prepared to give a very convincing reason for his eccentric activity."[34] "Night was a criminal time that filled every statute," Camporesi observes. The legal system, partly influenced by folk mythologies about the terrors of night, stiffened the punishments for certain crimes if they were perpetrated after nightfall.[35]

Although, the act ends with a fine extended *lazzo* including ladder high jinks and a noisy chase, the scene does not play an integral role in the plot of the pregnant girls except in so far as it delays it. The ruckus does motivate Pedrolino's revenge on Arlecchino in the next act, which succeeds, in the most elaborate way, in warding off the complication of Flaminia's having to take the medicine. Andrews lists this scenario as one of what he calls "third-act scenarios," scenarios in which there is only sufficient action for one act; the rest serves at best as a delaying tactic.[36] However, it is the passage of time that works against the plight of the outrageously pregnant girls, and Carnival becomes an active adversary. It eventually involves not only Arlecchino, who is central to the resolution, but also Pedrolino, the plot manipulator. It prevents them both from helping the girls, who are in imminent danger of delivering bastard children and thus of destroying the honour of both their houses.

It is as accurate, however, to see this scenario, with its four extended and memorable *lazzi* (three of which end each of the three acts), as a scenario about Carnival as much as it is about the plight of the lovers who, in fact, have very little onstage time after that plot is established. Their plight serves as the framework for the highly theatrical and carnivalesque antics. Carnival overtakes the action and contrasts with the melodramatic plight of the pregnant girls.

The roles of the policemen could have been played by the actors playing Pedrolino and perhaps either Graziano or Franceschina. Neither has been on stage since act 1, scene 9, and an interlude of music or dance between acts would have allowed for their costume change.

All the characters and their problems and intentions have been introduced in the first act. The night has been variously used as cover for lovers, as fear-inducing for the Capitano, as evidence of Pantalone's desperation, and as opportunity for Arlecchino's behaviour to be particularly inept and suspect.

Most of the exits have been motivated. The comic, romantic, and action scenes have not always been readily distinguished and do not follow any regular pattern.

Second Act

1. PEDROLINO	*[says] he has heard lots of noise, [says] he wants to go for the medicine, simply [in order] to give colour to the business and to [humour] Pantalone, away.*

Scala specifies that the scene after this be set during daylight. So this scene, reminding us of the close of the first act, apparently takes place just before dawn. Pedrolino enters from Pantalone's house. The only reason to have extended the night into the second act is to make clear that Pedrolino has been kept awake by the night's antics and is accordingly tired and irritated. The trick that he later plays on Arlecchino is motivated, at least in part, by this irritation.

Again, there seems to be a time compression as Pedrolino now exits, early in the morning, to fetch the medicine. It is all too apparent that he did nothing last night to help the pairs of lovers. Moreover, his intention to humour Pantalone intensifies the impending complication of the medicine. We hear nothing of the lovers' urgent plight for six scenes.

DAY

2. GRAZIANO FRANCESCHINA	*that they have slept in the house [of] the brother, saying that they have sent the wine and a ciambellone, and he says he wants to taste the wine; they knock at the house.*

The carnival mood continues. Graziano establishes that it is now early morning. In anticipation of the later festivities he has returned early and already wants to taste the wine. The ring-shaped cake that he has ordered is a traditional Easter bread-like cake. Michael Bristol observes the extent to which "carnival permitted and actually encouraged the unlimited consumption of special foods, drunkenness, and a high degree of sexual license, and it often led to street violence and civil commotion."[37] All but street violence and sexual licence – the latter having occurred before the action begins – are represented in this scenario.

The door is barred from the inside. In an effort to get Arlecchino to answer it, Franceschina calls and simulates loud and hard bangs on it. In Scala's scenarios it was, at least in the first instance, the job of the servant to knock on the door. Here Pantalone may have to knock as well. Much silliness and hollering accompanies the banging. Arlecchino, sound asleep after the night's binge drinking, is virtually impossible to rouse.

3. ARLECCHINO *answers, then comes out [and] receives the master, telling him the wine has come. Graziano gives him money to buy a pound of cheese to have for breakfast and to taste the wine; he goes inside with Franceschina. Arlecchino remains*

Indeed, the wine has come; Arlecchino, probably feeling its morning after-effects, is hardly in shape to run an errand, and he remains on stage.

4. PEDROLINO *with the medicine, makes Arlecchino believe it is malmsey. Arlecchino drinks some, becomes nauseous, and leaves. Pedrolino laughs about it; at that*

Pedrolino does not wish Flaminia to take the medicine, fearing its ill effects. Always quick to seize advantage of a situation, he gets the idea to preclude this complication and to take his revenge on Arlecchino for having disturbed his sleep, by offering him what he pretends is a sweet wine.

In Baldesar Castiglione's distinction between two kinds of practical jokes, this is one in which a little bait is offered and the victim causes his own downfall. Later Pedrolino and Arlecchino, in conspiracy, effect the other kind on the old fathers, in which someone is cleverly tricked in an adroit and amusing fashion. As distinct from the original audience, we are unlikely to regard the first of these *beffe* as but "an amicable deception regarding things that give little or no offence."[38]

It would have been hard for Arlecchino to refuse the supposed malmsey regardless of his present condition or Pedrolino's means of persuasion.

Although employed, Arlecchino would have been ill paid and regularly in a state of deprivation,[39] and the present brimming-over abundance would have been irresistible. Camporesi even argues that ritual ceremonies of eating and drinking provide a different perception of time: long days of the most meagre nourishment punctuated with interminable excesses, dietary orgies and colossal feasts, disorder, and drunkenness.[40] Sick as he is, it is hard to imagine him going anywhere but home.

5. PANTALONE *in despair because of his daughter, sees Pedrolino with the jar of medicine; he sends him into the house to give it to Flaminia. Pantalone remains.*

Pedrolino has disposed of the medicine just in time. Pantalone, within, perhaps having heard Pedrolino and Arlecchino, enters lamenting the condition of his daughter and probably disturbed that Pedrolino took so long to return from the pharmacy. There is an opportunity for Pantalone, always conscious of money, to enquire the cost and for Pedrolino to play with Pantalone's obtuseness about the pregnancy. Pantalone anxiously awaits the physician.

6. PHYSICIAN *arrives. Pantalone caresses him, entreating him to heal his daughter; at that*

The physician arrives as needed. No sooner has his prescribed medication been done away with than he himself arrives, potentially adding a new complication. Pantalone fawns over him and probably promises him what seems to Pantalone to be a large sum of money given his perpetual tale of financial woe. Pantalone naively describes and, no doubt, again gestures to demonstrate the daughter's problem.

7. PEDROLINO *[comes] out; Pantalone orders him to lead the physician to Flaminia, so that he can better examine her illness, and away. Physician has Flaminia called. Pedrolino into the house, then returns with*

8. FLAMINIA [PEDROLINO] *[comes] out, is examined by the physician; in the end she confesses she is pregnant by Orazio; at that*

Scala needs Pantalone offstage for the examination that reveals Flaminia's pregnancy. No mention of his exit is made, but he is probably sent into the house.

It is hard to imagine that a medical examination would have been conducted in the street, as the fixed outdoor setting required. However, as we know, houses afforded little privacy, and physicians relied on detailed patient histories (in addition to uroscopy) to make diagnoses, not on physical examination. The only physical examination at the time seems to have been pulse taking.[41]

Pedrolino brings the reluctant Flaminia outside. She does not wish her true condition to be revealed to her father and is thus a frightened and uncooperative patient. Her condition is surely obvious to the physician. Nonetheless, he can go through all kinds of skilful cross-examination, which she evidently evades until it is no use. A medical history could include biographical statistics, symptoms, periodicity of the disease, what the patient and relatives thought was the cause, her social and family relations, her bowel, urinary, and menstrual habits, and her diet and exercise.[42] Pedrolino is evidently present to supply verbal asides or silent takes on the account provided by Flaminia.

9. GRAZIANO *who, off to the side, has heard everything. Physician consoles her, sends her into the house, and he, away with Pedrolino. Graziano says that Orazio, his son, is a scoundrel,* and that this is why he stayed out in the country [so] willingly; at that*

Graziano would have most focus were he to enter when the physician is on the stage alone. It is odd that there is no stage direction for his entrance at that point or elsewhere. The direction here comes too late for an actor to have acted upon it.[43] He enters, perhaps with a wine glass in hand, seeking Arlecchino's return with the breakfast cheese. We know that he has already begun drinking for Carnival because later he tells Arlecchino that he wants to try the *other* wine. Seeing the physician, he hides, maybe behind his door, in order to find out why the physician is there. His interest and his response, verbal and aside or silent, upon learning that Orazio has impregnated Flaminia is part of the scene. Graziano now speaks about his irresponsible son. Graziano is a lover of the good life, but his son has impregnated his friend's daughter, deceived his own father, and negotiated no dowry. Graziano has not provided the obstacle to the relationship between his daughter Isabella and Flavio, like Pantalone's between his daughter Flaminia and Orazio, which we might well have expected, the parallels between the two sets of lovers having been so strongly established. Rather, Graziano is upset with his son.

10. ORAZIO *arrives; Graziano banters with Orazio about love, about the countryside, and about getting women pregnant. Orazio immediately pretends that he is having a fit, away. Graziano remains.*

Orazio has not been seen since act 1, scene 6. Perhaps he enters trying to see or talk to Flaminia. Time is of the essence, and nothing has been heard regarding Pedrolino's scheme. Graziano is not sober, and his joking may be obscene. In self-defence, Orazio becomes the third lover to feign madness.

11. PANTALONE *arrives. Graziano: that he has heard about Flaminia's illness and, to heal her, he asks her father Pantalone [to give] her as wife to his son Orazio. Pantalone refuses. Graziano: that if he wants her healthy, that he give her to Orazio. Pantalone, in a rage, leaves to find the physician. Graziano remains.*

Pantalone enters, probably from the house, anxious to learn the doctor's diagnosis and cure. Graziano hints broadly at the appropriate cure and probably emphasizes the urgency of the matter. Pantalone is as much in denial as he has been all along. He reiterates his strong disapproval of the suggestion, already made by Pedrolino at the outset, that Flaminia marry Orazio. He seeks to learn the diagnosis from the physician.

12. ARLECCHINO *with the cheese, gives it to Graziano, vomiting all over for having drunk some of the medicine. Graziano: that he come into the house to taste the other wine. Arlecchino remains, vomiting; at that*

Arlecchino vomits throughout this and the next five scenes. The extended vomiting is another *bravura* performance. The medicine proves to be an emetic and purgative.[44]

Graziano's expansive mood suggests something of the spirit in which he advised Pantalone. That Arlecchino cannot accept an official invitation to drink wine with and courtesy of his master makes clear how wretched he is.

13. FRANCESCHINA *calls him to tap the cask. He vomits, and [says] that his stomach aches. Franceschina goes inside; Arlecchino pauses.*

At the end of the scenario Franceschina and Arlecchino marry, and their relationship, which contrasts with the precious relationships of the upper-class lovers, had best be established here. Franceschina is probably enticing and in a cheerful carnival mood, to which, by contrast, Arlecchino is too sick to respond. He may stink of vomit as well. He continues to vomit and curse the physician and Pedrolino.

14. PEDROLINO *says the physician is a good man. Arlecchino complains about him, vomiting and straining to make a bowel movement; at that*

Carnival emphasizes bodily orifices. It gives focus to the belly and the buttocks, literally and figuratively the lower parts of the body, to "eating, drinking, defecation and other elimination ... as well as copulation, [and] pregnancy."[45] Pedrolino, facetiously, takes pleasure in the revenge that he has effected on Arlecchino through the medicine. Their moods contrast. Although Pedrolino has successfully prevented Isabella from ingesting the medicine, he has not taken the promised action to solve the girls' problems.

The scenario's focus on the obscene may suggest why, sometime between 1570 and 1580, the Grand Duke of Florence wanted and provided for himself secret access to a place from which he and his familiars could privately view *commedia dell'arte* performances that were intended for the public.[46] No doubt, performing troupes could pick and choose scenarios from their extensive repertory and tailor them to suit the local authorities and audience at hand and may have tailored bits of business as well. But this is a scenario representing Carnival; it is essentially about the body.

15. GRAZIANO *from inside calls Arlecchino, asking him who is with him. He says: "Pedrolino." Graziano calls him, that he come to drink. Pedrolino goes inside, Arlecchino remains; at that*

Graziano's mood becomes even more expansive. He invites in the servant of his neighbour. With drink and Carnival, he overlooks the class barriers. We probably hear him partying in the house. Pedrolino is once again distracted from his promise to the wretched, trusting, helpless lovers.

16. CAPITANO *arrives, Arlecchino wants the fifty scudi for having thrown the letter through the window; at that*

The Capitano, the nuisance whom we have not seen since the end of act 1 and have probably forgotten, returns to find out how his affair is progressing. Arlecchino, always impoverished and, in his clothing of patches, representing the many poorly paid unskilled and often marginally employed labourers in the cities, is not sick enough to forget that he is owed money. The Capitano has no intention of paying anything, having promised a ridiculous sum, being probably impoverished himself, and lacking moral rectitude. He may begin some elaborate excuse, including perhaps blaming Arlecchino for the unhappy incident with the police. Another common ploy was to insult the person asking for money by calling him a spy, a scoundrel, or a slut. "This tactic," social historian Elizabeth Cohen explains, "shifted the onus from the debtor to the creditor whose honour and reputation were now called into question, probably undeservedly."[47]

17. GRAZIANO *eating, to call Arlecchino; he sees the Capitano and leads him into the house to have breakfast; Arlecchino, vomiting, follows them.*

It does not seem likely that Arlecchino would go in to drink or eat. Graziano must still want Arlecchino to open the other cask. The Capitano is a stranger, but Graziano's carnival mood becomes even more expansive, and he invites him in, thus saving the Capitano from his promise to pay Arlecchino.

18. PANTALONE [PHYSICIAN] *asks the physician for [his] opinion about his daughter's illness. Physician tells Pantalone that he [should] marry his daughter to the one she wants, doing otherwise he [warns] is to have grief and dishonor in short order, and that the sensible men know how to make [good] choices, and away. Pantalone remains, pondering the word honour; he remembers what Graziano had told him; he hears singing and drinking of toasts in his house; knocks.*

When last we saw Pantalone, he exited to find the physician. For the third time and by men of increasing authority – first his servant, then his friend, and now the doctor – Pantalone has been told that to save his daughter and his honour he must marry her off quickly and not to a man of his choosing. In his profound denial of the situation he still does not understand. While he is trying to reason the matter through, given his disposition, which is generally more choleric than that of Graziano, and in his present state of mind, Pantalone is likely to be extremely disturbed by the carousing, perhaps including the singing of lewd songs. His anger at the noise, and his confusion, would contrast nicely with the sounds of the revellers. No resolution to Flaminia's problem is forthcoming from him.

19. GRAZIANO	*eating and drinking, and as drunk as monkeys.*
CAPITANO	*Pantalone reproaches Graziano, who falls on the*
PEDROLINO	*ground drunk, after many acts of a drunken kind;*
FRANCESCHINA	*and thus, one after the other, all fall on the ground.*
	Pantalone is surprised; at that

This act, like the last, ends with an extended *lazzo.* The carnival merriment in Graziano's house bursts out into the street. The characters carouse, and one by one, in their different ways pertaining to character and prop, drop to the ground. They are shown transformed through drink as they are in other scenarios transformed through disguise and love. The transformed states afford opportunity for acting virtuosity and, to judge by their number and kind, provided great pleasure for the audience.

Pantalone cannot believe such indulgence. Indeed, that very characteristic prevents him from being able to understand Flaminia's problem. He is not specifically Jewish, although his hook-nose, skull cap, miserliness, and calculating capitalism suggest the influence of that stereotype, as does his failure here to participate in the spirit of communality, free expenditure, and careless exuberance characteristic of Carnival. He is its antithesis. In Shakespeare's *Merchant of Venice,* Shylock admonishes his daughter Jessica: Do not "thrust your head into the public street / To gaze on Christian fools with varnish'd faces; / But stop my house's ears, I mean my casements; / Let not the sound of shallow foppery enter / My sober house. By Jacob's staff I swear / I have no mind of feasting forth to-night" (act 2, scene 5, lines 32–7).

20. ARLECCHINO	*drags [or carries] them, one by one, into the house in various ridiculous ways; in the end he comes back, wants to grab Pantalone, who runs away along the street. Arlecchino [goes] inside the house,*

and here the second act ends.

Arlecchino must move quickly lest this comic ending flag. The *lazzo* clears the stage for the act break. Pedrolino is obviously too drunk to act on behalf of the girls and has apparently forgotten them.

Third Act

1. ORAZIO [FLAVIO] *tells Flavio he suspects that his father might know something about his love, because of the words that he had just spoken to him; at that*

We have seen nothing of the youths since act 2, scene 10. They enter together from the street. Flavio serves to remind the audience that in act 2 his father, Graziano, had made jokes with him about love, about the countryside, and about impregnating women. The youths, it is clear, have made no progress whatever. In fact, Graziano is now perturbed about Orazio's licentiousness. The sombre mood contrasts with the close of act 2.

2. PEDROLINO *half asleep from the drunkenness; the lovers complain about him because he is taking too long to further the business. Pedrolino: that they should leave it to him; at that*

Pedrolino conveniently enters. Here, in another scene that foregrounds the parallels between the two sets of lovers, they complain about Pedrolino's long failure to deliver on the promise to fix everything, pending since the middle of act 1. The delay, together with his present condition, can hardly be reassuring either to the young men or to the audience. How soon before the inevitable births? David Wiles provides examples of jests in which clowns win audiences precisely by extracting themselves from a situation of hopeless disadvantage.[48] But here the threat is prolonged far beyond a jest. Carnival has sandbagged both Pedrolino and Arlecchino, and the reputations of two families hang in the balance.

3. CAPITANO ARLECCHINO *tells Arlecchino that he will satisfy him, greets the lovers, telling them how the Doctor had given him a present of some very good wine, away. Pedrolino sends Arlecchino into the house to tell the women that soon they will be happy; then, speaking into the lovers' ears, he sends them to their friend the costumer to disguise themselves as ghosts. They, away. Pedrolino remains.*

Logically, all the revellers would enter from Graziano's house. The Capitano and his condition, like Pedrolino's, refers us back to the end of the second act. Arlecchino's plea and the Capitano's evasion, now with a promise of future payment, have become a running joke. Once again, as with the entrance of Graziano, the Capitano sidesteps the matter of his debt by redirecting his attention to characters of a class that is higher than that of Arlecchino, making it difficult for Arlecchino to press his case. Douglas Biow explains that gifts were a recognition of status in a very stratified society. Gifts of food, in a culture where hunger was so real, were significant. The recipient would point not only to the gift and its copiousness but also to the giver as a measure of his own worth. Conspicuous consumption was enviable.[49] The Capitano might justify his previous drunken behaviour and his likely present disarray by observing the magnanimity of his host and his own discerning taste in wine. At this point, Scala abandons the story of the Capitano's quest for Flaminia, which the audience would not have taken seriously anyway. He has not managed to interact in any significant way with a single one of the principals, not even Flaminia towards whom he now makes no move. His pursuit of her was only another of his fantasies.

Pedrolino has finally sprung into action. There is no indication of the means by which he enlists Arlecchino's cooperation after having so recently ill treated him. Arlecchino may accept that the score has been evened.

Pedrolino's whispering must be loud enough for the audience to hear. The youths seem reassured that Pedrolino has finally set to work. We cannot tell in which direction they exit but probably not in the same direction as the Capitano or from where they entered. Costume makers were readily available at Carnival time. A ghost costume would not have been a usual request and might have raised some questions. Scala is careful to specify that the costumer is a friend.

In scenes 7 and 8 we learn that each of the women are in their separate houses, so it is not clear how Arlecchino might inform them by entering one of the houses, presumably his own. But his entrance into one house suffices to show that he is carrying out the appointed task.

4. PANTALONE *scolds Pedrolino because he gets himself drunk and does not attend to the house. Pedrolino blames the Doctor; then he tells him he has found someone who will heal his daughter for him; at that*

Pantalone comes into the playing space from his house and details the tasks that Pedrolino has omitted, and the result. Thus, once again, the offstage space is made real. Pantalone has been dishonoured by Pedrolino's failure to perform his appointed tasks; he is a disobedient servant. Pedrolino deflects Pantalone's attack, first by blaming Graziano and then by promising a cure. We still do not know Pedrolino's plan, only that we can look forward to the youths disguised as ghosts.

5. GRAZIANO *arrives; Pantalone reproaches him. Graziano apologizes, saying he [was acting in a way] fit for Carnival. Pedrolino again says that he has found someone who will heal both their daughters. Graziano entreats him on behalf of his own [daughter], but starts laughing about Pantalone's, saying that she will never recover if she does not have his son Orazio as husband. Pedrolino sends them to the Apothecary of the Chamber Pot to wait for him, and [says] that they [are] not to say anything at all about the sorcerer, because he does not want to be known. They, away; Pedrolino remains.*

Graziano enters, probably from his house. Neither of the old men comprehends the true condition of his daughter despite the overwhelming evidence. Pantalone, who is losing control of his life, is upset that his house is not in order. Graziano, while concerned about his daughter, has not passed up the opportunity to celebrate Carnival.

This is the first mention of the sorcerer. Pedrolino enlists the old men in secrecy, just as he had enlisted the youths. The secrecy adds to the suspense and suggests the modesty of the sorcerer. Moreover, magic, particularly black or demonic magic, which employed the help of evil spirits, was a dangerous art to practise.[50] The Italian Inquisitions and other ecclesiastical courts, backed by legislation and Church decrees, fought what they regarded as superstitious practices.[51] The data from Inquisition tribunals in Venice and Friuli show that, by a wide margin, accusations and denunciations of magic led all others.[52] "Practitioners of magic had to exercise great caution for fear of prosecution."[53]

Pedrolino must get the old men offstage. Since many, if not most, ailments were diagnosed by examination of the contents of the chamber pot, Scala, comically and perhaps somewhat satirically, calls the apothecary "The Apothecary of the Chamber Pot." It was recognized that to some extent uroscopy, and thus the medications prescribed on the basis of diagnoses made from it, was quackery and that the drugs, as we have seen, could be dangerous.[54] Indeed the cure does not come from there.

6. *ARLECCHINO* *arrives; Pedrolino tells him he wants to free their mistresses from worry and play a prank on the old men. He sends him to disguise himself as a sorcerer, and that, [on] coming [back], he will tell him what he should do, advising him that, when he is before Pantalone, he should pretend to conjure spirits. Arlecchino, away. Pedrolino knocks to inform the women.*

Arlecchino enters, probably from the house. Already enlisted into Pedrolino's service, he is now to be a co-conspirator. He must be flattered. From what the audience has seen of him, they have reason to have serious reservations about his abilities. Characteristically, Pedrolino will manipulate from behind the scene. The suspense continues. The plan is not spelled out; we still know only that the sorcery will be demonic; it will involve ghosts. In the scenario this dangerous business is clearly fake because necromancy was condemned by the Church.

Probably Arlecchino must also go to a costume shop, exiting in the same direction as the youths. How he might pay the costumer is not a detail with which Scala bothers.

7. *ISABELLA* *at the window.*

8. *FLAMINIA* *at the window. Pedrolino informs the women that they should not be afraid of what they will see because everything will be fake, and that then it will all lead to their happiness; women, cheerful, withdraw. Pedrolino [goes] to find the lovers, away.*

The young women, again at their windows, appear to have full confidence in Pedrolino. We cannot be so sure. From the scenario we know only that he has managed to trick the gullible Arlecchino and then waste more time partying. The scene with the two women cheerful in their windows contrasts nicely to the scene in act 1 when we last saw them there in despair.

9. *ARLECCHINO* *with Mercury's caduceus, with the winged cap, and with the winged ankle boots, says he has thought up [a] double trickery; calls Franceschina.*

Arlecchino has become very involved in his role; he has elaborated on it, having added Franceschina to it, further taking time to set up the trick and delay the resolution. Arlecchino must display the items and explain that they are part of the costume of Mercury. The popularizing of classical myth and its imagery became a staple of secular public festivals, and from these festivals and from second-hand print descriptions the non-learned spectators became familiar with them.[55]

10. FRANCESCHINA	*[comes] out, receives the stuff, and the plan is [spoken into] her ear, while she is pointing to the loggia of the house. She goes inside, and he [goes] to disguise himself, away.*

Franceschina enters from Graziano's house, perhaps at Arlecchino's call or other signal. Here, as before, they probably show a sexual relationship. She seems to have been impressed with his plan, whatever it is, and pleased and excited that it includes her. There was likely considerable intimate physical contact and merriment.[56] Her pointing builds anticipation.

11. PANTALONE [GRAZIANO]	*tells Graziano that he wants to marry off his daughter, right away, once she has recovered, refusing to give her to Orazio, since out in the country he had said that he would have her despite him. Pantalone says that if Graziano wants to give him Isabella as wife, when she has recovered, that he agrees to give Flaminia to his son Orazio. Graziano agrees; at that*

Deep in conversation, the two men return from the apothecary. Whatever transpired there (probably reassurances from the apothecary about the efficacy of the drug) leaves them optimistic that their daughters will recover. The result, surprisingly, is a new complication. While Scala does not prepare us for this complication, we can understand that it must seem both logical from Pantalone's point of view and shrewd. He accedes to the pressure from several sources to marry his daughter to Orazio and, at the same time, negotiates something for himself in return: marriage to a young girl. Indeed, particularly if he can negotiate a good dowry, he must relish the idea. From the point of view of both the fathers this is a good marital arrangement. They are friends who are financially well off and will cement their bond through it. They shake hands.[57] The young are bargaining chips in a negotiated arrangement, their required assent assumed. There is a contrast between the seeming immorality of the young men, who, in fact, are honourably seeking to marry the girls they love, and the old men who bargain the girls away. And Pantalone has hardly shown himself to be a good catch despite his money. The old men will deserve to be tricked, but it is hard to imagine how sorcery can overcome their pact.

Pantalone, evidently, objects neither to Orazio's family nor to his financial situation. His objection, we finally learn, results from Orazio's disrespect for his authority, a slight to his honour – no small thing. However, given Flaminia's condition, the audience cannot take Pantalone's objection seriously because he risks the more serious loss of honour that an illegitimate grandchild would bring. Orazio's behaviour was not a character flaw but rather an offer of salvation for Pantalone's honour. The clarification of Pantalone's objection to Orazio and his acceptance of him as a son-in-law, albeit on his disgusting terms, paves the way for the resolution.

12. PEDROLINO	*all out of breath, says he has lost sight of the sorcerer; at that*

That Pedrolino enters out of breath suggests that he has been searching hither and yon. He may mention landmarks of the particular city in which the scenario was being performed. This brief scene serves to heighten our anticipation of the entrance of Arlecchino. It also heightens our fear of the failure of Pedrolino's plan. Even if Arlecchino does appear, we continue to wonder whether he is up to the job. The potential for failure is great.

13. ARLECCHINO	*[dressed] as a sorcerer, conjuring the spirits, speaks to the old men, tracing two circles, one on one side of the stage, and the other on the other, inside of which he makes Pantalone and Graziano enter, ordering that, whatever they might see or hear, they are not to move. At that Arlecchino conjures, calls the spirits.*

In the nick of time, or so it seems, Arlecchino appears. He separates the old men. Neither will have the other to turn to, and the sorcery will fill the whole of the stage. Magic circles, traced by the magician, who at the same time chants or says special words, contain the energy raised by him and keep out unwanted energies. Pantalone, especially, has shown himself to be easily self-deceived. Arlecchino, whom we have seen only as drunk and himself deceived, outdoes himself. His words, figures, and incantations all have magical powers. He appears to be so authoritative and his effects so great that the two old men are thoroughly cowed and fooled. Their fear and credulity make them receptive to the magic.

It is not surprising that Arlecchino is familiar with magic; magic was widely practised, despite its prohibition.[58] The world was not seen as materialistic, static, and limited but rather as "closely and deeply integrated with a complex, dynamic, and powerful spiritual world."[59] Magic was a means of transformation that was well suited to theatre.

14. ORAZIO FLAVIO	*dressed as spirits, walking around the circles, scaring the old men and Pedrolino. Then, each of them goes inside the house [of] his woman. Old men make gestures of astonishment. Arlecchino, looking at the sky, calls Mercury, messenger of the gods, that he come on top of the house.*[60]

The ending of the scenario is spectacular and perhaps a little frightening, even for the audience. Although the Inquisition played an important role in propagandizing for and enforcing a withdrawal of the spiritual, ghosts, which were generally understood to be condemned souls who forebode eternal damnation, continued to be genuinely frightening to many people.[61] Just as Orazio upset Pantalone by circling round him at the beginning, so does he here again. The terrified fathers may fall to their knees. Only the magic circles protect them.

Ghosts "walk without moving their legs, they haunt the places which they used to like, unable to forget the delights of life which have now become alien to them. They have neglected to accomplish something important during their lifetime, or committed evil, or have taken a secret with them to the grave."[62] Ordinarily figures of the night, the ghosts appear here during daylight hours because the scenarios' happy resolutions are, for the most part, set in the day. And Orazio and Flavio operating in tandem, are, after all, only pretend ghosts. Franceschina ostensibly stands in for a *deus ex machina.*

15. FRANCESCHINA	*dressed as Mercury; [the] sorcerer asks her the will of the gods regarding the marriage of the old men's daughters. Franceschina says that the gods want Flaminia to be*

Orazio's, and Isabella to [be] Flavio's, and that if the fathers do not agree, those spirits that had appeared must lead them to hell. Old men agree; Franceschina, away; at that, and right away

Franceschina appears at the top of Graziano's house. Scala apparently envisions a substantial structure. In renderings from the period, Mercury appears either virtually nude or robed.[63] I do not know what would have been tolerated on stage beyond female breast baring. The appearance of Mercury may well have been accompanied by offstage music and incense. A particular kind of music was assigned to each of the planets.[64] According to D.P. Walker, sixteenth-century magic in every way borrowed heavily from the magic of the mass "with its music, words of consecration, incense, lights, wine, and supreme magical effect – transubstantiation."[65] The caduceus, like the magician's wand, was no doubt used to great dramatic effect. It is Mercury who orders the marriages in the name of the gods; the power ordering the marriages, twice removed from the magician, who merely conjures the messenger, is that much greater.

16. ISABELLA	*comes out saying: "Signor father, I am healthy, and I do not want [any] other husband than the one who is in the house"; at that, and right away*
17. FLAMINIA	*[comes] from the house, says the same. Old men say they do not want to become family with devils. Sorcerer: that he wants them to know his value; conjures again.*

This is an instance in which Scala refers to the character as he or she appears. Arlecchino is referred to as the sorcerer just as in other scenarios a girl disguised as male may be referred to by the pronoun for a male, suggesting the extent to which Scala is visualizing rather than explaining.

The young women's bellies are as distended as ever, but apparently in their terror the benighted old men overlook this. They never have any recognition of their daughters' condition.

18. ORAZIO	*in his [own] form*
19. FLAVIO	*the same. Arlecchino has them marry, then he frees the old men from the circle; they would like to give him a reward. He: that he wants no reward other than Franceschina; in agreement, they call her.*

The young men provide a final symmetrical picture. One daughter marries a nobleman, and the other the son of her father's close friend; therefore, they make good marriages and at the same time preserve the family honour. Arlecchino shows his true love for Franceschina by, improbably, forgoing a reward.

20. FRANCESCHINA *pretends to be afraid, then she agrees. Arlecchino commands that they must forgive a certain Pedrolino for some trickery. Old men agree; he pretends to conjure, then he takes his fake beard off of his face, reveals himself; at that*

Franceschina appears now, quickly changed into her own clothing. The old men are freed from their circles, and there are congratulations all round. So grateful are they that their daughters have been "cured" that no mention is made of the marriage bargain they had previously made. Pedrolino's wit, coupled with Arlecchino's skill, solves the problem of the pregnant women not a moment too soon. Typically, Pedrolino, like the playwright, has worked his magic behind the scenes. The spirit of Carnival gives way to the celebration of social order. But one can readily infer that the happy ending could only have been brought about by magic.

21. PEDROLINO *confesses all of the trickery done to satisfy the young lovers and to preserve the honour of their houses; everyone praises him,*

and here the comedy ends.

The scenario would suitably end with a wedding or, technically, after the Council of Trent in 1563, with a betrothal dance, here with very pregnant brides.

chapter seven

Day 25: The Jealous Isabella

The Jealous Isabella can be more clearly identified with a single source play than can most of Scala's scenarios, namely *Gl'ingannati,* written in 1532 by a member or members of the Academy degli Intronati di Siena. Andrews helpfully details the relationship between *Gl'ingannati* and *The Jealous Isabella.*[1] I examine the scenario, quite different from *Gl'ingannati,* in its own right as one of Scala's very inventive works, just as others have examined *Twelfth Night,* Shakespeare's play, also based on *Gl'ingannati. Gl'ingannati* went through fifteen editions before the end of the sixteenth century and was perhaps the most influential Italian play of the period. Nonetheless, despite its wide popularity we cannot be certain that Scala, much less Shakespeare, knew *Gl'ingannati* directly rather than through intermediate borrowings.

Unlike the two previous scenarios, the action of which I have attempted to reconstruct, *The Jealous Isabella* has no tricks. There are two major misunderstandings that intertwine the two plots, one resulting from a disguise. No conflict is established until scene 5. The scenario is nonetheless very tightly plotted.

Day 25
The Jealous Isabella
COMEDY

Argument

In Rome there lived a Venetian merchant named Pantalone Bisognosi, a man who liked to have a good time [and was] given to overindulgence and conversations. The aforementioned Pantalone had two children by his wife in one load [i.e., twins], a male named Fabrizio, and a female called Isabella. The boy had been taken away from her by one of his [Pantalone's] brothers, about whom no news at all was ever received; the girl lived in his house, with habits very different from those of the father.

And, while she remained thus idle, it came about that she fell in love with a very modest young man of means, named Orazio, who likewise lived in love with the aforementioned young lady.

They went through infinite travails in their loves; in the end, her brother, named Fabrizio, returning to his home city, was mistaken for her because of the great similarity between them; finally he was recognized by his father, and she was married with her lover.

Scala seems to suggest that upper-class girls' lack of useful activity and their confinement to needlework and devotional literature led to the romantic involvements their fathers so feared.

Characters in the Comedy	***Properties for the Comedy***
PANTALONE Venetian *ISABELLA daughter* *FABRIZIO son, who looks just like Isabella* *PEDROLINO servant* *GRAZIANO Doctor* *FLAMINIA daughter* *FRANCESCHINA servant* *ORAZIO and* *FLAVIO gentlemen friends* *CAPITANO SPAVENTO* *ARLECCHINO servant* *BURATTINO innkeeper* *ROME CITY*	

First Act

NIGHT

1. ISABELLA	*at the window, wondering at the lateness of Orazio, her lover;* at that*

Isabella must establish that she has great love for Orazio, she has been waiting a long time, and it is night. She is alone. There is no indication that she acknowledges the audience. A number of commentators have observed that the elaborate language of *commedia dell'arte* lovers can at different times elicit both admiration and amusement.[2] In this case Isabella needs to elicit our sympathy, before she turns, as she soon does, to anger and desperate acts that are intended to protect her misguided sense of honour, because in the end she marries the long-suffering Orazio and we are to rejoice in that outcome.

2. PANTALONE GRAZIANO [BURATTINO]	*leave Burattino's inn, saying they have dined very well. Burattino: that another evening they will enjoy themselves even more, and that he will find them each a beautiful courtesan. They agree to the plan and go to the party of a friend of theirs; away. Isabella reproaches Burattino for wanting to be her father's pimp. And he: that, if need be, he will do the same for her too, and goes inside. She remains; at that*

This scene, reaffirming the night-time, leaves Isabella still waiting. It sharply disrupts her yearning and the quiet of the night and contrasts her chaste romantic love with the old men's lechery.

According to Antoni Maczak, there were three hundred and sixty inns in Rome in 1615, one for about every three hundred people.[3] It is unlikely that Scala would have known such figures, but he would have known how common inns were in cities frequented by travellers. In Rome "the 'innkeeping industry' and prostitution dominated other branches of trade and production."[4] There were more registered courtesans than any other group "active in a profession," including wine merchants, carpenters, and cloth and haberdashery merchants. Rome was renowned throughout Europe for its courtesans.[5] They were elegantly dressed women, often skilled poetesses and musicians, who catered to gallant travellers, patricians, and well-to-do merchants and provided them not only with sex but with the illusion that they themselves were well mannered and learned.[6] Travellers and men who were unmarried because of their family's interest in keeping the patrimony intact were especially reliant on the presence of prostitutes. In addition, because the average age of marriage for males was late twenties to early thirties, and women frequently died in childbirth, prostitution at every level flourished in the cities of Italy. It would not have been unusual for an innkeeper to arrange such amenities.[7]

Burattino's suggestion and the widowers' response are shocking only because they are out in the open, because they contrast so suddenly with Isabella's virtue and confinement, and because Isabella, who makes clear her relationship to Pantalone, is witness to her father's violation of patriarchal decorum. Burattino's suggestion to a lady, however, is improperly bawdy. It serves as her come-uppance for her having upbraided him. Burattino interprets Isabella's anger as sexual frustration.

3. SERVANTS	*with lighted torches, followed by*

The servants are evidently present to maintain the idea that it is night and that Flavio and Orazio are gentlemen, Orazio wealthy enough to be an acceptable marriage partner for Isabella. They do not appear again and are not mentioned in the list of characters, perhaps because they do not speak and were thus overlooked in the process of editing. Not mentioned also were the torches and lamps used to establish that it is night. These would have been on hand because of the frequency of night scenes in the Scala scenarios.

4. FLAVIO [ORAZIO] [FLAMINIA] [FRANCESCHINA]	*who is leading Flaminia laughing because Orazio has led Franceschina to believe that he is in love with her. Orazio begs Franceschina to bed him. She: that if her mistress agrees, she will; they laugh again. Flaminia ceremoniously excuses herself and goes inside with Franceschina, who likewise makes a show of flirting with Orazio. Orazio signals to Isabella, as had been agreed between them.*

The characters in scenes 3 and 4 enter from other than from where Graziano and Pantalone have exited; they do not encounter the old men.

Scala does not provide the entrance for Orazio that Isabella has led us to anticipate. He enters not as a romantic lover who has been unfortunately delayed, but as one who has had a night on the town with friends and is jovially propositioning a serving woman. Apparently Franceschina is not taken in by Orazio, because at scene 11 she speaks lovingly to Orazio from the window, in darkness, and in Isabella's voice rather than her own. "If the social distance between the man and the woman was great, ... women ... were expected to be aware of the fact that the word of a man in such circumstances, no matter how serious it might sound, was not serious."[8]

Gl'ingannati was written to be performed during Carnival and is set at Carnival time. Whether this scenario is also intended for performance during Carnival, a time of much theatre, cannot be said, but the general night-time merriment, drunkenness, and licentiousness in the first act is carnivalesque. The idea that it is Carnival – coupled with Graziano's child-rearing practices in other scenarios, explicitly more casual than Pantalone's – may explain Flaminia's presence in the street at night with male companions, albeit under the watch of the serving woman Franceschina. Flaminia's amusement at Orazio's proposition, to which there is no indication that she assents, is consistent with the general character of the night; Isabella, unable to share in it, is intolerant, suspicious, and unforgiving.

Flavio and Flaminia are friends. Flavio has no love interest in the scenario and functions only as Orazio's friend, as in Day 6. Flaminia serves primarily at the end as a marriage partner for Fabrizio, but Scala carefully brings her into the action at the onset.

We know that while Isabella's chastity must be protected and she is thus confined to the house, the serving woman Franceschina is not so protected, because it was necessary for her to run errands and because, unlike Isabella, she is in no position to serve as a vessel for the transmission of family wealth. The class difference between her and the other characters, evident from her clothing, must also be clearly established by the actors. Franceschina's self-confident and later even brazen behaviour may suggest that she is older and more knowledgeable than are Flaminia and Isabella, who would have been in their teens. Her easy manner in front of her mistress contributes to the high spirits of the night and indicates that she is on good terms with Flaminia.

The reversals characteristic of Carnival are consistent with the idea that Franceschina may have been played by a man, provided that the troupe, as some did, had a male actor for the role. If it was played by a man, her agreement to Orazio's proposition, her imitation of Flaminia's elaborate leave taking, and Isabella's jealousy would have been all the funnier.

Orazio's signal is audible and must be something romantic, a bird call (improbable late at night) or a song fragment perhaps. In *Alessandro*, 1543, attributed to Alessandro Piccolomini, Lucilla directs Cornelio to "whistle the signal which Querciuola will teach you." In Scala's play *Il finto marito* the signals in the dark include loud repeated throat clearings and the sound of rocks being knocked together.[9]

5. ISABELLA *who had remained at the window the entire time, reveals herself, saying that he should go make love to his maidservant since he deserves to be in the kitchen more than in the bedroom, and, without listening to him at all, she withdraws. Astonished, they remain; at that*

At scene 4, Isabella's longing and worry quickly turn to anger upon seeing the interaction between Orazio and Franceschina. Her anger serves as counterpoint to the scene in the street below. For contemporary viewers, her quick temper and her jealousy would have revealed the depth of her love (see chapter 2, note 148). From our perspective and that of Burattino, it also reveals her pent-up sexuality. The direction that Isabella has remained at the window, although positioned so that she is visible only to the audience, not to Orazio, would have been too late for the actress playing the role.

We do not know whether the "they" who remain "astonished" includes the servants with lighted torches or only Orazio and Flavio. Scala specifies no exit for the servants, and it is not obvious where it might take place if not as part of the melee at scene 7, where there is no mention of them. However, the presence of servants at the entrance of the Capitano and Arlecchino would steal some focus from them, weighting the stage too heavily with the servants and Orazio, and Flavio. It seems unlikely that non-speaking actors would have been hired just for this appearance. The actor playing Pedrolino would have been free to double as one of the servants. The actors playing the Capitano and Arlecchino would also have been available if the servants exited soon enough for them to enter again as Capitano Spavento and Arlecchino at scene 6.

6. CAPITANO *with a lighted lantern; at that*
ARLECCHINO

Arlecchino must hold the lantern and light the way, not only to maintain the fiction that it is night but also to establish that he is the Capitano's servant.[10] There may be opportunity for interplay between Arlecchino and the Capitano to further establish their relationship and perhaps the Capitano's fear of the night and his reason for his appearance in it.

7. ISABELLA *again at the window, tells him [Orazio] to go to the maidservant and not make her wait any longer. Capitano asks*

Isabella what is the matter with her; who tells him she has been betrayed and cut to the quick. Capitano blusters*; Orazio and Flavio thrust their hands [raise their swords] against him, and, fighting, they go up the street; Isabella at the window; at that*

Isabella provides a speech on love betrayed. Always ready to help a lady in distress who might yield to his bravado, the Capitano threatens Orazio and Flavio. He must make clear his instant infatuation with Isabella at this point, probably as she speaks, and not for the first time at scene 16 where he enters in order to tell Isabella that for the sake of her love he has killed a number of her lovers. He evidently assumes (see scene 16) that both Orazio and Flavio have betrayed her. Whatever she says now should allow for this possibility. Orazio and Flavio, defending the honour of Orazio, draw their weapons against the Capitano. In a new complication Orazio is now beset by the meddling Capitano as well as by Isabella.

The image of Isabella at the window and pent up in the house is prolonged to act 2, scene 12, thus making emphatic her entrapment at a time when others make merry. This entrapment goes far to explain her otherwise rather extravagant jealousy. Her jealousy must not turn our sympathies against her, because our interest in her defensive behaviour and Orazio's devotion to her, despite all he is put through, depends on it. Everyone else including Flaminia can roam the streets on what is perhaps a Carnival night, can engage in sexual joking, and can physically defend his honour, something that Isabella later attempts to defend as a man, free of her confinement.

8. PEDROLINO *at the window [in Pantalone's house] with a lamp.*

It is unusual for Scala's scenarios to have more than one functional window per house. Here Pantalone's house has two. Pedrolino probably seeks to learn the cause of the commotion. Scala will need him at the window for scene 10 and carefully establishes him there now.

9. FRANCESCHINA *the same [at a window in Graziano's house]. Isabella, seeing her, says: "There she is, that fine thing that is the cause of everything!" Franceschina answers her back. And Isabella: that she does not speak to slatterns, and goes inside. Franceschina says she knows the source of all this; she goes inside. Pedrolino remains at the window.*

Both women and men defame women by focusing narrowly on their sexual integrity or, rather, their lack thereof.[11] Not surprisingly, the freedom to insult here belongs to someone of higher status than the woman insulted. Franceschina, like Burattino, suggests Isabella's sexual frustration. Isabella now feels that she has been aggrieved by both Orazio and Franceschina.

10. ORAZIO — *returns, complaining about Isabella; sees Pedrolino [and] calls him, asking him to come down with the lamp, thinking that he has been wounded [in the fight]. Pedrolino: that he [is to] wait; at that*

11. FRANCESCHINA — *inside the window near that of Isabella, speaks amorously soto voce with Orazio, pretending to be Isabella; at that*

Orazio has been wounded offstage in the process of defending his honourable intentions towards Isabella. He returns because he loves her. In different ways in this scenario Isabella, Orazio, Pantalone, Franceschina, and Capitano Spavento all strive to uphold their honour.

That Franceschina must speak at a window close by that of Isabella for the deception of Orazio to work may suggest that Scala ideally envisioned actual separate structures, not just openings in curtains. The houses of Graziano and Pantalone are set close to one another, probably on one side of the stage, with the inn on the other for balance. That at scene 13 Isabella closes the window in Orazio's face also suggests an actual structure with shutters, but we cannot be certain.[12]

The many window scenes in this act reinforce the idea that it is night and that people have retired to their houses.

12. ISABELLA — *at the window, stays there and listens; at that*

13. PEDROLINO — *[comes] outside with the lamp; and Isabella says: "Ah traitor, I've finally caught you talking with your sweetheart!" Franceschina, laughing, withdraws. Orazio would like to apologize to Isabella, who, incensed, does not want to listen to him, she shuts the window in* *his face. Orazio remains, pained,* with Pedrolino; at that*

Orazio's call to Pedrolino at scene 10 informs the audience that he has been wounded. Pedrolino's delayed entrance gives full focus to Franceschina and Isabella. The lamp illuminates Orazio, making clear to Isabella to whom Franceschina has spoken and his loving response, he assumes, to Isabella. As the scenario shows, the senses are deceptive. The resolution could be just an apology away, but Isabella will not hear it. Her belief that she has been betrayed is only reinforced. Her indignation increases.

Scala seems to have designed the Capitano's uncharacteristic engagement in conflict so that Orazio can show himself wounded. I would like to believe that Pedrolino binds Orazio's wound and thus Orazio has a visible scenario-long badge of his love and suffering for Isabella. No props are listed for this scenario, however. In any case, Isabella seems unmoved by Orazio's wound, and, wounded already, Orazio is very vulnerable to her rejection.

14. PANTALONE GRAZIANO	*with lamp, both of them drunk; Orazio away. Pedrolino reproaches Pantalone for his wicked ways, and [says] that one night he will find his daughter pregnant. Pantalone, laughing, goes inside. Graziano has [Pedrolino] knock at the [door of his] house. Pedrolino knocks.*

Orazio, trying to keep his relationship with Isabella secret from Pantalone, hurriedly exits other than from where Pantalone enters. The relationship, even limited as it is to communication through the window, impugns Isabella's virtue and so Pantalone's honour.

The lanterns make clear that it is still night. The return of Pantalone and Graziano from their party marks the passage of time. The men are now very drunk, and there is opportunity here, in a scene that contrasts in mood with scene 13, to play with the darkness by having them bump into one another and fail to find their own doors. Graziano's behaviour, along with his age and characteristic pedantry, serves to make us feel that Pantalone's later arrangement of Isabella's marriage to him is particularly regrettable. In *Gl'ingannati* the marriage arranged for the young girl is with a man in his fifties.

Ordinarily, the honour of the household was reflected in the obedience and subservience of the servants. Perhaps the servant Pedrolino can upbraid the master Pantalone because both have an interest in his daughter, whom Pantalone has left alone and unsupervised during the night on the town, and perhaps because it is Carnival. Pedrolino speaks about the influence of the behaviour of the parents on that of the children as did Erasmus: "What chance have your children of having decent moral standards when they are undermined by you?"[13]

The knocking is almost always a *lazzo.* Such knocking, invariably loud and lengthy, here disrupts the night and may include the drunken Graziano.

15. FLAMINIA *reproaches her father for his drunkenness. Graziano hugs her and leads her into the house. Pedrolino, laughing, remains; at that*

While we have probably already inferred from the house to which he has returned that Graziano is Flaminia's father, that inference is confirmed here. Graziano's drunkenness is evident to Flaminia as soon as she opens the door, from which she probably does not move far. To no effect, she very likely echoes some of the words of Pedrolino to Pantalone. Graziano's drunken embrace cannot have been pleasant for her.

The continued carnivalesque merriment contrasts with the mood of Isabella, who feels utterly betrayed, and now with the mood of the wounded and misunderstood Orazio.

16. CAPITANO [ARLECCHINO] *blustering*, orders Pedrolino to call Isabella, to whom he wishes to say that, for love of her, he has killed many of her suitors. Pedrolino laughs at this; at that*

Capitano, who enters from where he exited, greatly exaggerates his bravery and accomplishments as usual; Orazio is not seriously wounded, and, if in a general melee, it may not even have been clear by whom. Pedrolino's laugh assures us that the Capitano is fabricating, and, moreover, at scene 17 Flavio appears intact.

Arlecchino has opportunity to encourage the vain Capitano's braggadocio, while at the same time characteristically undercutting it without the Capitano's cognizance.

17. FLAVIO *who has heard his bragging, tells him that he lies in the throat. He draws [his] hand [sword] against him; Capitano runs away; Flavio goes after [him], Arlecchino [does] the same. Pedrolino, laughing, goes back into the house,*

and here the first act ends.

Again the specification of the timing of Flavio's entrance would be too late to serve the actor.

Social historian Edward Muir explains that a precise succession of steps preceded a duel: "When one party insulted or accused another of a dishonorable deed, the accused had to respond by 'giving the lie,' that is by stating loudly and clearly, 'You lie in the throat.'" At this point, the original speaker was to formally challenge the other to a duel by throwing down some pledge such as a glove, ring, dagger, or belt.[14] Instead, the fearful Capitano flees and, by not upholding the chivalric ethos, dishonours himself. The exit reminds us of the similar one at scene 7, and the exit may be off in the same direction. The fight provides an exciting ending for the act, one that Scala often uses, and leaves us in suspense as to its outcome. The laughter of Pedrolino, who is not involved in the action, underlines the spirit in which we are to take it.

Both comic and serious scenes, provided in an unpredictable pattern, have furthered the action of the scenario.[15] The primary misunderstanding that resulted in Orazio's wound has now been introduced, as have all of the characters, except Fabrizio. The night has been finely imagined and used.

Second Act

DAY

1. ORAZIO *[says] that he has not gone to bed that entire night, just thinking how greatly mistaken Isabella is;* at that*

In a scene reminiscent of Isabella's at the opening of the scenario, but in a speech about love despised, Orazio makes clear that it is morning and affirms his love for Isabella. He also summarizes for the audience's benefit the events that have befallen him, thus relating the first act to the second. Again, there is no indication that he speaks to the audience. Scala does not specify Orazio's exit from this scene, but there is no reason for him to remain on stage hidden or otherwise. His overhearing of all the scenes until scene 7, when his presence is certain, would not serve them.

2. PANTALONE [PEDROLINO] *hears from Pedrolino that Isabella is in love with Orazio. Pantalone, speaking loudly, says: "It seems impossible to me that my daughter Isabella could be in love with Orazio"; at that*

Pantalone and Pedrolino enter from the house, it being early the next morning. As they enter, we likely hear the conclusion of the scene that began inside, in which Pedrolino tells Pantalone of Isabella's love for Orazio. The audience would thus be encouraged to envision ongoing life in the offstage space. The motive for Pedrolino's surprising disclosure of Isabella's love remains unclear until scene 8. It serves here to bring Pantalone into the plot.

3. FRANCESCHINA *tells Pantalone that it is true, and of having seen them several times speaking amorously together; at that*

Pantalone's fervent denial is so loud that Franceschina, perhaps coming to the window in the adjacent house, can hear it. The many scenes that follow before Pantalone comes to realize the fact of the relationship between Isabella and Orazio make clear how emphatic his denial is.

Franceschina is still trying to restore her honour by getting back at Isabella, but now she goes further, telling Pantalone about the relationship between Orazio and Isabella. In *Gl'ingannati* the serving woman, albeit alone, says: "Recently she's fallen so madly in love and become so lathered up that she can't find any peace, day or night. She's always scratching between her legs, stroking her thighs, or running up onto the porch or over to the window or running down the stairs or up the stairs."[16] It seems unlikely that Franceschina here says anything quite as raw because if she did, Flaminia would have a hard time defending her at scene 6. However, I do suppose that she adds something quite colourful to what Pedrolino has said.

4. FLAVIO *reproaches Franceschina, having first listened to everything; Franceschina, angry, says that he will be sorry and goes inside. Pantalone tells Flavio not to consider the words of a maidservant, and leaves with Pedrolino; Flavio remains.*

The faithful friend Flavio tries to protect Isabella, fearing that the illicit relationship between her and Orazio will be seen by Pantalone as evidence of his failure to maintain his patriarchal authority and uphold his honour. Surprisingly, the disclosure of the relationship, now even with two people from separate households having testified to it, does not complicate the plot with a recognition on Pantalone's part. His denial is profound.

Pantalone and Pedrolino do not exit into the house; they are on their way somewhere. We know this because at scene 8 Pedrolino enters, out of breath.

5. ISABELLA	*shows that she has heard everything from the window, thanks Flavio for his help* and [says] that she did not want to respond to that wretch Franceschina; at that*

Scala does not specify that Isabella appears at her window until after the fact. Pantalone's loud denial at scene 2 is the logical place for the entrance of Isabella as well as that of Franceschina.

There is opportunity here for a set speech on friendship. The scene is reminiscent of act 1, scene 9, in which Isabella called Franceschina a slut. Isabella is still trapped in the house and is feeling increasingly betrayed. Franceschina has divulged her secret. And the behaviour of Orazio, in Isabella's eyes, compares very poorly with that of Flavio's.

6. FLAMINIA	*at the window tells Isabella that she should not insult her maidservant like that. Isabella apologizes; Flavio [does] the same. Flaminia tells Flavio that she has known for a while that he cares little about the things that concern her, and, angry, goes inside. Flavio remains, upset; Isabella consoles him, saying that Orazio, that traitor, is the cause of all the trouble, and goes inside. Flavio remains.*

If at scene 3 Franceschina appeared at the window, this act carries over the three-window pattern of the first act. Repetition, as we have seen, provides an important pattern of organization in the scenarios.

Flaminia's close relationship with Franceschina, established in their casual good fun at their first entrance in act 1, scene 3, is reaffirmed by Flaminia's defence of Franceschina. There may be some suggestion here that Flaminia is attracted to Flavio but that he has been oblivious to this. If so, her later sudden sexual relationship with Fabrizio is more strongly motivated.

Isabella, who has thanked Flavio for his friendship and loyalty, in turn comforts Flavio who has just provided these for her.

7. ORAZIO *having heard what Isabella said, despairs; Flavio consoles him;*

The timing of the actor's entrance is again specified too late for an actor to utilize. Scala's repeated use of the past perfect in this scenario reveals the extent to which he was recollecting the scenario for readers. Orazio enters in time for a kind of plot summary, at least from Isabella's point of view, which is provided just before the plot becomes more complicated with Pantalone's inevitable realization of the relationship between Isabella and Orazio. Both scenes 6 and 7 serve to delay his realization. The faithful Flavio, just comforted by Flaminia, now comforts Orazio. The gaiety of the carnival-like night opening has vanished. Orazio, Isabella, Flaminia, and Flavio have all been made unhappy as a result of Isabella's jealousy. Flaminia's anger at Flavio seems unmotivated except by Scala's interest in bringing both characters back into the scenario, paralleling the anger of Isabella at the window with that of Flaminia, and achieving a total turn of mood from the night to the day. Nothing subsequently comes of Flaminia's outburst.

8. PEDROLINO *panting, looks for Orazio; sees him, and tells him how he told Pantalone that Isabella was in love with him, and that he realizes he has done something he should not have done, since he was expecting one thing but the outcome was quite another, namely, that her father is trying to marry her off. Orazio despairs*; then they all leave to find a solution to the problem. Away.*

Here is another instance of Pedrolino's entering out of breath, adding to a sense of speed and to our appreciation of the performance as performance. Pedrolino enters from the direction in which he exited. In his effort to salvage the relationship between Isabella and Orazio by revealing it to her father, he has made things worse. This is not the trickster Pedrolino who skilfully manipulates the plot to its happy conclusion as he often does.

Pantalone, who has at long last come to accept the servants' word about the relationship between his protected Isabella and Orazio, urgently wants to get Isabella married off; her virginity is at risk. Pantalone's long-anticipated recognition is offstage. We are left to imagine its vehemence. Pantalone does not intend that Orazio be the husband.

Here, as well as at scene 7, there is opportunity for Orazio to provide a set speech of despair. Throughout there is ample opportunity for him to despair. The actor could judiciously vary the length of such speeches so as not to interrupt the flow of the action. The audience's pleasure in extravagant speeches of despair, however, seems to have been considerable.

9. CAPITANO ARLECCHINO	*come blustering about the previous night's fighting; at that*

The Capitano, in what is now a running joke, enters boasting about his war-like abilities, this time, as we are reminded, in the fight that ended act 1. In fact, we recall that he and Arlecchino ran away from the fight in fright. Here Arlecchino appears to identify with, rather than undercut, the Capitano. His arrogance in act 3, scene 3, is further consistent with the idea that he identifies with his master. The Capitano enters in the hopes of encountering his new beloved.

10. FABRIZIO	*Isabella's brother, who also looks just like her, has come from Sicily to find his father. Capitano believes he is Isabella; Arlecchino, the same. Capitano amorously pleads with ["] her. ["] Fabrizio, indignant, thrusts his hand [draws his sword]. Capitano: that he does not fight women. And away. Arlecchino the same, and leaves. Fabrizio, to the tavern and inn of Burattino.*

The Capitano does not find Isabella but rather Fabrizio. His hope of encountering Isabella, together with Fabrizio's looks, leads him to believe that Fabrizio is Isabella. The only character to whom the ridiculous and eager Capitano manages to make amorous advances is male. The implied homoeroticism derides the Capitano. The sexual misidentification of both Fabrizio and Isabella throughout the rest of the scenario is, of course, a theatrical convention but not one that an audience would find at all hard to accept, because of the perceived androgyny of adolescents.[17] The secondary plot neatly serves as complication for the primary one. Again, Scala, evidently seeing the characters in his mind's eye, refers to them by the sex that they appear to be. He does not provide the accommodation to the reader provided by the quotation marks in this translation.

Fabrizio, one of the two main characters and the object of the scenario's second plot of misunderstanding (like the first, based on the confusion between appearance and reality), is not introduced until the middle of act 2. The reader is prepared for Fabrizio's appearance by the Argument. Unless the viewing audience is similarly informed about his return in a prologue, the entrance of this long-lost relative is completely unexpected, as it is in *Gl'ingannati.* Andrews points out that here, as in *Gl'ingannati,* Isabella and Fabrizio are played by a single performer. In both play and scenario this even bigger surprise is not revealed until Fabrizio's first appearance. We know that the roles were played by the same performer because the action is designed so that Fabrizio never appears onstage with Isabella and he does not appear onstage in the final scene of family reunion, reconciliation, and marriages as one would expect.

Unlike in the source play, where both twins are played by a single male, Fabrizio and Isabella in *The Jealous Isabella* are played by a female. This is altogether remarkable, for while women in other scenarios, like Isabella in this scenario, don the disguise of a male, they revert in the end to their real modest, subservient, female selves. In this case, not only is a woman on the stage, and portraying Isabella playing a man for a period of time, but she must convincingly establish her other character, Fabrizio, and retain it. Later in the scenario we are even explicitly invited to envision Fabrizio's male genitalia and then to imagine the actress's marriage as a male.

11. BURATTINO *[comes] outside, receives him, asking him from where he comes and who he is. Fabrizio explains everything to him, then goes inside. Burattino says that is [actually] Isabella, Pantalone's daughter, and that the wicked ways of the fathers often cause their children's ruin, and leaves to find Orazio.*

The audience can reasonably assume that Fabrizio will be made known to his father. We do not know when or how.

The audience is asked to recall what it has seen of Pantalone in act 1, thus tying together the dissolute behaviour of the father with what here appears to be, and then actually comes to be, the behaviour of the daughter. Dressing in men's clothes suggested whoredom.[18] Pantalone's vehement and loud denial at act 2, scene 2, prolonged thereafter, may indicate his own fear that he is indeed responsible for Isabella's apparent moral failings.

Naturally, the stranger stays in the inn; indeed he necessitates its presence, which Scala also skilfully makes use of at the beginning of the scenario. The innkeeper, Burattino, someone outside the action, is the ideal character to hear Fabrizio's account, provided for the audience, of who he is. Scala's specifying at scene 10 that Fabrizio has arrived from Sicily suggests that Fabrizio's narrative should include this information. It is logical that Burattino, having already understood Isabella's sexual frustration, discounts Fabrizio's story and takes him for Isabella dressed as a man and seeking sex. He believes that Orazio can save her from her frustration and thus from her inappropriate behaviour. Burattino makes the same point as did Graziano about how the wicked ways of the fathers are taken up by the children. Fathers should model the behaviour they hope for in their offspring.

12. ISABELLA *dressed as a man, having gotten the costume in a play which she and the other young girls had put on. She wanting to look for Orazio to prove to him that he is a traitor; sees her father coming; leaves.*

The actress playing Fabrizio just entered the inn. With the time provided by Burattino's discourse on Pantalone's bad habits, she can move to a new entrance. Isabella, in her first appearance into the street, enters from the house of her father, Pantalone. Twins constitute a kind of repetition, Isabella's disguise constitutes another, and so does the doubling of roles. Further, Isabella's disguise would have resonated with the cross-dressing of Carnival. The rapidity of the actress's transformation is central to its interest. It must be clear to the audience from her acting that she is now not the male Fabrizio but Isabella pretending to be a man. Her entrance from the house reinforces this distinction. The dual roles, as in *Gl'ingannati,* provide a star turn for the performer.

Art historian David Summers observes that of all the terms of praise used by authors writing in the early modern period, perhaps none is more frequent or more important than *difficultá.*[19] This term of admiration can be applied not only to visual artists but to the work of the actress and of Scala. The proximity of the scenes here, not present in the source play, draws our attention to the daring and skill of both. We are called on to admire the act of representation itself.

Fabrizio appears first because it is easier for the audience to accept the actress first as a man and then as Isabella playing a man, rather than the other way round. A quick costume change, not so great as to disabuse the characters of their confusion, would help the audience distinguish between the two. Seeing the characters in immediate succession would allow the audience to become aware of the distinction.

Scala's explanation of Isabella's means for obtaining the costume makes sense for a convent-educated girl, which she would surely have been as a motherless girl from a well-to-do family. In the convents the novices and the boarding-school girls, in particular, performed in plays including in male roles in male dress.[20]

Isabella dons the costume of a man so that, free from the woman's confines of the house and without being recognized, she can seek out Orazio and, as we shall see, defend her honour, as would a man in a duel. She is willing to risk her life for her honour.

Isabella's costume, like Fabrizio's or any gentleman's, includes a sword. Her disguise, even if not her skill at swordplay, gives her power and some measure of safety in the streets. Although her presence in the masculine domain of the streets in her mannish dress also signals to others that she is a loose woman, nothing could actually be further from her mind. Her sexual energy is turned towards revenge.

Women disguised as men appear in eighteen of Scala's scenarios. The actual donning of male disguise by courtesans, actresses, and those who were obliged to travel or were left on their own gave credibility to the stage convention.[21] Whether Scala intended it or not, the constructedness of Isabella's role as male, based on little more than dress, and her and the actress's success in playing it raise questions about the naturalness and inevitability of the social constructions of men's and women's "nature" and their relative placement in the gender hierarchy.

13. PANTALONE [PEDROLINO]	*asks Pedrolino what business he had with Orazio and with Flavio. Pedrolino makes excuses. Pantalone: that he wants to marry her to Graziano. Pedrolino reproaches him. He [Pantalone]: that he wants to do things his way; knocks.*

There is no indication that Pantalone was present at act 2, scene 8, the scene in which Pedrolino, Orazio, and Flavio are together. The audience was, of course, and so may naturally assume that Pantalone shares their knowledge of that scene. The audience is reminded that, when last seen, Pedrolino, Orazio, and Flavio were going to plot to save the situation. They evidently have not managed to do so.

We learn, finally, to whom Pantalone plans to marry Isabella. His choice of Graziano for Isabella threatens her happiness even more than she has herself. Given his low status, Pedrolino is not appropriately deferential in his resistance to the plan. Again, Carnival may allow him to breach the customary respect and deferential language expected of servants.[22] Pedrolino's sympathies are aligned with the young, and ours with them.

The knock on Graziano's door now serves as foreboding.

14. GRAZIANO *hears from Pantalone that he is offering him Isabella, along with the inheritance of all that is his, if his son Fabrizio never returns. [Fabrizio was] born at the same time as Isabella, [and was then taken away by one of his [Pantalone's] brothers about whom he never received any news. Graziano agrees; at that*

Not only is it the norm for a marriage to be arranged by the families, but Graziano is Pantalone's friend and an older man whose financial position is secure. Isabella's girlish passions are not to be a consideration in the marital arrangement, except in the urgency that Pantalone now feels to marry her off. Isabella's dowry would be quite small relative to the amount left for a son; Pantalone's offer is very attractive. His account of Fabrizio's history prepares us for the reunion of father and son.

15. BURATTINO *who has heard that Graziano is to be the bridegroom, makes fun of him and goes inside the house. Pantalone says that it would be appropriate [for Graziano] to touch hands with Isabella; at that*

Burattino, his search for Orazio unsuccessful, returns to the inn from the direction in which he went to seek him.

The holding of hands, signifying consent to marry, had to be witnessed by the consenting parents. In this case, the father, the only living parent, will be present. Because Isabella seems all too ready to marry someone other than Orazio, if she enters now, her fate with Graziano as husband may be all but sealed – unless Fabrizio is discovered. Burattino makes fun of the idea of Graziano as Isabella's husband. His ridicule makes clear how we are to regard the marriage arranged between the old man and the young girl and points to the unlikelihood of it.

The audience knows that in the scenarios, in marked contrast to actual cultural practice where marriages were arranged as matters of family financial and social security and advancement, young love will find a way. This persistent fantasy served as wish-fulfilment and, as Laura Giannetti argues for the earlier written comedy, as a critique of the social system.[23] Again, it does so whether or not this was Scala's intention.

16. BURATTINO *[comes back out and] says, laughing, that in the inn there is a lad who says he would like to speak to a Venetian. Pantalone: that he should tell him to come out, and sends Pedrolino to call Isabella. Pedrolino goes inside and returns saying Isabella is not in the house. Pantalone despairs*; at that*

Pantalone agrees to see the young man but, primarily intent on Isabella's marriage, he also sends for Isabella. Burattino, still believing that Fabrizio is Isabella, laughs in expectation of what Pantalone and Graziano will see of what the bride-to-be has become. The audience, knowing that Isabella and Fabrizio are played by one and the same actress, for a moment must wonder how the conflicting demands on the actress can be met. Our hope is that it is Fabrizio who will arrive and that his timely arrival will nullify the marriage agreement.

Pantalone, so jovial in act 1, now like Isabella and Orazio, despairs until the scenario's resolution. The despair in the scenario is set in contrast to the framing laughter.

17. BURATTINO [FABRIZIO] *shows the lad, Fabrizio, to Pantalone, who, believing ["] her["] to be Isabella, scolds him; the Doctor does the same; they try to catch ["]her["]; Fabrizio cries out for help; at that*

Fabrizio's call for help reminds us that the character is played by a female. It also leads even Orazio to believe that Fabrizio is a woman, his Isabella. The audience's hope that Fabrizio's arrival will nullify the marriage agreement is dashed.

18. ORAZIO *arrives; Fabrizio says: "Sir, free me from the hands of these people!" Orazio draws his sword; he makes them all run away. Fabrizio thanks Orazio, who, believing him to be Isabella, begs his forgiveness for the offences done to her without meaning to. Fabrizio laughs about this and [says] that he does not know him, and goes inside the inn. Orazio, in despair,* leaves,*

and here the second act ends.

It is important for Orazio to appear before the end of act 2 to remind the audience of the problem with which the scenario began and after which it is named. To Orazio's mind, he has not only saved Isabella but begged her pardon, and still she denies him. His case seems hopeless, not only because of Pantalone's plans for her but also because "she" treats him like this. This is an occasion that might elicit Pantalone's tears.

At the close of the act, Orazio is miserable; Isabella is intent on killing him; Pantalone has arranged for her to marry Graziano; Fabrizio has neither been recognized as who he is nor recognized by his father.

Until act 3, scene 10, everyone but the audience takes Fabrizio to be Isabella. The discovery of his identity is delayed as long as possible.

Third Act

1. CAPITANO [ISABELLA]	*complains to Isabella of having been insulted by her.* Isabella says that she has not seen him since she has been dressed in these clothes. Capitano goes on, then he hears from her that she is in these clothes because she wants to prove to Orazio that he is a traitor, asking him [Capitano] to convey a challenge to him [Orazio], promising him [Capitano], if she survives [the duel], to be his [Capitano's] wife. Capitano agrees;* she, [goes] away [planning] to return. Capitano remains.*

We have not seen Isabella since act 2, scene 12, when she went off to seek Orazio to show him what a traitor he is. So the time passed seems long, but there is no reason to think that much time, if any, has elapsed between acts 2 and 3. The whole of the action takes less than twenty-four hours.

Isabella has not found Orazio and enters from other than the house, likely from the direction in which she exited in search of him, in order to keep the story straight for the audience. Capitano enters, once again seeking Isabella. At act 2, scene 10, the hapless Capitano mistook Fabrizio for Isabella. Now he mistakes Isabella for Fabrizio.

If Isabella will not be forced to marry old Graziano, she arranges an even less suitable match for herself, as must be made clear by the Capitano's usual poverty and his endless hollow speech-making about his prowess, now probably also with women. He has become not merely comic relief but a plot complication.

2. FLAVIO *arrives; Capitano, seeing him, tells him to hold off, since there must be between them a word of truce for a few days until another difference has been resolved; he asks about his friend Orazio. Flavio: that he does not know. Capitano, huffing;* away. Flavio says he is troubled because Orazio told him that Isabella is dressed as a man; at that*

Delaying the confrontation between the Capitano and Orazio and allowing the Capitano more grandiosity to heighten our anticipation of this confrontation, Orazio does not enter now; rather Flavio does. The Capitano has reason to avenge himself against Flavio, who drew his sword on him at the end of act 1. Characteristically, however, and now that Isabella has held out the promise of marriage to him, he, not unreasonably, backs off the fight while bragging of his capabilities as a warrior. To our knowledge, Flavio has seen neither Orazio nor Isabella since act 2, scene 8, and in his limited role as the faithful friend he must be very concerned about them.

3. ARLECCHINO *arrives, and in an arrogant manner asks Flavio about his master. Flavio, seeing his rudeness, gives him a beating; at that*

4. FRANCESCHINA *reproaches Flavio for beating Arlecchino. Flavio, enraged, wants to give her [a beating] too. Arlecchino lifts her up and takes her away; Flavio remains.*

We have seen neither Arlecchino nor Franceschina for some while: Arlecchino since act 2, scene 9, and Franceschina since act 2, scene 3. It is good structurally that we see them again. This is the first time we see Arlecchino without the Capitano, so it is logical that he is in search of him. Arlecchino identifies with his master's supercilious ways. Franceschina reasserts her sauciness. Moreover, if she has described Isabella's behaviour in private in anything like the terms in *Gl'ingannati*, in the moral economy of the scenario she deserves at least this threat of a beating. (Servants are beaten; gentlemen engage in duels.) In any case, Flavio takes out his frustration on the lower class, which, indeed, is not appropriately subordinate.

The real reason for Arlecchino's presence without the Capitano, and this beating *lazzo,* which otherwise does nothing to further the action, is to allow the scene's surprising conclusion in which Arlecchino picks up Franceschina and carries her off. The conclusion prepares us for the subsequent sexual intercourse and marriage of Arlecchino and Franceschina. If there is any suggestion of a potential rape, that rape would hardly be regarded as criminal for the lower end of society.[24]

If Franceschina is played by a man, her being carried by Arlecchino is funnier; conventionally, men do not carry other men. Jean Howard has observed that "a man ... who theatricalizes the self as female, invites playing the woman's part in sexual congress."[25]

5. PANTALONE	*in despair about his daughter,* *[26] *sees Flavio and complains to him about Orazio having come to the aid of his daughter. Flavio makes excuses for Orazio and pleads with him to forgive Isabella; at that*
6. ISABELLA	*arrives; Pantalone sees her right away and, in a rage, asks her why she is dressed in those clothes. She boldly states that at one time, she was in love with Orazio, and that, because of a wrong that he has done her, she has put on these clothes in order to fight him with weapons. And away. Pantalone, weeping, begs Flavio to follow her and change her mind. Flavio away. Pantalone remains; at that*

The tension mounts; the action speeds up. Isabella enters immediately after she is discussed. Pantalone recognizes Isabella, who is disguised; he has not recognized Fabrizio, who is not disguised. Not only has Isabella taken to the streets alone and dressed in men's clothing and so is unsafe, she now speaks in a bold immodest manner that is wholly unbecoming to a girl and risks her life in a duel. While she believes that she is defending her honour, Pantalone believes that she is behaving licentiously, destroying the honour of the family. She has denied him his patriarchal control, possibly her life, and his consolidation of his social situation with the marriage that he has arranged for her. Pantalone speaks downstage of the inn, where he cannot see Fabrizio enter.

7. FABRIZIO	*comes out of the inn. Pantalone, not seeing him come out but seeing him later, believes he is Isabella and again begins to plead with ["]her["] not to start a fight. Fabrizio laughs at this, saying that he does not know him; at that*

Pantalone's preceding scene with Flavio allows plenty of time for the actress who is playing Isabella to exit, make a minor costume change, and then enter from the inn as Fabrizio.

If Pantalone, in his grief at scene 6, does mention the missing Fabrizio, Scala has Fabrizio, like Isabella, arrive pat to the occasion, but alas, speaking at cross-purposes, father and son, who are finally brought together after all these years, do not recognize one another. The patriarch is reduced to pleading.

8. PEDROLINO *reproaches Fabrizio, taking him for Isabella, saying to him that he should do as his father wishes. Fabrizio mocks him; at that*

While characters' exits are generally motivated by their action or character, in this scenario, and particularly in this act, characters arrive on the scene to suit the story. Here and at scene 9, Pantalone continues to be upset as the characters enter. Pedrolino likely enters from Pantalone's house; it is important whenever possible to aid the audience in keeping clear the relationships between characters. He joins the growing chorus of those mistaking Fabrizio for Isabella.

Having first inadvertently made things worse for Isabella and Orazio by trying to help them, and then having vowed to help Orazio and Flavio to solve the mounting problems, Pedrolino has evidently done nothing. Matters have deteriorated.

9. FLAMINIA *tells Fabrizio (mistaking) [him for Isabella] that, though she has good reason to be angry with her, because she does not like seeing her, as a woman, in those clothes that, if she does not want to go to her father's house, she should go with her [Flaminia] into her house. Fabrizio asks the old man if he agrees. Pantalone: [says] yes. And embracing, they go inside the house. Pantalone and Pedrolino leave to find Orazio and resolve the matter.*

Fabrizio is evidently immediately attracted to Flaminia. He has no need, otherwise, to join her. Such obvious attraction and the embrace signal what is to come. That Fabrizio asks Pantalone's permission to go with Flaminia into her house makes no sense unless he assumes that Pantalone is Flaminia's father, but it does allow Pantalone to inadvertently sanction his son Fabrizio's impending relationship with and marriage to Flaminia; it also makes clear Pantalone's desperately failing authority. He cannot get his daughter back into his house, so at least to get her safely off the street and to protect his honour he agrees to have "her" go inside with Flaminia. The weakening of his authority will, in the end, make him more accepting of Isabella's choice of Orazio.

10. BURATTINO	*who has seen everything, says that it would be a fine thing if that were a man; at that*

Scala neglects to specify when in the course of scene 9 Burattino entered. Coming from the inn, he is the logical person to anticipate that Fabrizio might be a man, because at act 2, scene 11, Fabrizio gave him a full account of the truth. The audience has seen Flaminio and Fabrizio embrace. The audience is also encouraged by Burattino's suspicion to imagine what might be going on between Flaminia and Fabrizio in the house. Throughout, Burattino is attuned to lust.

11. FRANCESCHINA ARLECCHINO	*quarrelling, since, having enjoyed Franceschina, he does not want to give her more than one lira. They make Burattino the judge who says that they should let him try the merchandise, that then he will set a price; at that*

The audience's expectation that Fabrizio's sexual identity will be discovered at this point is cleverly delayed by this scene in which we are invited to visualize a sexual entanglement, but between servants and perhaps between men. If between men, Arlecchino, would have a particularly strong reason not to meet the price; the audience could imagine Burattino, now blinded by lust, being similarly misled and disappointed.

Scala carefully set up this action at scene 4 where Arlecchino carried off Franceschina. It is not merely a *lazzo* imported from some other source, as it may seem. It allows time for the action offstage between Flaminia and Fabrizio, describes an action that is parallel to it, thus keeping sexual intercourse in focus, and further prepares us for the wedding of Arlecchino and Franceschina that specifically parallels in honour that of Flaminia and Fabrizio.

12. CAPITANO [ORAZIO] [FLAVIO]	*tells Orazio of Isabella's challenge. Orazio [is] enraged. Flavio steps in so that things can be resolved [by negotiation]. (Franceschina goes into the house; Arlecchino away; Burattino, into the inn.) Capitano: that they cannot be resolved [that way]; at that*

Still the audience does not find out what is happening behind closed doors between Flaminia and Fabrizio. The ridiculous Capitano, anxious to claim Isabella as his reward, intervenes.

Andrews posits that the exits of the lower-class characters, which Scala here specifies in parentheses, again too late for actors, were actually to precede the entrance of those in scene 12.[27] This makes sense because the scene with the servants needs to be crisply resolved: Franceschina exits in disgust; Arlecchino gets off without paying; and Burattino does not get to "try the merchandise." Further, their exit would be too distracting once scene 12 begins.

Flavio's role, as it has been throughout, is that of the faithful and reasonable friend.

13. FRANCESCHINA *comes outside, saying that Isabella has turned into a man; at that*

Finally, Scala yields to our curiosity. We do not know all that Franceschina says in addition to expressing the deep-seated fear that clothes do make the man, but Andrews calls attention to the fact that the description in *Gl'ingannati* is salacious.[28] It is worth quoting the serving woman in that play, Pasquella, at length:

> My mistress had the person down on the bed, and she called me to help her while she held his hands. And he was letting her win, so I opened the front of his clothes, and suddenly I felt something slap my hand, and I wasn't sure whether it was a large pestle or a big stick or that other thing. But whatever it was, it was in great shape. And when I saw how big it was, I took off, believe me, and locked the door behind me.[29]

We know that Franceschina is a woman who doesn't hold back and who's seen some. Laura Giannetti usefully terms recognitions like Franceschina's "phallic revelations/celebrations."[30]

Maggie Günsberg points to the fact that in *Gl'ingannati* the all-female dynamic introduces not only heterosexual female desire but also, in addition to the masturbation suggested by Pasquella (quoted in my commentary for act 2, scene 3), the possibility of lesbianism. She observes, however, that in that play the fact of male actors performing the roles diffuses this possibility and that it is even further diffused by the male voyeurs who provide commentary on the scene within. This, she observes, "is the classic patriarchal recuperation of lesbianism, a sexuality dangerously excluding male membership ... The dynamic of sexual desire is thus continually returned to the male domain and particularly that of homoeroticism."[31] In this scenario Graziano's voyeurism in the next scene, and perhaps Franceschina's if she is played by a male, is also. But the fact remains that the lovers within, Flaminio and Fabrizio, are played by women. If the scenario was written for Carnival, the imagined scene may be more excusable.

14. PANTALONE GRAZIANO *arrive; Franceschina tells Graziano of having found a lad embracing his daughter Flaminia. Pantalone tells Graziano that is Isabella his daughter in men's clothes. Graziano goes inside to see. Pantalone pleads with Orazio to calm Isabella; that he will give her to him as wife. Capitano: that such a thing cannot be; at that*

We are left to imagine what Graziano sees. Meanwhile, so desperate has Pantalone become about his daughter's behaviour that, with Graziano safely offstage, he offers her to Orazio. Pantalone's disagreeable choice of the lecherous old and perhaps pedantic Graziano and the unjust treatment of the faithful Orazio make us wish for Orazio's success. But a conflict between Graziano and Pantalone looms. And Isabella still will not accept Orazio as a husband. Her promise to marry the Capitano, made without the authority of her father, cannot be taken seriously. The Capitano, with his pretensions, is again a nuisance.

15. FABRIZIO GRAZIANO *come out of the [Graziano's] house [both] yelling at the same time. Fabrizio: that he is a man and the son of Pantalone de'Bisognosi, taken away as a child by his uncle, whose death has caused him to come to see if his father lives. Pantalone with great happiness recognizes him. Capitano says he is going [to look] for Isabella. Fabrizio goes inside to touch the bride's hand; and goes inside. Pantalone again pleads with Orazio to appease Isabella; at that*

Graziano enters, yelling about his discovery that there is a man with his daughter. Fabrizio enters, probably hastily trying to reassemble his clothing. Whether, after his original account to Burattino, Fabrizio was so beset that he could not provide the account of himself again, it is critical to our pleasure that the recognition and joyful reunion of father and son have been delayed until now and that, meanwhile, matters have been complicated.

Fabrizio's apparent double entrance into the house suggests the possibility of his bringing Flaminia to the doorway so that the couple can touch hands in this transitional or liminal space in view of both elders and then of their going into Graziano's house. The premarital sex is overlooked because marriage follows it. This ending for the subplot would be dramatically satisfying and would make sense in the culture, but Scala does not mention Flaminia's appearance.

16. PEDROLINO *arrives, saying that the Capitano is bringing Isabella, resolute in wanting to do battle with Orazio. Pantalone despairs; at that*

Isabella's story has yet to be resolved. The entrance of Pedrolino only to announce that of Isabella and the Capitano gives additional time for the actress to enter as Isabella in the next scene and builds anticipation for her intended fight with Orazio. That it is the Capitano who brings her and Orazio to the same place, as he was charged to do by Isabella in order to marry her, heightens the idea that Isabella will continue to resist Orazio and marry the Capitano.

17. ISABELLA [CAPITANO] *immediately upon arrival draws her sword against Orazio, calling him traitor. Orazio throws himself onto his knees, telling her that he has not erred. She reminds him of the amorous words spoken to Franceschina, and he tells her that he said them in jest to tease the maidservant. Franceschina confesses how she mimicked Isabella's voice at the window and that she did all of this to annoy her. Flavio and all plead with Isabella to forgive Orazio; she, accepting his explanation, agrees to forgive him and to take him as husband. Capitano blusters, saying that Isabella is his by her own word. Orazio grasps his sword, saying whoever wishes to take Isabella, will have to take his life first. Capitano calms down. Orazio marries Isabella; Arlecchino, having enjoyed her, [marries] Franceschina; all say that they will go [inside to] visit Fabrizio, Isabella's brother, returned to his homeland; and they all go inside Graziano's house for the nuptials,*

and here the comedy ends.

Everyone has now been brought onstage for the resolution of Isabella's jealousy, all but Fabrizio and Flaminia. No gentleman can attack a man on his knees, so the anticipated fight is quickly averted. Franceschina evidently feels that she has done enough to get even for the way Isabella treated her, and, anyway, comedy characteristically does not belabour its ending. The primary misunderstanding that has motivated the action is cleared up. The recognition of Fabrizio intertwines the two plot lines, absolves Pantalone of his promise of Isabella to his friend Graziano, and at the same time lets Graziano down easy; his family will still inherit all of Pantalone's wealth except for Isabella's dowry. Thus, his daughter has a good match. Pantalone is happy to get his son back and grateful to have Isabella safely off the streets and his honour saved. Orazio's absolute fidelity, evidenced by his willingness to give even his life for Isabella, proves his worthiness and is rewarded. The Capitano, with some unexpected final bluster, disrupts the impending, and now seemingly inevitable, happy resolution. The disruption or threatened complication is only momentary; not surprisingly, the cowardly Capitano, faced with determined, more youthful, and vigorous opposition, backs down. His retreat is undoubtedly accomplished with some preposterous boast. Castiglione emphasized the need for a soldier's physical courage: "Just as once a woman's reputation for purity has been sullied it can never be restored, so once the reputation of a gentleman-at-arms has been stained through cowardice ... even if only once, it always remains defiled in the eyes of the world and covered with ignominy."[32]

The actress playing Isabella must turn to love from the jealousy and anger that are violent enough to kill. Isabella reverts finally to conventional womanhood and becomes a wife, indeed perhaps a more loving wife than she would otherwise have been; it was oddly believed that her affection was increased by her suspicion of her beloved. In this sense, there is character development. Isabella may have indicated her transformation by covering the breeches, in which she disguised herself as a male in the middle of act 2, with a skirt.[33]

Servants are commonly paired at the end of Scala's comic scenarios. In this case, Franceschina is made an honourable woman. It seems to be simply assumed that that is what she would want.

Isabella takes up the role of the good wife, but she has, in a small way, rewritten her role within the patriarchy. Nothing bad has come of her having dressed in men's clothing, spoken in public, stood up to her father, moved freely about the streets, or having acted on her own initiative, however misguided. In effect, the audience has witnessed a dramatized debate between the traditional and the evolving notion of women.[34]

We do not see Isabella reunited with her brother. And at the conclusion the audience continues to know something that the characters do not. The actress's role as Fabrizio necessarily remains intact within Graziano's house. The rule of the fourth-century drama theorist Evanthius that at the end everything should be made known to everyone is violated. The patriarchal recuperation of the role that Günsberg observes in *Gl'ingannati* is not provided.

The exit of eleven characters through a door or even a curtain takes time and lacks the appropriate dynamic. For this reason, here and in other scenarios with the same ending, the final exits were probably accompanied by dancing, acrobatics, and singing.

The pedant who delivers the epilogue to Vergilio Verucci's *Li diversi linguaggi*, 1627, a play for amateur performance written in imitation of *commedia dell'arte*, declares that parents of marriageable children should not intervene by arranging marriages of convenience between young women and older men, as the old men in that play attempted to do.[35] There is no indication of whether or not *The Jealous Isabella* was followed by an epilogue. It might have been observed, as in many another Italian fiction, that faithfulness in love, at least for males, is a virtue rewarded.[36]

I have shown both the care with which the scenario was constructed and the extent to which it represented the culture of its time. The scenario, quite apart from its performance, makes clear what would have interested its contemporary audience.

chapter eight

Day 36: Isabella [the] Astrologer

The genre to which *Isabella Astrologa* belongs, *commedia grave*, was developed by playwrights in the latter half of the sixteenth century, notably by Sforza Oddi and Giambattista Della Porta. They borrowed from the romances and *novelle* of the period to show heroic intent, tragic potential, and exalted self-sacrifice. They began with an unhappy situation that was attributed to fortune and typically subjected their strong female heroines to various trials and adventures, throughout which they exhibited their constancy in love. Consistent with the relative seriousness of the scenario, the plot unravelling depends not on trickery but on the resourcefulness of an extremely capable woman; on benevolence; and, more than in other of the scenarios I have examined here, on Divine Providence, which provides escape from a near tragic end. *Commedia grave* plays, like this scenario, could feature upper-class characters generally within the purview of tragedy. In his second prologue to *Prigione d'Amore* (*Love's Prison*), 1589, Sforza Oddi provided the rationale for this mixed genre: "In the bitterness of tears there is yet hidden the sweetness of delight; and I who wish in every way to give delight often make thus a most lovely mixture of both tears and laughter, and the bitterness of weeping makes more joyous the sweetness of laughter."[1]

The same rationale seems to lie behind *Isabella Astrologa.* The tone is very different from that of the other scenarios whose actions I have reconstructed. More than any other of the scenarios in the collection it incorporates the business of a city, and one with international trade. It is necessarily set in its specified locale. In a number of the comedies in the latter part of the collection, as I have suggested, Scala seems more experimental than in those in the earlier part. At the same time that this scenario seems to be a considerable departure from those earlier in the collection, its structure is at times mechanical, motivated by dramatic convenience rather than by the story. Perhaps it was envisioned as a one-time extravaganza to be funded and performed, as Andrews suggests, before a princely court.[2] It aligns that court, probably Spanish, with Divine Providence, judicial restraint, personal forgiveness, peace, and harmony.

Day 36
Isabella [the] Astrologer

COMEDY

Argument

In Naples a most noble gentleman from Spain named Lucio Cortesi held the office of the Regent of the Vicariate. He had a most noble daughter named Isabella with whom a gentleman, called Orazio Gentili, fell in love. It happened that her brother (whose name was Flavio) became aware of the courtship he was paying to his sister, therefore, overcome and moved by the greatness of Spain and by honour, he had thoughts of attacking him in the night and killing him; on the other side, the young Orazio had the same thought; and, encountering each other one night, they attacked each other; in this brawl Flavio was left wounded, [taken for] dead and thrown into the sea; by twist of fate he saved himself, and for shame he went off lost in the world, wandering for a long time. The aforementioned Orazio was caught by the [forces of the] law and condemned to death; and, while awaiting death, Isabella, daughter of the said Regent, who was in love with him, saved him with the help of the prison guard, and ordered him to prepare a frigate, with which she intended to escape with him. The unlucky lover went and, preparing everything, stayed in the frigate waiting for his woman to come with the guard, when, he was brought out to sea by a sudden storm; he was made a slave by pirates from the Barbary coast, and brought to Algiers; then hearing this news caused the grief-stricken lover to desperately board a ship, whose sails at that point were unfurling towards Alexandria of Egypt; having arrived there, she set about being a servant to a very great Arab philosopher and astrologer, who lived there; and because she was much inclined towards speculative matters, and [already] understood some of its principles, in not much time she learned a large part of the true astrology.

Flavio, after he found himself thrown into the sea by his enemy Orazio, supporting himself on top of a piece of wood, was driven by a sudden storm from the shore into the sea, and, found by pirates, he was made a slave, and he too was brought to Alexandria, and there was purchased from these same pirates by a very rich Alexandrian merchant. Flavio was liked by the daughter of the said Arab astrologer, who lived in a villa near that of his master; and such was their love that he, having secret relations with her, got her pregnant. It happened that the said merchant abruptly decided to board a ship from Alexandria going to Naples, to trade merchandise, and with him he brought Flavio, who was not able, as he [had] wished, to say goodbye to the young Turkish woman. The young woman seeing herself at that point abandoned and betrayed, spoke to the said Isabella, who was her friend – and from her [Isabella] hearing how, because of her master's [the astrologer's] death, she wanted to go to Italy, she entreated her to be so kind as to take her along. So agreed, having left and having arrived in Italy, after much time they get to Naples, [with] Isabella meanwhile, like a perfect astrologer, practising the art of astrology. Orazio arrived in Naples (and almost at the same time); [he was] captured by the galleys of Naples, while he went along with his master plundering the seas. For fear of the law, he said he was Turkish, nor did he wish for freedom. Finally, after many twists and turns of the tale, we reach a very fortunate and happy end.

The scenario's long Argument is very complicated, and its overlong sentences and organization make it hard to follow. Part of the difficulty may be that, unlike in the scenarios where the Argument explains a sequential action, the Argument in this case tries to relate in linear fashion the two strands of action that happened simultaneously.

The Argument is also not altogether self-consistent. In the first paragraph Scala states that after Flavio attempted to murder Orazio in order to preserve the family honour and failed, for shame he went off, lost in the world and wandering about. In the second paragraph we are told, instead, that he was immediately found by pirates and enslaved.

While the time that passes in the scenario is very short, the time that passes in the Argument is long. Its various parts need to be narrated piecemeal by different characters at specified points in the scenario, and this suggests that the audience was interested in narrative form as well as in drama. Spavento's windy tales in other scenarios, as well as other narratives to be supplied at indicated points in other scenarios, also testify to the audience's interest in narrative. Commenting on the comedies of Aretino, Andrews observes, "It is a commonplace to say that Renaissance rhetoric made a large contribution in Renaissance dramaturgy: perhaps we should consider whether on some occasions a dramatic spectacle was really a disguised form of rhetoric."[3] In this scenario it is, but the spectacle is itself striking and provides a kind of grandeur and ceremony that would befit a presentation before dignitaries.

We do not know that the scenario was, in fact, ever presented. If it was, it had to have been funded by someone very wealthy and probably for a single occasion, perhaps in Naples, where it is set – a city, the scenario suggests, with which Scala had some familiarity. The scenario requires a very large number of extras (who would have to have been carefully rehearsed), their costumes, a singular set with a fine palace expressly rendered in perspective, and a suitably grand chair. This is one of the few scenarios in which, as in *The Jealous Old Man*, seating for characters is specified.

Naples was under direct Spanish rule from 1503 to 1707. It was not mandatory that the Regent of the Vicariate in Naples, the judicial official presiding over the main court in the kingdom, be Spanish, but in practice he likely was.[4] Orazio's attentions to the Regent's daughter were out of bounds, not only for the usual reason that their courtship was not authorized by her father but also because, in this case, the woman is from the Spanish ruling class. Characteristically, Orazio is Italian and upper middle class. Flavio perceived that the honour of his family was threatened by Orazio's secret courtship of his sister, not only because it lacked parental approval but also because marriage was regarded as a tool for the social advancement of the family and a means for the exchange of material resources. He must have had words with Orazio, words that led Orazio to believe that his honour too was threatened. The code of honour required that threats to honour be avenged.

After the murderous encounter between Orazio and Flavio, through many coincidences that Scala takes pains to explain, their fates run parallel: both Neapolitans have been separated from their true loves and both live under assumed names – one as a slave to an Alexandrian merchant; the other, first as a galley slave on a Barbary pirate ship, and then, pretending to be "Turkish, " in the galleys of Naples, part of the Spanish fleet that operated primarily out of Naples and Sicily. Flavio and Orazio were both picked up by galleys near the coast. The large number of men needed to outfit galleys required that they hug the coast in order to be able to stop repeatedly to take on water and food.[5]

In 1600, in Algiers, where Scala specified that Orazio was brought, there were thirty thousand to forty thousand Christian slaves, of whom perhaps a third to a half were Italian.[6] Although the Barbary slavers ranged most widely and employed the most sophisticated of means, virtually everybody in the sixteenth-century Mediterranean was trying to enslave some other group. Christians took Muslims in numbers that were comparable to those of their Muslim counterparts.[7] Muslim and sub-Saharan African slaves were common in southern Italy, the majority, like Christian slaves, being victims of piracy or warfare. Most male slaves served as rowers on galleys, along with convicts and a few others desperately in need of any form of employment. The powerful Spanish fleet required vast numbers of rowers. In the seventeenth century, between 20 and 30 per cent of the crews of the galleys of Spanish Italy were slaves. Female slaves, relatively less numerous, served as domestic help.[8]

When Orazio and Flavio return to Naples at the same time, coincidentally their loves, Isabella and Rabbya, also arrive. However, Isabella does not appear as she did when she was last in Naples; she has become an astrologer, having learned part of the true astrology (*vera astrologia*). Astrology, the means for determining the nature of the alliance between the events on earth and the stars, was seen as key to predicting fortune and was widely accepted. But much of astrology came in conflict with the Church. The belief that the destiny of human beings was irrevocably governed by the position or pattern of stars and planets was inconsistent with the doctrine of free will, the belief in Divine Providence, including the influence of Divine Grace, and the value of intercessory prayer. It left no way for the Church to teach moral responsibility, to promise eternal rewards, or to threaten eternal punishments.

Under Pope Pius IV, the Council of Trent in 1564 produced an index of banned books on astrology. More leniently, the papal bull of Sixtus V in 1586 repudiated all books on judicial astrology, that is, astrology that dealt with the influence of the stars and planets upon human events, declaring that God alone knew the future. The Church permitted only natural astrology, that is, opinions and natural observations written in the interest of navigation, agriculture, or medical art. In practice, the distinction between the two was not clear cut, and judicial astrology continued to penetrate deeply into the lives of most people, including some popes. As Lynn Thorndike observes, even the bull of 1586 inadvertently signalled that the force of the stars on humans was fact, by affirming that each human soul has a guardian angel to aid it against the stars.[9] The more lenient *Index librorum prohibitorum* of 1596 allowed books containing judicial astrology by Christians, provided they were corrected or expurgated in so far as they claimed that contingent future events in human lives were certain, even in cases where the author denied that he was making any claim of certainty. Books on judicial astrology by pagan authors, the ones that would have been the source of Isabella's learning, curiously enough, were permitted.[10] Thus the Neapolitan dramatist Giambattista Della Porta in the preface to his tragedy *Ulisse*, 1614, ducked the prohibition with the following defence:

> The present tragedy is performed by pagans. Therefore one finds in it the following words: fate, destiny, luck, fortune, the force and compulsion of the stars, gods, etc. This has been done to accord with their ancient customs and rites. The latter, however, according to the Catholic religion, are all folly since one must attribute all outcomes and events to our Blessed Lord, the supreme and universal cause.[11]

We cannot know how much Scala knew about changing Church doctrine. We know that in other of the scenarios he played it safe, steering wide of anything that might in any way offend the Church. In Day 26, Flaminia, disguised as a gypsy, pretends to read in Pedrolino's palm what she has secretly overheard. Similarly, in Day 32, Pedrolino claims to identify Flavio by means of fortune telling, when in fact he has just overheard Flavio speak his own name.

In *Isabella [the] Astrologer* almost all of the knowledge that Isabella attributes to her special powers appears to be a function of her common sense. There seems to me a distinct possibility that a number of scenes in which she claims to have extraordinary knowledge are meant to be comic. She is never called upon to predict the future. The action of the play in no way depends upon her professed skills in astrology. The turns in the Argument and the scenario are determined by a number of forces that were given great credence in the sixteenth century: Fortune, Love (here that of Orazio, Isabella, and Flavio), and Reason, a force "more powerful than Fortune" (that of Pedrolino and, more importantly, of Isabella).[12] The resolution depends upon forgiveness, grace, and finally on the force regarded as the most powerful: Divine Providence.

Characters in the Comedy

The REGENT of the Vicariate
FLAMINIA daughter
PEDROLINO servant with
many other servants

GRAZIANO physician
CINTIO his son

Turkish MERCHANT from Alexandria
MEMMII his slave, then FLAVIO, son
of the Regent
< *Turkish SERVANTS* >

ISABELLA Astrologer, then daughter
of the Regent, under the Turkish name
HAUSSÁ

RABBYA, a Turkish girl, her companion,
with a newborn baby

AGUZZINO overseer of galley slaves
of the galleys of Naples
AMETT slave, in the end, Orazio
Turkish SLAVES eight in number
CAPTAIN of the galley

ALECCHINO pimp, alone

< *COPS* >

NAPLES

Properties for the Comedy

Slave costumes and iron chains

Barrels for water, eight

A fine chair for the Regent
A fine palace in perspective on
stage with its colonnade,
and the chair off to one side

Graziano's role can be played by
Pantalone

The translation provided here differs in significant respects from that of Andrews.[13] In the cast of characters we have left untranslated the name Aguzzino, much as we have left untranslated the names given in the Argument, Cortesi, meaning kind and gracious, and Gentile, meaning courteous and kind. *Aguzzino* can mean either the overseer of galley slaves or a (usually cruel) jailer. *Galere* is here translated as "galley." Only later, when galleys were no longer in use, did it come to mean "jail";

elsewhere (act 2, scene 12) Scala uses the word *carcere* for jail. As I show, information about the use of jails at the time and the story itself require that *galere* mean "galley." Accordingly, and again because the logic of the story requires it, we take *Capo,* later referred to as *Capitano di galera,* to mean "Captain of the Galley." In Andrews's translation he is the governor of the prison. Andrews takes *Capo della galera* listed in the cast of characters and the *guardino* in the Argument to be one and the same. We do not. Our choices have depended on close reading of the scenario and, as will become clear, on cultural history.

The Regent is the only political personage to appear in a comic Scala scenario, and he is safely presented as a very dignified and reasonable person, a far remove from the laughable Capitano Spavento, who in other of the scenarios is the hungry and haughty Spaniard swaggering as a noble cavalier over the peninsula. The Spanish ship captain, who makes only a brief appearance, is all business. The merchant from Alexandria is no Pantalone but rather an upstanding and gracious man, not withstanding his keeping of Orazio as a slave and his desire for a prostitute. Neither would have been a source of disapproval. The aversion and animosity that mercantile activities prompted in the past, inviting performers to make Pantalone a figure of fun, are not in play. In 1585 Spain signed a peace treaty with the Ottoman Empire, but whether at war or at peace, the extensive and highly profitable trade between Italy and the Ottoman Empire continued, often on very friendly terms.[14] An Alexandrian merchant would have been a familiar and desirable figure in Naples.

This is the only comic scenario in which Pantalone does not appear. Perhaps it is for this reason that Scala specifies that the role of Graziano can be played by Pantalone. Evidently either mask would do. At the lower end of the social spectrum, Scala represents the only pimp in his collection. There are also slaves. Altogether, it is clear that in this scenario Scala does not confine himself to imitating the actions of private citizens of moderate social rank, their servants, and children. Contrary to Aristotle's dictum, the characters do not appear to be worse than those in ordinary life: Pedrolino is a loyal servant; Graziano has a serious role.

Four important new characters are created: a Spanish dignitary (the Regent), an Alexandrian merchant, the Turkish woman Rabbya, and the captain of the Spanish galley. This is one of Scala's two comic scenarios in which a baby appears.

Isabella, very different from the Isabella in, say, *The Fake Sorcerer,* works to support herself and manipulates the plot. Arlecchino, in a minor role as a pimp, is an independent literate contractor.

The list of properties makes clear that Scala, at least for this scenario, envisioned scenery using perspective painting.

First Act

1. AGUZZINO [SLAVES] [AMETT, SLAVE]	*comes with the galley slaves to get water from the well of the palace of the Regent, sends the slaves in to get water, and remains with Amett [who is really Orazio] sitting on top of two barrels; asks the slave why he sighs every time they come to that palace to get water and stays reluctantly. Amett tells him that in Algiers he had a friend, named Orazio, who was a slave because of Love. Several times he [the friend] had told him the story of his misfortune; here he tells all that had happened [to him], as is written in the argument of the fable, adding that he sighs out of pity for his friend. Aguzzino: that he remembers that case, which happened many years ago. Amett then tells how the said Orazio died. Aguzzino: that it would be good to give this news to the father of the one who had been killed by Orazio, because they would get a tip out of it; at that*

The entrance and then, in the next scene, the exit of a chorus of eight slaves in chains and carrying barrels provide an arresting frame for the long narration during which the speaking characters are seated and thus rather static. Visually striking entrances and exits substitute for dramatic action and, along with the narrations and seated figures, establish a measured ceremonial pace. Each of the first five scenes entails entrances and exits of either multiple slaves or servants. Remarkably, no action begins until scene 10 and then only in the tertiary plot. Urgent action only comes into play at the end of the second act.

Maps of Naples from 1550 and 1572 show the urban area of Naples all very close to the shore. The bay would have been a presence from much of the town.[15] An actual castle, Castel Nuovo, was very near the port (see figure 8.1).[16] At the time Scala wrote, it served as an important military fortress, did not have the colonnade specified by Scala for the Regent's palace, and would have been too vast (even without the pictorial exaggeration in figure 8.1) for the palace of the Regent, but its location may have been suggestive to Scala. It would have been a logical place for a galley of Naples, as part of the Spanish fleet harboured there and directly under Spanish control, to get water.[17]

In Roman drama, the entrance to the harbour and foreign parts was

8.1 Tavola Strozzi, *View of the City of Naples in Italy from the Sea, 1470* (depicting the naval victory of Alfonso V of Aragon over John of Anjou). Museo di San Martino, Naples. Public domain.

stage left, and the entrance to the city proper was stage right.[18] It is impossible to know whether Scala was familiar with this convention and employed it here, but his scenarios do show that he carefully visualized offstage spaces and thus would have had some such means of defining them for the actors and the audience.

Orazio is enslaved by and as a result of Love. His determination to find Isabella, like hers to find him, is long-standing. He evidently is not enchained and has not been assigned the hard labour of the other galley slaves but is, rather, at liberty to sit and talk. Scala motivates his long exposition by Aguzzino's query about his sighs. Given the small-town quality of life in even large Italian cities, and the facility with which gossip spread,[19] Aguzzino would have known about the fight between Flavio and Orazio, about Orazio's escape from the law, and about the storm that brought the frigate out to sea. Breaking up Orazio's narration, Aguzzino can tell, reiterate, or enhance those parts of the story and make clear the relationship of Flavio to the Regent. His interest in the story, to "get a tip out of it," promptly arrests the sadness of the tale and the tone of its delivery and shows that he does not realize that Amett is Orazio.

If the audience is not enabled to deduce or know in advance that Amett is Orazio, the scenario seems to me seriously diminished. The scenes that follow from Orazio's story about his own death must be appreciated at the time of their performance and not just in retrospect, otherwise the audience can take no pleasure in his disguise and indeed would feel deceived by him and by Scala. What means Amett might use to convey the information that he is Orazio is not clear. We cannot rule out the possibility that at least this part of the Argument was provided in a prologue.

In the second half of the sixteenth century there was an increased interest in comedy that included stories of lost children, pirate raids, shipwrecks, abductions, the misfortunes of war, abandoned lovers, presumed deaths, and the exotic people discovered in the course of maritime exploration and commerce. Similar increasing interest in such misadventure and travel is revealed in Scala's scenarios, and when, as here, the misadventures are central to the action, they tend to darken its tone.

2. SLAVES *return with the barrels full of water, and all together with Aguzzino as guard they go to the galleys, away.*

The sad narration is long enough for the slaves to have filled the water barrels.

3. ALEXANDRIAN MERCHANT [MEMMII HIS SLAVE] [TURKISH SERVANTS]	*lets Memmii, his slave, know that he wants to leave for Alexandria in two days, having purchased beautiful fabric of silk and gold, and that he wants to take the ship from Ragusa [Dubrovnik] which is to leave soon, and that he [Memmii should] make a list of typical things from Naples to be used as gifts in Alexandria, and away with the servants. Memmii, left alone, says that this is his native land, [and that] he does not want to reveal himself to his [family] because they would forbid his return to Alexandria, where he left his beloved though [she is] Turkish; at that*

It seems unlikely that any of the men just having exited in chains, carrying barrels, could readily reappear as servants following a costume change, particularly because the space they would take up in exiting suggests that the Merchant and his entourage would enter from the opposite side of the stage.

That the Merchant, again in a sudden departure, intends to board a ship from Dubrovnik makes clear that the port of Naples was of enormous commercial and maritime importance[20] and that Scala intended to represent it as such. The Merchant's urgency suggests that there is urgency to the action although neither we nor Flavio (Memmii) know that Flavio's love is in Naples and that in leaving Naples, he would be leaving her. The captain likely exits towards the ship, ostensibly to see to his departure and to allow the number of people in the next scene to enter from the city side, laden with goods.

The typical things from Naples that a merchant might seek as gifts included velvets, laces, braids, frills, trimmings, light fabrics, fine linens, and silk clothes.[21] Memmii is a trusted slave who, having come from an upper-class family, can read and write.

In this narration, barely separated from the one that opened the scenario, the audience learns that Memmii is Flavio in disguise, alive and present in Naples. That he would logically experience internal conflict about being a slave in his native land where he is comfortably the son of a high-ranking dignitary makes the monologue more interesting than would mere exposition, and motivates it. We are set to anticipate the meeting of the mortal enemies, Orazio and Flavio.

It is difficult to determine whether or not the character addresses the audience directly. Apart from a single sentence at the end of act 2 in

Day 37, Scala's comic scenarios provide no clear evidence of direct address (see p. 276 note 59). Plautus used direct address; Terrence did not. Andrews demonstrates that in the learned comedy, which *commedia dell'arte* imitated, Donatus's prohibition of direct address was not strictly followed.[22]

4. PEDROLINO [SERVANTS] *buyer for the Regent, with servants loaded with stuff, he sends them into the palace, then he is interrogated by the slave and asked if the father of a certain Flavio, called Lucio Cortesi, [the] Regent, is alive, and if a sister of his [Flavio], named Isabella, lives. Pedrolino is surprised, he tells him he [the Regent] is alive, but that the sister ran away from Naples, nor have they ever been able to get news [of her]. The slave tells him that he had known Flavio in Alexandria, and that he is alive; at that*

Now comes another procession of men carrying things. At least in this instance there has clearly been time enough for the slaves, or some of them, to reappear here as servants, probably from the opposite side of the stage in order to represent more clearly the new characters. Pedrolino must identify the palace of the obviously wealthy Regent and his own role relative to the Regent. Having introduced Orazio and his story, and Flavio and his, the latter by means of a response to Flavio's query, Scala now introduces the Regent and explains in yet another long narration the events that caused Isabella to leave the country. Flavio must surreptitiously be relieved that his father is alive and disturbed that his sister has run off.

5. MERCHANT [SERVANTS] *arrives and, seeing Pedrolino speaking with his slave, he asks him what his profession is. Pedrolino: that he is a pimp. Merchant: that he find him a beautiful Spanish courtesan. Pedrolino promises. Merchant, away with Memmii and servants. Pedrolino stays, unsure whether he should tell the Regent about Flavio or not; at that*

In another scene with an entourage, the Merchant returns with his servants. Scala provides a comic break from the long, sad narrations. Pedrolino, in his only and little trick, misleads the Alexandrian merchant into thinking that he is a pimp. The Merchant wants the best of prostitutes, a courtesan, and a Spanish one at that. Nothing comes of this request, but

Arlecchino and his business are introduced by means of it, and later another character does make use of Arlecchino's services. Arlecchino turns out to be a character with whom a significant number of the characters interact, thus providing one of the means that make the actions cohere.

Pedrolino's uncertainty about whether to report to the Regent that Flavio is alive may tell us something about the Regent's present state of mind regarding his son's supposed death and lead us to anticipate his learning that he is alive.

6. ARLECCHINO *professional pimp. Pedrolino asks him for the courtesan for the merchant. Arlecchino names a number of courtesans from different countries, having written them all down on a list, and [says] that when it gets late, he will give him a very beautiful one; on condition that Pedrolino get him permission from the Regent for him to go around at night without a light; so agreed, Pedrolino, in[to] the palace; Arlecchino, praising the art of the pimp, leaves.*

Conveniently, an actual procurer appears, presumably from his place of business, to establish it as such for the audience. His place of business would not have been distinguished from other houses. Dianne Ghirardo explains that

> everything about both the activity [of prostitution] and its settings revealed constant and irresolvable contradictory impulses. At once shameful and endemic, officially unacceptable but a useful complement to the imperative of female chastity, prostitution was both an everyday activity that blended almost seamlessly with the rest of civic life and the most readily available scapegoat for a variety of social, economic, and cosmological ills.[23]

The procurer's brothel, although inconspicuously intermixed with other dwellings, would have been located not far from the market or some other good business location, like the port.

One of the few successful activities for entrepreneurs in Spanish Naples was prostitution, owing particularly to the influx of Spanish troops and the destitution of the urban poor, although prostitutes frequently came from elsewhere in search of both work and anonymity. Thus, a list of prostitutes in Rome included names like Antonia Fiorentina, Francesca Ferarese, and Narda Napolenta.[24] Such names on Arlecchino's list would have added to the actor's comic turn. He might also have added prices as in the famed *Catalogo di tutte le principale et più honorate cortigiane di Venezia*, 1565.[25] One contemporary observer commented that the freedom the prostitutes had to live in Naples meant that they were much in evidence, including in the best streets and squares, and had come from all over the world.[26] Arlecchino very likely dealt in common prostitutes, however he may have referred to them.[27]

Prostitutes generally worked under male protectors.[28] Arlecchino, the businessman, provides a list of goods of another sort than that the Merchant has asked Flavio to make. The repeated showing or mention of goods and services and the processions of their bearers give coherence to the scenario and suits the port city.

Arlecchino's praise of the art of pandering may lend itself to song. Again, we do not know whether the speaker directly addresses the audience. His doing so would increase the lightness that his scene adds to the scenario. He leaves, presumably looking for new "stuff" (*robbe*) for his shop, as we see in scene 8.

7. *ISABELLA [RABBYA]*	*dressed in Syrian style, acting as an astrologer, with the Turkish woman her companion, and her son in swaddling clothes, narrates to her companion how she still carries within her the memory of her [Rabbya's] father – most perfect astrologer among the Arabs, from whom she learned the art of astrology – and how before his death he made her an astronomical chart, telling her that he had learned [from it] that she would return to her native land and be happy and content, but that so far this has not yet come to pass; telling her [Rabbya] again the story of her misfortune, as it is written in the argument of the fable, and lastly she tells her how she too will be happy one day, although she [Rabbya] has never wanted to tell her who the father of the child was. Rabbya: that one day she will know; at that*

The male lovers have been introduced one at a time, one in a dialogue, one in a monologue. Scala now introduces the two women together along with Rabbya's male child, the women's relationship, and the story of Isabella's misfortune. The narrations of extreme events have the added appeal of their narrators' being in disguise as slaves or as an astrologer. The narrations have been punctuated by Aguzzino's suggestion of an action at the end of scene 1, by Pedrolino's pretending to be a pimp, by a real pimp, by processions of slaves and servants, and by a "Turkish" woman carrying a baby. These breaks in the narration of the primary action add activity and vividness to the city, and they add comedy to the otherwise, thus far, slow-moving scenario. Along with the narrations, and perhaps Rabbya's withholding of information, to add a little suspense, these seem easily sufficient to hold an audience's attention for the time being.

What the astrologer told Isabella and now what she tells Rabbya, namely, that each would be happy one day, may depend as much on faith and hope as on astrology. The promised happiness, as Isabella reminds us, has yet to come to pass. However, the playwright, the real fortune-teller, here reliably foretells that the sad predicaments thus far narrated will be resolved happily.

All the central players have now been introduced at least by name. A familiar return motif has providentially brought the four dispersed lovers to Naples at the same time. They have yet to meet. No major conflict has been introduced. The audience must strongly suspect that Rabbya is Flavio's beloved and anticipate their meeting.

8. ARLECCHINO *looking for new stuff for his shop, sees the women, he wants to lead them to the store of shame. They: that they are not of that sort. Isabella tells him that she is an astrologer, and, looking at him, by palmistry and by physiognomy tells him that he is a pimp, and that the galley and the gallows threaten him. Arlecchino wants to lead them into his house by force; at that*

Now in another comic interlude, suggesting the perils of women on their own, Arlecchino tries to lure them into his place of business, perhaps quite indirectly, in language full of *double entendres.* His manner will, nonetheless, betray him, and Isabella requires no palmistry or reading of physiognomy to know him for what he is. If she pretends to require such skills here, the effect is comic. This is the first display of the gumption of Isabella that is manifest in the Argument.

Isabella's threat of a punishment of the galley for Arlecchino cannot be a reference to a prison sentence. Prisons only held people until their cases were decided. Cost-effectiveness suggested quick punishments: penances, fines, floggings, mutilation, time on the galleys, expulsion, or the gallows.[29] Not only was time on the galleys a cost-effective punishment, but it also served the naval fleet and thus was a frequent punishment for serious and even petty crimes.[30]

9. REGENT [SERVANTS] *comes out of palace, threatens Arlecchino, who runs away frightened, then, turned towards the women, he asks them what they are doing. Isabella: that she is an astrologer and that she comes from Syria. Regent, in jest asks her what astrology is. Isabella gives an account of the whole art of astronomy, divided into many categories. Regent is amazed by this, and all the more, when she calls him by name, telling him she knows all of his business better than he does, and away. Regent remains stunned, then orders that while he stays in [is at] the Vicariate to attend to criminal matters, the servants should lead her to his house, because he wants to converse with her again; they go away.*

The Spanish authorities taxed the earnings from prostitution, but as Scala's scenario suggests, prostitution, though regarded as a necessary social evil, was increasingly viewed with opprobrium.[31] Moreover, Arlecchino is found trying to force the women.

In the Argument, Isabella is said to have come from Egypt dressed in Syrian style. Here she says she comes from Syria. It was all "Turkish" to Scala because, at the time, the term was broadly used to refer to anyone who was Muslim or from the Ottoman Empire.

In this first meeting of any of the plot's major constituents the benevolent Regent saves the women. He does not recognize his daughter, and she does not acknowledge him as her father. Contrary to any expectation that women should remain in the house, silent, with head bowed, Isabella lectures at length to a high-ranking man in a public place. Moreover, contrary to all belief that science, philosophy, and rhetoric were not appropriate topics for women, Isabella demonstrates her formidable knowledge of astrology. There were in fact some very learned women and even a very few female philosophers who wrote about astrology. Isabella's outspoken mental ability was earlier a feature of the women in plays by the Academy of the Intronati, in which, Laura Giannetti observes, women, given the opportunity to study, were shown to be as competent as men.[32] Their confident mental agility was excused by disguises and by the constancy in true love for which they undertook their risky ventures.[33]

Isabella's identification of the Regent by name requires no astrology; he is her father and he has entered from her house. The Regent probably exits in one direction towards the Vicariate (located, actually, in Castel Capuano), and the servants, seeking Isabella, in the other.

10. GRAZIANO *hears from Cintio his son [about] his love for Flaminia, daughter of the Regent, and how he longs to have her as wife. Graziano reproaches him, and [tells him] that he wants to meet the [same] end that Orazio already met many years before. Cintio: that he is loved by Flaminia in return. Graziano: that this does not satisfy him, and leaves. Cintio remains in despair, worrying about what his father has told him; at that*

We are introduced to another father and son, who perhaps enter from a third onstage building, and finally to a conflict, in a tertiary plot line, entailing a third set of lovers. Graziano points to the potential story parallel between Cintio and Orazio. We hear, or hear again, about the class and ethnic differences as well as the failure of the fathers to give their assent to the sought-after love matches. The cast list specifies that Graziano is a physician. Perhaps this is made clear here. Left alone, in another long monologue, Cintio does not resist his father's admonitions as do sons in other Scala scenarios, but worries, rather, that they are appropriate, thus suggesting the dignity of Graziano's role.

11. PEDROLINO *aware of his love, consoles him, telling him he has a [piece of] good news to give him, but that he does not want to tell it if not in the presence of Flaminia; enters into the palace to tell her to come to the window, then returns; at that*

Pedrolino comes out onto the street from the palace. When he returns inside the palace, Cintio will have to fill the time with expression of his fears and hopes. Scala finds a reason to introduce Flaminia at this point because she does not appear again until the third act and because her response and Cintio's response to Pedrolino's idea make a highly emotional closing for the act.

12. FLAMINIA *at the window, with Pedrolino as chaperone, converses with Cintio, performing [a] love scene*; then Pedrolino gives the news to the lover, telling him that he is to go to the Regent and tell him: "Sir: if I were to bring news to Your Most Illustrious Lordship that Flavio your son were alive, would you do me the particular favor of granting me your Lady Flaminia as wife?" And if by chance the Regent says yes to him, that he should freely tell him Flavio is alive. Flaminia,* *believing that a joke is being played on her, withdraws weeping. Cintio complaining about Pedrolino because he is playing a joke on him, and [saying] that it is impossible that Flavio is alive, goes inside in a rage, away. Pedrolino follows him to tell him that he is not being deceived,*

and the first act ends.

Scala's directions for the action are very explicit and include dialogue. Pedrolino, having found a way to use the information he has that Flavio is alive, no longer hesitates to have it provided. By means of it, Scala points towards a meeting between the Regent and Flavio and interweaves two plot lines. In Pedrolino's characteristic interest in serving the young in their affairs of the heart – here Flaminia – he goes so far as to forgo any reward he might receive, by providing the information himself. Having seen Flavio, the audience knows that Pedrolino's information that Flavio is alive is reliable; however, it seems impossible to the lovers. With weeping and rage, some tension is established finally at the very end of the first act.

Second Act

1. *REGENT [SERVANTS]* — *returns from the Vicariate to go to the palace, asks the servants if they have found the Astrologer. They: that they have not; at that*

There is no indication that the barrels are used for seats after act 1, scene 1. At what point they have been removed is not clear, perhaps even by Aguzzino and Orazio at act 1, scene 2. In any case, they are unlikely to be present in this act.

We are reminded of where the Regent went at act 1, scene 9, and that when he left, he was seeking the astrologer in order to question her. Scala delays and builds suspense for this meeting with her. We do not know from where the servants appear.

2. *AGUZZINO [AMETT]* — *greets the Regent, giving him news that Orazio, who killed his son Flavio, has died in Algiers, [a] slave in chains. Amett confirms [this], and [tells] how he died at his [galley] bench. Regent: that they [should] return after the meal, that he will give them a very good tip, and goes inside the palace. Amett sighing, promises Aguzzino that he will have him earn some additional tips, and away they go.*

The overseer of the galley now comes to earn the reward that he had proposed at the end of act 1, scene 1. Orazio, still fearing punishment for having killed the son of the Regent (as he thinks), provides what is probably a gruesome tale of his own death on the galley bench. In contrast to this slave is the Regent, whose presence is enhanced by servants. The Regent goes into the palace with them. Orazio in his present state apparently has little hope in life but to generate further tips for Aguzzino. How he can do so is unclear; he has already provided the news that the Regent would most like to hear. Scala seems to want to add suspense and a nice exit line.

3. GRAZIANO [CINTIO]	*hears from Cintio what Pedrolino has ordered him to tell the Regent. Graziano: that he should not trust him, and he [Cinzio] adds that Pedrolino is the go-between in his affair with Flaminia and how she does not trust anyone else but him; at that*

The audience is reminded of this tertiary plot, but it is not further advanced by this scene except in so far as Cintio seems to be trying to persuade himself and his father of the trustworthiness of Pedrolino and therefore of his claim that Flavio is alive, and that he should act upon that claim. The scene prepares for the next one in which Graziano hears Pedrolino's assurance directly from him.

4. PEDROLINO	*who is going [around] looking for the Astrologer, sees Graziano, to whom he says that Flaminia, his mistress, is in love with his son Cintio, and that she wants no other husband but him, and he asks him [Cintio] if he has spoken to the Regent, and told him all that he had been ordered to. Cintio: that he has not. Pedrolino urges him again. Cintio, goes into the palace to tell him. Graziano, away. Pedrolino says: "Where the devil will I find this Astrologer?"*

The search for the Astrologer is now becoming a running joke and conveniently provides Pedrolino with an opportunity to further persuade Cintio to action, which now he takes, leaving us to anticipate conflict. Graziano, whose resistance to that action has evidently been lessened by the words of Cintio in scene 3 and now by those of Pedrolino, seems not to protest it further; he exits.

Pedrolino functions primarily as a loyal servant. His role as plot manipulator and *mezzano*, or go-between, is slight. Commenting on the work of Sforza Oddi, Robert Leslie notes that the reduction of the role of the go-between in plot manipulation is characteristic of *commedia grave*[34] because the great force is Divine Providence.

5. *ISABELLA* *immediately says: "I am here." Pedrolino: that his master the Regent wants to converse with her again, and wants to know from her if a certain Orazio is alive or not, having been told by one Aguzzino and by a slave that he died in Algiers. Isabella: that for now she cannot come, but that in one hour she will go to the Regent and will be able to tell him everything. Pedrolino gives her two scudi, entreating her to tell him if one Flavio, son of the Regent, is alive or dead, because a certain Alexandrian Merchant has told him that Flavio is alive. She is amazed by the news and promises Pedrolino that she will be able to tell him the truth. Pedrolino, away. Isabella, remaining alone, laments her fortune, because the truths of astrology show themselves to be uncertain. By the power of the stars she has always known Orazio to be alive; she resolves to converse with Aguzzino, with the slave and with the Alexandrian Merchant, one and all, to learn the truth of what was said by Pedrolino, whom she recognized very well, and away.*

Isabella, like the pimp before her, appears fortuitously. Pedrolino's searching everywhere for her builds our anticipation for her entrance and for her powers and serves to herald her. The Regent seeks her to learn whether Orazio is alive. Owing to the extreme difficulty in getting a letter through, spell casters and charm chanters were frequently asked whether those missing were alive, slave, free, or turned Turk (that is, converted to Islam).[35] Isabella's surprise upon hearing that Flavio is alive must be hidden from Pedrolino because she would ostensibly have no knowledge of who he is. Her response to the news, however, must be evident to the audience.

His search complete, Pedrolino presumably returns to the palace. Significantly, Isabella is not called upon to predict the future but only to state what is in the present. The truths of astrology are uncertain; Isabella will ask around to learn the answers to the questions put to her. Her meeting with the Regent is delayed, and the suspense is increased.

6. ALEXANDRIAN MERCHANT [MEMMII, SLAVE] [SERVANTS] *asks his slave the reason for his sadness, and why he has not had lunch. Slave says he is not feeling too well; at that*

The scene recalls act 1, scene 1, in which, at Aguzzino's urging, Orazio explains why he sighs. It forebodes Flavio's fall to the ground in the next scene and partially motivates it; Orazio has had no lunch and feels ill. The servants need to be onstage in this scene only to carry Flavio off after his collapse in the next scene.

7. RABBYA, TURKISH [WOMAN] *with her little son in her arms. Merchant, seeing her dressed in the Turkish [style], asks her about herself. She says she is a native of Alexandria and the daughter of an Arab astrologer and Muslim named Amoratt, and how her father when he was alive kept her in a villa of his not far from the city; the slave looks at her, and, as if filled with wonder, he falls to the ground unconscious. Merchant is surprised and has him taken away to the ship, and leaves with them. Rabbya, having recognized her lover, complains of his betrayal of her;* at that*

The lovers have each had a scene in which to explain their backgrounds. Rabbya had exchanged her honour / material good for the honour/ word of Flavio. The transaction was inherently unequal. In giving away her honour, she gave away the one asset essential to her contracting a respectable marriage. A young woman who succumbed to a man promising marriage often found herself as abandoned as Rabbya feels here.[36] The lovers have miraculously found one another, but there is no interaction.

8. ISABELLA *hears from the Turkish woman how she has seen that traitor who is the cause of her misfortune and who took away her honour, the father of her child. Isabella entreats her to tell her more about the story of her misfortune. Rabbya: that there will be no shortage of time, and goes to take a rest. Isabella wonders about the Turkish woman's great steadfastness in keeping [the source of] her torment hidden. Then, returning to her own particular [case], she says she has learned, by way of a new chart she has made, that Orazio is alive, and by way of another, this one made for Flavio, that he too is alive, but in great mortal danger; at that*

Isabella presumably returns from the search she conducted to learn whether Flavio and Orazio are alive. There is no reason, except dramatic, for Rabbya to keep denying Isabella her full story. The departure of Rabbya with her baby to rest serves to allow Isabella to be onstage alone. It is unclear whether Isabella has learned that Orazio and Flavio are alive by way of diagrams as she says or whether she expresses her hope and faith. The audience already knows that Flavio is alive.

It is Orazio who is about to be in grave danger. Scala seems to have provided Flavio's name in error. Orazio's impending danger is a new potential plot complication arising just when a resolution seems to be in the offing. It is the one clear prediction that Isabella makes in the scenario and then only to herself.

9. AGUZZINO [AMETT] *with Amett, the slave, on their way to the Regent for the tip. Isabella immediately withdraws; then he [Aguzzino] tells him they are too early, and that he wants to go into the pimp Arlecchino's house to stay [for a while] and that he [Amett] wait for him at the door; at that*

Scala further delays the meeting of Isabella with the Regent and with Orazio. He reintroduces Arlecchino and his whorehouse and brings them together now with Aguzzino and Orazio. It is Aguzzino, not the higher ranking, more respected Merchant, whom we see actually making use of Arlecchino's services. Aguzzino likely knocks on Arlecchino's door. The audience must be made aware that Isabella, who has withdrawn, sees Orazio. At what point she recognizes him is not clear. She must indicate to the audience that she has.

10. ARLECCHINO *[comes] out, leads Aguzzino into the house. Amett remains at the door to wait for him; at that*

There is opportunity here for a brief comic scene involving Aguzzino's sexual interest and Arlecchino's promise of untold pleasures. Arlecchino serves to get Aguzzino offstage for the next scene.

11. ISABELLA *comes forward, and, seeing the slave, asks him where he is from. He: from Algiers. She asks him whether he might have known any Neapolitan slaves in that city. He: that he had known a certain Orazio from Naples, who had died in his arms. Isabella asks him if he was the one who had given such news to the Regent. Slave says yes. She: that he is lying, and that she knows by way of the art of astrology that Orazio is alive, and that he said what he said in order to earn [a tip], threatening him. So the slave tells her: "Since you know so much, tell me the truth, is that Isabella of his alive or dead?" She answers him: "She is dead." The slave makes her repeat this several times; in the end, overcome by grief, he says: "And am I alive? And do I breathe? I am Orazio, I am the murderer!," and, while he goes [on] crying out, Isabella observes him; at that*

It requires no astrology for Isabella to know that Orazio is lying about his death because she recognizes him. She knows from having overheard his conversation with Aguzzino at act 2, scene 9, that the two of them were attempting to earn a tip from the Regent by reporting that death. In pretending to be dead, Orazio, from Isabella's perspective, effectively denies his relationship with her. Thus, in despair and anger, she declares herself dead. The two women, both feeling betrayed, have now recognized their lovers, the most important of the women last. Their lovers have yet to recognize them. The audience will know that Orazio's response to hearing that she is dead proves his faithfulness and devotion to her. Her despair and anger seem to prevent her from understanding this until too late.

12. REGENT [SERVANTS] [CINTIO] *arrives; Orazio immediately kneels down, reveals who he is and his [real] name [that] he had concealed by using the name Amett and by [pretending to be] Turkish; [he was] nabbed by the galleys of Naples. He says that, because he has heard that his Isabella is dead, he resolves that he too will end his life. Regent is surprised by Orazio's steadfastness and has him taken to the prison. Regent remains with Cintio, talking about his [Orazio's] action; at that*

The Regent comes out of his palace with Cintio and servants. The servants have rather awkwardly to be present to lead Orazio away. Isabella must have withdrawn again because the Regent, who has been in search of her since act 1, scene 9, never so much as acknowledges her. But she is clearly present onstage, reacting to Orazio's plight. It is not obvious where she might exit.

The potential conflict between Cintio and the Regent seems to have been resolved successfully offstage. With the news that Flavio is alive, the Regent has evidently been willing to overlook any possible obstacles to his daughter Flaminia's marriage and has given his assent to it. Both he and Cintio are pleased. Without complication, the tertiary plot is all but resolved.

Orazio by contrast, believing Isabella to be dead, finds no reason to go on living and, on his knees before the Regent, gives himself up as Flavio's murderer. The kneeling pattern will be repeated with Flavio on his knees before Rabbya, Pedrolino on his knees before Isabella, and Isabella on her knees before the Regent. The scenario is marked by the humility of its characters.

Orazio is taken off to jail to await trial.[37] The scene between Cintio and the Regent reveals their new relationship and reiterates the story of the presumed murder and of Orazio's escape from jail, aided by Isabella and the prison guard, whom we never see. Enough time is passed by their conversation to make plausible the return of the servants and the police who meanwhile have been wholly moved by Orazio's tale of all that he suffered for true love.

13. SERVANTS [COPS]	*bring with them many cops and tell the Regent how Orazio has made all those who have heard his case weep; at that*

Men could weep openly in public on certain occasions, as we know, without seeming unmanly.

14. AGUZZINO [ARLECCHINO]	*arrives; Regent has Aguzzino taken prisoner. Arlecchino wants to defend him, cops take Arlecchino prisoner too, and the second act ends.*

The Regent is perturbed, having just learned that Orazio is alive, and must presume that Aguzzino has been lying about Orazio's death and has been knowingly harbouring the criminal all the while. On this account, Aguzzino is taken prisoner (*prigione*). Arlecchino may be arrested for obstructing justice. Prostitution, as I said, was a legal activity, one in which the Regent already knew that Arlecchino was involved.

The second act ends with three men being jailed prior to their sentencing. Given the nature of his supposed crime, the sentence for Orazio is likely to be execution.

Third Act

1. ISABELLA	*mad at herself for not having revealed herself to him [Orazio], having seen his love and his faith [to be] still pure and intact, and having suffered at seeing him be taken prisoner; goes about thinking of various ways to free him, or to die with him; at that*

Isabella reminds us of what happened at the grievous end of the second act. She reacted too late to Orazio's response to her declaration of her death. As with Orazio's prior arrest (the one narrated in the Argument), she seeks to free him. Failing any present rescue, without him she is as willing to die as he is.

2. RABBYA, TURKISH [WOMAN]	*with her child, unsettled by what she has seen of her lover the slave, sees Isabella, who again entreats her to tell her who it was who took her honour. She: that she does not know his Christian name, telling her in brief how that slave was the slave of an Alexandrian merchant, who had a villa near that of her father of blessed memory, and how he so knew just what to do and just what to say, that he went [to bed] with her, with the promise of taking her as wife, [once] she became a Christian, and how he went away from Alexandria with his master; and she has never seen him again, nor does she know where he may be. Isabella consoles her again, telling her that she has seen by way of her art how she will soon be happy; at that*

This narration further reminds us of events in the second act. Finally our strong suspicion that Flavio is the father of Rabbya's child is confirmed, and the details of their relationship are supplied. Here, as in several of Scala's scenarios, it is conversion to Christianity, not ethnic difference, that matters. Isabella, while herself very unhappy, reassures Rabbya that she will soon be happy. Flavio, in his devotion to Rabbya, is, we know, disguised and a slave. We deduce that Flavio, alone empowered to restore Rabbya's honour, will do so by marrying her.[38]

3. MEMMII *slave of the merchant, looking for the Astrologer, since she is the companion of Rabbya, the Turkish woman, his beloved; she [Rabbya] sees him and, having recognized him very well, calls him traitor, throwing in his face all that she has always done for him. Slave, on his knees, apologizes telling how his master led him away by way of the sea, and how he did not have [enough] time [to be able] to visit her. She does not accept his apologies. Slave begs her companion the Astrologer [to help him], telling her that Naples is his native land, and that in order to be able to return to Alexandria to visit his beloved, he did not reveal himself to his father, who is the principal Lord of the city. Isabella makes sure that this is her brother Flavio, [and] entreats the Turkish woman to entrust her with [resolving] all their differences. Turkish woman agrees. Isabella has them reconcile and [has him] embrace his little child, on condition however that he agree to forgive two people for whatever wrong they may have done him. Slave agrees. Isabella tells him to forgive Orazio, who finds himself in very great danger of losing his life. Slave holds back for some time, then, [as] his Rabbya commands him, he agrees, takes his child in his arms, and, everyone cheerful, away.*

Again, an entrance is motivated by a search for the astrologer, about whom everything seems to revolve. Evidently, Flavio speaks in an aside about his intention to find her: in order to make Rabbya's immediate confrontation of him plausible, she must see him before he sees her. During their interchange Isabella quickly conceives of an ambitious plan. She thinks of a way to resolve all their problems, not as an astrologer, but as the daughter of the Regent and the sister of Flavio. It remains to be shown who might be the second person Isabella wants forgiven.

4. GRAZIANO [CINTIO] *hears from Cintio his son how Orazio, the one who killed Flavio the son of the Regent, is a prisoner for [taking] his life, and that the following morning they will kill him, as he has already been tried and everything, and how the Regent has promised him Flaminia, since he brings him news that Flavio is alive; at that*

In the small world of the neighbourhood, news travels fast. Cintio makes a point of explaining for the audience's sake the speed with which Orazio has been tried and sentenced and is to be executed. The whole action, after so many delays, now rushes towards a crisis.

5. PEDROLINO	*in despair since he can find neither the Alexandrian merchant and slave, nor the Astrologer, and he [says] how they want to kill Orazio; at that*

Scala repeats the refrain of Pedrolino's not being able to find the astrologer and of her arriving pat to the occasion in the next scene. It is not clear why Pedrolino seeks the merchant and his slave except that Scala needs to bring all the characters back onstage for the ending.

6. ISABELLA	*arrives; Pedrolino immediately entreats her on his knees to free Orazio from death with her art (if she can), and moreover to tell him, as she had promised him, if Flavio is alive or dead. She consoles them all, saying affirmatively Flavio is alive, and that she wants to converse at length with the Regent. Cintio, cheerful, says that the hour of the public audience is near; at that*

Isabella has no need of astrology to know that Flavio is alive; she has just seen him.

There is no indication of any exit for Cintio and Graziano after act 3, scene 4, or of their participation in this scene, and their presence onstage, presumably to begin to mass the characters for the scenario's conclusion, is awkward.

7. REGENT [CAPTAIN OF THE GALLEY] [SERVANTS]	*with the Captain of the galley, asks what he wants. The Captain tells him he wants his Aguzzino, and his slave Amett, who are imprisoned – it being [the case] that his Most Illustrious Lordship does not have power over the men of his galley, and galley of his King of Spain. Regent reveals to him that Amett is not Turkish, but is that Orazio who killed Flavio his son, who kept himself [hidden] under the Turkish name so as not to be recognized, but that he will give him back Aguzzino. The Captain agrees; at that*

Evidently the Regent is now seated for his public audience.[39] It is not certain when the chair might have been brought on, perhaps by the servants at this point.

This is the first appearance of the Captain. His relationship with the Regent is cordial.[40]

8. ISABELLA	*presents herself before the Regent, telling him she has come [before him] to make him happy and console him, although at first sight it will all seem to him to be the opposite. Regent receives her gladly. Isabella entreats the Regent to have that Orazio who killed his son Flavio brought before him. Regent sends for Orazio. Pedrolino and the servants go away for Orazio. While they are going to get Orazio, Isabella makes a speech on morals, showing that all of the trials that come to us from the heavens are for the greater happiness of humankind; at that*

Isabella's speech makes plausible the passage of time that is required to fetch Orazio. More important, it makes clear that all the tribulations have been the working out of a heavenly plan for human happiness. Louise George Clubb notes that in play after play of the *commedia grave* "it is expressly stated that the seeming chaos and confusion of the intrigue are in fact part of a plan above change, a divine pattern implicitly or explicitly Christian, guiding the characters ... to perfect order." In the second prologue to his *Prigione d'amore* Sforza Oddi explains that *commedia grave* teaches people, especially lovers, not to despair, because even in their darkest confusion the pattern for their happiness is taking shape.[41] Their fidelity seems to deserve divine intervention. We await Isabella's plan.

9. ALEXANDRIAN MERCHANT [MEMMII, SLAVE] [SERVANTS]	*having been informed of everything by Flavio, his slave, bows before the Regent, telling him that, when he has finished his business, he wishes to talk to him about something very important; at that*

The audience already knows all that the merchant has learned, but for the merchant's role in act 3, scene 11, it must be clear that he knows. The merchant is discreet and respectful. We await his important disclosure.

10. RABBYA	*with her child in her arms, bows before the Regent, saying she is appearing before him seeking justice; at that*

Rabbya's honour is at stake.

11. SERVANTS [PEDROLINO] [COPS] *who are bringing Orazio, [who is] tied, before the Regent; he [Orazio] asks for death as an act of grace and justice. Regent: that he does not want to delay until the following morning, but that he wants to put him to death on this day. Isabella tells the Regent that she wants to prove to him that Orazio cannot be put to death, having received a pardon from his enemies, and she shows the pardon, in Flavio's handwriting. Regent is astonished, asks where Flavio may be. Merchant presents Memmii, saying "Lord, this is Flavio your son." Regent, with greatest joy, receives him. Isabella presents his little grandchild and his daughter-in-law to him, telling him briefly who she [Rabbya] is, and how she must become a Christian and take Flavio as husband. Regent rejoices [even] more. Pedrolino calls Flaminia.*

Now for the first time Orazio appears as a prisoner, bound. By having moved back the time of his execution, the Regent intensifies the crisis and serves to confine the action to within twenty-four hours. The lost son, presumed dead, has been found. That Rabbya has borne a son rather than a daughter makes her, as well as her child, more acceptable. Perhaps even more important is the fact that Rabbya is the daughter of a well-respected and influential man. Isabella has resolved the secondary plot.

12. FLAMINIA *[comes] from palace, embraces her brother, her Turkish sister-in-law and her little nephew. This being done, Isabella gets the Regent to give Flaminia to Cintio, as he has promised, which is immediately done; then, turned towards Flavio, she tells him: "It is up to you to perform the second act of grace, to forgive the second person, and moreover to have her father forgive her." Flavio: that he is a very ready executor; at that Isabella on her knees reveals herself, narrating just what she did and what she said (summing up all that is written in the argument of the comedy) and lastly asking for Orazio's life, or for death for both of them. Regent, weeping, gets up, embraces her, forgives Orazio, who, reconciled with Flavio, asks his forgiveness; he obtains it, and at the same time obtains his [Flavio's] sister Isabella as wife – and [she is] so much dearer [to him] as he finds her again [now] so talented and learned in the art of astrology. The Regent promises the ransom for Flavio to the merchant. Merchant: that he does not want anything at all. Flavio: that he will give him very beautiful gifts to take to the Pasha of Alexandria on his behalf; they have Aguzzino and Arlecchino released.*

For Flaminia, Isabella will have to identify her brother, whom she has not seen for a long time, and his wife and their child, about whose existence she has been unaware. In a quick ceremony of hand-holding, Flaminia and Cintio are espoused. Scala provides the words that Isabella now addresses to Flavio, "A voi sta di fare la seconda grazia, di perdonare alla seconda persona, et inoltre farle perdonare al padre," presumably because of the importance of their being spoken just so; at the beginning of the sentence we still do not who the person to be forgiven is and must be surprised when, a little later in the sentence, the person is identified as female and, finally, as none other than herself. Just as Pedrolino often sums up the action of a scenario, including his role in it, so Isabella's summary of all that she said and did leaves no doubt as to her centrality in the action and allows the audience the pleasure of reliving the action. Having just learned that his son is alive, having satisfactorily married off one of his daughters, and having been reunited with his son, the Regent (in the last of the scenario's weeping, this time for joy) is in a forgiving mood and willingly gives Isabella to Orazio. Following a series of linked revelations, the whole family is reunited, and Orazio is accepted into it. The last and most important of the plots comes to a happy end. Quite surprisingly, having learned about Isabella's great capabilities, Orazio values her more. But then, again, she did all that she did out of love for him.

As usual, there is one last small matter to resolve. The merchant, as charitable as is the Regent, forgoes the remuneration that might make up for Flavio's original purchase price. The gifts for the Pasha that Flavio will provide are more than financial recompense; they will serve as proof of the Merchant's personal contacts in Naples and of his elevated status there.[42] Moreover, the goodwill offering to the Pasha will facilitate trade between the two empires.

13. AGUZZINO thank the Regent,
ARLECCHINO

and the comedy of Isabella [the] Astrologer ends.

The tag ending prolongs even more the great grace and joy of the conclusion that makes up for all that has gone before.

Conclusion

I began, in Mark Edmondton's words, to befriend Scala's scenarios. I read them as Scala said he wanted them to be read, as a mirror of life, making clear what that would have meant for him in the context of the ideas about representation in the period. I read them, as Scala's close friend Francesco Andreini referred to them, as plays, in all but the words. I read them not merely as iterations of earlier literature, dramatic and otherwise, although they surely are that, but as we might read any literature, as independent works of art. I read them in their cultural context. In so doing, I showed that our distance from that period had left many of the cultural references in the scenarios either too easy to overlook because they had been lost to us or not given the same weight they had likely been given by their original audience. These cultural references in the scenarios I examined make clear that the scenarios are much more tightly constructed than has been supposed and that they take up the tensions in personal relationships in daily lives at the time. I hope to have made it difficult to continue to describe the scenarios, albeit not fully scripted, as *skeletal* or as merely full of all the tricks, devices, and plot elements of comedy found in the earlier plays. I have argued that the Scala scenarios are central to our understanding of *commedia dell'arte* in its golden age, are full of the life of their time, and bear close analysis in terms of their cultural context and the aesthetic principles they employ.

I encourage others to provide reconstructions of other Scala compositions and of other scenarios to be found in manuscript collections, many now published. Through such reconstructions I believe that, with respect to the Scala scenarios, they will become convinced that, just as the actors were not freely improvising their words but rather calling upon vast stores of memorized material in order to speak, so they were not improvising actions to anywhere near the extent that has been supposed. While then as now there was nothing to stop performers from using a scenario in any way they wished, the value of a Scala scenario – a combination of accretion and invention (like all art and, certainly, all art in the period in which Scala was working) – did not lie solely "in what a company was able to do with it." The scenarios are, in many cases, carefully crafted, and on that account their performance could not be "radically different with different performers." The evidence defies the well-worn, and still popular, premises with which I began to teach my acting class.

Appendix: List of All Scala Scenarios

Following is the complete list by days of the scenarios included in Flaminio Scala's *Il teatro delle favole rappresentative.* Those discussed in detail in chapters 5–8 of this book are shown in bold.

Giornata I *Li duo vecchi gemelli* Comedia	Day 1 *The Two Old Twins* Comedy
Giornata II *La fortuna di Flavio* Comedia	Day 2 *Flavio's Fortunes* Comedy
Giornata III *La fortunata Isabella* Comedia	Day 3 *The Fortunate Isabella* Comedy
Giornata IV *Le burle d'Isabella* Comedia	Day 4 *Isabella's Pranks* Comedy
Giornata V *Flavio tradito* Comedia	Day 5 *Flavio Betrayed* Comedy
Giornata VI ***Il vecchio geloso*** **Comedia**	**Day 6** ***The Jealous Old Man*** **Comedy**

Giornata VII *La cruduta morta* Comedia	Day 7 *The Woman Believed to Be Dead* Comedy
Giornata VIII *La finta pazza* Comedia	Day 8 *The Fake Madwoman* Comedy
Giornata IX *Il marito* Comedia	Day 9 *The Husband* Comedy
Giornata X *La sposa* Comedia	Day 10 *The Bride* Comedy
Giornata XI *Il Capitano* Comedia	Day 11 *The Captain* Comedy
Giornata XII *Il cavadente* Comedia	Day 12 *The Tooth Puller* Comedy
Giornata XIII *Il dottor disperato* Comedia	Day 13 *The Despairing Doctor* Comedy
Giornata XIV *Il pellegrino fido amante* Comedia	Day 14 *The Pilgrim and Loyal Lover* Comedy
Giornata XV *La travagliata Isabella* Comedia	Day 15 *The Troubled Isabella* Comedy
Giornata XVI *Lo specchio* Comedia	Day 16 *The Mirror* Comedy

Giornata XVII
Li duo capitani simili
Comedia

Day 17
The Two Captains Who Look Alike
Comedy

Giornata XVIII
Li tragic successi
Comedia

Day 18
The Tragic Events
Comedy

Giornata XIX
Li tre fidi amici
Comedia

Day 19
The Three Loyal Friends
Comedy

Giornata XX
Li duo fidi notari
Comedia

Day 20
The Two Loyal Notaries
Comedy

Giornata XXI
Il finto negromante
Comedia

Day 21
The Fake Sorcerer
Comedy

Giornata XXII
Il creduto morto
Comedia

Day 22
The Man Believed to Be Dead
Comedy

Giornata XXIII
Il portalettere
Comedia

Day 23
The Letter Carrier
Comedy

Giornata XXIV
Il finto Tofano
Comedia

Day 24
The Fake Tofano
Comedy

Giornata XXV
La gelosa Isabella
Comedia

Day 25
The Jealous Isabella
Comedy

Giornata XXVI
Li tappeti Alessandrini
Comedia

Day 26
The Alexandrian Carpets
Comedy

Giornata XXVII
La mancata fede
Comedia

Day 27
The Promise Not Kept
Comedy

Giornata XXVIII
Flavio finto negromante
Comedia

Day 28
Flavio the Fake Sorcerer
Comedy

Giornata XXIX
Il fido amico
Comedia

Day 29
The Loyal Friend
Comedy

Giornata XXX
Li finti servi
Comedia

Day 30
The Fake Servants
Comedy

Giornata XXXI
Il pedante
Comedia

Day 31
The Pedant
Comedy

Giornata XXXII
Li duo finti zingani
Comedia

Day 32
The Two Fake Gypsies
Comedy

Giornata XXXIII
Li quattro finti spiritati
Comedia

Day 33
The Four Fake Possessed Men
Comedy

Giornata XXXIV
Il finto cieco
Comedia

Day 34
The Fake Blind Man
Comedy

Giornata XXXV
Le disgrazie di Flavio
Comedia

Day 35
Flavio's Misfortunes
Comedy

Giornata XXXVI
Isabella astrologa
Comedia

Day 36
Isabella [the] Astrologer
Comedy

Giornata XXXVII *La caccia* Comedia	Day 37 *The Hunt* Comedy
Giornata XXXVIII *La pazzia d'Isabella* Comedia	Day 38 *The Madness of Isabella* Comedy
Giornata XXXIX *Il ritratto* Comedia	Day 39 *The Portrait* Comedy
Giornata XL *Il giusto castigo* Comedia	Day 40 *The Proper Punishment* Comedy
Giornata XLI *La forsennata prencipessa* Tragedia	Day 41 *The Deranged Princess* Tragedy
Giornata XLII *Gli avvenimenti comici, pastorali e tragici* Opera mista	Day 42 *The Comic, Pastoral and Tragic Events* Mixed Drama
Giornata XLIII *L'Alvida* Opera regia	Day 43 *Alvida* Royal Drama
Giornata XLIV *Rosalba incantatrice* Opera eroica	Day 44 *Rosalba [the] Enchantress* Heroic Drama
Giornata XLV *L'innocente Persiana* Opera reale	Day 45 *The Innocent Persian Woman* Royal Opera
Giornata XLVI *I Parte-Dell'orseida* Opera reale	Day 46 *Orseis, Part I* Royal Opera

Giornata XLVII *II Parte-Dell'orseida* Opera reale	Day 47 *Orseis, Part II* Royal Drama
Giornata XLVIII *III Parte-Dell'orseida* Opera reale	Day 48 *Orseis, Part III* Royal Drama
Giornata XLIX *L'arbore incantato* Pastorale	Day 49 *The Enchanted Tree* Pastoral
Giornata L *La fortuna di foresta prencipessa di Moscovia* Opera regia	Day 50 *The Fortunes of Foresta, Princess of Moscow* Royal Drama

Notes

1. Befriending the Text

1 Scala's full title is *Il teatro delle favole rappresentative, overo la ricreatione comica, boscareccia, e tragica: divisa in cinquanta giornate* (Venice: Battista Pulciani, 1611). All my citations are from Ferruccio Marotti's 1976 edition entitled *Il teatro delle favole rappresentative* by Flaminio Scala.

2 Other terms were *commedia Italiana* or *commedia degli zanni*, and *commedia delle maschere*. The first documented use of the term *commedia dell'arte* (professional comedy) seems to have been Carlo Goldoni's, in 1750. See Richard Andrews, "Molière, *commedia dell'arte*, and the Question of Influence in Early Modern European Theatre," 445. I use the term *commedia dell'arte* throughout because it is best known, the professional players worked not only from scenarios but also from scripts, and they were, accordingly, not always improvising. Unfortunately, the term *commedia dell'arte*, even though *commedia* can mean "play" as well as "comedy," may also be misleading because, while most *commedia dell'arte* scenarios were comic, the players also worked in other genres, as Scala's collection makes clear (see appendix).

3 Louise George Clubb, "Italian Renaissance Theatre," 128–9.

4 Henry Salerno, *Scenarios of the Commedia dell'Arte: Flaminio Scala's Il Teatro Delle Favole Rappresentative* was printed by New York University in 1967 and subsequently by Limelight in 1989, 1992, and 1996. Sadly, for Salerno's undeniably considerable labour in translating all of Scala's scenarios, Kenneth McKee wrote a foreword stating the then common view that the scenarios are "not worth saving" and are of "no artistic value," xvi, xvii.

5 Richard Andrews, "How – and Why – Does One Print Scenarios? Flaminio Scala, 1611," 36.

6 Richard Andrews, in Scala, *The Commedia dell'Arte of Flaminio Scala*, xviii.

7 Ibid. For Andrews' argument, see especially vii, xxxv.

8 Richard Andrews, "Writing as Re-arranging." Courtesy of the author.

9 Flaminio Scala, first prologue to *Il finto marito*, cx.

10 Tim Fitzpatrick, *The Relationship of Oral and Literate Performance Processes in the Commedia dell'Arte*, 104.

11 Quirino Galli, *Gli scenari di Flaminio Scala*, 122. The analytic vocabulary of the two men differs. Fitzpatrick's analysis is in terms of schemas, sub-schemas (both diachronic and synchronic), categories, and words. Galli's is in terms of words, fragments, episodes, plot intrigue, and variants. One moves from the larger units to the smaller; the other, from the smaller to the larger.

12 See for instance, Kenneth Richards and Laura Richards, *"Commedia dell'Arte"*, 111, and Andrews, in Scala, *The Commedia dell'Arte of Flaminio Scala*, vii.

13 Fitzpatrick, *Relationship of Oral and Literate Performance Processes*, 104. Galli, *Gli scenari di Flaminio Scala*, 122.

14 Andrews, in Scala, *The Commedia dell'Arte of Flaminio Scala*, xiv.

15 Robert Henke, *Performance and Literature in the Commedia dell'Arte*, 181–96.

16 Flaminio Scala, "L'autore a' cortesi lettori," and Francesco Andreini, "Cortesi lettori," in *Il teatro delle favole rappresentative* by Flaminio Scala, ii, xiii. Henke, *Performance and Literature in the Commedia dell'Arte*, 13.

17 Corsini, ii. 43; Corsini i. II; Correr, no. 21 in K.M. Lea, *Italian Popular Comedy*, vol. 2, at 582, 601, and 607.

18 Mark Edmundson, "Against Readings," 62–3.

19 Roberto Tessari, *La commedia dell' arte nel Seicento: "Industria" e "Arte giocosa" della civiltà* barocca, 116.

20 Ruzante, *Teatro: Prima edizione completa*, xxvii. Richard Helgerson, in keeping with this idea, remarks that, unlike the later drama he considers, the *commedia dell'arte* presented "the nonaristocratic home as a scene of extravagant folly meant to provoke mirth." He posits a clear-cut distinction between public and private in the material he examines. Richard Helgerson, *Adulterous Alliances*, 3.

21 Richard Andrews, *Scripts and Scenarios*, 106.

22 Guido Ruggiero, "Marriage, Love, Sex, and Renaissance Civic Morality," 15, 28, and *passim*. Laura Giannetti has provided a spirited and persuasive re-evaluation of the *commedia erudita* based on Ruggiero's extensive studies of sex and marriage in early modern Italy (Giannetti, *Lelia's Kiss*).

23 John Jeffries Martin, *Myths of Renaissance Individualism*, 16.

24 Ibid.

25 Flaminio Scala, second prologue to *Il finto marito*, cxvii. Both Fitzpatrick and

Galli claim, but do not show, that within their "conventionalized fictional world" the Scala scenarios deal with everyday concerns. Fitzpatrick, *Relationship of Oral and Literate Performance Processes*, 349; Galli, *Gli scenari di Flaminio Scala*, 135.

26 In Siro Ferrone, *Comici dell'arte: Corrispondenze*, 451–587.

27 Flaminio Scala, *Il finto marito*, in *Commedi dei comici dell'arte*, ed. Laura Falavolti.

28 Andreini, "*Cortesi lettori*," vol. 1, 12.

29 Scala, first prologue to *Il finto marito*, cxv. Emphasizing this same point more than three hundred years later, a guide for would-be playwrights emphasizes that "a professional playwright spends more time on the scenario either on paper or in his head, than upon the actual writing of the dialogue." Marian Gallaway, *Constructing a Play*, 313.

30 Bernardino Telesio (1509–80), for instance, one of the founders of the empirical movement, "insisted that observation alone, not reason or authority, was the path to true knowledge." William Eamon, "The Scientific Renaissance," 420.

31 Scala, first prologue to *Il finto marito*, cx–cxiv.

32 Janet Levarie Smarr, *Italian Renaissance Tales*, xxxiii.

33 The Ingram Bywater translation of Aristotle's *Poetics* reads as follows: "Now the action (that which was done) is represented in the play by the Fable or Plot. The Fable, in our present sense of the term, is simply this, the combination of the incidents, or things done in the story." Aristotle, *Aristotle on the Art of Poetry*, 16.

34 "The Prologue is normally the part where the plot is narrated." Flaminio Scala, second prologue to *Il finto marito*, cxviii.

35 Andrews, "How – and Why – Does One Print Scenarios?" 38.

36 For this debate see Ferruccio Marotti, "Il teatro delle favole rappresentative: Un progetto utopico."

37 I borrow the term that Henry Kamen uses for non-aristocratic elites. He uses it because it does not carry the baggage of the term *bourgeoisie*, although, as he admits, the term is not ideal; there is no lower elite. Henry Kamen, *Early Modern European Society*, 97.

38 I use the terms as seems appropriate in the particular context. The word *youths*, as we shall see, is often and suitably used in the early modern period for those whom we would now consider to be young men. At the time, there was considerable ambiguity in positing the length of adolescence. Some designations continued it until age thirty. See Rudolph M. Bell, *How to Do It*, 331n4. For Richard C. Trexler's extensive use of the word *youths* to mean "*giovani*," see his *Public Life in Renaissance Florence*, 388–9, and the whole of

his chapter 13. See also Guido Ruggiero, "Marriage, Love, Sex, and Civic Morality," 23–4.

39 Scala added other characters, probably as actor availability, character doubling, and finances allowed and as the story required. From time to time some actor whose character was not in the scenario might have taken another role in it. In Day 36, Scala explicitly tells us that the role of Graziano may be played by the actor who ordinarily plays Pantalone.

40 Ferdinano Taviani, "Positions du masque dans la Commedia dell'Arte," 126.

41 M.A. Katritzky shows masked upper-class women as well. Their masks seem to denote their class rather than their character. M.A. Katritzky, *The Art of Commedia*, 202–4.

42 John Jeffries Martin, "The Myth of Renaissance Individualism," 215.

43 Guazzo, *La civil conversazione*, 177.

44 Jay Tribby, review of *Stefano Guazzo e la civil conversazione.*

45 The revelatory term *theatregram* was introduced by Louise George Clubb ("Theatregrams," 15–33). See my chapter 4 section on imitation and invention.

46 As a shorthand, I often refer to a scenario only by its Day. A list of scenario titles in both Italian and English can be found in the appendix to this work.

47 Francesco Andreini, "*Cortesi lettori*," 12.

48 Up to his death in 1983 Ludovico Zorzi sought, with the aid of students, to transcribe all the extant scenarios. This work remains incomplete and unpublished.

49 The edition of fifty-one in Italian from 1996 is *Gli scenari Correr: La commedia dell'arte a Venezia*, ed. Carmelo Alberti (Rome: Bulzoni, 1996). *La Commedia dell'Arte*, edited and introduced by Cesare Molinari (Rome: Istituto poligrafico e Zecca dello Stato, 1999), includes a selection of scenarios from Scala, Correr, and Magliabecchiana manuscript collections. Francesco Cotticelli, Anne Goodrich Heck, and Thomas F. Heck provided *The Commedia dell'Arte in Naples: A Bilingual Edition of the 176 Casamarciano Scenarios = La commedia dell'arte a Napoli: Edizione bilingue dei 176 scenari Casamariano*, 2 vols. (Lanham, MD: Scarecrow Press, 2001). Annamaria Testaverde edited *I canovacci della commedia dell'arte* (Turin: Giulio Einaudi, 2007), which includes selections of scenarios by Scala, by Basilio Locatelli, and from a number of anonymous collections in various libraries. Prior to these, in 1880, Adolfo Bartoli published the twenty-two scenarios from the Magliabecchiana manuscript (*Scenari inediti della Commedia dell'Arte contributo alla storia del teatro popolare italiano Scenari inediti* (Florence: G.C. Sansoni, 1880). During most of the twentieth century only isolated *scenari* were printed here and there. In 1934 Kathleen Lea provided a limited sample of scenarios in English in *Italian Popular Comedy*, vol. 2.

2. Character Relationships

1 The English theologian William Perkins (1558–1602) explained that one is "a person in respect of another": a "husband, father, mother, daughter, wife, lord, subject." William Perkins, *The Work of William Perkins*, 382.

2 Middle elites in cities were variously referred to as *cittadini* in Venice, *popolo* or *ceto civile* in Naples, *popolo grosso* (people of substance) in Genoa, and more generally as "those of the middling sort" (*quelli dell sorte mediocre*). By and large these groups included those who enjoyed an independent income, those who worked in the courts of law, and merchants, and craftsmen who were especially esteemed such as goldsmiths, printers, physicians, and architects. Domenico Sella, *Italy in the Seventeenth Century*, 69.

3 Scala, first prologue, *Il finto marito*, cxi.

4 Aelius Donatus, "On Comedy and Tragedy," 79.

5 Domenico Bruni, "Prologue to *Lo Speccio*," 414. Bruni wrote prologues, including this one, to plays he never wrote.

6 Debora Shuger, "The 'I' of the Beholder," 22. It is significant in this context that Renaissance mirrors were not flat but convex.

7 Scala, second prologue to *Il finto marito*, cxvii.

8 See Madeleine Doran, *Endeavors of Art*, 77–8. Doran observes that this was more strictly the case with Italian plays than with Elizabethan ones.

9 Alessandro Piccolomini, "Annotationi nel libro della poetica d'Aristotle" (Venice, 1575), in *Italian Comedy in the Renaissance* by Marvin T. Herrick, 108.

10 John M. Najemy, "Giannozzo and His Elders," 57.

11 Guido Ruggiero, "Marriage, Love, Sex, and Renaissance Civic Morality," 28.

12 Dale Kent, *Friendship, Love, and Trust in Renaissance Florence*, 367.

13 Trexler, *Public Life in Renaissance Florence*, 16, 367. Trexler suggests further that the patriarchs of Florence hired foreign mercenaries to do their fighting, not because of cost-effectiveness but because they feared that an army of local "youths" would turn arms inward against the regime (390).

14 Edward Muir, *Ritual in Early Modern Europe*, 129.

15 Ian Frederick Moulton, "The Illicit Worlds of the Renaissance," 503.

16 Northrop Frye, *Anatomy of Criticism*, 165.

17 In 1589 Nicolo Gozze cautioned in his *Governo della famiglia* that, for reasons of modesty and honour, fathers should admonish and instruct their children and train their wives in the home, not in public outside the home: "This is one of the reasons for which houses have been built" ("Introduction: Approaching the Italian Renaissance Interior" by Marta Ajmar-Wollheim, Flora Dennis, and Ann Matchette, 623).

18 Proverb quoted in Anthony Molho, *Marriage Alliance in Late Medieval Florence*, 13.

19 Gene Brucker, *Giovanni and Lusanna*, 107.

20 Niccolò Machiavelli, "How a State is Ruined Because of Women," chap. 26.

21 Guido Ruggiero, "Marriage, Love, Sex, and Renaissance Civic Morality," 13.

22 Francesco Guicciardini, *Maxims and Reflections of a Renaissance Statesman (Ricordi)*, series C, 68, 106. Guicciardini was also a statesman and a diplomat.

23 Guido Ruggiero, "Witchcraft and Magic," 479.

24 John Hale, *The Civilization of Europe in the Renaissance*, 439. See also Jackson I. Cope, *Secret Sharers in Italian Comedy from Machiavelli to Goldoni*, 5: "What we, the viewers, agree to silence is our awareness that events at the 'end' are not closed back in a great circle that creates a renewed social harmony but open onto vistas of disruption and deception that belie the ludic ritualized release and restoration that have been the historic seedbed and pattern of New Comedy. The effect is a play more cynical than carnivalesque."

25 Giannetti, *Lelia's* Kiss, chap. 5.

26 Ibid., 23.

27 See, for instance, Stanley Chojnacki, *Women and Men in Renaissance Venice*; Ferraro, *Marriage Wars in Late Renaissance Venice*; and Eric R. Dursteler, *Renegade Women*.

28 Hale, *The Civilization of Europe in the Renaissance*, 438.

29 Brian Richardson, "'*Amore maritale*': Advice on Love and Marriage in the Second Half of the Cinquecento," 194.

30 William P. Roberts, "Christian Marriage," 210.

31 See Daniela Hacke, "'*Non lo volevo per marito in modo alcuno*'," 208. Hacke cites Volker Hunecke, *Der venezianische Adel am Ende der Republik, 1646–1797: Demographie, Familie, Haushalt* (Tübingen, Germany: M. Niemeyer, 1995), 141.

32 Joanne M. Ferraro, *Marriage Wars in Late Renaissance Venice*, 160.

33 Brucker, *Giovanni and Lusanna*, 102.

34 Paul F. Grendler, *Books and Schools in the Italian Renaissance*, 199–200.

35 Claudione, the tutor in Day 34, is a wholly undeveloped character with but a single brief appearance.

36 Paul F. Grendler, *Schooling in Renaissance Italy*, 124, citing Erasmus, *Ciceronianus*, 1528.

37 Paul F. Grendler, *Critics of the Italian World*, 148.

38 Scala, *Il teatro delle favole rappresentative*, vol. 2, 275; vol. 1, 107.

39 Henry Kamen, *Early Modern European Society*, 107. Hilde de Ridder-Symoens, "Training and Professionalization," 170-2.

40 Kamen, *Early Modern European Society*, 99.

41 Alberto Tenenti, "The Merchant and the Banker," 156.

42 Bernardino de Siena (1380–1444), Paula Findlen, "Understanding the Italian Renaissance," in *The Italian Renaissance*, 8.

43 Richard A. Goldthwaite, *The Economy of Renaissance Florence*, 586.

44 Gene Brucker, *Giovanni and Lusanna*, 106, and *Florence*, 91.

45 Tenenti, "The Merchant and the Banker," 160.

46 Christopher R. Friedrichs, *The Early Modern City, 1450–1750*, 191. Tenenti, "The Merchant and the Banker," 170.

47 Hale, *The Civilization of Europe in the Renaissance*, 438. Jan de Vries, *European Urbanization, 1500–1800*, 213. Joanne M. Ferraro, "Family and Clan in the Renaissance World," 174.

48 Tenenti, "The Merchant and the Banker," 165.

49 Paul F. Grendler "Form and Function in Italian Renaissance Popular Books," 453.

50 Ferrone, "La nevrosi postale," 37–43. The considerable fear of the letters being delayed, lost, or stolen expressed in this correspondence is reflected in the scenarios.

51 Leon Battista Alberti, *The Family in Renaissance Florence* (*I libri della famiglia)*, 160. Alberti's treatise on the family was written between 1433 and 1440 and disseminated in manuscript form but was not published until 1843. Although it was written one hundred and fifty years before Scala wrote, the views of Alberti in the passages I cite are consistent with those expressed by Italian humanists at the end of the sixteenth century but are more incisive. I therefore use it often.

52 Camporesi, *Bread of Dreams*, 171.

53 Ibid., 118. Croce is being facetious, but Camporesi cites him extensively as a true expression of a style of life that many people had to observe from stark necessity. See also the unsourced quote provided by D.V. and F.W. Kent:

> Always complain about your tax: how you didn't deserve half as much, how you are burdened with debt, how you have enormous expenses, obligations from your father's bequests, that you have lost money in trading, that your crops are poor, that you will have to buy grain and wine and wood and other necessities. However, don't let these complaints be so outrageous as to make a fool of you: tell a lie which is near to the truth so that you will be believed and not be seen to be a liar.

Such complaints were regarded as moral behaviour: self-protection. D.V. and F.W. Kent, *Neighbours and Neighbourhood in Renaissance Florence*, 54.

54 Peter Burke, *Culture and Society in Renaissance Italy, 1420–1540*, 239.

55 Guido Ruggiero, "Marriage, Love, Sex, and Renaissance Civic Morality, 23.

56 Hale, *The Civilization of Europe in the Renaissance*, 438.

57 Thomas Kuehn, *Law, Family, and Women*, 136.

58 Marsilio Ficino's 1455 "*Epistola ad fratres vulgaris*," in *Supplementum ficinianum*, ed. P.O. Kristeller, 2 vols. (Florence: Olschki, 1937), vol. 2, 122, quoted in F.W. Kent, *Household and Lineage in Renaissance Florence*, 47.

59 Alberti, *The Family in Renaissance Florence*, 41.

60 Ibid.

61 Torquato Tasso, *Tasso's Dialogues*, 61.

62 In Palmieri's division of life into six parts, adolescence was followed by the stage of virility, and old age began at fifty-six. Matteo Palmieri, *Della vita civile trattato di Matteo Palmieri*, 28, first published as *Libro della via civile* (Florence: Giunti, 1529), and in three subsequent sixteenth-century editions in 1534, 1535, and 1536.

63 Moulton, "The Illicit Worlds of the Renaissance," 497. Up to the age of eighteen or twenty, males could assume the passive role in anal intercourse. After that, "manly" norms required the male to be the sodomizer. What mattered was that the behaviour was age appropriate. John Jeffries Martin, introduction to Michael Rocke, "Gender and Sexual Culture in Renaissance Italy," 140.

64 Guido Ruggiero, "Marriage, Love, Sex, and Renaissance Civic Morality," 23.

65 Alberti, *The Family in Renaissance Florence*, 160.

66 Rocke, "Gender and Sexual Culture in Renaissance Italy," 142.

67 In response, Pantalone wants to know who, then, *is* corrupting his son. It seems not to be conceivable to him that his son is responsible for his own behaviour. Adovardo Alberti, in Leon Battista Alberti's, *The Family in Renaissance Florence*, comments on such obtuseness: "For some reason that I don't know, however, something like excessive love veils and blinds the father's eyes. He rarely sees the faults of his children until they have already grown obvious and serious" (80). The fear of sons being corrupted by the company they keep is several times expressed in Alberti. Lorenzo Alberti says, "Sometimes they are inspired to evil and wholly ruined by the bad conversation and customs around them" (36).

68 Christopher Carlsmith, *A Renaissance Education*, 290.

69 Lorenzo Alberti in Alberti, *The Family in Renaissance Florence*, 36.

70 Doran, *Endeavors of Art*, 22.

71 Ibid., 236.

72 Torquato Tasso, *Tasso's Dialogues*, 83.

73 Rocke, "Gender and Sexual Culture in Renaissance Italy," 141. See also Jean E. Howard, "Cross-Dressing, the Theater, and Gender Struggle in Early Modern England," 25.

74 Margaret L. King, "The Woman of the Renaissance," 223. Women in convents presented no issues for the patriarchy nor, then, for comedy. There are poorly documented cases of lay spinsters, women under the supervision of brothers or other relatives. These suggest that such women were often no more than unpaid servants or nurses and badly treated at that. Federica Ambrosini, "Toward a Social History of Women in Venice," 424–5.

75 In Florence the law required that a woman needed a guardian in order to take part in legal transactions. This *mundualdus* could be any designated male. For a married woman the husband served in that role. Kuehn, *Law, Family and Women,* 204.

76 Elissa B. Weaver, "Gender,"190.

77 King, "The Woman of the Renaissance," 223.

78 Diana E. Henderson, "The Theatre and Domestic Culture," 181. "Nature and human reason taught mankind the necessity of having a spouse, both to increase and continue generations and to nourish and preserve those already born," says Lionardo in Alberti, *The Family in Renaissance Florence,* 111.

79 Ludovico Dolce, *Dialogo della institution delle donne,* in "The Lady and the Laurel" by Anne Christine Junkerman, 49.

80 Paula Findlen, "Introduction to Part IV," in *The Italian Renaissance,* 169.

81 Dilwyn Knox, "Civility, Courtesy, and Women in the Italian Renaissance," 6. Ludovico Dolce analogized an unmarried girl's body to a ship floating in a sea of many dangers, all the orifices of which have to be closed so that these dangers cannot penetrate into the inner parts." Lodovico Dolci, *Dialogo della istitutione delle donne* (Venice: Giolito, 1560), fol. 9v., in Bonnie Gordon, "The Courtesan's Singing Body as Cultural Capital in Seventeenth-Century Italy," 188.

82 Marta Ajmar, "Exemplary Women in Renaissance Italy," 246.

83 Gabriella Zarri, "Christian Good Manners," 88.

84 Lena Cowen Orlin, "Three Ways to Be Invisible in the Renaissance," 185. Handiwork kept the woman occupied, out of public view with head lowered, appropriately modelling and proving her self-abnegation. See also King, "The Woman of the Renaissance," 237.

85 King, "The Woman of the Renaissance," 223.

86 Alberti, *The Family in Renaissance Florence,* 207.

87 Paolo Caggio, "Iconomica del Signor Paolo Caggio, gentil'huomo di Palermo," in Bell, *How to Do It,* 346n1.

88 Grendler, *Schooling in Renaissance Italy,* 102.

89 Ibid., 88.

90 Grendler, "Form and Function," 453.

91 Thomas Frederick Crane, *Italian Social Customs of the Sixteenth Century, and Their influence on the Literatures of Europe*, 249.

92 Fra Sabba Castiglione, 1554, in Grendler, *Schooling in Renaissance Italy*, 88.

93 Daniela Hacke, *Women, Sex, and Marriage in Early Modern Venice*, 164, 187.

94 Alessandro Piccolomini, "Alessandro," 306.

95 Christiane Klapisch-Zuber, *Women, Family, and Ritual in Renaissance Italy*, 108–9.

96 Ibid., 111. Owing to inferior care and sometimes outright neglect, the infant mortality rate for girls who were farmed out to wet nurses was higher than that of boys with in-house wet nurses. Rudolph M. Bell disputes this view, inferring from advice books of the period that "girls as well as boys were cherished" and that "abandonment or indifference were not frequent." Bell, *How to Do It*, 145.

97 Stanley Chojnacki, "'The Most Serious Duty,'" 181.

98 Christopher F. Black, *Early Modern Italy*, 113.

99 Ann Crabb, *The Strozzi of Florence*, 190, 205.

100 Sharon T. Strocchia, "Gender and the Rites of Honour in Italian Renaissance Cities," 43.

101 Chojnacki, "'The Most Serious Duty,'" 182.

102 Tanya Pollard sees the relationship between the considerable interest in drugs of various kinds in early modern theatre as expression of the rising concern about "the rapidly changing and controversy-ridden world of early modern pharmacy" together with a comparable concern about the power of theatre, which was frequently analogized to drugs. Pollard observes that opium, brought from the New World, was increasingly used to induce sleep, particularly for plague victims, but that its use called attention to the too-fine line between drug-induced sleep and death. Tanya Pollard, *Drugs and Theater in Early Modern England*, 4, 18, 66–7.

103 Desiderius Erasmus, *Erasmus on Women*, 17.

104 Grendler, *Books and Schools in the Italian Renaissance*, 11. The most popular story was *Orlando furioso*. From the first edition in 1516 to the end of the century, by Grendler's count, there were perhaps as many as 183 printings.

105 E.R. Chamberlin, *The World of the Italian Renaissance*, 192.

106 Strocchia, "Gender and the Rites of Honour in Italian Renaissance Cities," 44.

107 King, "The Woman of the Renaissance," 214.

108 Dennis Romano, *Housecraft and Statecraft*, 10.

109 Days 30 and 36 each call for a baby in arms. No other young children appear in the Scala scenarios.

110 See, for instance, "Widows, Legal Rights, and the Mercantile Economy of Early Modern Milan," by Jeanette M. Fregulia, 233–8.

111 King, "The Woman of the Renaissance," 215.

112 Kamen, *Early Modern European Society*, 20, table 1.1.

113 Christine Meek, "Women Between the Law and Social Reality," 184.

114 Ibid.

115 King, "The Woman of the Renaissance," 213.

116 Giannetti, *Lelia's Kiss*, 69.

117 Over age forty, a woman became virtually unmarriageable. Klapisch-Zuber, *Women, Family, and Ritual*, 119.

118 Caroline Castiglione, "Mothers and Children," 382.

119 Widows with no prospects for marriage were sent to convents. Otherwise, their independence, like that of an unmarried daughter, would have posed a threat to the family. Najemy, "Giannozzo and His Elders," 55.

120 See, for instance, Ferraro, *Marriage Wars in Late Renaissance Venice*, 154.

121 Castiglione, "Mothers and Children," 386.

122 If the male offspring did not survive, his patrimony went to the paternal agnates – uncles and grandfathers – who, accordingly, may not always have acted in the best interests of the offspring. Giulia Calvi, "Widows, the State, and the Guardianship of Children in Early Modern Tuscany," 213.

123 Exemplified in the engraving from the Recueil Fossard provided by Pierre Louis Duchartre, *The Italian Comedy*, 320. Katritzky, *The Art of Commedia*, dates these engravings from the 1580s, 108.

124 Rocke, "Gender and Sexual Culture," 149.

125 Ferraro, "Family and Clan in the Renaissance World," 179.

126 Strocchia, "Gender and the Rites of Honour," 44.

127 Romano, *Housecraft and Statecraft*, 159.

128 Robert C. Davis, "The Geography of Gender in the Renaissance," 22. They were also subject to everyday street violence. Davis reports that washerwomen typically had to do the laundry at wells located in the middle of public spaces, where they were frequently caught in the midst of youths fighting one another. They risked serious injury and even death. To prevent this, cities like Perugia built enclosed wash-houses from which teasing and provocative youths and men stopping to water their horses were banned. Ibid., 30.

129 Rocke, "Gender and Sexual Culture," 149.

130 Trevor Dean, "Fathers and Daughters," 95.

131 Ibid., 89. In real life, he may also have chosen the husband.

132 Flaminio Scala, *Il teatro delle favole rappresentative*, vol. 1, 56. Verona Eisenach reports that because of the almost certain disabilities that a concubine would suffer if she were simply abandoned once the relationship had ended, the men who kept them often helped them to marry, providing a dowry, a husband, and a proper celebration, thus allowing them to re-enter

respectable society. Eisenach speculates that this arrangement may have been the chief attraction of concubinage for many women. Verona Emlyn Eisenach, *Husbands, Wives, and Concubines,* 134, 153.

133 Sandra Cavallo and Simona Cerutti, "Female Honor and the Social Control of Reproduction in Piedmont between 1600 and 1800," 78.

134 Dean, "Fathers and Daughters," 95

135 Scala, *Il teatro dell favole rappresentative,* vol. 1, 53. Adultery was a crime prosecuted primarily against women, and the punishments could be severe. Giannetti, *Lelia's Kiss,* 209.

136 Crane, *Italian Social Customs of the Sixteenth Century,* 146.

137 Ibid., 146, 251.

138 Pietro Bembo, *Gli Asolani,* 48.

139 Brian Vickers, *In Defence of Rhetoric,* 303.

140 Hale, *The Civilization of Europe in the Renaissance,* 325.

141 Peter Burke, *The Italian Renaissance,* 162.

142 Rosalind Kerr, "Isabellla Andreini (Comica Gelosa 1562–1604)," 71–92.

143 Andrews's assertion that the fathers in the scenarios "opposed the desired matches [of the lovers] either for selfish reasons (avarice, or wanting one of the young women for themselves), or else out of an automatic hostility to any marriage proposal which they had not initiated. In some of Scala's scenarios no reason is given why a father forbids a betrothal: it is a knee-jerk authoritarian reaction which does not demand explanation." This is true as far as it goes but minimizes the significance of marriage relative to the preservation of the patriarchy in the society. Richard Andrews, in Scala, *The Commedia dell'Arte of Flaminio Scala,* xxxiii.

144 Ruggiero, "Witchcraft and Magic," 479.

145 Bembo, *Gli Asolani.* By 1600, *Gli Asolani (1497–1504),* one of the most influential books of the Renaissance, had appeared in at least twenty-two Italian editions.

146 This scenario is a tour de force for the actress playing Isabella, who goes mad following Orazio's betrayal. It also allows Orazio an emotional conflict, not so fully developed in other scenarios. If it is hard for contemporary readers to accept the usual happy marriage after Isabella's murders and Orazio's vacillation between two women, we have to take into account that the murders took place only in the antefact and before Isabella was a Christian; they serve as part of the motivation for Isabella's madness, and we are to appreciate her devotion to and suffering for Orazio. For his part, Orazio is a victim of Love.

147 Paula Findlen, "Introduction to Part III," in *The Italian Renaissance,* 95.

148 Crane, *Italian Social Customs of the Sixteenth Century,* 146, 35, and 145. For

a debate on the role of jealousy in love see Sperone Speroni, "Dialogue on Love," revised version of 1575; I am grateful to one of the anonymous readers for the University of Toronto Press for calling this dialogue to my attention.

149 Crane, *Italian Social Customs*, 35, 420.

150 Domenico Pietropaolo, "The Theatre," 17.

151 Battista in Alberti, *The Family in Renaissance Florence*, 96.

152 Often for a tip. See Giovanni Maria Cécchi, *The Horned Owl* (*L'assiuolo*), 77.

153 Guazzo, *La civil conversazione*, 237.

154 Hacke, *Women, Sex, and Marriage*, 189.

155 Thomas V. Cohen, *Love and Death in Renaissance Italy*, 62.

156 Richard Andrews finds the presence of Capitano here mere padding "in scenes which have no connection with the main plot," added because the story of Cataldo, the pedant, "is not sufficient to fill a whole three acts." Andrews, in Scala, *The Commedia dell'Arte of Flaminio Scala*, 190. In my reading, Isabella's behaviour gives her character depth and adds suspense. Her behaviour is neither inconsistent nor one-dimensionally "virtuous" as Andrews claims (in Scala, *The Commedia dell'Arte of Flaminio Scala*, 191). At the end of the second act when the tutor kisses Isabella and she goes into the house happy, the prior scene with the Capitano leaves the audience wondering whether she will be unfaithful with the more ready-to-hand tutor. Isabella's sexual frustration is displaced onto Pedrolino, who seeks revenge for the beating she gives him, which, like Isabella's frustration, in the end is also displaced satisfactorily onto the pedant.

157 Thomas V. Cohen, *Love and Death in Renaissance Italy*, 195.

158 Baldesar Castiglione, *The Book of the Courtier (Il cortegiano)*, 138.

159 Leon Battista Alberti, *The Family in Renaissance Florence*, 95.

160 Kent, *Friendship, Love, and Trust*, 6.

161 Leon Battista Alberti, *The Family in Renaissance Florence*, 41.

162 Ibid., 282.

163 Findlen, "Introduction to Part III," in *The Italian Renaissance*, 95.

164 Kent, *Friendship, Love, and Trust*, 6, 9, 13.

165 Ibid., 218.

166 Ibid., 13.

167 Giovanni Morelli, *Ricordi*, ed. Vittore Branca (Florence, 1956), 226, in Kent, *Friendship, Love, and Trust*, 157.

168 In Day 3 the friend simply gives up the one love interest for another. In Day 30 Flavio does not forgive, but his love interest turns out to be his own sister.

169 Doran, *Endeavors of Art*, 22, 235–6.

170 Alberti, *The Family in Renaissance Florence*, 306–7.
171 Black, *Early Modern Italy*, 97.
172 Romano, *Housecraft and Statecraft*, 107–8.
173 Ibid., 110, 116.
174 Ibid., 167.
175 Tasso, *Tasso's Dialogues*, 101, 105.
176 Romano, *Housecraft and Statecraft*, 31.
177 Ibid., 32.
178 Ibid., 16.
179 Crane, *Italian Social Customs*, 295. Romano, *Housecraft and Statecraft*, 31.
180 Alberti, *The Family in Renaissance Florence*, 218.
181 Romano, *Housecraft and Statecraft*, 13, 12.
182 F.W. Kent, "'Be Rather Loved Than Feared': Class Relations in Quattrocento Florence," 48.
183 They could also be removed from the will. Apparently, promises of inclusion in the will and threats of removal from it played a role in discipline. Romano, *Housecraft and Statecraft*, 207.
184 Marta Ajmar-Wollheim and Flora Dennis, eds., *At Home in Renaissance Italy*, 151.
185 According to Guazzo, *La civil conversazione*, vol. 1, 254.
186 Romano, *Housecraft and Statecraft*, 8, 40.
187 Guazzo, *La civil conversazione*, vol 1, 253–4, translated by Crane, *Italian Social Customs*, 295. Guazzo's work was very popular, having been translated into Latin, French, and English and reprinted as late as 1738. The book first appeared In English as *The Civile Conversation of M. Steeven Guazzo*, books 1–3 translated by George Pettie, 1581, and book 4 translated by Barth Young, 1586, with an introduction by Edward Sullivan. London: Constable and Co, 1925.
188 Romano, *Housecraft and Statecraft*, 24.
189 F.W. Kent, "Be Rather Loved Than Feared," 48.
190 Romano, *Housecraft and Statecraft*, 222.
191 Ibid., 216, 222.
192 Ajmar-Wollheim and Dennis, *At Home in Renaissance Italy*, 222.
193 Romano, *Housecraft and Statecraft*, 222; emphasis Romano's.
194 Ibid., 223.
195 Ibid.
196 Sella, *Italy in the Seventeenth Century*, 78.
197 Ibid., 207.
198 Karl Appuhn, "Tools for the Development of the European Economy," 261.

199 Ibid.

200 Friedrichs, *The Early Modern City*, 133. This number does not take into account the high mortality rate of the poor, many of them crowded into disease-infested quarters. Appuhn, "Tools for the Development of the European Economy," 261.

201 Romano, *Housecraft and Statecraft*, 226.

202 Ibid., 220.

203 Ibid., 153.

204 Ibid., 226.

205 James R. Farr, "Honor, Law, and Custom in Renaissance Europe," 134.

206 The black-faced mask of Arlecchino seems to be a reference to his peasant background. The term *nigredo* was used to describe the peasant and serf, as well as the devil. If the peasant was a good for nothing, he was referred to as a "black *leccatore* [sponging] rustic." His brow was low, his nose flat. He was subhuman, monstrous; "an unheard-of filthy blackness afflicted" him all over. Piero Camporesi, *The Land of Hunger*, 36.

207 Guicciardini, *Maxims and Reflections of a Renaissance Statesman*, series B, 106, 39.

208 Peter Burke, *The Historical Anthropology of Early Modern Italy*, 9.

209 Richard Andrews, "Shakespeare and Italian Comedy," 138.

210 Robert Henke, "Representations of Poverty in the *Commedia dell'Arte*," 235.

211 Peter Burke, "The Historical Geography of the Renaissance," 92.

212 De Vries, *European Urbanization*, 213. Burke "The Historical Geography," 92.

213 Michael Mallett, *Mercenaries and Their Masters*, 18.

214 Robert C. Davis, "The Renaissance Goes Up in Smoke," 400.

215 Ibid.

216 Tommaso Astarita, *Between Salt Water and Holy Water*, 97.

217 Stefonao Carboni, *Venice and the Islamic World, 828–1797*, 72.

218 Astarita, *Between Salt Water and Holy Water*, 98.

219 Ibid., 182.

220 Robert C. Davis, *Christian Slaves, Muslim Masters*, 23–4.

221 Astarita, *Between Salt Water and Holy Water*, 97. For my discussion of slavery by Christians see my chapter 8, "Day 36, *Isabella [the] Astrologer*."

222 Davis, *Christian Slaves, Muslim Masters*, 144.

223 Tommaso Astarita reports that Christians in Muslim lands who converted to Islam, as many did, could ascend to prominent positions in the Muslim world. Astarita, *Between Salt Water and Holy Water*, 98. There is also record of those who pretended to convert. See Eric R. Dursteler, *Renegade Women*, 17, 115, 118.

224 Sella, *Italy in the Seventeenth Century*, 1. See also Thomas James Dandelet, *Spanish Rome, 1500–1700.*

225 Mallett, *Mercenaries and Their Masters*, 18.

226 Niccolò Machievelli, *History of Florence and the Affairs of Italy.*

227 Felix Gilbert, *Machiavelli and Guicciardini*, 92.

228 Francesco Guicciardini, *The History of Italy*, 32. The book was first published in Florence in 1561 and subsequently in 1562 and 1599. Lodovico Alamanni, 1516, ascribed "the present state and shame of serfdom of Italy" to the "habit of using mercenary soldiers," in Gilbert, *Machiavelli and Guicciardini*, 130.

229 Niccolò Machiavelli, *The Prince*, 1532, chap. 12.

230 Between 1532, the date of its first publication, and 1611, the date of Scala's collection, Machiavelli's *The Prince* had been printed twenty times. Mallett, *Mercenaries and Their Masters, 208.*

231 Recent scholars have argued that the disunified Italian states were no match for a national army in any case.

232 Coluccio Salutati in Mallet, *Mercenaries and Their Masters*, 208.

233 Machiavelli, *The Prince*, chap. 12. See also Machiavelli, *Discourses*, book 1, chap. 43.

234 Niccolò Machiavelli, *The Art of War* (*Arte della Guerra*, 1521), 189.

235 Guicciardini, *The History of Italy*, 52.

236 Geoffrey Trease, *The Condottieri*, 18.

237 Mallett, *Mercenaries and Their Masters*, 3.

238 Michael D. Bristol, "Theater and Popular Culture," 232.

239 Sella, *Italy in the Seventeenth Century*, 52.

240 Thomas F. Arnold, "Violence and Warfare in the Renaissance World," 461.

241 Castiglione, *The Book of the Courtier*, 58.

242 Davis, "The Renaissance Goes Up in Smoke," 399.

243 At one time the *condottieri* used the configuration of the three-soldier mounted *lancia* (that is a head or a *capo-lancia*, a groom, and a boy). Arlecchino, when accompanying the Capitano, seems to play the role of that groom.

244 Michael Mallett, "The Condottiere," 41.

245 Henke, "Representations of Poverty," 229–46.

246 Black, *Early Modern Italy*, 25.

247 Hale, *The Civilization of Europe*, 455–6.

248 Black, *Early Modern Italy*, 25.

249 Thomas F. Van Laan sees middle-elite characters, who are frequently shown dressing down, as in the process of losing themselves to find themselves. Van Laan, *Role-Playing in Shakespeare*, 105. David Bevington, influ-

enced by Victor Turner, aligns this process with ritual initiation (David Bevington, *Action Is Eloquence*, 4 and *passim*). Recently Peter Hyland has argued that the prevalence of disguise on the early modern stage reflects broader current questions about the stability of the self, particularly provoked by the rise of the upwardly mobile classes (*Disguise on the Early Modern English Stage*, 30, 141). In Scala the middle elites dress down. I can think of two instances in Scala in which a servant dresses up: In Day 9 Isabella's nurse disguises herself as a gentleman, husband to Isabella, to help her mistress prevent an unwanted marriage while she awaits her true love; and in Day 26 Pedrolino momentarily costumes himself as a Levantine merchant in order to help his master.

250 Scala was certainly familiar with the term *lazzi*: the Stranger, adversary to the Player in the first prologue of *Il finto marito*, uses it (p. cviv).

251 Camporesi, *The Land of Hunger*, 120. Camporesi also observes that in real life "tricks, expedients and techniques ... belong to the repertoire of the art of hunger, [the] great inventor of swindling subtleties" (ibid, 116–17).

252 Ray Porter, preface to *Bread of Dreams* by Piero Camporesi, 14–15.

253 Robert Garapon, *La Fantaisie verbale et le comique dans le théâtre français du Moyen Âge à la fin du XVIIe siècle*, 87; in Camporesi, *Bread of Dreams*, 81.

254 Hale, *The Civilization of Europe*, 456.

255 Black, *Early Modern Italy*, 105.

3. The Setting and Life in the Street

1 Andrews, "Shakespeare and Italian Comedy," 127.

2 Ibid. See also Richard Andrews, "Anti-feminism in *Commedia Erudita*," 17.

3 Fynes Moryson, *An Itinerary Containing His Ten Yeeres Travell through the Twelve Dominions of Germany, Bohmerland, Sweitzerland, Netherland, Denmarke, Poland, Italy, Turky, France, England, Scotland & Ireland*, vol. 1, 70.

4 Donald Beecher, *Renaissance Comedy*, vol. 1, 12.

5 Domenico Pietropaolo, "The Stage in the Text," 38.

6 Leon Battista Alberti, *On Painting*, 75.

7 Samuel Beckett deliberately turned the convention of the street setting on its head where, on a road in *Waiting for Godot*, "nothing happens, nobody comes, nobody goes, it's awful" (Estragon, act 1).

8 Maggie Günsberg, *Gender and the Italian Stage*, 46.

9 For this argument see Pietropaolo, "The Stage in the Text," 38.

10 Likewise, Ludovico Ariosto in his prologue to *Il Negromante* (1509) explains that the same set that he used for Ferrara in his *La Lena*, namely the fixed stage set of the ducal theatre in Ferrara, now represents Cremona (215).

11 Francesco Andreini, "Cortesi Lettori," 13.

12 Corsini manuscript illustrations, in Vita Pandolfi, *La commedia dell'arte,* vol 5, reproduced in an unnumbered twenty-six-page supplement between pages 256 and 257; and, much smaller, in Katritzky, *The Art of Commedia,* 543–9.

13 Stefano Mengarelli, "New Developments in Commedia Research," 214.

14 Similarly an ink-and-wash representation, "?French School c. 1575–1600. A scene from the *commedia dell'arte,*" in Katritzky, *The Art of Commedia,* 592, fig. 305, shows a man playing a mandolin partially behind the front building. For other figures within the set, but not behind the front buildings, see the engraving by Jacques Callot, "Scapino takes centre stage," 1618–20, in Katritzky, *The Art of Commedia,* 590, fig. 301; also the woodcut shown as "C. Gonzaga, *Gli inganni,*" in Peter Brand, "Disguise in Renaissance Comedy," 68. For a figure in a doorway on the perspectival street see 34v in "Curzio Gonzaga, *Gli inganni,* 1592," reproduced in Louise George Clubb, "Pictures for the Reader," 271. Clubb also attributes the work to Curzio Gonzaga. At the present time the play, in accordance with its prologue, is seen as the collective work of the Academy of the Intronati of Siena to which Gonzaga belonged. For a figure knocking on the door in the perspectival street, see the anonymous illustration for act 3, scene 3, in Orazio Vecchi, *L'amfiparnaso,* 1597, no page number.

15 Scala, Day 19, act 3, *Il teatro delle favole rappresentative,* 203.

16 Lodovico Castelvetro, *Poetica d'Aristotele vulgarizzata e sposta* (Basel, 1576), 535, in Marvin Carlson, *Theories of the Theatre,* 49.

17 Pietro Aretino, *La cortigiana,* 53. In *La calandra* the argument tells us that "the city that you see here before you is Rome. That city, once so large, spacious, and great that with all its triumphs it encompassed many cities, countries, and rivers, now has become so small that, as you see, it can be easily contained in your city" (4).

18 Vecchi, *L'amfiparnaso,* no page number.

19 This point is made by Salvatore Di Maria, *The Italian Tragedy in the Renaissance,* 138.

20 Kenneth Richards and Laura Richards, "*Commedia dell'Arte,*" 112.

21 Burke, *Culture and Society,* 252.

22 For population figures see Edward Muir and Ronald F.E. Weissman, "Social and Symbolic Places in Renaissance Venice and Florence," 82, and Burke, *The Italian Renaissance,* 226.

23 De Vries, *European Urbanization,* 181.

24 Muir and Weissman, "Social and Symbolic Places," 82.

25 Kamen, *Early Modern European Society,* 20, table 1.1.

26 From Marsilio Ficino's "Epistola ad fratres vulgaris," 1455, in F.W. Kent, *Household and Lineage in Renaissance Florence,* 47.

27 Eisenach observes that the nuclear family isolated women from the control, influences, and oversight of the extended kinship group (*Husbands, Wives, and Concubines*, 85).
28 E.R. Chamberlin, *Everyday Life in Renaissance Times*, 80–2.
29 Muir, *Ritual in Early Modern Europe*, 33.
30 Günsberg, *Gender and the Italian Stage*, 21.
31 Bernardo Dovizi da Bibbiena, *La calandra* (*The Comedy of Calandro*).
32 Chamberlin, *Everyday Life in Renaissance Times*, 83; Chamberlin, *The World of the Italian Renaissance*, 201–2.
33 Andrea de Jorio, *Gesture in Naples and Gesture in Classical Antiquity*, cv.
34 Hale, *The Civilization of Europe in the Renaissance*, 147.
35 Michael Talbot, "*Ore Italiane*," 58–9.
36 Sabba Castiglione, *Ricordi overo ammaestramenti*, in Camporesi, *Bread of Dreams*, 95.
37 Robbery and murder, including revenge killings, were endemic in Italy at the time. Davis, "The Renaissance Goes Up in Smoke," 399.
38 Talbot, "*Ore Italiane*," 58.
39 Ibid., 57.
40 Ghosts appear "all too often in Scala's ... scenarios." Richard Andrews, in Scala, *The Commedia dell'Arte of Flaminio Scala*, 287, also 309. Jeremy Lopez comments that "there is something theatrically exuberant about making live bodies seem extravagantly dead, and also about representing ghosts with indisputably corporeal actors." Jeremy Lopez, "Imagining the Actor's Body on the Early Modern Stage," 195.
41 Martin, "The Myth of Renaissance Individualism," 38.
42 Camporesi, *Bread of Dreams*, 94.
43 David Wiles, *A Short History of Western Performance Space*, 107, 120.
44 Tim Fitzpatrick sees a convention of unmotivated exits in Scala's scenarios, which he interprets as "more or less natural returns to 'home base' [off-stage]." Fitzpatrick, *The Relationship of Oral and Literate Performance Processes*, 111. In my reading, most of the exits are, in fact, motivated; entrances, however, often serve only plot convenience; the *piazza* is "home base."
45 F.W. Kent, *Household and Lineage in Renaissance Florence*, 241–2.
46 D.V. Kent, *Friendship, Love, and Trust in Renaissance Florence*, 6.
47 Ibid.
48 Muir and Weissman, "Social and Symbolic Places," 88, 90.
49 D.V. Kent and F.W. Kent, *Neighbours and Neighbourhood in Renaissance Florence*, 2. Peter Burke reiterates the analogy: The city was "a stage," upon which was played out, in public view, many activities, which today are conducted behind the privacy of walls. Burke, *The Historical Anthropology*, 119.
50 Adam Kendon in de Jorio, *Gesture in Naples*, cii.

51 Muir, *Ritual in Early Modern Europe*, 102.
52 James S. Ackerman and Myra Nan Rosenfeld, "Social Stratification in Renaissance Urban Planning," 46. See also Muir and Weissman, "Social and Symbolic Places," 88.
53 Moulton, "The Illicit Words of the Renaissance," 494.
54 Peter Burke, *The Art of Conversation*, 78.
55 Alberti, *The Family in Renaissance Florence*, 207.
56 Burke, *The Historical Anthropology*, 10.
57 Romano, *Housecraft and Statecraft*, 167.
58 Davis, "The Geography of Gender," 22.
59 Muir, *Ritual in Early Modern Europe*, 109.
60 Burke, *The Historical Anthropology*, 9.
61 The Italian fascination with the beguiling allusion extends literally to facades in which simulated marble, cleverly disguised concrete, and a cunning assortment of ashlar (thin stone slabs applied to resemble weighty blocks) feign the real thing.
62 Burke, *The Historical Anthropology*, 10.
63 Alberti, *The Family in Renaissance Florence*, 47.
64 Alexander Cowan, "Cities, Towns, and New Forms of Culture," 107.
65 Dursteler, *Renegade Women*, 17.
66 Paolo Sarpi, letter to Jacques Gillot, 1609, in Jon R. Snyder, *Dissimulation and the Culture of Secrecy in Early Modern Europe*, 59.
67 Snyder, *Dissimulation and the Culture of Secrecy*, 6.
68 Ibid., 59, 5.
69 *Le Banquet ou apres-dinée du comte d'Arète* (Paris: Guillaume Bichon, 1594), 4, in Snyder, *Dissimulation and the Culture of Secrecy*, xiv.
70 Alberti, *The Family in Renaissance Florence*, 266.
71 Linda Woodbridge, "Renaissance Bogeymen," 453.
72 Alberti, *The Family in Renaissance Florence*, 149.
73 Edward Muir, *Mad Blood Stirring*, 255. Muir cites the dialogue on honour of Annibale Romei. See also Farr, "Honor, Law, and Custom," 127.
74 D.V. Kent, *Friendship, Love, and Trust*, 136.
75 Agostino Ventura, *Misc. Gregolin*, 1572, in Ugo Tucci, "The Psychology of the Venetian Merchant in the Sixteenth Century," 368.
76 Guido Ruggiero, "Marriage, Love, Sex," 12.
77 Elizabeth S. Cohen, "Honor and Gender in the Streets of Early Modern Rome," 617.
78 Weaver, "Gender," 190.
79 Farr, "Honor, Law, and Custom," 128.
80 Crabb, *The Strozzi of Florence*, 193.

81 Jeffrey Masten, "Playwrighting," 359.
82 Gregory Hanlon, *Early Modern Italy, 1550–1800*, 28.
83 Davis, "The Geography of Gender," 23.
84 Ibid., 17.
85 The effort to keep the family's wealth intact meant that many men never married. Scala's comedies do not include these men, except perhaps in the case of the Capitano. Nor does he represent unmarried women in convents, the number of whom increased with dowry inflation.
86 Guido Ruggiero, "Marriage, Love, Sex," 23.
87 Guido Ruggiero, "Witchcraft and Magic," 478.
88 Strocchia, "Gender and Rites of Honour," 53–4.
89 Burke, *The Historical Anthropology*, 108, 99.
90 Guido Ruggiero, *Binding Passions*, 60.
91 Baldesar Castiglione, *The Book of the Courtier*, 195.
92 Guido Ruggiero, *Binding Passions*, 96-7. Also Strocchia, "Gender and the Rites of Honour," 54.
93 Strocchia, "Gender and the Rites of Honour," 57–8.
94 Peter Burke, *Popular Culture in Early Modern Europe*, 200.
95 Strocchia, "Gender and the Rites of Honour," 53.
96 Bristol, "Theater and Popular Culture," 235.
97 Arnold, "Violence and Warfare," 466.
98 Gregory Hanlon, "Violence and Its Control in the Late Renaissance," 140.
99 Hale, *The Civilization of Europe*, 456.
100 Hanlon, *Early Modern Italy*, 29.
101 Arnold, "Violence and Warfare," 463.
102 Hanlon, "Violence and Its Control," 140.
103 V.G. Kiernan, *The Duel in European History*, 117.
104 Arnold, "Violence and Warfare," 461.
105 Hale, *The Civilization of Europe*, 422.
106 Muir, *Mad Blood Stirring*, 256.
107 Hale, *The Civilization of Europe*, 422.
108 Kiernan, *The Duel in European History*, 118.
109 Muir, *Mad Blood Stirring*, 255. For the intimate relationship between honour, violence, and concepts of manliness in our own society see James Gilligan, *Violence, passim.*
110 Hanlon, "Violence and Its Control," 140.
111 Edward Muir, "The Double Binds of Manly Revenge in Renaissance Italy," 71.
112 Arnold, "Violence and Warfare," 465.

113 Donald Weinstein, “Fighting or flyting? Verbal Dueling in Mid-Sixteenth-Century Italy,” 212.

114 Hanlon, *Early Modern Italy*, 28.

115 Thomas Kuehn, “Inheritance and Identity in Early Renaissance Florence,” 138–9.

116 Guicciardini, *Maxims and Reflections*, series C, 60, 74.

117 Kiernan, *The Duel in European History*, 118.

118 Arnold, “Violence and Warfare,” 465.

119 Burke, *The Historical Anthropology*, 11. For a very vivid and amusing account of the theatrical nature of quarrels in the streets of Naples, two hundred years after Scala wrote, see de Jorio, *Gesture in Naples*, ciii.

120 Muir, *Mad Blood Stirring*, 256.

121 Muir, *Ritual in Early Modern Europe*, 141.

122 Twenty-fifth session, Council of Trent, 1563, chap. 19. On the effect of duelling manuals see Weinstein, “Fighting or flyting?,” 215.

123 Scala's Day 6, *The Jealous Old Man*, and Day 37, *The Hunt*, both portray hunters. Hunting was a violent activity that was central to the early modern period; the killing of other living things was regarded as a pleasurable activity. Thomas Arnold argues that among the upper classes “familiarity and the sensation of inflicting physical hurt on another living thing was first won and most often reinforced by the experience of the hunt.” Arnold, “Violence and Warfare,” 465.

124 Jane Tylus, “Women at the Windows,” 325.

125 Ibid., 331.

126 Louise George Clubb, “Italian Stories on Stage,” 42.

127 Rudolf M. Dekker and Lotte C. van de Pol, *The Tradition of Female Transvestism in Early Modern Europe*, 8, 99. Other motivations listed by Dekker and van de Pol are migration and following, remaining with, or escaping a husband or family. These are not utilized in Scala.

128 Giannetti, *Lelia's Kiss*, 117–18. Giannetti notes that in Italy the male characters who cross-dressed as female could appear in the Italian drama as they could not in the English drama, largely because the males who cross-dressed were invariably youths who had not renounced male privileges or superiority, for the simple but telling reason that society did not see them as having either as yet.

129 Howard, “Cross-Dressing, the Theater, and Gender Struggle,” 25.

130 Laura Giannetti Ruggiero, “When Male Characters Pass as Women,” 757.

131 M.A. Katritzky, *Women, Medicine, and Theatre, 1500–1750*, 243.

132 Ferdinando Taviani and Mirella Schino, *Il segreto della commedia dell'arte*, 416.

133 Howard, "Cross-Dressing, the Theater, and Gender Struggle," 41.
134 Giannetti, *Lelia's Kiss*, 15.
135 For this debate see Brand, "Disguise in Renaissance comedy," 84. Brand is also very good on the social effects of transsexual disguise, 86.

4. Invention

1 Flaminio Scala's letter to readers that prefaces his scenario collection, *Il teatro delle favole rappresentative*, 10.
2 Leon Battista Alberti, *Leon Battista Alberti on Painting*, 75.
3 Andrews, in Flaminio Scala, *The Commedia dell'Arte of Flaminio Scala*, vii.
4 Ireneo Sanesi maintained that the *commedia dell'arte* is a "popular adaptation or travesty of the learned comedy" (*La commedia*, vol. 1, 515).
5 Flaminio Scala, first prologue to *Il finto marito*, cx, cxiii.
6 Thomas M. Greene, *The Light in Troy*, 1.
7 Hayden White, for instance, argues that "narrativity ... is intimately related to, if not a function of, the impulse to moralize reality, that is to identify with the social system that is the source of any morality that we can imagine," and that the "demand for closure ... is a demand ... for moral meaning, a demand that sequences of real events be assessed as to their significance as elements of a moral drama" (*The Content of the Form*, 14, 21). We know that the Renaissance mirror showed events in moral terms. See the introduction to my chapter 2.
8 Mary Carruthers, *The Book of Memory*, 237.
9 Quintilian in Greene, *The Light in Troy*, 54.
10 Mary Carruthers, *The Craft of Thought*, 23.
11 Greene, *The Light in Troy*, 31.
12 Carruthers, *The Book of Memory*, 14–15.
13 Ibid., 93, 195, 14.
14 Ibid., 113, 21–2.
15 Ibid., 240.
16 Seneca's letter to Lucilius in Greene, *The Light in Troy*, 73–4.
17 Greene, *The Light in Troy*, 39.
18 Carruthers, *The Book of Memory*, 272–3.
19 Francesco Petrarch, *Le familiari*, 33.19, in Francesco Petrarch, *Letters from Petrarch*, 199. Letters are identified by volume and number according to Petrarch's original division.
20 Petrarch, *Le familiari*, 23.19, in Greene, *The Light in Troy*, 98.
21 Petrarch, *Le familiari*, 1, 8, in Greene, *The Light in Troy*, 99.
22 Scala, first prologue to *Il finto marito*, in *Il teatro delle favole rappresentative*, cx.

23 Carruthers, *The Book of Memory*, 272.
24 Louise George Clubb, "Looking Back on Shakespeare and Italian Theatre," 4.
25 She was writing about Shakespeare, after all.
26 The late Ludovico Zorzi's effort, following Vladimir Propp, to ambitiously count the number of what Propp called "narratemes" that were employed in all of *commedia dell'arte*, while highly enlightening, similarly suggests reshuffling. Ludovico Zorzi, "Intorno alla Commedia dell' Arte," 70.
27 Richard Dawkins, *The Selfish Gene*, chap 11.
28 Steven Johnson, *Where Good Ideas Come From*, 29.
29 Ibid., 31.
30 Marjorie Perloff, *Unoriginal Genius*, 3. Perloff cites a *TLS* review by Edgell Rickword of T.S. Eliot's "The Wasteland," when the poem first appeared in 1923: "One's 'magic-lantern show' [a term, Perloff observes, that was no doubt derived from Proust] should not consist of 'slides made by others.' A poem as a 'set of notes,' most of them 'borrowed' from other texts: such 'mere notation' can only be 'the result of an indolence of the imagination.'" Edgell Rickword, *TLS*, 20 September 1923, 49.
31 Charles Bernstein, "Manifest Aversions, Conceptual Conundrums, and Implausibly Deniable Links," *Poetry*, February 2009, in Marjorie Perloff, *Unoriginal Genius*, 1.
32 Scala, first prologue to *Il finto marito*, in *Il teatro delle favole rappresentative*, cxiii; Andreini, "*Cortesi lettori*," in *Il teatro delle favole rappresentative*, 13.
33 Quintillian, *Institutio Oratatoria*, x. vii. 7, in Carruthers, *The Book of Memory*, 109.
34 Scala, first prologue to *Il finto* marito, cxiii.
35 Richard Andrews, in Scala, *The Commedia dell'Arte of Flaminio Scala*, xii–xiii.
36 Giovanni Battista Andreini, at the end of his play, *Le due comedie in comedia*, 1623.
37 Testaverde reads Francesco Andreini's praise thus. Annamaria Testaverde, "Introduzione," *I canovacci della Commedia Dell' Arte*, xxv.
38 Barbara Mowat observes that a number of plays by Shakespeare (like some plays by Marlowe) can be considered as dramatizations of particular literary works and that others (like some plays by Jonson, Greene, and Marlowe) instead weave together language, characters, and incidents from a variety of works. "Even in the case of William Shakespeare, then, the matter presented on the early modern stage had absorbed and transmuted many a printed quarto and folio page. " Barbara A. Mowat, "The Theater and Literary Culture," 223–4.
39 Natalie Crohn Schmitt, "Improvisation in the *Commedia dell'Arte* in Its Golden Age," 225–50.

40 Jeremy Lopez, *Theatrical Convention and Audience Response in Early Modern Drama*, 134.

41 Neil Rhodes, *The Power of Eloquence and English Renaissance Literature*, 46.

42 Vickers, *In Defence of Rhetoric*, 258.

43 Lodovico Castelvetro, *Poetica d'Aristotele vulgarizzata e sposta* (Basel, 1576), 29, in Carlson, *Theories of the Theatre*, 49.

44 Testaverde discusses the "obsession with doubles" in *commedia dell'arte*, particularly as it shows itself in puns and in the characters, especially twins. She usefully analyses scenarios in terms of "redoubling and the trick of disguise" ("Introduzione," *I canovacci della Commedia Dell' Arte*, xlvii–liii).

45 I am paraphrasing Longinus's (?) description of the effect of Demostenes's *hyperbata*, in *On the Sublime* in Vickers, *In Defence of Rhetoric*, 298–9.

46 Marvin T. Herrick, *Comic Theory in the Sixteenth Century*, 149.

47 Aristotle, *Poetics*, xv, 6; Horace, *Ars poetica*, II, 191–2. Madeleine Doran has observed that, while Renaissance critics universally condemned the *deus ex machina*, their emphasis on the clever denouement put a premium on surprise. All that was required was that its improbability be skillfully concealed. Doran, *Endeavors of Art*, 324.

48 The scenario is set in Venice where impoverished peasants from the region around Bergamo came to work. Indeed, in Day 10 Burattino and Pedrolino discover that they are from the same village near Bergamo and thus probably both spoke with a Bergamasque dialect. In Day 28 Burattino and Pedrolino are again from the same area as are Arlecchino and Pedrolino in Day 31. So in each of these scenarios the two characters are likely to have spoken with the same dialect.

49 Andrews helpfully delineates Scala's frequent use of "the bad disguise trick," one in which a character is persuaded to disguise himself in a way that will result in his harm or ridicule. We might usefully extend Andrews's idea to Spavento in Scala's Day 37, where he is persuaded to go about without his sword and is then mocked and beaten; to Burattino in Day 27, who is advised to stay mute and as a result is repeatedly beaten; and to Malvolio in *Twelfth Night*, who woos in cross-garters. Andrews, in Scala, *The Commedia dell'Arte of Flaminio Scala*, 190.

50 Lopez, *Theatrical Convention*, 70.

51 Ibid., 182.

52 Roberto Tessari, *La commedia dell'arte nel Seicento*, 125.

53 See the views of Castelvetro and Robortello in Carlson, *Theories of the Theatre*, 49.

54 William G. Crane, *Wit and Rhetoric in the Renaissance*, 4.

55 Heinrich Wölfflin, *Principles of Art History*, 166.

56 In act 2 of Day 14, Fabrizio, actually a woman in disguise, confesses herself

to be overcome by the power of Love and, in so doing, refers the audience back to the opening scene and calls upon them to reinterpret it.

57 In revenge for the beating, Pedrolino had previously tried to pimp Isabella as his "wife" to the Capitino and, in claiming that he weeps for his wife, he may be fantasizing a most unfortunate end for Isabella, who has mistreated him.

58 The second of these lazzi also serves to allow time to pass while Isabella goes to gather a crowd for the humiliation of the pedant.

59 Terence, unlike the earlier Plautus, and favoured by early modern playwrights, discouraged direct address to the audience as unrealistic. http://www.britannica.com/EBchecked/topic/587857/Terence (accessed 25 January 2014). There is only very limited direct evidence in Scala's scenarios of the audience's being acknowledged, but we cannot know the extent of such acknowledgment in performance. Pantalone bows to the audience here at the end of act 1 in Day 26, and at the end of act 2, Day 37, the Capitano bows to the people (presumably to the audience, there being no one else on stage) and says "May it do you good, Gentlemen." Scala, *Il teatro delle favole rappresentative*, vol. 2, 381.

60 Doran, *Endeavors of Art*, 235–6.

61 Joel Altman makes the point that those who studied Terence's plays viewed each as "a running controversy waged by characters whose ruminations, inquiries, laments, and rejoicings were imaged responses to the need for proof required to win the argument." Joel B. Altman, *The Tudor Play of Mind*, 143.

62 The entertainment value of the scenario itself argues against the negative views of theatrical performance put forth in the scenario.

63 Alessandro Striggio, *La caccia*, liner notes with compact disc entitled *Banchieri, Il Festino del Giovedi Grasso; Striggio, La caccia*, Concerto Italiano directed by Rinaldo Allessandrini.

64 Lucia Marchi, "Chasing Voices, Hunting Love," 13–31. I am grateful to Marchi for calling attention to this essay, and the pen-and-ink drawing I include here, and for lending me a copy of the compact disc of Striggio's *La caccia*.

65 Andrews, in Scala, *The Commedia dell'Arte of Flaminio Scala*, 222.

66 Lucia Marchi, personal communication, 24 June 2013.

67 Lopez, *Theatrical Convention and Audience Response*, 4.

68 J.L. Styan, *Drama, Stage, and Audience*, 218. Jeremy Lopez has suggested that the opulent texture of the drama provided "a surfeit of stimulus and complexity ... akin ... to sexual excitement" (*Theatrical Convention and Audience Response*, 118).

69 Cicero, *De oratore*, 142.

70 Quintilian, preface to the seventh book of *Instituto oratoria*, in Herrick, *Comic Theory*, 96.

71 Giovanni Battista Guarini, prologue to *The Dropsical Lady* (*L'idropica*), 1583, in Herrick, *Italian Comedy*, 158. This idea was also shared by Della Porta, Giraldi, Castelvetro, and Beni. See Doran, *Endeavors of Art*, 278.

72 Desiderius Erasmus, 1512, *Copia*, 24: 302.

73 Janet Levarie Smarr, *Italian Renaissance Tales*, xxxiii.

74 Jacob Burckhardt, *The Civilization of the Renaissance in Italy*, part 4, 439.

75 Henke, "Representations of Poverty," 242.

76 The speaker is Bibbiena, known for his love of practical jokes. Baldesar Castiglione, *The Book of the Courtier*, 188.

77 Perhaps we need to keep in mind that poor dental care, fisticuffs, and dentistry itself meant that many people were missing teeth. However, infection was one of the top five killers, and tooth pulling, as unsanitary as it was, could result in death. Rotten teeth must have made bad breath, a subject of Scala's Day 12 and Day 20.

78 Donald A. Beecher, "Intriguers and Tricksters," 62.

79 Scala, *Il teatro delle favole rappresentative*, vol. 2, 332.

80 Quintilian, *De Institutio Oratoria*, 6.1.2 in Herrick, *Comic Theory in the Renaissance*, 31.

81 The last ten of the fifty scenarios go even further afield, not only into tragedy, pastoral, and what Scala calls "heroic" and "royal," or "mixed," but to a work extending over three days. See the appendix.

82 Taviani, "*Positions du masque dans la Commedia dell'Arte*," 126, 121. M.A. Katritzky observes that masked or veiled female characters are, in fact, represented in the iconography of the *commedia dell'arte* (*The Art of Commedia*, 202–3). These masks seem to denote membership in the upper class rather than character.

83 In Day 20 Pedrolino and in Day 16 Laura do not seem self-consistent but merely functionaries of the plot.

Method

1 Henke, *Performance and Literature*, 120.

2 Bembo, *Gli Asolani*, 126.

5. Day 6: The Jealous Old Man

1 See, for instance, Ferruccio Marotti, ed., *Il teatro delle favole rappresentative*, lvi–lviii; Roberto Tessari, *La commedia dell'arte nel Seicento*, 127–9; Cesari Molinari, "'Le favole rappresentative' di Flaminio Scala," 134–5.

2 Isabella Andreini, in *Masks and Marionettes*, by Joseph Spencer Kennard, 52. See also Isabella Andreini, "Biasimo di I vecchi innamorati," in *La Commedia dell'Arte*, 977. Madonna Oretta, in Giovanni Maria Cécchi's, *The Horned Owl* (*L'assiuolo*), IV, 3, provides a similar *malmaritata* (complaint about bad marriage):

> How many pleasures we are deprived of, and under what cruel tyranny we must live our lives. When men have to take a wife, they nearly always take whoever they please. We, on the contrary, must take whoever is given us. Sometimes, and I for one can vouch for it, poor me, we must take one who, to say nothing of his age which would make him our father rather than our husband, is so rough and inhuman ... I find myself married to Messer Ambrogio, who could be my grandfather! He's rich yes. But this doesn't mean I eat any better! Besides having a husband who's old, there's the problem of having one who's jealous, wrongly jealous. And there's no one who's more jealous than him. So, because of his jealousy I'm deprived of pleasure outside the house, and because of his age, of pleasure inside the house. (47)

Notable feminist writers of the period, Lucrezia Marinella (1571–1653) and Moderata Fonte (1555–92), denounced both arranged marriages and forced monacization. Ferraro, "Family Clan," 182.

3 A theorbo is a long-necked lute, virtually indistinguishable from the chitterone that Scala references later.

4 In the list of characters for Days 26, 28, and 29, Scala specifies policemen who speak, and for Day 30, servants who speak, thus suggesting a difference in pay scale and the possibility of employing non-speaking extras on occasion for small roles.

5 Muir, *Ritual in Early Modern Europe*, 102.

6 Antonio Venuti's preface to *De agricoltura opusculum* (Venice: Orso, 1546), 3rd ed., in Tucci, "The Psychology of the Venetian Merchant in the Sixteenth century," 350.

7 Alberti, *The Family in Renaissance Florence*, 193. Amanda Lillie makes clear how widespread and long-lived has been the idea of the idyllic life at a villa ("The Humanist Villa Revisited," 193–4).

8 Crane, *Italian Social Customs*, 251.

9 The theme of the young girl unhappily married to an older husband with whom she has little rapport and a young, unmarried male eager for a sexual affair appears in many *novelle*.

10 David Gentilcore, *Medical Charlatanism in Early Modern Italy*, 181–8. I am grateful to musicologist Martha Feldman for this reference.

11 Romano, *Housecraft and Statecraft*, 118.

12 Michael Rocke provides a quotation from Matteo Palmieri, *Vita civile*, 1433 (published in 1529), that could easily serve as a set speech at this point for Pantalone. Rocke, "Gender and Sexual Culture," 141.

13 Jean Baptiste Molière, *The School for Wives* (*L'école des femmes*), 140.

14 Rocke, "Gender and Sexual Culture," 155.

15 David R. Coffin, *The Villa in the Life of Renaissance Rome*, 18.

16 The Medici palace actually had toilets with drain pipes. Marta Ajmar-Wollheim and Flora Dennis, ed., *At Home in Renaissance Italy*, 36. These seem unlikely in this scenario.

17 Leon Battista Alberti, *Dinner Pieces* (*Intercenales*), 141.

18 Ajmar-Wollheim and Dennis, *At Home in Renaissance Italy*, 38.

19 Andrea Perrucci, *A Treatise on Acting, from Memory and by Improvisation*, 70.

20 Coffin, *The Villa in the Life of Renaissance Rome*, 141. In the course of the sixteenth century not only did firearms decimate the wildlife, but game habitat was turned into gardens and pasture. Coffin, *The Villa in the Life of Renaissance Rome*, 111, 124.

21 The dance steps provided by Fabritio Caroso, *Il ballarino*, 1581, can be found at http://jducoeur.org/IlBallarino/Book2/Ballo%20del%20Piantone.html. The music from Caroso can be heard at http://www.pbm.com/~lindahl/del/music/caroso_il_piantone_susan.mid. The site also provides the sheet music.

22 Perrucci, *A Treatise on Acting*, 70.

23 In Giovanni Maria Cécchi's play *L'assiuolo* (The Horned Owl) the old husband, locked outside in the garden, dutifully makes the call of an owl while the young lovers within enjoy the pleasure of their lovemaking, which is enhanced by the trick on the old man.

24 Men could be similarly punished but sometimes had the option of paying a fine. Moulton, "The Illicit Worlds," 492. See also Cohen, *Love and Death*, 198: "Adultery was punishable by death in some law codes; in Ferrara the guilty woman was to be burned alive, but not the man. In practice the courts often took a much more lenient view, as in sixteenth-century Venice, though the honour of offended aristocratic families might encourage the murder of both male and female offenders, with little consequence for the murdering cuckold or his supporters." See also Eva Cantarella, "Homicides of Honor," 229–44. Michael Rocke reports that punishment could also include forfeiture of the woman's dowry to her husband and children ("Gender and Sexual Culture," 158). The dowry was often her sole means of subsistence in widowhood, as well as a mark of her honour.

25 Comedies of adultery were not in the majority, but some of them are

well known: Ariosto's *La lena,* Machiavelli's *La mandragola,* and Cécchi's *L'assiuolo.* In Scala's Day 39, there is scant reassurance that the wives, with their young lovers, will not continue to be blissfully unfaithful to their foolish old husbands.

26 Alessandro Piccolomini, *La Raffaella ovvero Dialogo della bella creanza delle donne,* ed. Giancarlo Alfano (Rome: Salerno, 2001), 108, in Giannetti, *Lelia's Kiss,* 193.

27 Ruggiero, "Marriage, Love, Sex," 13, 15.

28 The comedy of old men and their inappropriate sexual passion for young girls is taken up by playwright Andrea Calmo, 1510–71, who himself specialized in the role of a mature Venetian merchant who loses his dignity to "senile passion and gross stupidity." It is also taken up by Gigio Giancarli, *La cingana,* 1550, and by Adriano Banchieri, *La pazzia senile* (*The Madness of Old Age*), 1598. See Andrews, *Scripts and Scenarios,* 147, and Ferraro, *Marriage Wars,* 63.

29 John Walter Hill, *Roman Monody, Cantata, and Opera from the Circles around Cardinal Montalto.* vol. 1, 75. I am grateful to musicologist Robert L. Kendrick for this reference.

30 Ibid., 75, 121, 129.

31 Francesco Rasi, *Virtuoso Italian Vocal Music: Monteverdi, Carissima, Caccini, Frescobaldi,* performed by Catherine Bott. Liner notes with compact disc. I am grateful to musicologist Lucia Marchi for having explained the Roman style to me and for having lent me this compact disc.

32 Hill, *Roman Monody,* vol. 1, 236.

33 At this point the scenario is reminiscent of *The Decameron,* III, 6.

34 Richard Andrews notes that English dramatists, unlike Italian ones, used the bed trick only to get men in bed with their "rightful" mates, not for adultery ("Shakespeare and Italian Comedy," 140).

35 In Bibbiena's *La calandra,* 1513, Calandro, who foolishly believes that the young Santilla is in love with him and seeks his favours, is placed by a servant in a darkened room with an ugly prostitute instead. The maid in the fourth story on the eighth day in *The Decameron* is also very ugly. Perhaps Pasquella is ugly too or perhaps she was played by a man.

36 The form of *The Decameron* and of other collections of fables and the frequency of writing set in dialogue form reflect the extent to which writing was regarded as speech written, whereas today we think of performance as writing spoken.

37 Ferruccio Marotti in Scala, *Il teatro,* d*elle favole rappresentative,*viii.

38 Hacke, *Women, Sex and Marriage,* 147.

39 "According to canon law, a marriage that could never be consummated was

not valid" (Ferraro, *Marriage Wars,* 10). In Cécchi's *L'assiuolo,* act 5, scene 6, in which the adultery is similarly celebrated, one of the characters observes, "Old men are like a gardener's dog: it never eats the lettuce nor lets anyone else eat it" (70).

40 Daniela Lombardi, "Intervention by Church and State in Marriage Disputes in Sixteenth- and Seventeenth-Century Florence," 143–5.

41 Guido Ruggiero, *The Boundaries of Eros,* 97.

42 Cohen, *Love and Death,* 147.

43 Van Laan, *Role-Playing in Shakespeare,* 223.

44 Muir, *Ritual in Early Modern Europe,* 33.

6. Day 21: The Fake Sorcerer

1 Kenneth Burke, *Counter-Statement,* 125.

2 Mikhail Bahktin, *Rabelais and His World, passim.*

3 Roger Caillois, *Man, Play, and Games,* 87.

4 Spavento (meaning "fear") is the captain Francesco Andreini, Scala's friend, made famous in performing with the Gelosi. There is no evidence that Scala wrote for the Gelosi. Rather he seems to have used this name in his printed versions of the scenarios to honour his friend and to capitalize on his reputation in that role.

5 Ruggiero, "Marriage, Love, Sex," 18.

6 In a source play, Girolamo Bargagli's *La pellegrina,* ca 1567, two women in similar situations hide their clandestine marriages; one woman is pregnant and pretending to be mad, and the other is cross-dressed as a man. But in 1563 the Council of Trent proclaimed that clandestine marriage was invalid. Scala played it safe.

7 In *La pellegrina,* Lespida's nurse fears that if the father realizes she is pregnant, he will disown her (act 1, scene 2).

8 The renowned Isabella Andreini, for instance, who bore seven children and died in childbirth with her eighth, must often have been performing pregnant. We do not know for whom the role was written. Pantalone's daughter is most often Isabella, not Flaminia.

9 "Folly, melancholy, madness, are but one disease, delirium is a common name to all." Robert Burton, *The Anatomy of Melancholy,* vol. 1, 273.

10 Paolo Valesio, "The Language of Madness in the Renaissance," 217.

11 Anne MacNeil, *Music and Women of the Commedia dell'Arte in the Late Sixteenth Century,* 49.

12 Carol Thomas Neely, *Distracted Subjects,* 50. In Scala's only examples of mad speech, in his scenario *The Madness of Isabella,* there is no underlying

psychology. Louise George Clubb suggests that mad Isabella's reference to "Isola" (that is, Isabel or, in English, Elizabeth) in "'a clister for Isola of England who couldn't piss' is probably an echo of Catholic anti-Tudor calumny referring to various physical abnormalities attributed by rumor to the Virgin Queen." Thus, the possibility for political commentary, at least safe political commentary, is suggested. Louise George Clubb, "The State of the Arte in the Andreini's Time," 270.

13 Valesio, "The Language of Madness," 203; Duncan Salkeld, *Madness and Drama in the Age of Shakespeare*, 67, 76.

14 Pierto Aretino, *La cortigiana*, 70, act 1, scene 7.

15 Burton, *The Anatomy of Melancholy*, vol. 1, 389, 394.

16 In a mad speech written by Isabella Andreini, the character responds to phantasms. Isabella Andreini, *Fragmenti di alcune scritture*, 58–60.

17 Ludovico Ariosto, *Orlando Furioso*, 572, 592.

18 Valesio, "The Language of Madness," 203; Salkeld, *Madness and Drama*, 109. Conversely, sumptuary law forbade people from dressing above their station.

19 M.A. Katritzky, *The Art of Commedia*, 546, fig. 43.

20 Robert Henke, "The Italian Mountebank and the *Commedia dell'Arte*," 4.

21 Hale, *The Civilization of Europe*, 543. Hale has observed that by the late fifteenth century doctors were expected to be able to discriminate between twenty varieties of colour and density in urine. See also William I. White, "A New Look at the Role of Urinalysis in the History of Diagnostic Medicine," 122.

22 White, ibid.

23 It was believed that the urine of a pregnant woman, after several days, developed a pearly film on top. In 1928 it was proven that hormones in the urine of pregnant women stimulate bacterial growth that results in such a film. Laurinda S. Dixon, *Perilous Chastity*, 75.

24 White," A New Look at the Role of Urinalysis," 122.

25 Ibid., 123.

26 Neely, *Distracted Subjects*, 6.

27 Don Gregorio Paniagua Rodriguez (conductor), *Tarentule-Tarentelle*, The Atrium Musical de Madrid, compact disc with liner notes.

28 Maps from the period show no Porta della Cavena. The old site of Porta Capena borders the current district of Ripa. *Grande Dizionario Garzanti* gives the first definition of *caneva* as a shop that sells wine and other foodstuffs (regional use); and the second, as the warehouse for storage of wheat and other provisions (archaic). I am grateful to Margherita Pieracci Harwell for her help in this matter.

29 Romano, *Household and Statecraft*, 159.

30 Burke, *Culture and Society*, 238.

31 Crane, *Italian Social Customs*, 146.

32 Romano, *Housecraft and Statecraft*, 24.

33 In Day 29 Scala uses Arlecchino's fall from a ladder to end act 1. M.A. Katritzky notes that ladders were popular professional stage props figuring in scenarios not only by Scala but by Diancolelli and others. A French courtier at Fontainebleau recorded in his diary in 1608 that the *commedia dell'arte* actor Cola "climbed straight up a ladder that was not leaning against anything, and then fell its full length doing somersaults without getting a scratch." In M.A. Katritzky, *Healing, Performance, and Ceremony in the Writings of Three Early Modern Physicians*, 169.

34 Chamberlin, *Everyday Life*, 121.

35 Camporesi, *Bread of Dreams*, 98–9.

36 Scala, *The Commedia dell'Arte of Flaminio Scala*, 129.

37 Michael D. Bristol, "Theater and Popular Culture," 235.

38 Castiglione, *The Book of the Courtier*, 188.

39 Sella, *Italy in the Seventeenth Century*, 78.

40 Camporesi, *Bread of Dreams*, 82.

41 Neely, *Distracted Subjects*, 73; Jerome J. Bylebyl, "The School of Padua," 350.

42 Ronald Sawyer, "Patients, Healers, and Disease in the Southeast Midlands, England, 1597–1634," 207–11.

43 Instances like this have fuelled the debate about whether Scala wrote for readers or for actors.

44 We do not know the doctor's diagnosis. Black hellebore, a supposed cure for dropsy, also caused vertigo, emesis, and catharsis among other things. In *The Madness of Isabella*, Scala introduces it as a cure for madness. Women's mental disturbances, it was widely believed, were frequently caused by a failure to menstruate, too much blood in the uterus: Neely, *Distracted Subjects*, 94 and *passim*. For this there were "menstrual regulators." These same drugs, available in every apothecary shop, were effective abortifacients, even for late-term pregnancies, although, because they were strictly forbidden by the Church, they were not openly referred to as such. John M. Riddle, *Eve's Herbs*, 124, 147–8. I do not know their side effects.

45 Bahktin, *Rabelais and His World*, 21, 317. The eighteenth-century Dutch artist, G.-J. Xavery, in illustrations for *The Marvellous Malady of Harlequin* represents Harlequin vomiting and then, in another image, defecating. Duchartre, *The Italian Comedy*, between p. 56 and p. 57.

46 Robert Henke, "Towards Reconstructing the Audiences of the *Commedia dell'Arte*," 213.

47 Cohen, Honor and Gender," 601.
48 David Wiles, *Shakespeare's Clown*, 16–17, 129–30.
49 Douglas Biow, "Food," 503, 511.
50 Peter Burke, "Worldviews," 184. Peter Burke defines magic as "the attempt to produce material changes in the world as the result of performing certain rituals and writing or uttering certain verbal formulas ('spells,' 'charms' or incantations) requesting or demanding that these changes take place" (ibid.).
51 Camporesi, *Bread of Dreams*, 203.
52 Black, *Early Modern Italy*, 201.
53 Douglas Radcliff-Umstead, "The Sorcerer in Italian Renaissance Comedy," 75.
54 Neely, *Distracted Subjects*, 124. See also Pollard, *Drugs and Theater*, 18.
55 Hale, *The Civilization of Europe*, 262.
56 The Recueil Fossard woodcut, from the mid-1580s, shows very explicit sex play between Harlequin and Francisquina, in Duchartre, *The Italian Comedy*, 320.
57 "The handshaking ritual among merchant elite ... took place between the relatives of the betrothed couple and represented only the first step of a complex series of negotiations, which involved the bride-to-be only in the final stages." Lombardi, "Intervention by Church and State," 145.
58 D.P. Walker, *Spiritual and Demonic Magic from Ficino to Campanella*, 17.
59 Guido Ruggiero, "Witchcraft and Magic," 481.
60 In alchemy, Mercury is the medium of conjunction or the reconciliation of opposites. He is also the protector of thieves.
61 Guido Ruggiero, *Binding Passions*, 17. The spiritual and material world continued to seem very close. Guido Ruggiero, "Witchcraft and Magic," 477. Scala uses essentially the same disguise trick several times: in Day 20 the youths enter their love's houses as notaries, in Day 37 as doctors.
62 Kurt Seligman, *The History of Magic*, 303.
63 Peter Whitfield, *Astrology*, 139, 140, 164.
64 Walker, *Spiritual and Demonic Magic*, 18.
65 Ibid. Walker observes that part of the reason for the Church's objection to magic was that it imitated the trappings of the mass: "The church has her own magic; there is no room for any other." Ibid.

7. Day 25: The Jealous Isabella

1 Andrews, in Scala, *The Commedia dell'Arte of Flaminio Scala*, 148–9.
2 See, for instance, Pietropaolo, "The Theatre," 17.

3 Antoni Maczak, *Travel in Early Modern Europe*, 63–4.
4 Ibid., 64.
5 King, "The Woman of the Renaissance," 22. Lynne Lawner estimates that throughout the sixteenth century prostitutes and courtesans in Rome constituted about 10 per cent of the population. Lynne Lawner, *Loves of the Courtesans*, 6. See also Maczak, *Travel in Early Modern Europe*, 247, and Moulton, "The Illicit Worlds of the Renaissance," 496.
6 Guido Ruggiero, *Binding Passions*, 42.
7 "Anyone who works as an innkeeper, as you do, must fill the clients' beds as well as their bellies." Girolamo Bargagli, *The Female Pilgrim* (*La pellegrina*), act 2, scene 3.
8 Guido Ruggiero, *Binding Passions*, 64.
9 Piccolomini, "Alessandro," (act 1, scene 5), 314. Scala, *Il finto marito*, 328–9.
10 Christopher Black estimates that about one-third of households had at least one servant, so it is not surprising that even the Capitano, whose means were modest, had one. Christopher F. Black, *Early Modern Italy*, 97.
11 Strocchia, "Gender and Rites of Honour," 54.
12 The windows would not have had glass.
13 Erasmus, *Erasmus on Women*, 17.
14 Muir, *Ritual in Early Modern Europe*, 150.
15 Unlike Virginia Scott in *The Commedia dell'Arte in Paris, 1644–1697*, 124, I do not find any regular alternation of scene types in Scala.
16 Laura Giannetti and Guido Ruggiero note that "this description of a young woman madly in love uses the language of contemporary love spells." Accademia intornati di Siena, *Gl'ingannati*, act 2, scene 2, line 228.
17 Laura Giannetti Ruggiero, "When Male Characters Pass as Women," 743–60.
18 In one of Pietro Aretino's dialogues, 1534, an experienced prostitute advises her daughter that to warm up a sluggish customer she should put on his clothes: "'No sooner does the gentleman see you transformed from a woman into a man than he will leap on you as hunger does on a hot loaf.'" Aretino, *Ragionamenti*, 206, in Cathy Santore, "Julia Lombardo, 'Somtuosa Meretrize,'" 57–8.
19 David Summers, *Michelangelo and the Language of Art*, 177.
20 Brian Richardson, *Printing, Writers and Readers in Renaissance Italy*, 111. No men would have been present. Women were not sent to schools that provided training in Latin. When they were schooled at all, they were taught in convents or at home. For upper-middle-class girls the convent route was not unusual. See also Elissa Weaver, *Convent Theatre in Early Modern Italy*, 61, 88; Diana Robin, "Humanism and Feminism in Laura Cereta's Public Letters," 369; and Grendler, *Schooling in Renaissance Italy*, 88.

21 M.A. Katritzky, "Reading the Actress in *Commedia* Imagery," 136.
22 Friedrichs, *The Early Modern City*, 250.
23 Giannetti, *Lelia's Kiss*, chap. 5.
24 Guido Ruggiero, *The Boundaries of Eros*, 97.
25 Howard, "Cross-Dressing," 25.
26 The father in *Gl'ingannati* despairs:

> Is this the honor she pays me? Oh, how unlucky I am! I've worked so hard to overcome my evil fortune, and for this? To see my patrimony without heirs; to see my house ruined; to see my daughter a whore; to become the subject of common gossip; to be unable to show my face in public; to be pointed out by children in the streets; to be held up as a warning by the old; ... to be made an example of in tales; and to be made the subject of the gossip of every woman in this city? Maybe these women aren't gossips, eh? Maybe they don't like to malign others, eh? But I imagine it doesn't really matter, because everyone knows everything already. Actually, I'm certain, for if even one woman knows it, in three hours the whole town knows it. I'm a disgraced father, a miserable and sad old man who has lived too long! What can I do? What should I think?

(Accademia degli Intornati di Siena, *Gl'ingannati*, act 3, scene 3, lines 248–9).
27 Andrews, in Scala, *The Commedia dell'Arte of Flaminio Scala*, 150.
28 Ibid., 149.
29 Accademia degli Intornati di Siena, *Gl'ingannati*, act 4, scene 5, lines 266–7.
30 Giannetti, *Lelia's Kiss*, 142–52.
31 Maggie Günsberg, "Gender Deceptions," 343. By the statute of the Holy Roman Empire enacted in 1532, the sentence for sexual acts between women was death by burning. See Judith C. Brown, *Immodest Acts*, 7, 13. In practice, because there could be no penetration, the possibility of sexual activity between women was often not taken seriously.
32 Castiglione, *The Book of the Courtier*, 57.
33 M.A. Katritzky observes iconography in which the inamorata wears breeches under her dress. Katritzky, *The Art of Commedia*, 202.
34 Di Maria makes this same point relative to written tragedy, in *The Italian Tragedy in the Renaissance*, 102.
35 Vergilio Verucci, *Li diversi linguaggi*, 205.
36 Richard Andrews, "Theatre," 294.

8. Day 36: Isabella [the] Astrologer

1 Translated by James E. Hirsh, in *The Structure of Shakespearean Scenes*, 203. Torquato Tasso, in the first canto of his highly influential epic poem *Gerusa-*

lemme liberta (1581), pronounced, in a modification of Horace, that poetry is like a medicine offered to sick children, in a glass with an appealingly sweetened rim but that can effect its curative powers. It both delights and teaches. Torquato Tasso, *Gerusalemme liberata*, vol. 1, canto 1, verse 3, page 4. Similarly, *commedia grave* was seen as having redemptive powers.

2 Andrews, in Scala, *The Commedia dell'Arte of Flaminio Scala*, 213.

3 Richard Andrews, "Rhetoric and Drama," 153–68.

4 Peter Mazur, personal communication, 16 January 2010.

5 Hanlon, *Early Modern Italy*, 182.

6 Ibid., 183.

7 Davis, *Christian Slaves*, 206n10.

8 Astarita, *Between Salt Water and Holy Water*, 98.

9 Lynn Thorndike, *A History of Magic and Experimental Sciences*, vol. 6, 157.

10 Ugo Baldini, "The Roman Inquisition's Condemnation of Astrology," 95. Subsequently, in 1633, the bull *Inscrutabilis* of Urban VIII unmistakably branded all astrology as heresy. Whitfield, *Astrology*, 163.

11 Giambattista Della Porta, *Teatro*, ed. Raffaele Sirri (Naples: Scientifiche Italiane, 1978), 1, 315, in Robert W. Leslie, "Sforza Oddi and the Commedia Grave," 531.

12 On fortune see Whitfield, *Astrology*, 156. On love, see Guido Ruggiero, "Witchcraft and Magic," 479. "Reason is more powerful than Fortune," and "Fortune has in her hand only the man who submits to her." Alberti in *The Family in Renaissance Florence*, 30, 28. The interplay between fortune and reason was a common motif.

13 Andrews's translation, in Scala, *The Commedia dell'Arte of Flaminio Scala*, 204–14.

14 Carboni, *Venice and the Islamic World*, 66. The author observes that even today "orientation" has positive connotations, whereas "disorientation" does not. Ibid., 70.

15 Jordan Lancaster, *In the Shadow of Vesuvius*, 92.

16 My illustration is a painting from 1470. I have chosen it for its clarity. Numerous subsequent plans and views of Naples from the bay were "published on paper or painted on walls (like the geographic gallery in the Vatican palace) that would have been seen by all educated men." Personal communication, art historian Martha Pollak, 28 July 2013. Such a map of Naples, *Neapolis*, is by Sebastian Münster, *Cosmographei* CCLXX (Basel: H. Petri, 1550).

17 Hanlon, *Early Modern Italy*, 183.

18 George E. Duckworth, *The Nature of Roman Comedy*, 86.

19 Hanlon, *Early Modern Italy*, 15.

20 Lancaster, *In the Shadow of Vesuvius*, 92. The town Ragusa in Italy is landlocked.

21 Hanlon, *Early Modern Italy*, 86.

22 Andrews, "Rhetoric and Drama," *passim*.

23 Dianne Yvonne Ghirardo, "The Topography of Prostitution in Renaissance Ferrara," 424.

24 Ibid., 405.

25 For a modern "edition" of this catalogue see Rita Casagrande di Villaviera, *Le cortigiane veneziane del Cinquecento*. See also Margaret F. Rosenthal, *The Honest Courtesan, passim*. I am grateful to one of the anonymous referees of my manuscript for this reference. Rudolph M. Bell, *How to Do It*, 333n12, asserts that the purpose of such catalogues was satirical – like Arlecchino's.

26 Lancaster, *In the Shadow of Vesuvius*, 107.

27 Traveller and writer Thomas Coryat estimated that there were twenty thousand courtesans in Venice but that "many are esteemed so loose, that they are said to open their quivers to every arrow," *Coryats Crudities*, 1611, in Patricia Fortini Brown, *Private Lives in Renaissance Venice*, 161.

28 Moulton, "The Illicit Worlds of the Renaissance," 493.

29 Black, *Early Modern Italy*, 196. "The care of prisoners was largely left to their own families and to religious organizations." Historian Peter Mazur, personal communication, 16 January 2010.

30 Davis, "The Renaissance Goes Up in Smoke," 99.

31 Lancaster, *In the Shadow of Vesuvius*, 107. Hacke, *Women, Sex, and Marriage*, 20.

32 Giannetti, *Lelia's Kiss*, 84.

33 Louise George Clubb, *Romance and Aretine Humanism in Sienese Comedy, 1516*, with Robert Black and Giovanni Pollastra, 169.

34 Leslie, "Sforza Oddi and the Commedia Grave," 529.

35 Carboni, *Venice and the Islamic World*, 144.

36 Cavallo and Cerutti, "Female Honor," 77.

37 There would have been no reason for Orazio, when he was seen as a Turk who had committed no crime, to have been arrested. After his escape from jail, explained in the argument, he disguised himself successfully to keep from being jailed again. His re-arrest in this scene constitutes a crisis for Isabella and of the scenario.

38 Hacke, *Women, Sex, and Marriage*, 18, 187.

39 An etching by Jacques Callot for a series on the siege of La Rochelle, *The Inhabitants of La Rochelle Asking Pardon of the King Louis XIII*, shows the king seated out of doors at the side of an open area. Jacques Callot, *Callot's Etchings*, print 227.

40 Were this captain the governor of the prison and the same man as the guard who had arranged for Orazio's escape, as he is in Andrews's trans-

lation, it is hard to imagine the Regent being on cordial terms with him. More likely, the prison guard who arranged for Orazio's escape from prison would have suffered very serious consequences. It is also hard to imagine why the governor of the prison would be much interested in pulling rank on the Regent to secure the return of Aguizzino and Amett to prison or that Amett in prison served as a slave under Aguizzino.

41 Sforza Oddi, second prologue to *Prigione d'amore* in Louise George Clubb, *Italian Drama in Shakespeare's Time,* 62.

42 Carboni, *Venice and the Islamic World,* 101, 114.

Selected Bibliography

The bibliography includes works used, rather than just cited. Images that are not represented, sound recordings, and dance steps are listed separately at the end.

Texts

Accademia degli Intornati di Siena. *Gl'ingannati* (*The Deceived*). In *Five Comedies from the Italian Renaissance,* translated and edited by Laura Giannetti and Guido Ruggiero. Baltimore, MD: John Hopkins University Press, 2003.

Ackerman, James S., and Myra Nan Rosenfeld. "Social Stratification in Renaissance Urban Planning." In *Urban Life in the Renaissance,* edited by Susan Zimmerman and Ronald F.E. Weissman, 21–49. Newark, DE: University of Delaware Press, 1989.

Ajmar, Marta. "Exemplary Women in Renaissance Italy: Ambivalent Models of Behaviour?" In *Renaissance Characters,* edited by Eugenio Garin, 244–64. Chicago: University of Chicago Press, 1991.

– *See also* Ajmar-Wollheim, Marta.

Ajmar-Wollheim, Marta, and Flora Dennis, eds. *At Home in Renaissance Italy: Art and Life in the Italian House, 1400–1600.* London: Victoria and Albert Museum Publications, 2006.

Ajmar-Wollheim, Marta, Flora Dennis, and Ann Matchette. "Introduction: Approaching the Italian Renaissance Interior; Sources, Methodologies, Debates." *Renaissance Studies* 20, no. 5 (2006): 623–8.

Alberti, Leon Battista. *Dinner Pieces* (*Intercenales*). Translated by David Marsh. Binghamton, NY: Renaissance Society of America, New York, 1987.

– *The Family in Renaissance Florence* (*I libri della famiglia*). Translation and introduction by Renée Watkins. Columbia: University of South Carolina Press, 1969.

– *Leon Battista Alberti on Painting*. Translation, introduction, and notes by John R. Spencer. New Haven, CT: Yale University Press, 1966.

Alessandrini, Rinaldo (director). *Alessandro Striggio: La Cacci*. Concerto Italiano. Compact disc with liner notes.

Altman, Joel. *The Tudor Play of Mind: Rhetorical Inquiry and the Development of Elizabethan Drama*. Berkeley: University of California Press, 1978.

Ambrosini Federica. "Toward a Social History of Women in Venice." In *Venice Reconsidered: The History and Civilization of an Italian City-State, 1297–1797.*, edited by John Martin and Dennis Romano. Baltimore, MD: Johns Hopkins University Press, 2000.

Andreini, Francesco. "Cortesi lettori." In *Il teatro delle favole rappresentative* by Flaminio Scala, ed. Ferruccio Marotti. 2 vols. Milan: Il Polifilo, 1976.

Andreini, Giovanni Battista. *Le due comedi in comedia*. Venice, Imberti, 1623. In *Commedie dell'Arte*, edited by Siro Ferrone, vol. 2, 17–105. Milan: Mursia, 1986.

Andreini, Isabella. "Biasimo di I vecchi innamorati." In *La Commedia dell'Arte*, edited by Cesare Molinari and Renzo Guardenti, 977. Rome: Istituto poligrafico e Zecca dello Stato, 1999.

– *Fragmenti di alcune scritture*. Edited by Francesco Andreini and Flaminio Scala. Venice, Combi, 1617. In *La commedia dell'arte: Storia e testo*, edited by Vito Pandolfi, vol. 2 of 6, 58–60. Florence: Sansoni, 1957–61.

Andrews, Richard. "Anti-feminism in *Commedia Erudita*." In *Contexts of Renaissance Comedy*., edited by Janet Clare and Roy Eriksen, 11–31. Oslo: Novus, 1997.

– "How—and Why—Does One Print Scenarios? Flaminio Scala, 1611," *Italian Studies* 61, no. 1 (2006): 36–49.

– Introduction to *The Commedia dell'Arte of Flaminio Scala: A Translation and Analysis of 30 Scenarios*, by Flaminio Scala, ix–lvi. Edited and translated by Richard Andrews. Lanham, MD.: Scarecrow Press, 2008.

– "Molière, *commedia dell'arte*, and the Question of Influence in Early Modern European Theatre." *Modern Language Review* 11, no. 2 (2005): 444–63.

– "Rhetoric and Drama: Monologues and Set Speeches in Aretino's Comedies." In *The Languages of Literature in Renaissance Italy*, edited by Peter Hainsworth, Valerio Lucchesi, Christina Roaf, David Robey, and J. R. Woodhouse, 153–68. Oxford: Clarendon Press, 1988.

– *Scripts and Scenarios: The Performance of Comedy in Renaissance Italy*. Cambridge: Cambridge University Press, 1993.

– "Shakespeare and Italian Comedy." In *Shakespeare and Renaissance Europe*., edited by Andrew Hadfield and Paul Hammond, 123–48. London: Arden Shakespeare, 2005.

– "Theatre." In *Cambridge History of Italian Literature,* edited by Peter Brand and Lino Pertile. Cambridge: Cambridge University Press, 1996.

– "Writing as Re-Arranging: Flaminio Scala in 1611." Unpublished conference paper, University of Strathclyde, Glasgow, 27 October 2006.

Anonymous. *Gli scenari Correr: La commedia dell'arte a Venezia* . Edited by Carmelo Alberti. Rome: Bulzoni, 1996.

Appuhn, Karl. "Tools for the Development of the European Economy." In *A Companion to the Worlds of the Renaissance,* edited by Guido Ruggiero, 259–78. Oxford: Blackwell, 2002.

Aretino, Pierto. *La cortigiana.* Translation by J. Douglas Campbell and Leonard G. Sbrocchi. Introduction by. Raymond B. Waddington. Ottawa: Dovehouse, 2003.

Ariosto, Ludovico. *La lena.* Edited by Guido Davico Bonino. Turin: G. Einaudi, 1976.

– *Il Negromante. Tutte le opera di Ludovico Ariosto: Commedie.* Vol. 4, edited by Angela Casella, Gabriella Ronschi, et al. Cesare Segre, general editor. Milan: Mondador, 1974.

– *Orlando Furioso.* Translated by David R. Slavitt. Cambridge, MA.: Harvard University Press, 2009.

Aristotle. *Aristotle* on *the Art of Poetry.* Edited and translated by Ingram Bywater. Preface by Gilbert Murray. Oxford: Clarendon Press, 1920.

Arnold, Thomas F. "Violence and Warfare in the Renaissance World." In *A Companion to the Worlds of the Renaissance,* edited by Guido Ruggiero, 460–74. Oxford: Blackwell, 2002.

Astarita, Tommaso. *Between Salt Water and Holy Water: A History of Southern Italy.* New York: W.W. Norton, 2005.

Bahktin, Mikhail. *Rabelais and His World.* Translated by Helene Iswolsky. Bloomington: Indiana University Press, 1968.

Baldini, Ugo. "The Roman Inquisition's Condemnation of Astrology: Antecedents, Reasons, and Consequences." In *Church, Censorship, and Culture in Early Modern Italy,* edited by Gigliola Fragnito, translated by Adrian Belton, 79–110. Cambridge: Cambridge University Press, 2001.

Banchieri, Adriano. *La pazzia senile.* Stuttgart: Cornetto, 1997.

Bargagli, Girolamo. *The Female Pilgrim* (*La pellegrina*). Translation, introduction, and notes by Bruno Ferraro. Ottawa: Dovehouse Editions, 1988.

Bartoli, Adolfo. *Scenari inediti della Commedia dell'Arte contributo alla storia del teatro popolare.* Florence: G.C. Sansoni, 1880.

Beckett, Samuel. *Waiting for Godot.* London: Faber, 2010.

Beecher, Donald A. "Intriguers and Tricksters: The Manifestation of an Archetype in the Comedy of the Renaissance." In *Comparative Critical Approaches to Renaissance Comedy*, edited by Donald Beecher and Massimo Ciavolella, 53–72. Ottawa: Dovehouse, 1986.

– "Introduction: 'Erudite' Comedy in Renaissance Italy." In *Renaissance Comedy: The Italian Masters*, edited by Donald Beecher, vol. 1 of 2, 3–35. Toronto: University of Toronto Press, 2008.

– ed. *Renaissance Comedy: The Italian Masters*. Vol. 1. Toronto: University of Toronto Press, 2008.

Bell, Rudolph M. *How to Do It: Guides to Good Living for Renaissance Italians*. Chicago: University of Chicago Press, 1999.

Bembo, Pietro. *Gli Asolani*. Translated by Rudolf B. Gottfried. Bloomington: University of Indiana Press, 1954.

Bevington, David. *Action Is Eloquence: Shakespeare's Language of Gesture*. Cambridge, MA: Harvard University Press, 1984.

Bibbiena, Bernardo Dovizi. *La calandra*. In *Five Comedies from the Italian Renaissance*, translated and edited by Laura Giannetti and Guido Ruggiero, 1–70. Baltimore, MD: Johns Hopkins University Press, 2003.

Biow, Douglas. "Food: Petro Aretino and the Art of Conspicuous Consumption." In *The Renaissance World*, edited by John Jeffries Martin, 501–16. New York: Routledge, 2007.

Black, Christopher F. *Early Modern Italy: A Social History*. London: Routledge, 2001.

Boccaccio, Giovanni. *The Decameron*. Edited and translated by Frances Winwar. New York: Modern Library, 1955.

Brand, Peter. "Disguise in Renaissance Comedy." *Comparative Criticism* 10 (1988): 68–92.

Bristol, Michael D. "Theater and Popular Culture." In *A New History of Early English Drama*, edited by John D. Cox and David Scott Kastan, 231–50. New York: Columbia University Press, 1997.

Brown, Judith C. *Immodest Acts: The Life of a Lesbian Nun in Renaissance Italy*. Oxford: Oxford University Press, 1986.

Brown, Patricia Fortini. *Private Lives in Renaissance Venice: Art, Architecture, and the Family*. New Haven, CT: Yale University Press, 2004.

Brucker, Gene. *Florence: The Golden Age, 1138–1737*. New York: Abbeville Press, 1984. First published as *Firenze: 1138–1737; L'impero del fiorino*. Milan: Arnoldo Mondadori, 1983.

– *Giovanni and Lusanna: Love and Marriage in Renaissance Florence*. Berkeley: University of California Press, 1986.

Bruni, Domenico. Prologue to his *Lo specchio*, 1621. In *La commedia dell'arte e la societa barocca: La professione del teatro*, edited by Feruccio Marotti and Giovanna Romei, 413–5. Rome: Bulzoni, 1991.

Burckhardt, Jacob. *The Civilization of the Renaissance in Italy.* Translated by S.G.C. Middlemore. Part 6. London: S. Sonnenschein, 1904.

Burke, Kenneth. *Counter-Statement.* University of Chicago Press, 1968. First published 1931.

Burke, Peter. *The Art of Conversation.* Ithaca, NY: Cornell University Press, 1993.

– *Culture and Society in Renaissance Italy, 1420–1540.* New York: Charles Scribner, 1972.

– *The Historical Anthropology of Early Modern Italy: Essays on Perception and Communication.* Cambridge: Cambridge University Press, 1987.

– "The Historical Geography of the Renaissance." In *A Companion to the Worlds of the Renaissance,* edited by Guido Ruggiero, 88–104. Oxford: Blackwell, 2002.

– *The Italian Renaissance: Culture and Society in Renaissance Italy, 1420–1540.* Revised second edition. Princeton, NJ: Princeton University Press, 1999.

– *Popular Culture in Early Modern Europe.* New York: Harper and Row, 1978.

– "Worldviews: Some Dominant Traits." In *The Italian Renaissance,* edited and introduced by Harold Bloom, 177–202. Philadelphia: Chelsea House, 2004.

Burton, Robert. *The Anatomy of Melancholy.* , Vol. 1 of 3. New York: Everyman, 1964.

Bylebyl, Jerome J. "The School of Padua: Humanistic Medicine in the Sixteenth Century." In *Health, Medicine, and Mortality in the Sixteenth Century,* edited by Charles Webster, 335–70. Cambridge: Cambridge University Press, 1979.

Caillois, Roger. *Man, Play, and Games.* Translated by Meyer Barash. New York: Free Press, 1961.

Calvi, Giulia. "Widows, the State, and the Guardianship of Children in Early Modern Tuscany." In *Widowhood in Medieval and Early Modern Europe,* edited by Sandra Cavallo and Lyndan Warner, 209–19. New York: Longman, 1999.

Camporesi, Piero. *Bread of Dreams: Food and Fantasy in Early Modern Europe.* Translation by David Gentilcore. Chicago: University of Chicago Press, 1989. Originally published as *Il pane selvaggio.* Bologna: Il mulino, 1980.

– *The Land of Hunger.* Translation by Tania Croft-Murray with the assistance of Claire Foley. Italian dialect and Latin text translation by Shayne Mitchell. Cambridge: Polity Press, 1996. Originally published as *Il paese della fame.* Bologna: Il Mulino, 1978.

Cantarella Eva. "Homicides of Honor: The Development of Italian Adultery Law over Two Millennia." In *The Family in Italy from Antiquity to the Present,* edited by David L. Kertzer and Richard P. Saller. New Haven, CT: Yale University Press, 1991.

Carboni, Stefano. *Venice and the Islamic World, 828–1797.* New Haven, CT: Yale University Press, 2007.

Carlsmith, Christopher. *A Renaissance Education: Schooling in Bergamo and the Venetian Republic, 1500–1650.* Toronto: University of Toronto Press, 2010.

Carlson, Marvin. *Theories of the Theatre: A Historical and Critical Survey, from the Greeks to the Present.* Expanded edition. Ithaca, NY: Cornell University Press, 1993.

Carruthers, Mary. *The Book of Memory: A Study of Memory in Medieval Culture.* Revised second edition. Cambridge: Cambridge University Press, 2008.

– *The Craft of Thought: Meditation, Rhetoric, and the Making of Images, 400–1200.* Cambridge: Cambridge University Press, 1998.

Castiglione, Baldesar. *The Book of the Courtier* (*Il cortegiano*). Translation and introduction by George Bull. New York: Penguin, 1976.

Castiglione, Caroline. "Mothers and Children." In *The Renaissance World*, edited by John Jeffries Martin, 381–97. New York: Routledge, 2007.

Cavallo, Sandra, and Simona Cerutti. "Female Honor and the Social Control of Reproduction in Piedmont between 1600 and 1800." Translated by Mary M. Gallucci. In *Sex and Gender in Historical Perspective*, edited by Edward Muir and Guido Ruggiero, 73–109. Baltimore, MD: Johns Hopkins University Press, 1990.

Cécchi, Giovanni Maria. *The Horned Owl* (*L'assiuolo*). Translated by Konrad Eisenbichler. Waterloo, ON: Wilfrid Laurier University Press, 1981.

Chamberlin, E.R. *Everyday Life in Renaissance Times.* New York: Perigree, 1980.

– *The World of the Italian Renaissance.* London: Allen and Unwin, 1982.

Chojnacki, Stanley. "'The Most Serious Duty': Motherhood, Gender, and Patrician Culture in Renaissance Venice." In *The Italian Renaissance: The Essential Readings*, edited by Paula Findlen, 173–91. Oxford: Blackwell, 2002.

– *Women and Men in Renaissance Venice: Twelve Essays on Patrician Society.* Baltimore, MD: Johns Hopkins University Press, 2000.

Cicero, Tullius. *De oratore.* Translated by E.W. Sutton. Cambridge, MA: Harvard, Loeb Classical Library, 1942.

Clubb, Louise George. *Italian Drama in Shakespeare's Time.* New Haven, CT: Yale University Press, 1989.

– "Italian Renaissance Theatre." *The Oxford Illustrated History of Theatre*, edited by John Russell Brown, 107–41. Oxford: Oxford University Press, 1995.

– "Italian Stories on Stage." In *The Cambridge Companion to Shakespearean Comedy*, edited by Alexander Leggatt, 32–46. Cambridge: Cambridge University, 2002.

– "Looking Back on Shakespeare and Italian Theatre." *Renaissance Drama* 36/37 (2010): 3–19.

– "Pictures for the Reader: A Series of Illustrations to Comedy, 1591–92." *Renaissance Drama*, 9 (1966): 265–78.

– *Romance and Aretine Humanism in Sienese Comedy, 1516: Pollastra Parthenio at the Studio di Siena.* With Robert Black and Giovanni Pollastra. Siena and Florence: La Nuova Italia, 1993.

– "The State of the Arte in the Andreini's Time." In *Studies in the Italian Renaissance: Essays in Memory of Arnolfo B. Ferruolo,* edited by Gian Paolo Biasin, Albert N. Mancini, and Nicholas J. Perella, 263–79. Naples: Società Editrice Napoletana, 1985.

– "Theatregrams." In *Comparative Critical Approaches to Renaissance Comedy,* edited by Donald Beecher and Massimo Ciavolella, 15–33. Ottawa: Dovehouse, 1986.

Coffin, David R. *The Villa in the Life of Renaissance Rome.* Princeton: Princeton University Press, 1979.

Cohen, Elizabeth S. "Honor and Gender in the Streets of Early Modern Rome." *Journal of Interdisciplinary History* 22, 4 (1992): 597–625.

Cohen, Thomas V. *Love and Death in Renaissance Italy.* Chicago: University of Chicago Press, 2004.

Cope, Jackson L. *Secret Sharers in Italian Comedy from Machiavelli to Goldoni.* Durham, NC: Duke University Press, 1996.

Cowan, Alexander. "Cities, Towns, and New Forms of Culture." In *The Renaissance World,* edited by John Jeffries Martin, 101–17. New York: Routledge, 2007.

Crabb, Ann. *The Strozzi of Florence: Widowhood and Family Solidarity in the Renaissance.* Ann Arbor: University of Michigan Press, 2000.

Crane, Thomas Frederick. *Italian Social Customs of the Sixteenth Century and Their Influence on the Literatures of Europe.* New York: Russell and Russell, 1971. First published 1920 by Johns Hopkins University Press.

Crane, William G. *Wit and Rhetoric in the Renaissance: The Formal Basis of Elizabethan Prose Style.* Gloucester, MA: Peter Smith, 1964.

Dandelet, Thomas James. *Spanish Rome, 1500–1700.* New Haven, CT: Yale University Press, 2001.

Davis, Robert C. *Christian Slaves, Muslim Masters: White Slavery in the Mediterranean, the Barbary Coast, and Italy, 1500–1800.* New York: Palgrave, 2003.

– "The Geography of Gender in the Renaissance." In *Gender and Society in Renaissance Italy,* edited by Judith C. Brown and Robert C. Davis, 19–38. London and New York: Longman, 1998.

– "The Renaissance Goes Up in Smoke." *The Renaissance World,* edited by John Jeffries Martin, 398–409. New York: Routledge, 2007.

Dawkins, Richard. *The Selfish Gene.* Revised edition. Oxford: Oxford University Press, 1989. First published 1976.

Dean, Trevor. "Fathers and Daughters: Marriage Laws and Marriage Disputes in Bologna and Italy, 1200-1500." In *Marriage in Italy, 1300–1650,* edited by Trevor Dean and K.J. P. Lowe. Cambridge: Cambridge University Press, 1998, 85–106.

de Jorio Andrea. *Gesture in Naples and Gesture in Classical Antiquity* (*La mimica degli antichi investigata nel gestire napoletano*). Translation and introduction by Adam Kendon. Bloomington: Indiana University Press, 2000.

Dekker, Rudolf M., and Lotte C. van de Pol. *The Tradition of Female Transvestism in Early Modern Europe.* New York: St Martin's Press, 1989.

de Vries, Jan. *European Urbanization, 1500–1800.* Cambridge, MA: Harvard University Press, 1984.

Di Maria, Salvatore. *The Italian Tragedy in the Renaissance: Cultural Realities and Theatrical Innovations.* Lewisburg, PA: Bucknell University Press, 2002.

di Villaviera, Rita Casagrande. *Le cortigiane veneziane del Cinquecento.* Milan: Longanesi, 1968.

Dixon, Laurinda S. *Perilous Chastity: Women and Illness in Pre-Enlightenment Art and Medicine.* Ithaca, NY: Cornell University Press, 1995.

[Donatus, Aelius?]. "On Comedy and Tragedy" (*De Comoedia et Tragoedia).* In *Sources of Dramatic Theory,* edited and annotated by Michael J. Sidnell. Cambridge: Cambridge University Press, 1991.

Doran, Madeleine. *Endeavors of Art: A Study of Form in Elizabethan Drama.* Madison: University of Wisconsin Press, 1954.

Dovizi da Bibbiena, Bernardo. *La calandra.* In *Five Comedies from the Renaissance,* translated and edited by Laura Gianetti and Guido Ruggiero. Baltimore, MD: Johns Hopkins University Press, 2003.

Duchartre, Pierre Louis. *The Italian Comedy: The Improvisation, Scenarios, Lives, Attributes, Portraits, and Masks of the Illustrious Characters of the Commedia dell'Arte.* Translated by Randolph T. Weaver. New York: Dover, 1966. Originally published 1929.

Duckworth, George E. *The Nature of Roman Comedy: A Study in Popular Entertainment.* Princeton: Princeton University Press, 1952.

Dursteler, Eric R. *Renegade Women: Gender, Identity, and Boundaries in the Early Modern Mediterranean.* Baltimore, MD: Johns Hopkins University Press, 2011.

Eamon, William. "The Scientific Renaissance." In *A Companion to the Worlds of the Renaissance,* edited by Guido Ruggiero, 403–24. Oxford: Blackwell, 2002.

Edmundson, Mark. "Against Readings." *Profession* 2009, 56–65.

Eisenach, Emlyn. *Husbands, Wives, and Concubines: Marriage, Family, and Social Order in Sixteeth-Century Verona.* Kirksville, MO: Truman State University Press, 2004.

Eramus, Desiderius. *Copia: Foundations of the Abundant Style.* In *Collected Works of*

Erasmus, edited by Craig R. Thomson, translated and edited by Betty I. Knott. Toronto: University of Toronto Press, 1970.

– *Erasmus on Women.* Edited by Erika Rummel. Toronto: University of Toronto Press, 1996.

Farr, James R. "Honor, Law, and Custom in Renaissance Europe." In *A Companion to the Worlds of the Renaissance*, edited by Guido Ruggiero, 124–38. Oxford: Blackwell, 2002.

Ferraro, Joanne M. "Family and Clan in the Renaissance World." In *A Companion to the Worlds of the Renaissance*, edited by Guido Ruggiero, 173–87. Oxford: Blackwell 2002.

– *Marriage Wars in Late Renaissance Venice.* Oxford: Oxford University Press, 2001.

Ferrone, Siro. "La nevrosi postale." In *Comici dell'arte: Corrispondenze: G.B. Andreini, N. Barbieri, P.M. Cecchini, S. Fiorillo, T .Martinelli, F. Scala*, edited by Claudia Buratelli, Domenica Landofi, and Anna Zinanni, directed by Siro Ferrone, 37–43. Florence: Le Lettere, 1993.

Findlen, Paula, ed. *The Italian Renaissance: The Essential Readings.* Oxford: Blackwell, 2002.

Fitzpatrick, Tim. *The Relationship of Oral and Literate Performance Processes in the Commedia dell'Arte: Beyond the Improvisation/Memorisation Divide.* Lewiston, NY: Edward Mellen Press, 1995.

Fregulia, Jeanette M. "Widows, Legal Rights, and the Mercantile Economy of Early Modern Milan." In *Early Modern Women: An Interdisciplinary Journal* 3 (2008): 233–8.

Friedrichs, Christopher R. *The Early Modern City, 1450–1750.* London: Longman, 1995.

Frye, Northrop. *Anatomy of Criticism: Four Essays*. Princeton: Princeton University Press, 1957.

Gallaway, Marian. *Constructing a Play.* New York: Prentice Hall, 1950.

Galli, Quirino. *Gli scenari di Flaminio Scala: Lingua e teoria teatrale.* Salerno: Pietro Laveglia, 2005.

Gentilcore, David. *Medical Charlatanism in Early Modern Italy.* Oxford: Oxford University Press, 2006.

Ghirardo, Dianne Yvonne. "The Topography of Prostitution in Renaissance Ferrara." *Journal of the Society of Architectural Historians* 60, no. 4 (2001): 402–31.

Giannetti, Laura. *Lelia's Kiss: Imagining Gender, Sex, and Marriage in Italian Renaissance Comedy.* Toronto: University of Toronto Press, 2009.

– *See also* Ruggiero, Laura Giannetti.

Gilbert, Felix. *Machiavelli and Guicciardini: Politics and History in Sixteenth-Century Florence.* Princeton: Princeton University Press, 1965.

Gilligan, James. *Violence: Reflections on Our Deadliest Epidemic.* London: Jessica Kinsley, 2000.

Goldthwaite, Richard A. *The Economy of Renaissance Florence.* Baltimore, MD: Johns Hopkins University Press, 2009.

Gordon, Bonnie. "The Courtesan's Singing Body as Cultural Capital in Seventeenth-Century Italy." In *The Courtesan's Arts: Cross-Cultural Perspectives*, edited by Martha Feldman and Bonnie Gordon, 182–208. Oxford: Oxford University Press, 2006.

Greene, Thomas M. *Light in Troy: Imitation and Discovery in Renaissance Poetry.* New Haven, CT: Yale University Press, 1982.

Grendler, Paul F. *Books and Schools in the Italian Renaissance.* Brookfield, VT: Variorum, 1995.

– *Critics of the Italian World, 1530–1560: Anton Francesco, Doni Nicolò Franco, and Ortensio Lando.* Madison: University of Wisconsin Press, 1969.

– "Form and Function in Italian Renaissance Popular Books." *Renaissance Quarterly* 46, no. 3 (1993): 451–85.

– *Schooling in Renaissance Italy: Literacy and Learning, 1300–1600.* Baltimore, MD: Johns Hopkins University Press, 1989.

Guazzo, Stefano. *La civil conversazione.* Edited by Amedeo Quondam. Vol. 1. Modena, Italy: Franco Cosimo Panini, 1993.

Guicciardini, Francesco. *The History of Italy.* Translated, edited, notated, and introduced by Sidney Alexander. New York: Macmillan, 1969.

– *Maxims and Reflections of a Renaissance Statesman* (*Ricordi*). Translation by Mario Domandi. Introduction by Nicolai Rubinstein. New York: Harper and Row, 1965.

Günsberg, Maggie. *Gender and the Italian Stage.* Cambridge: Cambridge University Press, 1997.

– "Gender Deceptions: Cross-Dressing in Italian Renaissance Comedy." In *Women in Italian Renaissance Culture and Society*, edited by Letizia Panizza. Oxford: Oxford University Press, 2000.

Hacke, Daniela. "'*Non lo volevo per marito in modo alcuno*': Forced Marriages, Generational Conflicts, and the Limits of Patriarchal Power in Early Modern Venice, c. 1580–1680." In *Time, Space, and Women's Lives in Early Modern Europe*, edited by Anne Jacobson Schutte, et al., 203–21. Kirksville, MO: Truman State University Press, 2001.

– *Women, Sex, and Marriage in Early Modern Venice.* Burlington, VT: Ashgate, 2004.

Hale, John. *The Civilization of Europe in the Renaissance.* London: Harper Collins, 1993.

Hanlon, Gregory. *Early Modern Italy, 1500–1800: Three Seasons in European History.* New York: St Martins, 2000.

– "Violence and Its Control in the Late Renaissance: An Italian Mode." In *A Companion to the Worlds of the Renaissance*, edited by Guido Ruggiero, 139–55. Oxford: Blackwell, 2002.

Helgerson, Richard. *Adulterous Alliances: Home, State, and History in Early Modern European Drama and Painting.* Chicago: University of Chicago Press, 2000.

Henderson, Diana E. "The Theatre and Domestic Culture." In *A New History of Early English Drama*, edited by John D. Cox and David Scott Kastan, 173–94. New York: Columbia University Press.

Henke, Robert. "The Italian Mountebank and the *Commedia dell'Arte.*" *Theatre Survey* 38, no. 2 (1997): 1–30.

– *Performance and Literature in the Commedia dell'Arte.* Cambridge: Cambridge University Press, 2002.

– "Representations of Poverty in the *Commedia dell'Arte.*" *Theatre Survey* 48, no. 2 (2007): 229–46.

– "Towards Reconstructing the Audiences of the *Commedia dell'Arte.*" *Essays in Theatre* 15, no. 2 (1997): 207–20.

Herrick, Marvin T. *Comic Theory in the Sixteenth Century.* Urbana: University of Illinois Press, 1950.

– *Italian Comedy in the Renaissance.* Urbana: University of Illinois Press, 1960.

Hill, John Walter. *Roman Monody, Cantata, and Opera from the Circles around Cardinal Montalto.* Vol. 1. Oxford: Clarendon Press, 1997.

Hirsh, James E. *The Structure of Shakespearean Scenes* . New Haven, CT: Yale University Press, 1981.

Howard, Jean E. "Cross-Dressing, the Theater, and Gender Struggle in Early Modern England." In *Crossing the Stage: Controversies in Cross-Dressing*, edited by Lesley Ferris, 20–46. London: Routledge, 1993.

Hyland, Peter. *Disguise on the Early Modern English Stage.* Burlington, VT: Ashgate, 2011.

Jarzombek, Mark. *On Leon Battista Alberti: His Literary and Aesthetic Theories.* Cambridge, MA: MIT Press, 1989.

Johnson, Steven. *Where Good Ideas Come From: The Natural History of Innovation.* New York: Riverhead, 2010.

Junkerman, Anne Christine. "The Lady and the Laurel: Gender and Meaning in Giogione's Laura." *Oxford Arts Journal* 16 (1993): 49–58.

Kamen, Henry. *Early Modern European Society.* London: Routledge, 2000.

Katritzky, M.A. *The Art of Commedia: A Study in the Commedia dell'Arte, 1560–1620, with Special Reference to the Visual Record.* Amsterdam: Rodopi, 2006.

– *Healing, Performance, and Ceremony in the Writings of Three Early Modern Physicians: Hippolytus Guarinonius and the Brothers Felix and Thomas Platte.* Burlington, VT: Ashgate, 2012.

– "Reading the Actress in *Commedia* Imagery." In *Women Players in England, 1500–1660: Beyond the All-Male Stage*, edited by Pamela Allen Brown and Peter Parolin, 109–43. Hampshire, UK: Ashgate, 2005.

– *Women, Medicine, and Theatre, 1500–1750*. Burlington, VT: Ashgate, 2007.

Kennard, Joseph Spencer. *Masks and Marionettes*. Port Washington, NY: Kennikat, 1967. First published 1935.

Kent, Dale V. *Friendship, Love, and Trust in Renaissance Florence*. Cambridge, MA: Harvard University Press, 2009.

Kent, Dale V., and Francis William Kent. *Neighbours and Neighbourhood in Renaissance Florence: The District of the Red Lion in the Fifteenth Century*. Locust Valley, NY: J.J. Augustin, 1982.

Kent, Francis William. "'Be Rather Loved Than Feared': Class Relations in Quattrocento Florence." In *Society and Individual in Renaissance Florence*, edited by William J. Connell, 13–50. Berkeley: University of California Press, 2002.

– *Household and Lineage in Renaissance Florence: The Family Life of the Capponi, Ginori, and Rucellai*. Princeton: Princeton University Press, 1977.

Kerr, Rosalind. "Isabella Andreini (Comica Gelosa, 1562–1604): Petrarchism for the Theatre Public." *Quaderni d'Italianistica* 27, no. 2 (2006): 71–92.

Kiernan, V.G. *The Duel in European History: Honour and the Reign of Aristocracy*. Oxford: Oxford University Press, 1988.

King, Margaret L. "The Woman of the Renaissance." In *Renaissance Characters*, edited by Eugenio Garin, translated by Lydia G. Cochrane, 207–49. Chicago: University of Chicago Press, 1991.

Klapisch-Zubar, Christiane. *Women, Family, and Ritual in Renaissance Italy*. Translated by Lydia Cochrane. Chicago: University of Chicago Press, 1985.

Knox, Dilwyn. "Civility, Courtesy, and Women in the Italian Renaissance." In *Women in Italian Renaissance Culture and Society*, edited by Letizia Panizza, 2–17. Oxford: University of Oxford Press, 2000.

Kuehn, Thomas. "Inheritance and Identity in Early Renaissance Florence: The Estate of Paliano di Falco." In *Society and Individual in Renaissance Florence*, edited by William J. Connell, 137–54. Berkeley: University of California Press, 2002.

– *Law, Family, and Women: Toward a Legal Anthropology of Renaissance Italy*. Chicago: University of Chicago Press, 1991.

Lancaster, Jordan. *In the Shadow of Vesuvius: A Cultural History of Naples*. London: I.B. Tauris, 2005.

Lawner, Lynne. *Loves of the Courtesans: Portraits of the Renaissance*. New York: Rizzoli, 1987.

Lea, Kathleen Marguerite. *Italian Popular Comedy: A Study in the Commedia dell'Arte, 1560–1620, with Special Reference to the English Stage*. Vol. 2 of 2. New York: Russell and Russell, 1962 (1934).

Leslie, Robert W. "Sforza Oddi and the Commedia Grave." *Comparative Drama* 30, no. 4 (1996–7): 525–51.

Lillie, Amanda. "The Humanist Villa Revisited." In *Language and Images of Renaissance Italy*, edited by Alison Brown, 193–215. Oxford: Oxford University Press, 1995.

Lombardi, Daniela. "Intervention by Church and State in Marriage Disputes in Sixteenth- and Seventeenth-Century Florence." In *Crime, Society, and Law in Renaissance Italy*, edited by Trevor Dean and K.J.P. Lowe, 142–56. Cambridge: Cambridge University Press, 1994.

Lopez, Jeremy. "Imagining the Actor's Body on the Early Modern Stage." In *Medieval and Renaissance Drama in England*, edited by S.P. Cerasano, 187–203. Madison, NJ: Fairleigh Dickinson University Press, 2007.

– *Theatrical Convention and Audience Response in Early Modern Drama*. Cambridge: Cambridge University Press, 2003.

Machiavelli, Niccolò. *The Art of War*. Translated and edited with commentary by Christopher Lynch. Chicago: University of Chicago Press, 2003.

– *Discourses*. Edited with an introduction by Bernard Crick. Translation by Leslie J. Walker. Book 1, chap. 43. New York: Penguin, 1970.

– *History of Florence and the Affairs of Italy* http://www.gutenberg.org/catalog/world/readfile?fk_files=227128&pageno=28.

– "How a State Is Ruined Because of Women." In *Discourses on Livy*, translated by Harvey C. Mansfield and Nathan Tarcov, book 3. Chicago: University of Chicago Press, 1996.

– *La mandragola (The Mandrake Root)*. In *Five Comedies from the Renaissance*, translated and edited by Laura Giannetti and Guido Ruggiero. Baltimore, MD: Johns Hopkins University Press, 2003.

– *The Prince*. Translation, introduction and notes by James B. Atkinson. Indianapolis, IN: Hackett, 2008. First published 1976 by Bobbs-Merrill.

MacNeil, Anne. *Music and Women of the Commedia dell'Arte in the Late Sixteenth Century*. Oxford: Oxford University Press, 2003.

Maczak, Antoni. *Travel in Early Modern Europe*. Translated by Ursula Phillips. Cambridge: Polity Press, 1995.

Mallett, Michael. "The Condottiere." In *Renaissance Characters*, edited by Eugenio Garin, translated by Lydia G. Cochrane, 22–45. Chicago: University of Chicago Press, 1997.

– *Mercenaries and Their Masters: Warfare in Renaissance Italy*. Totowa, NY: Rowman and Littlefield, 1974.

Marchi, Lucia. "Chasing Voices, Hunting Love: The Meaning of the Italian *Caccia*." *Essays in Medieval Studies* 27 (2011): 13–31.

Marotti, Ferruccio. "Il teatro della favole rappresentative: Un progetto utópico." *Biblioteca teatrale*, no. 15/16 (1976): 191–215.

Martin, John Jeffries. "The Myth of Renaissance Individualism." In *A Companion to the Worlds of the Renaissance*, edited by Guido Ruggiero, 208–24. Oxford: Basil Blackwell, 2002.

– *Myths of Renaissance Individualism.* New York: Palgrave, 2004.

Masten, Jeffrey. "Playwrighting: Authorship and Collaboration." In *A New History of Early English Drama*, edited by John D. Cox and David Scott Kastan, 357–82. New York: Columbia University Press, 1997.

Meek, Christine. "Women between the Law and Social Reality" In *Women in Italian Renaissance Culture and Society*, edited by Letizia Panizza, 182–93. Oxford: Oxford University Press, 2000.

Mengarelli, Stefano. "New Developments in Commedia Research: The Commedia all'improvviso Pictures in the Corsini Manuscript; A New Reading." *Early Theatre* 11, no. 2 (2008): 212–26.

Molho, Anthony. *Marriage Alliance in Late Medieval Florence.* Cambridge, MA: Harvard University Press, 1994.

Molière, Jean Baptiste. *The School for Wives* (*L'école des femmes*). In *Plays by Molière.* Introduction by Francis Fergusson. New York: Random House, 1950.

Molinari, Cesari. "'Le favole rappresentative' di Flaminio Scala." In *La Commedia dell'Arte*, 133–9. Milan: Arnoldo Mondadori, 1985.

Moryson, Fynes. *An Itinerary Containing His Ten Yeeres Travell through the Twelve Dominions of Germany, Bohmerland, Sweitzerland, Netherland, Denmarke, Poland, Italy, Turky, France, England, Scotland, & Ireland*, vol. 1. New York: MacMillan, 1907.

Moulton, Ian Frederick. "The Illicit Worlds of the Renaissance." In *A Companion to the Worlds of the Renaissance*, edited by Guido Ruggiero, 491–505. Oxford: Blackwell, 2002.

Mowat, Barbara. "The Theater and Literary Culture." In *A New History of Early English Drama*, edited by John D. Cox and David Scott Kastan, 213–30. New York: Columbia University Press, 1997.

Muir, Edward. "The Double Binds of Manly Revenge in Renaissance Italy." In *Gender Rhetorics: Postures of Dominance and Submission in History*, edited by Richard C. Trexler, 65–82. Binghamton, NY: Medieval and Renaissance Texts and Studies, 1994.

– *Mad Blood Stirring: Vendetta and Factions in Friuli during the Renaissance.* Baltimore, MD: Johns Hopkins University Press, 1993.

– *Ritual in Early Modern Europe.* Cambridge: Cambridge University Press, 2005.

Muir, Edward, and Ronald F.E. Weissman. "Social and Symbolic Places in Renaissance Venice and Florence." In *The Power of Place: Bringing Together Geographical and Sociological Imaginations*, edited by John A. Agnew and James S. Duncan. Boston: Unwin Hyman, 1989.

Najemy, John M. "Giannozzo and His Elders: Alberti's Critique of Renaissance Patriarchy." In *Society and Individual in Renaissance Florence*, edited by William J. Connell, 51–78. Berkeley: University of California Press, 2002.

Neely, Carol Thomas. *Distracted Subjects: Madness and Gender in Shakespeare and Early Modern Culture.* Ithaca, NY: Cornell University Press, 2004.

Orlin, Lena Cowen. "Three Ways to Be Invisible in the Renaissance." In *Renaissance Culture and the Everyday*, edited by Patricia Fumerton and Simon Hunt, 183–203. Philadelphia: University of Pennsylvania Press, 1999.

Palmieri, Matteo. *Della vita civile trattato di Matteo Palmieri* . Milan: N. Bettoni, 1830. Originally *Libro della via civile.* Florence: Giunti, 1529.

Pandolfi, Vito. *La commedia dell'arte: Storia e testo*. Edited by Vito Pandolfi. Vol. 2 of 6. Florence: Sansoni, 1957–61.

Perkins, William. *The Work of William Perkins.* Edited by Ian Breward. Appleford, UK: Suttor Courtenay Press, 1970.

Perloff, Marjorie. *Unoriginal Genius: Poetry by Other Means in the New Century.* Chicago: University of Chicago Press, 2010.

Perrucci, Andrea. *A Treatise on Acting, from Memory and by Improvisation. La Commedia dell'Arte a Napoli: Edizione Bilingue dei 176 Scenari Casamarciano.* Bilingual Italian and English edition. Edited and translated by Francesco Cotticelli, Anne Goodrich Heck, and Thomas F. Heck. Lanham, MD: Scarecrow, 2008.

Petrarch, Francesco. *Letters from Petrarch.* Translated by Morris Bishop. Bloomington: Indiana University, 1966.

Piccolomini, Alessandro. "Alessandro. "Translated by Rita Belladonna. In vol. 1 of *Renaissance Comedy: The Italian Masters*, edited and introduced by Donald Beecher. Toronto: University of Toronto Press, 2008.

Pietropaolo, Domenico. "The Stage in the Text: A Theatrical Stratification of Italian Renaissance Comedy. " In *Comparative Critical Approaches to Renaissance Comedy*, edited by Donald Beecher and Massimo Ciavolella, 35–51. Toronto: University of Toronto Press, 1986.

– "The Theatre." In *Harlequin Unmasked: The Commedia Dell'Arte and Porcelain Sculpture*, by Meredith Chilton, 9–32. New Haven, CT: George R. Gardiner Museum of Ceramic Art with Yale University Press, 2001.

Pollard, Tanya. *Drugs and Theater in Early Modern England.* Oxford: Oxford University Press, 2005.

Porter, Ray. Preface to *Bread of Dreams: Food and Fantasy in Early Modern Europe*, by Piero Camporesi, 1–16. Translated by David Gentilcore. Chicago: University of Chicago Press, 1989.

Radcliff-Umstead, Douglas. "The Sorcerer in Italian Renaissance Comedy." In *Comparative Critical Approaches to Renaissance Comedy*, edited by Donald Beecher and Massimo Ciavolella, 73–98. Ottawa: Dovehouse, 1986.

Rhodes, Neil. *The Power of Eloquence and English Renaissance Literature.* New York: St Martin's Press, 1992.

Richards, Kenneth, and Laura Richards. *The Commedia dell'Arte: A Documentary History.* Oxford: Basil Blackwell, 1990.

– "*Commedia dell'Arte*": *A History of Italian Theatre.* Edited by Joseph Farrell and Paolo Puppa. Cambridge: Cambridge University Press, 2006.

Richardson, Brian. "'*Amore maritale*': Advice on Love and Marriage in the Second Half of the Cinquecento." In *Women in Italian Renaissance Culture and Society*, edited by Letizia Panizza, 194–208. Oxford: Oxford University Press.

– *Printing, Writers and Readers in Renaissance Italy.* Cambridge: Cambridge University Press, 1999.

Ridder-Symoens, Hilde de. "Training and Professionalization." In *Power Elites and State Building*, edited by Wolfgang Reinhard, 149–72. Oxford: Clarendon Press, 1996.

Riddle, John M. *Eve's Herbs: A History of Contraception and Abortion in the West.* Cambridge, MA: Harvard University Press, 1997.

Roberts, William P. "Christian Marriage." In *From Trent to Vatican II: Historical and Theological Investigations*, edited by Raymond F. Bulman and Frederick J. Parrella, 209–26. Oxford: Oxford University Press, 2006.

Robin, Diana. "Humanism and Feminism in Laura Cereta's Public Letters." In *Women in Italian Renaissance Culture and Society*, edited by Letizia Panizza. Oxford: Oxford University Press, 2000.

Rocke, Michael. "Gender and Sexual Culture in Renaissance Italy." In *The Renaissance: Italy and Abroad*, edited by John Jeffries Martin, 139–58. London: Routledge, 2003. In slightly longer form in *Gender and Society in Renaissance Italy*, edited by Judith C. Brown and Robert C. Davis, 150–70. London: Longman, 1998.

Rodriguez, Don Gregorio Paniagua, conductor. *Tarentule-Tarentelle.* The Atrium Musical de Madrid. Compact disc with liner notes. Arles, France: Harmonia Mundi, 1977.

Romano, Dennis. *Housecraft and Statecraft: Domestic Service in Renaissance Venice, 1400–1600.* Baltimore, MD: Johns Hopkins University Press, 1996.

Rosenthal, Margaret F. *The Honest Courtesan: Veronica Franco, Citizen and Writer in Sixteenth-Century Venice.* Chicago: University of Chicago Press, 1992.

Ruggiero, Guido. *Binding Passions: Tales of Magic, Marriage, and Power at the End of the Renaissance.* New York: Oxford University Press, 1993.

– *The Boundaries of Eros: Sex Crime and Sexuality in Renaissance Venice.* Oxford: Oxford University Press, 1985.

– "Marriage, Love, Sex, and Renaissance Civic Morality." In *Sexuality and Gender in Early Modern Europe: Institutions, Texts, Images*, edited by Grantham Turner, 10–30. Cambridge: Cambridge University Press, 1993.

– "Witchcraft and Magic." In *A Companion to the Worlds of the Renaissance*, edited by Guido Ruggiero, 475–90. Oxford: Blackwell, 2002.

Ruggiero, Laura Giannetti. "When Male Characters Pass as Women: Theatrical Play and Social Practice in the Italian Renaissance." *The Sixteenth Century Journal* 36, no. 3 (2005): 743–60.

– *See also* Giannetti, Laura.

Ruzante [Angelo Beolco]. *Teatro: Prima edizione completa.* Edited by Ludovico Zorzi. Turin: G. Einaudi, 1967.

Salkeld, Duncan. *Madness and Drama in the Age of Shakespeare.* Manchester, UK:. Manchester University Press, 1994.

Sanesi, Ireneo. *La commedia.* Revised edition, 2 vols. Milan: F. Vallardi, 1954. Original edition 1911–35.

Santore, Cathy. "Julia Lombardo, 'Somtuosa Meretrize': A Portrait by Property." *Renaissance Quarterly* 41, no. 1 (1988): 44–83.

Sawyer, Ronald. "Patients, Healers, and Disease in the Southeast Midlands, England, 1597–1634." PhD diss., University of Wisconsin, 1986.

Scala, Flaminio. *The Commedia dell'Arte of Flaminio Scala: A Translation and Analysis of 30 Scenarios.* Edited and translated by Richard Andrews. Lanham, MD.: Scarecrow Press, 2008.

– *Il finto marito.* In *Commedi dei comici dell'arte* , edited by Laura Falavolti, 215–365. Turin: UTET, 1982.

– Prologues 1 and 2 to *Il finto marito.* In *Il teatro delle favole rappresentative,* by Flaminio Scala, edited by Ferruccio Marotti, vol. 1, cviv–cxvii. Milan: Il Polifilo, 1976.

– *Il teatro delle favole rappresentative.* Edited by Ferruccio Marotti, 2 vols. Milan: Il Polifilo, 1976.

Salerno, Henry. *Scenarios of the Commedia dell'Arte: Flaminio Scala's Il Teatro Delle Favole Rappresentative.* New York: Limelight, 1989.

Schmitt, Natalie Crohn. "Improvisation in the *Commedia dell'Arte* in Its Golden Age: Why, What, How." *Renaissance Drama,* n.s. 38 (2010): 225–50.

Scott, Virginia. *The Commedia dell'Arte in Paris, 1644–1697.* Charlottesville: University of Virginia, 1990.

Seligman, Kurt. *The History of Magic.* New York: Pantheon, 1948.

Sella, Domenici. *Italy in the Seventeenth Century.* London: Longmans, 1997.

Shuger, Debora. "The 'I' of the Beholder: Renaissance Mirrors and the Reflexive Mind." In *Renaissance Culture and the Everyday,* edited by Patricia Fumerton and Simon Hunt, 21–41. Philadelphia: University of Pennsylvania Press, 1999.

Smarr, Janet Levarie. *Italian Renaissance Tales.* Selection, translation, and introduction by Janet Levarie Smarr. Rochester, NY: Solaris Press, 1983.

Snyder, Jon R. *Dissimulation and the Culture of Secrecy in Early Modern Europe.* Berkeley: University of California Press, 2009.

Speroni, Sperone. "Dialogue on Love." Translated by Janet L. Smarr. In *Dialogue with the Other Voice in Sixteenth-Century Italy: Literary and Social Context for Women's Writing,* edited by Julie D. Campbell and Maria Galli Stampino, 202–64. Toronto: Centre for Reformation and Renaissance Studies, 2011.

Strocchia, Sharon T. "Gender and Rites of Honour in Italian Renaissance Cities." In *Gender and Society in Renaissance Italy,* edited by Judith C. Brown and Robert C. Davis, 39–60. London: Longman, 1998.

Styan, J.L. *Drama, Stage, and Audience.* Cambridge: Cambridge University Press, 1975.

Summers, David. *Michelangelo and the Language of Art.* Princeton: Princeton University Press, 1981.

Talbot, Michael. "*Ore Italiane*: The Reckoning of the Time of Day in Pre-Napoleonic Italy. *Italian Studies* 40 (1985): 51–63.

Tasso, Torquato. *Gerusalemme liberata.* Edited by Lanfronaco Caretti. Vol. 1 of 2. Bari: Laterza, 1967.

– *Tasso's Dialogues: A Selection, with the Discourse on the Art of the Dialogue.* Translation, introduction, and notes by Carnes Lord and Dain A. Trafton. Berkeley: University of California Press, 1982.

Taviani, Ferdinano. "Positions du masque dans la Commedia dell'Arte. " In *Le masque: Du rite au théâtre,* edited by Odette Aslan, Jean Louis Barrault, and Denis Bablet, 119–34. Paris: Centre national de la recherche scientifique, 1985.

Taviani, Ferdinando, and Mirella Schino. *Il segreto della commedia dell'arte: La memoria delle compagnie italiane del XVI, XVII, e XVIII secolo.* Florence: La Casa Usher, 1982.

Tenenti, Alberto. "The Merchant and the Banker." In *Renaissance Characters,* edited by Eugenio Garin, translated by Lydia G. Cochrane, 154–79. Chicago: University of Chicago Press, 1991.

Tessari, Roberto. *La commedia dell' arte nel Seicento: "Industria" e "Arte giocosa" della civiltà barocca.* Florence: L.S. Olschki, 1969.

Testaverde, Annamaria. "Introduzione." In *I canovacci della Commedia Dell' Arte,* edited by Annamaria Testaverde, xvii–lxxi. Transcription of the text and notes by Anna Evangelista. Preface by Roberto De Simone. Turin: Giulio Einaudi, 2007.

Thorndike, Lynn. *A History of Magic and Experimental Sciences.* Vol. 6. New York: Columbia University Press, 1941.

Trabotti, Arcangela. *Paternal Tyranny*. Translated by Letizia Panizza. Chicago: University of Chicago Press, 2004.

Trease, Geoffrey. *The Condottieri: Soldiers of Fortune*. New York: Holt, Rinehart, and Winston, 1971.

Trexler, Richard C. *Public Life in Renaissance Florence*. New York: Academic Press, 1980.

Tribby, Jay. "*Stefano Guazzo e la civil conversatione*." Book review in *MLN* 105, no. 5 (1990): 1091–3.

Tucci, Ugo. "The Psychology of the Venetian Merchant in the Sixteenth Century." In *Renaissance Venice*, edited by J.R. Hale, 346–78. Totowa, NJ: Rowman and Littlefield, 1973.

Tylus, Jane. "Women at the Windows: *Commedia dell'Arte* and Theatrical Practice in Early Modern Italy." *Theatre Journal*, 49 (1997): 323–42.

Valesio, Paolo. "The Language of Madness in the Renaissance." *Yearbook of Italian Studies*, 1 (1971): 199–234.

Van Laan, Thomas F. *Role-Playing in Shakespeare*. Toronto: University of Toronto Press, 1978.

Verucci, Vergilio. *Li diversi linguaggi*. In *Commedia ridicolosa: Comici di professione, dilettanti, editoria teatrale nel Seicento; Storia e testi*, edited by Luciano Mariti, 107–206. Rome: Bulzoni, 1978.

Vickers, Brian. *In Defence of Rhetoric*. Oxford: Clarendon Press, 1988.

Walker, D.P. *Spiritual and Demonic Magic from Ficino to Campanella*. London: Warburg Institute of the University of London Press, 1958.

Weaver, Elissa. *Convent Theatre in Early Modern Italy: Spiritual Fun and Learning for Women*. Cambridge: Cambridge University Press, 2002.

– "Gender." In *A Companion to the Worlds of the Renaissance*, edited by Guido Ruggiero, 188–207. Oxford: Blackwell, 2002.

Weinstein, Donald. "Fighting or Flyting? Verbal Dueling in Mid-Sixteenth-Century Italy." In *Crime, Society, and the Law in Renaissance Italy*, edited by Trevor Dean and K.J.P. Lowe, 204–20. Cambridge: Cambridge University Press, 1994.

White, Hayden. *The Content of the Form: Narrative Discourse and Historical Representation*. Baltimore, MD: Johns Hopkins University Press, 1987.

White, William I. "A New Look at the Role of Urinalysis in the History of Diagnostic Medicine." *Clinical Chemistry* 37, no. 1 (1991): 119–25.

Whitfield, Peter. *Astrology: A History*. New York: Harry N. Abrams, 2001.

Wiles, David. *Shakespeare's Clown: Actor and Text in the Elizabethan Playhouse*. Cambridge: Cambridge University Press, 1987.

– *A Short History of Western Performance Space*. Cambridge: Cambridge University Press, 2003.

Wölfflin, Heinrich. *Principles of Art History: The Problem of the Development of Style in Later Art.* Translated by M.D. Hottinger from the 7th German edition. New York: Dover, 1950. Originally published 1915 as *Kunstgeschichtliche Grundbegriffe.*

Woodbridge, Linda. "Renaissance Bogeymen: The Necessary Monsters of the Age." In *A Companion to the Worlds of the Renaissance,* edited by Guido Ruggiero, 444–59. Oxford: Blackwell, 2002.

Zarri, Gabriella. "Christian Good Manners: Spiritual and Monastic Rules in the Quattro-Cinquecento." In *Women in Italian Renaissance Culture and Society,* edited by Letizia Panizza, 76–91. Oxford: Oxford University Press, 2000.

Zorzi, Ludovico. "Intorno alla Commedia dell Arte." In *Arte della maschera nella Commedia dell'Arte,* edited by Donato Sartori and Bruno Lanata, 63–83. Milan: Palazzo Bagatti-Valsecchi, 1983.

Images

Anonymous. Corsini scenarios. Illustrated title pages. Biblioteca Corsiniana, Rome. In *La commedia dell'arte: Storia e testa,* by Vito Pandolfi, vol. 5, unnumbered 26 pages between 256 and 257. Florence: Sansoni, 1957–61. Also smaller in *The Art of Commedia: A Study in the Commedia dell'Arte, 1560–1620, with Special Reference to the Visual Records,* by M.A. Katritzky, 543–9. Amsterdam: Rodopi, 2006.

– Figure in a doorway. Image for Curzio Gonzaga, *Gli ingannati,* 1592. In "Pictures for the Reader: A Series of Illustrations to Comedy, 1591–92," by Louise George Clubb, *Renaissance Drama,* 9 (1966): 265–78.

– Illustration for Act 3, Scene 3. In *L'amfiparnaso,* by Orazio Vecchi, 1597. Edited by Hugo Leichtentritt (n.d., no publisher).

– Recueil Fossard. Woodcut (1580s). In *The Italian Comedy,* by Pierre Louis Duchartre, 320. New York: Dover, 1966.

– Woodcut in C. Gonzaga, *Gli ingannati.*" In "Disguise in Renaissance Comedy," by Peter Brand, *Comparative Criticism,* 10 (1988): 68.

Callot, Jacques. *Callot's Etchings.* Edited by Howard Daniel, print 227. New York: Dover, 1974.

– "Scapino Takes Centre Stage." Engraving. Archiginnasio, Bologna, 1618–20. In *The Art of Commedia: A Study in the Commedia dell'Arte, 1560–1620, with Special Reference to the Visual Record,* by M.A. Katritzky. Amsterdam: Rodopi, 2006.

Münster, Sebastian. "Neapolis." *Cosmographei* CCLXX. Basel: H. Petri, 1550. Hebrew University of Jerusalem and the Jewish National and University Library and http://historic-cities.huji.ac.il/italy/napoli/maps/munster_ger_1550_cclxx_b.jpg.

Xavery, G.J. Illustrations for *The Marvellous Malday of Harlequin.* In *The Italian Comedy,* by Pierre Louis Duchartre, ff. 56, plate II, top of page; plate III, foot of page. New York: Dover, 1966.

Sound Recordings, and Dance Steps

Caroso, Fabritio. Ballo del piantone. *Il ballarino,* 1581. Sound recording and sheet music. http://www.pbm.com/~lindahl/del/music/caroso_il_piantone_susan.mid

– Ballo del piantone. *Il ballarino,* 1581. Dance steps. http://jducoeur.org/IlBallarino/Book2/Ballo%20del%20Piantone.html

Index

www.ingramcontent.com/pod-product-compliance
Lightning Source LLC
LaVergne TN
LVHW041112090826
844660LV00061B/736/J

* 9 7 8 1 4 4 2 6 4 8 9 9 9 *